D1602796

THE SOUL
OF POLITICS

THE SOUL OF POLITICS

HARRY V. JAFFA

AND THE FIGHT
FOR AMERICA

GLENN
ELLMERS

Encounter
BOOKS

New York • London

First American edition published in 2021 by Encounter Books,
an activity of Encounter for Culture and Education, Inc.,
a nonprofit, tax-exempt corporation.
Encounter Books website address: www.encounterbooks.com

Manufactured in the United States and printed on
acid-free paper. The paper used in this publication meets
the minimum requirements of ANSI/NISO Z39.48–1992
(R 1997) (*Permanence of Paper*).

FIRST AMERICAN EDITION

LIBRARY OF CONGRESS CATALOGING-IN-PUBLICATION DATA

Names: Ellmers, Glenn, 1966– author.
Title: The Soul of Politics: Harry V. Jaffa and the Fight for America
By Glenn Ellmers. Description: First American Edition.
New York : Encounter Books, 2021.
Includes bibliographical references and index. | Identifiers: LCCN 2021001840 (print)
LCCN 2021001841 (ebook) | ISBN9781641772006 (Hardcover : acid-free paper)
ISBN 9781641772013 (eBook)
Subjects: LCSH: Conservatism—United States.
Political science—United States—Philosophy.
United States—Politics and government—Philosophy. | Jaffa, Harry V.
Classification: LCC JC573.2.U6 E57 2021 (print) | LCC JC573.2.U6 (ebook)
DDC 320.01—dc23
LC record available at https://lccn.loc.gov/2021001840
LC ebook record available at https://lccn.loc.gov/2021001841

Interior page design and composition by Bruce Leckie

To be a fellow citizen means not only to be able to accept the results of a free election but also to be willing to fight to preserve, protect, and defend the regime of free elections. A community of citizens is a community of those willing to fight for each other. Someone who will not fight for you, when you are willing to fight for him, cannot be your fellow citizen.

Finding the natural *aristoi*, providing for their education, and discovering the ways and means in particular circumstances to maximize their influence, is the task of political philosophy, whether in the ancient or modern world.

We cannot define our tasks by our powers, for our powers become known to us through performing our tasks; it is better to fail nobly than to succeed basely.

CONTENTS

FOREWORD

At first sight, this is a very academic sort of book. It is about a college professor. Although it gives the best account I have read of the *events* in the life of its subject, Harry Jaffa, it is not mostly about events. Professor Jaffa was born in 1918 and bears the middle name "Victor." Neither the victory in the First World War nor in the second comes into play. Jaffa lived through the Great Depression, the Korean War, and the Vietnam War. They come up, but in passing. With the rare exception of a Winston Churchill, the events in the lives of thinkers and writers are ordinary, filled not with battles but with books, not with odysseys except between the study and the classroom.

Nor is the classroom the same kind of place as the dramatic stage. Few professors prepare their classes with a beginning, a middle, and an end through which they climb to a peak of tension, understanding, and exhaustion. If you want to know what a professor thinks about a subject, the academic way is to take the course, which means sitting in a classroom for forty-five hours stretching over four months. Plus, there is plenty of reading and thinking to do outside the classroom. Recounting a lifetime like this can make a boring book.

Yet this book is not boring, because it is not about an ordinary sort of academic. Professor Jaffa was a *political* thinker in the school of classical political philosophy, and in him political passion was intense, qualified only by a greater devotion to knowledge. He learned from his teacher and from the classics that philosophy begins with the inescapable question: how should we live? This is the pressing form of the fundamental question, what is "good?", which itself raises questions both inescapable and urgent. The starting point for Plato and Aristotle is the opinions of ordinary people, especially the most authoritative opinions as they are expressed in the law. Thus, *political* philosophy.

We know from ancient political philosophy that the examination of the opinions of citizens and their laws can be dangerous, especially to the philosopher. Socrates, the father of political philosophy, was executed for treasons and impieties that he claimed he had not committed. Aristotle fled for his life from Athens to escape the same fate. Have you read the news these days about the hounding of professors from classrooms for the slightest violation of political correctness? Today as in classical times, the study of politics produces casualties. During Professor Jaffa's own career, on his own campus, radicals destroyed a building and maimed an employee with a pipe bomb. Professor Jaffa spoke out boldly and at risk against these evils and the college administrators who surrendered to them.

Professor Jaffa did not and would not willingly kill anyone, and he died peacefully at ninety-six. But the combat in which he engaged was fierce because it was consequential. One of Professor Jaffa's old friends exclaimed once in writing: "who will rid us of this pest a priest?" After Henry II uttered those words, some who heard them assassinated Thomas Becket. Professor Jaffa learned nothing from the example of Becket and returned immediately to the attack.

Like that of Socrates, Professor Jaffa's kind of philosophy operates very close to home. He had the insight of his life in his late thirties. By accident or providence, Professor Jaffa fell in love with Abraham Lincoln. He had a chance encounter with the text of the Lincoln-Douglas debates, and he saw in them the profundity of a Socratic dialogue. Those debates changed his life, the lives of his students, and the politics of our nation. From Lincoln, Jaffa worked his way back to the founding and discovered things in it that had been forgotten. He resurrected those things and made them compelling for his students, as they had been for the founders who articulated, fought for, and established the meaning of our nation. Professor Jaffa hoped for nothing less than the revival of a "scholarship of the politics of freedom," a reversal of the relentless march toward historicism. Only by that means could both freedom and civilization be made safe. Professor Jaffa succeeded with his students, as his teacher had succeeded with him. This he thought proved that a revival was as possible as it was necessary.

The central story of this book is in fact a grand drama involving the life and meaning of the greatest modern republic. Professor Jaffa loved the United States of America on a cosmic scale. He found its justification beyond it, in the heavens, where God or the idea of God influences human actions here below. He saw that the Declaration of Independence appeals to that very place in establishing the ground of our freedom and equality.

This means that Professor Jaffa was not simply a political thinker or simply an American thinker. His interests covered, like the works of Aristotle, the whole sweep of questions available to the human mind. His life's work was to integrate what he knew into an account of the meaning of his country.

RANGE

Professor Jaffa was not always the most organized teacher, but in this book one sees his strength in the classroom, how that radiated through his publications, and the range of his thought. His best classes might or might not be about the text being read. Rising from that text, from some question or comment from a student, or from who knows where, Professor Jaffa would embark on a sweep through the grand themes of political philosophy across the centuries. He could place them in order and explicate them with the familiarity of friendship—or the intensity of battle. What is a human? What is reason? What is good? What would you do if you had the power of mythical Gyges, of a ring to make you invisible to do whatever you pleased? Would you despoil or enslave others? Along a track that led through Shakespeare, Aristotle, Thomas Aquinas, Machiavelli, and the American Revolution, the professor led his students upon a circular march that ended back at the beginning, the basic question of the good.

These lectures would erupt as commonly when studying Aristotle as Lincoln, Xenophon as the founding. They would often go an hour or more beyond the schedule. No one would notice until emerging to find that it was getting dark. Then the students would retire to dinner talk about the class for hours. These classes were a microcosm of the teacher's entire career. He was working to make wisdom practical and therefore both vital and useful, not as a tool but as a light and a guide.

One cannot understand the meaning of Professor Jaffa's teaching without thinking about Aristotle. As Plato invented a new form of literature, the dialogue, to reproduce the conversations of Socrates, so Aristotle invented a different kind of treatise written in its own dialectical form. As one proceeds through the *Ethics*, Professor Jaffa's favorite book, one sees that the definitions of things change as the book proceeds. At each stage, it is written for one who knows just as much as has been covered, and in the next stage higher understanding emerges. When one perseveres to the end of the *Ethics*, he finds a vision of contemplative friendship, the highest human association.

One cannot understand the charm of Professor Jaffa without reading him on Shakespeare. For the Bard, Professor Jaffa had a special love born in his study of literature at Yale in undergraduate school. His classes on Shakespeare were always superb. He had the habit of listening to great recordings of the plays (in those days, on a turntable) and picking up the needle when a passage struck his fancy or someone had a question. I remember once studying Macbeth, and the scene came where Macbeth was in the chamber of the sleeping Duncan, his house guest and kinsman, about to commit his murder to get hold of the throne. Angels and demons cry out for and against the deed. Professor Jaffa picked up the needle and said: "Does not this man live in a richly populated moral universe?" By this explication of poetry, Professor Jaffa introduced his students to that same universe. Jaffa learned from Aristotle that history is indispensable for understanding reality, but poetry at its best reveals more.

As he explored the meaning of things and of America, Professor Jaffa perceived and resisted the movement of the nation toward its current dread divisions. He saw these divisions in light of the two turning points in American history: the American Revolution that replaced monarchy with republicanism, and the Civil War that expunged slavery and reaffirmed our commitment to the principles of the revolution. Professor Jaffa drew on Lincoln, especially, to elucidate the crisis of our time. In such a crisis, the whole regime and the way of life it protects are cast into doubt and controversy. Upon the outcome rests the freedom and the lives of millions.

This book explains how Professor Jaffa explored the soul of Lincoln and his response to the crisis of his time. He explains that the turning point Lincoln faced is related to the one we face today. In this, Glenn Ellmers performs a valuable service. It took Professor Jaffa decades, the teaching of many classes, and the writing of many books to develop both his understanding and his explanation. It has taken many of his students that same amount of time to understand and to extend his teaching. Glenn, one of those students, has brought it all together in one book, a splendid summary of a great life.

DEVELOPMENT

Ellmers is particularly concerned to follow the development of Jaffa's thought. Mind you, he does not see this as the product of outside influences upon Jaffa's mind but rather the working out of the internal logic of his discoveries. Ellmers makes this point explicit in a long and interesting discussion of Jaffa, Lincoln, and the philosopher Hegel, connections that Jaffa brings out in *A New Birth of Freedom.*

Jaffa changed his mind about some important things, and Ellmers explains those in detail. Was Lincoln a refounder or a restorer? If the former, Lincoln was an original as much as or more than Thomas Jefferson in the Declaration of Independence and the other founders. This is the position of Jaffa's groundbreaking *Crisis of the House Divided.* But by working his way over decades from Lincoln back through the founders, Jaffa surrenders this idea to something he came to regard as truer and nobler. Lincoln did not, he argues in *New Birth of Freedom,* remake America but restored and elevated it by understanding it more deeply.

Professor Jaffa was a man of argument. He loved the word "polemical," which derives from the Greek word for "war." He had fights with many famous people, such as Robert Bork, and Ellmers recounts these arguments ably. Also, he benefits greatly from three intelligent and respectful critics of Jaffa with whom Jaffa had extended arguments. They are Robert Kraynak, Michael Zuckert, and, in a different category, Charles Kesler. They all puzzle over the difference between Jaffa's first book about Lincoln, *Crisis of the House Divided,* and his second, *New Birth of Freedom.* It is Kesler who sees best that Jaffa was working out the teachings of natural and political right found especially in Jaffa's favorite,

Aristotle, and the career of Lincoln. Even the greatest human minds do not understand as the God in Aristotle's *Metaphysics*. We do not see everything at once but rather go step-by-step. The life of the scholar is a long march toward completeness; the best scholars go nearest to the end.

I am too old to have taken classes alongside Glenn Ellmers. I worked with him for many years at the Claremont Institute. Those were days of great growth and learning for all of us. Glenn matured quickly into a high-minded young man gathering knowledge and driven by noble intentions. If you want to see his character, read the "Note to the Reader" at the beginning of the book. There he names his audience, which I hope is you, the same as the audience for which Professor Jaffa aimed. Writing this book would be an achievement for anyone; it is Glenn's finest hour to date.

For those who knew and studied with Professor Jaffa, this book is a tour through fond memories that deepens the knowledge contained in those memories. For those young members of the "natural *aristoi*" to whom Glenn addresses this book, it is a gateway into a journey that leads up to high understanding and noble action.

Larry P. Arnn
PRESIDENT, HILLSDALE COLLEGE

A NOTE TO THE READER

It is the hope of most modern authors to write a best seller, purchased (and perhaps even read) by millions. Yet in writing this book, I have a particular audience in mind. It is my hope that at least some of you are young Americans who care about our country as I do and as Professor Jaffa did. You may see that it is in trouble. But perhaps you find that there is no adequate guidance available for how to think and how to act.

I am writing to you, spirited moral gentlemen, America's natural *aristoi*, because the crisis of our country is also the crisis of Western civilization, of civilization itself. It is so advanced that reasonable people are losing hope. Yet we must not, for despair is both a moral failing and an intellectual error. There is hope, and it depends on you. The cause for hope, and resolution, may be found in nature, particularly human nature, which supplies a permanent ground on which we can orient our thoughts and actions.

The common belief today, shaped by the technology that seems to govern our lives, is that the world is simply matter in motion. Everything, even nature, is in flux. This is not a new idea. In ancient Greece, a playwright named Aristophanes wrote in one of his plays, "Whirl is king." But this idea was refuted by another man named Socrates, as it was refuted in our time by the man who is the subject of this book.

One could spend a lifetime learning from both men. But Harry Jaffa was closer to us, and he spoke about ideas and institutions familiar, and dear, to us. One thing Jaffa taught is that each of us must think for himself, yet we each need the help of friends. I am inviting you, readers, into a world of thought that may help you to think, and act, in these momentous times. With luck, perhaps we can yet save what is best and highest in our country. There is nothing more beautiful, worthwhile, or fulfilling we could do.

Among the many truths about politics, philosophy, and life that Harry Jaffa imparted, perhaps the most important concerns what he called "the metaphysical freedom of the human mind." Without this, neither rational thought nor moral action is possible. In one essay, Jaffa wrote:

> According to the classical or Socratic perspective, the conditions for thinking clearly and well—e.g., intelligence, health, a certain amount of wealth, freedom, leisure—do not guarantee that one will think clearly and well. Nothing can guarantee understanding. Indeed, from this perspective nothing can guarantee a successful outcome to any human enterprise, practical or theoretical.... To say that the conditions of success—in thinking or anything else— necessarily produce success, would be to reduce man to a cipher of his environment. This is what in effect, the idea of the end of history does.

As Jaffa learned from Winston Churchill (and also from his great teacher Leo Strauss), we cannot guarantee success, but we can deserve it. And by acting in a way deserving of success, it may yet come, even if altogether unexpectedly.

BALLOTS, BULLETS, AND BOOKS

Then out spake brave Horatius,
The Captain of the Gate:
To every man upon this earth
Death cometh soon or late.
And how can man die better
Than facing fearful odds,
For the ashes of his fathers,
And the temples of his gods.

—THOMAS MACAULAY, *The Lays of Ancient Rome*

The bomb that detonated at Scripps College on the afternoon of February 26, 1969, didn't injure anyone, but an innocent young woman was badly maimed when another device exploded almost simultaneously in Carnegie Hall at adjacent Pomona College. Hidden inside a shoebox wrapped in brown paper, the second bomb left twenty-year-old Mary Ann Keatley blind in one eye and ripped two fingers from her right hand. Keatley, married just five months earlier to an undergraduate at Claremont Men's College, worked as the secretary for the Pomona political science department. These two explosions, and a third two weeks later, shattered windows and wrecked buildings. But they also rattled the confidence of those responsible for the academic mission and integrity of the Claremont Colleges.[1] The student unrest and mayhem of the late 1960s affected many campuses besides Claremont, but what happened there is notable for other reasons, particularly the response of the academic and administrative authorities and a small minority of faculty who opposed them.

Resistance to the Vietnam War motivated the campus violence in California and elsewhere, but so did the demands of the Black Power Movement, especially at Claremont, where protestors called for various new programs in ethnic studies as well as quotas for minority students. A leading member of this group had asked, shortly before a fire that destroyed Claremont McKenna's historic Story House (a separate incident, in addition to the bombings), "Do you want this campus burned down this summer or next summer?"[2]

Among the small group of faculty opposing those demands was a professor of political philosophy named Harry V. Jaffa. Though diametrically opposite in outlook and temperament, Jaffa and the radical students agreed at one level with the slogan, "No Justice, No Peace." Jaffa had studied with Leo Strauss, the brilliant Jewish émigré scholar who fled Nazi Germany in the 1930s. From Strauss, Jaffa learned that this apparently outrageous statement is in fact a true observation about human life: there *can't* be peace without justice, nor vice versa. Jaffa's philosophical reasoning and explanation for this observation were nearly polar opposite of the justifications invoked by the violent protesters. But he understood that the radicals, in their passionate commitment to building a new social order, perceived something essential about political life, a truth missed or suppressed by mainstream academic thought. The protestors had a conception of justice they were extreme in pursuing and saw no virtue in moderating their demands. This was a view Jaffa understood well.

Despite strong resistance and dire warnings from the small coterie of conservative professors, the administrators of the

Claremont Colleges opened negotiations with the radicals on the assumption that those responsible for the bombings shared their faith in compromise and dialogue. The leadership of the colleges granted nearly every demand of the protestors in the vain hope that capitulation would appease those who threatened to burn down the campus. (It didn't.) Not for the first or last time, the unwillingness of the academic establishment to defend the integrity of the university would remind Jaffa of the aphorism attributed to Winston Churchill: "You were given the choice between war and dishonor. You chose dishonor, and you will have war."[3]

Compromise, Jaffa noted later, "presupposes an end that the compromisers share and that it is more important to them than what they are asked to sacrifice in compromising."[4] The administrators' avowed principles evidently were less important to them than the commitment of the radicals to *their* principles. Jaffa expressed particular disappointment over how the rhetorical bravery of the "no-nonsense" businessmen on the board of trustees melted away when courage was really needed. In a letter to a colleague years afterward, Jaffa explained:

> We who opposed this policy of surrender, were very much in the position of the defenders of the Alamo. And ... I could not detect any prospect of relief emanating from the trustees. And this, notwithstanding the bold and uncompromising talk I had so often heard over brandy and cigars from conservative trustees when there was no danger to face. "You don't understand," [one trustee] declared, "Rome was not built in a day." "You don't understand," I replied, "Rome is not being built, it's being burned."[5]

At the time of the bombings, Jaffa, then fifty years old, already had established himself as a figure of controversy and an enemy of facile conciliation. Five year earlier, he had helped Republican presidential nominee Barry Goldwater jab a thumb in the eye of this same establishment crowd, those who seemed, both to Goldwater and Jaffa, too eager to sacrifice upon the altar of safety and expediency. Jaffa had grown up in a "high-spirited" Jewish family in New York, studied English at Yale, then earned a PhD in political philosophy under Strauss at the New School for Social Research. In 1963, he took a temporary leave from academic life to help advise the Goldwater campaign as a noted Lincoln scholar and student of American political thought.

At the Republican National Convention in San Francisco, he was recruited by Goldwater to write the bulk of the nomination acceptance speech. In a memo for the campaign prepared a few days earlier, after sitting through the debates of the platform committee, Jaffa had crafted the famous lines that caught Goldwater's attention and, reformulated for the speech, would become world famous: "I would remind you that extremism in the defense of liberty is no vice. And let me remind you also that moderation in the pursuit of justice is no virtue!" Though the crowd in the "Cow Palace" auditorium erupted in cheers, the mainstream establishment—including television commentators, prominent journalists, and moderate Republicans (not to mention Democrats)—reacted with alarm and consternation. Pat Brown, the liberal governor of California, embraced his own form of extremism and went so far as to say, "The stench of fascism is in the air."[6]

Today, looking back on these years from a distance of five decades, such scenes may seem depressingly familiar: social-justice warriors pulling to port and conservative demagogues keeling to starboard threaten to tear apart the ship of state. Moderation, tolerance, and civil debate are left to drown at sea. What, then, can be gained by retelling moldy stories about Jaffa's campus skirmishes from a half century ago? They seem only to remind us how little has changed and how fruitless must be any effort to affect the course of human affairs. The '60s radicals grew up and became the establishment. Goldwater morphed into Reagan and then into Trump. History carries us along on her tedious course, monotonously reenacting the same "crimes, follies, and misfortunes," and we ride as flotsam on the current.

And yet, the very fact that our politics are so divided and bitter today demonstrates that nothing, really, has been settled—despite a century of efforts by progressives, reformers, and well-educated experts to create a modern "administrative state" overseen by nonpartisan and professional bureaucrats. If the Donald Trump presidency revealed anything, it was that the superficial consensus that dominated postwar America was an illusion. But despite today's availability of 24-7 commentary, from every possible ideological perspective, there is little understanding of the deeper political and philosophical roots of our current crisis.

More so than Jaffa himself, his students have developed a body of scholarship, now built up over several decades, exploring how progressive ideas overturned the framers' constitutionalism. Yet as early as 1986, Jaffa himself observed, with astounding prescience, what was happening to consent and self-government. In a letter to his friend Lewis Lehrman, Jaffa noted "that elections are a necessary, but not a sufficient condition for the exercise of political power in our government as it really is."

> [The] preferences registered by the voters at the polls have been vetoed, in large part, by a combination of the media elite and the institutionalized pressure groups who control Congress and the bureaucracy. These people are, to paraphrase Keynes, the slaves of ideas that are, if not defunct, then moribund. But they are the ideas patronized by the universities, particularly those in the northeast whose prestige is the greatest. Even men as strong willed as Nixon and Reagan lose much of the confidence that they have had in the ideas they expressed before their election, when they are subject to the unrelenting bombardment of the Fourth Estate and its dependents.[7]

No nostalgia for "the Reagan revolution" clouded Jaffa's judgment about the march toward an unaccountable class of ruling elites. (In 1988, he would complain in a letter that "the last years of the Reagan presidency have turned into a disaster," describing "the old Man in the Oval Office" as "hen pecked.")[8] To be sure, Jaffa credited Reagan for his admirable resolution in leading the West's victory over the Soviet Union in the Cold War (an achievement of statesmanship perhaps underappreciated by those who did not live through the 1970s). But a recurring theme one finds in both Strauss and Jaffa is that triumph in arms is not necessarily triumph in minds. "That is why the present so-called victory of liberal democracy over Communism being trumpeted in Washington, London, Paris, etc. is such a delusion," Jaffa wrote in 1991.[9] As vital as it was to win the Cold War, there was still an ideological battle at home with which to contend.

Jaffa's student John Marini has devoted his career to expanding on Jaffa's observation about how the voters' preferences are overturned or ignored. Marini explored in great depth the theoretical basis and institutional contours of this "second constitution":

> In political practice, liberals and conservatives had established a kind of symbiotic relationship that made them appear as opposite sides of the same coin. The contemporary meaning of those terms had been derived from the theories and policies that had become embodied within the administrative state. There were disagreements over how certain domestic or foreign policies should be promulgated, or when they should take effect, or how much they should cost. However, there was little partisan disagreement as to whether those policies should have been pursued, or abandoned, because there was no political standard by which to judge results in terms of success or failure. Those decisions were put in the

hands of experts, or bureaucrats, whose knowledge established their authority. But the outcome of the decisions based on that supposed knowledge, whether successful or not, remained unquestioned by those who had political power.

The authority of the intellectuals had established a theoretical, or socially constructed, reality that appeared indifferent to reality as it revealed itself in practical or political life. It seemed as though liberal and conservative intellectuals could disagree when it came to practical means, but they were in apparent agreement concerning technical ends. But it was the ends—the results or failures—that brought about the political turmoil that led to the questioning of their authority. Much of official Washington rested on the authority of the knowledge that had been invested in those technical administrative positions. And nearly all concerned had a stake in maintaining the status quo.[10]

That is, until the big crack-up began in 2016. Although Antifa and other leftist radicals would surely bristle at the idea, the heartland unease that helped elect Trump has a common origin with the campus protest culture: they are both eruptions of the human concern for justice breaking through the artificial shell of the uniparty establishment. (Chapter 8 considers Jaffa's teachings in light of recent political developments.)

Jaffa spent his entire long career rejecting the false consensus of the status quo intellectuals because he had learned how unnatural and even impossible it was to suppress what Strauss called our "simple experiences regarding right and wrong."[11] Jaffa was accused of being a superficial moralizer, a potentially great scholar who frittered away the promise of his early work through a regrettable descent into florid patriotism. But such a view cannot seriously be entertained by anyone who has examined Jaffa's writings with any care. This book will reveal his appreciation for Churchill's ruthlessness, Shakespeare's Machiavellian poetry,

Aristotle's denigration of "mere" moral virtue, and Lincoln's keen appraisal of tyranny and its singular attractions. All of these stark portraits are drawn by Jaffa with unstinting candor, not sparing the unsettling implications.

In a fascinating paper delivered in 1986, Jaffa compares Shakespeare's *Coriolanus* with the Sherlock Holmes mysteries to show how men of intellect, ambition, and passion may locate their sense of justice in an all-consuming *self*-justification. The awareness of one's own compulsive need to escape stultifying conformity—the urge simply to *act* and feel alive—may be what matters most, regardless of which side one chooses. Literature's most famous detective is depicted living in the relative safety and comfort of Victorian London. But, as Jaffa observes, Holmes "is bored by it all. He cannot live without danger." His epic battle with his archrival, the master criminal Moriarty, reveals a curious similarity and a certain ambiguous, mutual dependence.

> Justice has been defined as the art of safekeeping and who knew better how to keep something safe than the one who best knew how to steal it? Holmes and Moriarty both had the art of the thief. What then can be the difference between them? Is Holmes the one who exercises his art justly, and Moriarty the one who does so unjustly? But is justice itself just? There is nothing in the conception of the art itself, to distinguish the just exercise of the art of justice from the unjust exercise of the art of justice.[12]

In Shakespeare's play, Coriolanus is an aristocratic Roman general. Returning from a hard-won victory over Rome's enemy, Aufidius, he refuses to grovel before the people in order to claim what he regards as his rightful title as consul. Spurned by the ungrateful and fickle mob, Coriolanus turns his back on his fatherland and joins forces with his former rival to exact vengeance. Jaffa elaborates the comparison between the unlikely pairs:

Holmes and Moriarty are related very much as Coriolanus and Aufidius, according to Shakespeare. Each is a representative of heroic virtue, and each is ambitious to be recognized as the supreme representative of such virtue, which is possible only by combat with the other. Each is a necessary means to the other's highest end—and in that sense is at once his dearest friend and bitterest enemy.[13]

"Coriolanus hates the plebs [common people]," Jaffa explains, because they are "preoccupied with the safety and comfort of their bodies. They care much for their freedom, but little for honor. They will fight if they must—to preserve their freedom, or for booty—but not for the honor of victory or the glory of conquest." Such low concerns are almost incomprehensible to the proud general, who thinks the plebs "do not deserve their freedom." The commoners "fill him with contempt."

Freedom belongs only to those who can use it well, and he thinks using freedom well requires virtue. He cannot understand those who want freedom without caring for virtue. He does not think that the people deserve to be free.[14]

Over and over in his scholarship, Jaffa returns to this theme. In his first great book on Lincoln, *Crisis of the House Divided*, he remarks on Lincoln's apparent contempt for "moral weaklings," a phrase he repeats four times in the span of eight pages. In fact, we will see that the heart of Jaffa's project was to demonstrate the shallowness and inadequacy of our modern conventional morality, which seeks to turn men into obedient sheep or mindless machines. "Purposeless politics is a human impossibility. All human beings act for the sake of ends. Action not for the sake of ends…is not possible."[15] Nor can such aspirations be mere creations of our whim or imagination.

An aimless life [is] bound to become frustrated at any time and place, no matter how perfect the opportunities offered to the human beings in that time and place. Man does not make himself, and therefore he cannot invent the ends that prescribe his well-being.... The act of self-deception, whereby one treats the ends one has invented as if they were real, leads to nothing but fanaticism, and to the unspeakable tyrannies that have in fact characterized our time.[16]

The attempt to avoid this problem by building a sterile regime of soulless men—the kind of regime imagined or desired by those university administrators in the 1960s, who thought everything could be negotiated—does not eliminate passion or courage; it can only make courage pointless. A purposeless world, in which all moral questions have been set aside in favor of "professional administration" simply results in the mindless slaughter represented perhaps most tragically in World War I's Battle of Verdun. Verdun, according to Jaffa, was "the apotheosis" of what happens when the dignity of courage is separated "from either wisdom or justice."

The "case against politics" in its starkest form is when the political alternatives are seen as a cowardice which knows no limits of baseness, and a courage which knows no limits of prudence. In truth, they do not constitute real alternatives at all, since one will inevitably lead to the other. Either is an extreme against which human nature rebels. No one really wants to live his life dominated every moment by the fear of death, and choosing only those ends which involve no danger. Neither do human beings want to seek out danger for its own sake, and fight and kill each other as the only way to become fully alive![17]

Jaffa writes with luminous force about this courageous human striving for some higher purpose. But this is hardly the end of the story. It is not even, to paraphrase Churchill, the beginning of the end. But it is perhaps the end of the beginning.

Breaking out of the tunnel of our artificial politics, and recognizing the human need for purpose and meaning, opens up a world of entirely new, and perhaps even more serious, challenges. Leo Strauss, invoking a famous image from Plato's *Republic*, memorably suggested that our blindness and delusions about human nature had placed modern man in a cave beneath the "natural" cave of ordinary politics. Strauss's project was to revive an older form of political and philosophic thought that could escape the socially constructed reality that turned politics into a merely technical exercise. But, mixing metaphors, this escape from the underground pit would be no more than a jump out of the frying pan. Even if it were possible to return to the natural cave, above the artificial cave, this would simply reopen the older and more fundamental questions: Whose justice? What is the best way of life? Who is entitled to rule? What is to be the basis of the political community? Such questions are nothing less than the discovery, or rediscovery, of political philosophy as practiced by Plato and Aristotle. It is through the rediscovery of these question that one is eventually led to ask, Is there something that is right or just, not merely by opinion or convention, but always and everywhere? Is there any *natural right*?

Strauss's rediscovery involved a kind of daring or boldness in even raising and taking seriously such questions. They had been buried for so long that the very possibility of asking them was (and still is) denied. But this rediscovery and reopening, once achieved, took on a life of its own. One notable effect for Jaffa was that the possibility of these questions, which had been studiously ignored by his professors at Yale, animated his intense confrontation with the Lincoln-Douglas debates. In studying those debates over the justice or injustice of slavery and its political fate, Jaffa began a lifelong meditation on the profound arguments that clarified, but could not prevent, the greatest war in American history.

As Jaffa was to discover in his study of American political history, it was partly the terrible suffering and losses incurred in the Civil War that led many intellectuals to embrace the utopian hope of forever removing violence and factionalism from political life. This impulse, in itself, is not hard to understand. In fact, this expectation has striking similarities with the sentiments of the founding fathers of 1776, who hoped that their new republic, a *novus ordo seclorum*, offered a solution to the bloody religious conflicts that had afflicted Europe. (A comparison of these two versions of American constitutionalism will be one theme of this book.)

Within less than a generation after the Union victory over the Confederacy, American political scientists, many of whom had studied in Germany or read books by German philosophers of history, had begun a project for building "the modern administrative state." Their goal, Marini explains, was "to establish the rational or technical means to carry out the will of the people." Commensurate with its boundless optimism, this project would exact an almost impossible price: "It required unlimited power in the state...to institutionalize rationality in the service of will through utilization of a universal class, the bureaucracy."[18] This development points to one of the great ironies of the Civil War and another element of tragedy in Lincoln's assassination. Though he managed to drive the Union to success on the battlefield, Lincoln did not live to translate that victory into a political program guided by his statesmanship.

> The Civil War, as Abraham Lincoln always insisted, was about the issue of slavery and was fought over the principle of equality. With

the victory of the Union armies, it seemed likely that Lincoln's understanding of the meaning of equality would prevail. In that case, equality would have remained the indispensable ground of national citizenship. But such was not to be the case. The Progressive intellectuals, and the new social science disciplines then being developed in the new research universities, denied the natural right foundation of the regime. They also rejected the social compact and the abstract principle of equality itself.[19]

The attempt by American political scientists to escape the challenge of natural right by putting all political decisions into the hands of nonpartisan experts was as naïve as it was disastrous, Jaffa thought. Such a project, he argued, was "the logical culmination of the quest by modern man, equipped by modern science, to solve the human problem by abolishing…the discipline of moral virtue."[20] It was precisely this misunderstanding of the true nature and limits of politics that had led most historians to overlook the real significance of the Lincoln-Douglas debates. To the degree that mid-twentieth century scholars noticed any enduring moral dimension to those debates, they considered it a *failure* of democracy.

In a 1958 essay, Jaffa responds to the argument of a professor who had asserted "the simple fact" that "issues dealing with right and wrong…do not lend themselves to the democratic process." But, as Jaffa notes, "if discussion is efficient only when there is nothing important to discuss, then democracy as a form of government is neither possible nor desirable." Only in Strauss's subterranean pit of self-delusion would political scientists attempt to create a government that avoided any discussion of right and wrong. Jaffa notes in the conclusion of his essay: "That men may be called upon to fight for [a] conviction cannot be called a failure of democracy. It would be a failure only if they refused to fight for it."[21]

There is no doubt Jaffa thought the violent campus radicals of the 1960s were wrong about almost everything; their ends were wildly unreasonable, their tactics cowardly and cruel, their arguments weak. Yet for all that, the very fact that these radicals were willing to make claims about right and wrong (however misguided) and argue for a conception of justice (however grounded in passion rather than reason) put them one small step closer to the light than the bureaucratic mole-men, with their blind faith in soothing platitudes. Thus, Jaffa's writings have something to offer the cynical and disaffected on both the left and the right, especially those young people who wonder what meaning they can hope to find in their lives as the establishment crumbles.

But what Jaffa teaches is neither easy nor comforting. So far from offering his students and readers idle chatter or shallow patriotism, Jaffa sought to reveal how natural right remains a living force, pulsing with great power, as long as there are men and women who would resist the burrowing mole-men seeking safety in denial. Precisely for this reason, the ancient world considered it very much an open question whether appeals to natural right should be seen as ultimately comforting or terrifying.

In antiquity, both Jerusalem and Athens emphasized the danger, even the sinfulness, of man's overly bold inquisitiveness. The Bible and Greek mythology each prescribe terrible punishment for peering behind the curtain of the revealed, divine law, the law that simply *is* and is not to be questioned. Genesis tells of the expulsion of Adam and Eve from the Garden of Eden for eating from the tree of knowledge of good and evil. The Greek myth of Prometheus recounts a similar parable of divine punishment for intellectual hubris. But whereas the Hebrews believed in a single creator God, the Greeks worshipped the squabbling Olympian divinities. They had, therefore, a rather different metaphor for the original sin of learning "the nature of things." Prometheus was not damned to eternal torment for giving mankind an apple; the knowledge he shared was symbolically represented by... fire.

2

THE OPEN DOOR

Using Freudian psychoanalysis to understand someone's character was not an approach that impressed Jaffa.[1] It would seem inappropriate then to begin this chapter attempting to do just that. Still, if we take its psychological influence with a grain of salt, the following anecdote is too good to pass up as a glimpse into the early development of Jaffa's personality.

In a long eulogy he wrote when his mother, Frances, passed away in 1984, Jaffa recounts an episode from when he was about five years old, while his family was living on Long Island, just outside New York City where his father would later own a successful nightclub. His mother decided to start a small business making high-end children's clothes. Harry was her mannequin and model. One particularly lavish costume was a velveteen suit with pearl buttons. Perhaps finding no buyers, or perhaps to showcase her creation to a wider audience, Frances sent Harry to school one day in this Little Lord Fauntleroy outfit. The teachers were impressed with his mother's handiwork and cooed over him. But the other students, especially the boys, were somewhat less besotted with Harry's finery. (This would have been around 1923.) Before the day was out, Jaffa recounts,

"I was in my first fight, and I never again went to school in any 'distinctive' garments."[2]

It was not his last encounter with recess fisticuffs. In tow to his father's various business ventures, Harry and his family moved several times to different parts of New York City and its suburbs. Each time he started a new school, he would be more or less compelled to scuffle with a few of the other boys on his first day. These events did not seem to leave him emotionally scarred or physically traumatized. He cheerfully joined the boxing team when he matriculated at Yale in 1935, where one of his coaches was a man named Gerald Ford, who would go on to a rather successful career in politics. (Contrary to some reports, Jaffa was never in the Golden Gloves.) But his career in the ring didn't last. Before his freshman year was out, Harry—according to family legend—"got a dent in his head" during one match and hung up his gloves for good. He continued the training, though, maintaining his proficiency with the jump rope well into middle age. Later, his passion for exercise switched to long-distance cycling. Of the several serendipitous coincidences that seemed to mark Jaffa's life and career, not the least was this early introduction to the necessity, even the nobility, of spirited self-defense.[3] Whether this meant, as Jaffa seemed to infer, that one should *seek out* fights ("my instincts have always been to spring right at the throat of objections") and embrace pugnacity as a virtue is another matter.[4]

There were other childhood indicators of his later interests. In a warm, reminiscing letter to Norman Podhoretz, the famous "neoconservative" and longtime editor of *Commentary* magazine, Jaffa recalls that his father's restaurant and jazz club

brought me often to the city as a teenager, and I remember watching and listening to political debates in Union Square as early as 1933. I began to become "politicized" by reading Lincoln Steffens'

Autobiography, which someone gave me for my Bar Mitzvah. I also received Beveridge's *Lincoln* on that occasion, but it did not "take" until much later.

But I went to Yale, not Columbia (or City College). I certainly became an enthusiastic New Dealer (as was my first instructor in political science, Harvey C. Mansfield, Sr.) If memory serves aright, some 60 to 80% of my class were for Landon in 1936. How times do change. But that was as far to the Left as I ever went. (Ronald Reagan's politics seem to have marched with mine over the years. We both cast our first votes for FDR, we both changed our party registration in 1962, and we both supported Goldwater in 1964....)

I read Hayek's *Road to Serfdom* in 1946, and became a rabid anti-socialist then and thereafter. But I loathe Hayek's philosophical libertarianism as much as I loathe the socialism he taught me to despise.[5]

Harry Jaffa was born in New York City on October 7, 1918, just a few weeks after Germany requested armistice talks with President Woodrow Wilson, hoping to end the hostilities of what was then called the Great War. With the defeat of the Imperial Powers imminent, Jaffa's parents gave Harry the middle name "Victor" (perhaps another fact that Freud would have found significant). Though the family was never wealthy, Harry's childhood was comfortable, safe, and what we today would call "enriching." Harry's mother was an impressive woman, with a formidable intellect, a love for the English language (especially proper elocution), and an impressive education. In high school, she had studied Latin and performed so well that she was invited to attend special early-morning sessions on Greek. She was admitted to Vassar, but her father thought it more practical to send her to secretarial school. In another time, Frances Jaffa might have earned a name for herself as an accomplished scholar. Nevertheless, she was able to satisfy her intellectual curiosity through the many opportunities for attending classes and seminars in and around New York City, including a lecture by the political theorist and economist Harold Laski at Columbia University. Frances passed on her love of learning to her son, though she never pressured him to pursue an academic career.

Harry's father, Sol, confined his cerebral activities to business. His restaurant and night club, with the wonderfully symbolic name The Open Door, operated in Greenwich Village from 1925 to 1955. A barrel-chested but gentle man, Sol tried to keep his family life—especially for his wife and Harry's sister, Lillian—insulated from the somewhat risqué world of a Manhattan nightclub. (The Open Door was one of the first white-owned establishments to feature African-American jazz artists.) Harry, betraying his study of English literature at Yale, once described the restaurant in New York as the world of novelist Damon Runyon, while at home his father tried to cultivate the sensibilities of Edith Wharton.

The club did well; Harry and Lillian never lacked for any necessities. But Sol's somewhat carefree attitude toward money (including an admirable generosity toward the needy) meant the family never rose above middle class. Still, unlike many of his generation, Harry had the luxury of turning his childhood "work" into a form of play. He and his cousin Hortense used puppets, constructed by his mother and his aunt, to perform marionette shows at children's parties, for which they earned the then-princely sum of $15. Under the tutelage of another aunt, Nettie, he learned to play the violin, a passion he would maintain into his twenties.

Among his large extended family, with many aunts, uncles, and cousins, Jaffa was immersed in his Jewish identity, with its roots in Old Europe and all its culturally imposing connotations. Though neither of his parents were especially devout, both his mother and grandmother dreamt often of visiting their ancestral homeland in Germany. With the Nazis' rise to power, however,

"Mom gave up her lifelong attachment to the superiority of Jewish life in Germany and transferred all her intellectual and cultural allegiance" to England and America. Jaffa's arrival at Yale was his first experience outside of a Jewish environment. This separation, he later remarked, was essential to his appreciation for the deeper meaning of his ancient faith "and America as a New Jerusalem."[6]

Before leaving his New York Jewish environment, however, Jaffa prepared for his Bar Mitzvah alongside his close childhood friend Joseph Cropsey. Some years later, Jaffa would introduce Cropsey to political philosophy (pulling him away from economics), and Joe would go on to become a colleague of and collaborator with Leo Strauss at the University of Chicago. As to the Bar Mitzvah classes, Jaffa recalled,

> I was the worst student in the class, while Joe was the best. I remember even that he conducted young people's services, which I never attended since, like Tom Sawyer, I never attended any religious services except under the sternest compulsion.[7]

Another adolescent friend was Francis Canavan, who would also become a professor of political philosophy, teaching for many years at Fordham University. But while Harry and Joe were studying Hebrew, young Frank was reciting Latin in preparation for his Rite of Confirmation and would eventually become a Jesuit priest.

Though a less than diligent student of the Torah, Harry's clear academic aptitude meant that, unlike his maternal grandfather, Sol and Frances never questioned that he would go to college. He was only sixteen when he arrived at Yale's New Haven, Connecticut, campus, turning seventeen a month into his first semester. In the courses he took for his major in English, he recounts that he read nothing but excellent books. (The reading material for his other interest, political science, was more disappointing.) Even many years later, Jaffa would speak fondly of his favorite Yale professor, a respected Milton scholar named Alex Witherspoon, who sponsored an unofficial Bible reading group. Jaffa claimed to have never missed a meeting in four years. In fact, he found it to be the best "course" he took since it gave him an ear for the many biblical allusions he would later encounter in Lincoln.

At the end of his freshman year, Harry decided on an academic career, although his father as well as his academic advisor, Harvey Mansfield, Sr., both warned him that his desired fields, English and political science, were at that time closed to Jews. Given the stubbornness he had inherited from both parents, this deterred him not in the least. After receiving his bachelor's degree in English in 1939, he remained at Yale to pursue graduate work in political science, but he found the courses intellectually arid. He would later describe the graduate department there as "a land of dead souls." The great thinkers of the past were examined not for any vital truth they might impart but as antiquarian curiosities. Studying political philosophy struck him at that time "like a tour through a wax museum." The modern, relativistic doctrine that "values" are merely personal preferences, radically distinct from empirical facts,

> [was as] unchallengeable as the doctrine of the Trinity was presumed to be in thirteenth-century Paris. While at that time I had no intellectual equipment to challenge the reigning assumptions, I had an instinct that told me that a career lived under their authority would not be a life worth living.[8]

But for a stroke of good fortune, which would occur a few years later, this might have been the end of Jaffa's academic career in political philosophy.

Fleeing Yale, he returned to New York in 1940 to look for work, but the lingering effects of the Great Depression meant that good jobs were scarce for a Jew with little more to show than an

English degree from Yale and moderate skills as a violin player. His most promising option was to work for the government, but that meant taking the civil service examination in public administration (still a formidable hurdle in those days). He had studied public administration at Yale and despised it. But necessity drove him to register for a two-semester graduate course at the New School for Social Research taught by the great German scholar and former judge Arnold Brecht. Like many of the professors at the New School, Brecht had relocated to New York after fleeing the Nazis. As Jaffa described it,

> The Graduate Faculty had been added in the thirties to the original New School, which had been founded in the twenties by some of the leading lights of the Progressive era as a progressive enterprise in adult education. The Graduate Faculty had been originally called the University in Exile, to provide a haven for distinguished scholars who were refugees from Hitler's Europe. Prestigious or not, that faculty in the forties, may have been, for a decade or more, the greatest faculty of its kind ever assembled under one roof, courtesy of Adolf Hitler. But it received little or no notice in the world of the elite universities.[9]

In April of 1941, Jaffa passed the civil service exam and moved to Washington, DC, in order to take up "salaried employment for the first time in my life." One morning, eating breakfast at his boarding house, he looked across the table and set his eyes on a young woman named Marjorie Etta Butler. He fell in love in that moment, "made a date for that night, and never looked back."[10] Jaffa would later joke, "I hadn't expected this: I was looking for a job, not a wife."[11] Thus began a lifelong love affair and a marriage that lasted an astonishing sixty-eight years. (They were married in 1942; Marjorie died in 2010.)

Jaffa landed a job doing what he regarded as tedious and

unimportant work with the War Production Board, overseeing the rationing of the silk-substitute, rayon. (The federal government had seized all silk production for military purposes.) He did, however, reconnect with his former faculty advisor from Yale, Harvey Mansfield, now an official in the Office of Price Administration.[12] Jaffa, who wore thick glasses his whole life, remained in Washington for most of the war after failing the eye exam for active military service three times. In 1944 he decided to return to graduate studies, and he and Marjorie moved to New York, where he had developed a good impression of The New School. Arnold Brecht, with whom Jaffa had taken the public administration class four year earlier, had achieved distinction as a jurist and government official in Weimar Germany and possessed "a tall, stately presence."[13] But Jaffa's life would be changed by a much less prepossessing figure. In his first semester, looking through the catalog, he signed up for a course on Jean-Jacques Rousseau taught by one "L. Strauss," a professor unknown to him (or virtually anyone else in the United States). Jaffa was impressed enough that he signed up the following semester for another Leo Strauss course, on Immanuel Kant and Aristotle, and it was here that Jaffa was thunderstruck. He recalls his experience this way:

> Strauss was a physically insignificant little man with a weak voice. His presence was as unimpressive as the dilapidated classrooms provided by the New School. But he was pure overwhelming intellectual force. After a few minutes into one of his seminars, the little man became a giant. Every great book was a kind of *Treasure Island*, or more particularly a map of an island holding a treasure. But you had to decipher the map, and do the work of discovery, overcoming the obstacles by which great art, imitating nature, trains the mind to be worthy of its gifts. One of Strauss's secrets was that he made you feel not a passive receptacle of his insights, but as his partner in a voyage of discovery. He was the captain of the ship. But you were part of the crew. And you sailed

together. Saul on the road to Damascus was not more stunned, nor more transformed than I, by my encounter with Strauss.[14]

The spring 1945 course on Aristotle, described in the New School catalogue as "Justice and Political Necessity (Ethics and Politics)," cemented Jaffa's lifelong interest in the Greek philosopher who wrote so memorably on those themes. In fact, Aristotle's *Nicomachean Ethics* and *Politics* would become the subjects of two of Jaffa's most significant scholarly accomplishments. During his decades in front of the classroom, he would return to Aristotle, especially the *Ethics*, as a constant theme of his lectures, and he seemed over the years to have absorbed the text into his bones. Many former students recall Jaffa's course on the *Ethics* as the best and most memorable of their college careers.[15] (Chapter 4 will address Jaffa and Aristotle in greater detail.)

This, however, was not the end of Strauss's soul-turning influence. The following semester his course "Readings in Political Philosophy: Utopias and Political Science" included Plato's *Republic*. Jaffa was not moved to transfer his deep interest in Aristotle to Plato. (In fact, on the most urgent questions, he thought what united the two thinkers was far more significant than what divided them). Yet a certain argument about justice presented in *The Republic* between Socrates and a character named Thrasymachus lodged itself in Jaffa's mind. Less than a year later, it would flash into his consciousness like a burst of lightning while he browsed in a second-hand bookstore.

It's appropriate to pause this narrative briefly in order to consider what Strauss said in that course. Later in his career, when his reputation had grown, Strauss's students began to record his lectures on audio cassettes. Many of these recordings have been transcribed and are available at the University of Chicago's Leo Strauss Center website.[16] When Jaffa studied Plato's *Republic* with Strauss in New York in 1946, this practice had not yet begun. However, the transcripts of Strauss's 1957 and 1961 courses on

The Republic are available, and although not identical they cover many of the same broad themes. (Strauss's remarks in class are also generally commensurate with his published commentaries on *The Republic*.) We have, therefore, some sense of what Jaffa would have learned at the New School.

Strauss begins the 1957 course by noting that "the city in speech" described by Socrates is a utopia. It is the "best regime" that is "demanded by the nature of man and yet that which is not necessarily actual." But, anticipating a common objection, Strauss asks, "What does this have to do with our concern as political scientists or political analysts for societies which *exist*?" "All political action," Strauss explains, "is concerned with improvement or preservation."

> To improve means to make better; to preserve means to retain that which is proving satisfactory. All political action is thus concerned with questions of better or worse.... The problem is that what we ordinarily think about good and bad is certainly not very clear. In any case, we may even be wrong about what we think. With this in mind we call this thing *opinion* about good and bad. With the realization that we do not really know about good and bad, however, comes the demand that we should seek for *knowledge* of good and bad. The completed knowledge, the fully developed knowledge of the good and thus of the bad is the best regime. Knowing the best regime, we would know what is good politically or humanly in an all-comprehensive way regarding the most important and most comprehensive matters.[17]

This emphasis on identifying what is highest or best, as the standard by which to judge any phenomenon, is the general approach toward political philosophy we find in the classical writers, including Aristotle—whose best regime we will examine later.

Before addressing the substance of Plato's dialectical investigation—*The Republic,* like all of Plato's books, is a dialogue,
not a treatise—Strauss raises another objection. Assuming an
examination of the best regime is a legitimate question: Can it be
answered? "The dominant view within the social sciences today,"
he explains, "is that it cannot be answered [because] all answers
to questions of good and bad, ultimately even of true and false,
depend on specific historical premises." This is a doctrine known
as historicism, which insists that all philosophic discoveries
are "evident not to man as man, but to a specific kind of man,
e.g., Western man, Greeks, Americans, or what have you." It is
worth noting the severity of Strauss's next remark: "We must
not underestimate the power of this *collective evil* of our time."
[Emphasis added.][18]

Strauss's interpretation of *The Republic* is subtle and complex.
We can summarize here only a small segment of what Strauss
says about the character Thrasymachus, a teacher of rhetoric who
bursts into the conversation in Book I and challenges Socrates's
musings about the nature of justice. Thrasymachus is most famous
for advancing the view that justice is "the advantage of the stronger," a weak, self-interested argument that Socrates quashes, as
expected, but perhaps a bit too easily. Thrasymachus accepts his
dialectical defeat and submits to Socrates's contention that justice
is not a matter of "might makes right." Socrates pointedly insists
that it is better (for one's soul, at any rate) to suffer injustice than
to commit it.

A few notable points from Strauss's commentary:

- Thrasymachus is a teacher of rhetoric and thus claims
  a kind of expertise in ruling or governing. But this
  self-interest colors his arguments about justice. Strauss
  compares this expertise to the self-interested claims
  of modern academics. "Thrasymachus stands and falls

with the contention that intelligence is necessary in politics. Compare this with the situation of the social scientist," who must always insist on the unique and objective insights of his profession. For a social scientist to challenge the premises of his discipline would be to "absolutely ruin himself in the eyes of the Rockefeller Foundation and all other foundations in the world." Strauss reminds his students not to "underestimate the vested interests which arise with the existence of such groups."[19]

- Partly related to this, Thrasymachus represents a view known as legal positivism. According to this doctrine, there is "no natural justice. The just is identical with the legal. Thrasymachus suggests that we cannot go beyond the idea that the just is the legal." Strauss elaborates on this later by noting, that "the hidden argument of the whole *Republic* [is] to transcend the positive law and go to a higher level," which is governed "not by positive law but by reason or a rational art."[20]

- Thrasymachus enters the dialogue as an accuser of Socrates. This, and the fact that he is a master of swaying crowds by inciting their passions, indicates that he symbolically represents the people *en masse* of Athens itself (the *demos*).

- The argument about the advantage of the stronger raises the question: Who is, or are, stronger? We should not simply assume it is the most powerful individual. Athens was a democracy, which, by a majority vote of its popular assembly, executed Socrates. Strauss mentions that in a democracy, "The many weak are the strong.... This is the democratic implication of Thrasymachus's doctrine." (One implication here is a warning against oppressive majoritarianism.)[21]

These brief hints do not by themselves reveal very much either about the infinite complexities of *The Republic* or its influence on Jaffa's thought. But the disputes over justice that Plato elaborates in this dialogue were central to his scholarship. I will explain these points in more detail as we dig into Jaffa's work on American politics, especially the Civil War.

When Strauss and Jaffa met in September of 1944, Strauss was about to turn forty-five; Jaffa would be twenty-six that October. Though Strauss had been with the graduate faculty of the New School since 1938, his great fame and influence as a teacher was still before him, and Jaffa was among his very first PhD students. Today, the ever-growing literature on Leo Strauss can fill a small library, and there are interpretations attributing to him almost every imaginable position. Depending on who you read, he was a liberal democrat, a self-styled Nietzschean *Übermensch*, a pious Jew, a nihilist who thought philosophy was impossible, a philosopher king, a quasi-fascist enemy of liberal democracy, a metaphysical theorist with no genuine interest in politics, or an atheistic theologian who devoted decades to proving the non-existence of God. In a strange burst of infamy during the 1990s and early 2000s, Strauss's name even came to the attention of the mainstream media, when he was accused of being the mastermind (beyond the grave) of George W. Bush's invasion of Iraq. Many of these extreme views have been concocted by ideologues who never met (or perhaps even read) Strauss. Among his actual students, views about his true beliefs tend to be more subtle and more reasonable. Nevertheless, even among the first generation of Straussians, there is a surprising amount of disagreement. (Chapter 7 addresses some of these disputes.)

We do know that Strauss was born outside Marburg in central Germany, was raised an observant Jew (and became, for a while, an ardent Zionist), and earned a doctorate in philosophy under Ernst Cassirer at the University of Hamburg. He also took classes at the University of Freiburg, where he studied with some of the great minds of prewar Germany, including Edmund Husserl and Martin Heidegger. Strauss was a brilliant analyst of the great philosophic texts, and he published nuanced (even abstruse) interpretations of Plato, Xenophon, Aristophanes, Maimonides, Machiavelli, Spinoza, Rousseau, Nietzsche, and others. Strauss was deeply concerned with the "crisis of the West" and believed that the recovery of classical political philosophy, particularly Plato and Aristotle, was necessary to rescue modern thought from the pit beneath the cave. Contrary to the nearly unanimous opinion of leading intellectuals and scholars, Strauss averred that the insights of Plato, Aristotle, and other great minds of the past might be *true*, and he challenged the historicist dogma that denied the possibility of any universal knowledge or permanent wisdom.[22]

Strauss's most famous book, *Natural Right and History* (1953), was partly a self-conscious challenge to Martin Heidegger's *Being and Time* (1927). Heidegger was the most sophisticated exponent of this historical relativism, or existentialism, which took on a superficial form in the "fact-value" distinction. In response to an essay about Strauss in the *New York Times* in 1985, Jaffa explained his own conversion away from this dogma.

> I had spent five years at Yale in the 1930s, as undergraduate and graduate student, where no one, so far as I knew, had ever doubted this orthodoxy. To study the Declaration of Independence—or Plato's *Republic*—meant to study the "climate of opinion," "the spirit of the times," the "weltanschauung" out of which the work came. Strauss however declared that we must understand the great works of the human mind as their authors understood them, before we try to understand them differently or better.... None of the great writers of the past had believed, either in the fact-value distinction, or in the historicist fallacy that the genesis of an idea was the key to the truth about it....

It is difficult to convey to anyone who has not shared such an experience the excitement I felt—now nearly forty years ago—when I realized that I had been emancipated from the dungeon of historicism, from that dark place of the soul in which the great questions, the only questions that make life ultimately worth living, are treated as "essentially meaningless."[23]

In Strauss's mind, modern political science, distorted by its imitation of quantitative natural science, was unwilling or unable to confront the problem of justice and was therefore useless in making distinctions between good and bad regimes. Above all, it could not educate, let alone inspire, citizens in the face of Nazi and Soviet tyranny. In one of his most striking and memorable lines, Strauss declared that only a "fool would call the new political science diabolic: it has no attributes peculiar to fallen angels." It did not even reach the intellectual seriousness of Machiavelli, "for Machiavelli's teaching was graceful, subtle, and colorful. Nor is it Neronian. Nevertheless one may say of it that it fiddles while Rome burns." And with a crushing blow, Strauss adds, "It is excused by two facts: it does not know that it fiddles, and it does not know that Rome burns."[24]

The rejection of Heidegger and the fact-value distinction was subsidiary to three main dichotomies that dominated Strauss's thinking: 1) what he called "the theological-political problem," 2) the quarrel between philosophy and poetry, and 3) the contrast between ancients and moderns. The first interpenetrated virtually all of Strauss's writing, according to Jaffa, and was also central to Jaffa's own scholarship. It will thus form a major theme of this book. In brief, the "problem" of theology and politics turns on whether the highest life for man consists in the pious obedience of the believer or the skeptical inquiry of the philosopher. (A related aspect—especially in the way Jaffa elaborated this theme—concerns the authority of the laws. Does every regime require some kind of divine sanction or support; and what happens when obedience to God conflicts with obedience to secular authority?)

As Jaffa wrote in a 1987 essay, Strauss's deepest thinking was guided by

> the only ultimate principles he recognized, between revelation and reason, the Bible and Greek philosophy, Jerusalem and Athens. Strauss saw Western civilization as constituted, at its core, by the confluence of what was represented by the two cities, Jerusalem and Athens.... By philosophy, Strauss meant not a subject matter but a way of life, above all the way of life of Socrates, the way of life of autonomous human reason. By revelation, he meant not Homer or Hesiod or any other poet (not even Shakespeare), but the Bible, the way of life of obedient love of the living God. He saw revelation and reason—the Bible and Greek philosophy—as in fundamental agreement both as to what morality was and as to the insufficiency of morality. He saw them as in fundamental disagreement as to what that X was which completed and justified morality.[25]

Strauss's second dichotomy addressed the tension between the rational teachings of philosophers and the stories and myths told by the poets (in our time the "poets" are Hollywood directors and pop stars). Human beings are never fully rational, societies even less so. This raises the question of whether (or to what degree) pure reason should try to correct the entertaining fictions and epic narratives that capture our imaginations and shape our views of the world.

The last distinction, between ancients and moderns, was partly chronological and partly philosophic. Strauss was concerned about the consequences of the modern attempt to solve the inevitable contradictions inherent in political life. The ancient thinkers held that every human community raises questions about the peak of virtue or the most admirable human type. In particular, this includes the dispute between piety and philosophy mentioned above. This natural and healthy tension took a problematic turn with the rise of Christianity as the official religion of medieval Europe. Again, this issue of secular versus religious authority was a topic of central importance for Jaffa and will be discussed in later chapters. By way of introducing the issue, we can say that in the sixteenth and seventeenth centuries certain radical thinkers attempted to deal with the problem of theocratic authority by insulating politics from "unrealistic" hopes about virtue or the good of the soul and lowering the focus of government to the needs and pleasures of the body. In part, the "modern project" as Strauss saw it was a highly questionable attempt to solve or overcome the question of the best way of life and thus eliminate the theological-political problem. Philosophers such as Thomas Hobbes, Benedict Spinoza, Francis Bacon, and René Descartes hoped that (as Jaffa describes it) "science would supply the goods that men wanted most—health, wealth, freedom—without any requirement of virtue, either in their acquisition or in their enjoyment."[26]

All three of these distinctions (theology/politics, philosophy/poetry, ancients/moderns) are connected with another important theme for which Strauss became famous (or notorious): "esoteric" writing.

To explain the baleful consequences of late-modern philosophy, Strauss's *Natural Right and History* traced a process of continuous radicalization, beginning with Niccolò Machiavelli's initial break from classical and Christian thought. In some cases, the thread had to be discerned in the subtle or indirect teachings of leading philosophers. Strauss believed that for various reasons (including the threat of persecution by religious or secular authorities), some great thinkers concealed their true intent in an esoteric subtext obscured beneath a more innocuous surface. His remarks about esoteric writing in the works of English philosopher John Locke, in particular, would eventually lead to considerable disputes among Strauss's students. Because of Locke's influence on the American founders, this question of "the esoteric Locke" also played an important part in Jaffa's scholarship. The editors of a posthumous collection of Jaffa's essays called *The Rediscovery of America* clarify what would be implied by one version of this hypothesis:

> The esoteric Locke viewed man as apolitical and possessed of rights by nature but having no obligations by nature. Man was, from Locke's point of view, a radical egoist. The American Founders, insofar as they placed any reliance on Locke, therefore incorporated this radical individualism into their notion of natural rights, particularly the right to property—which Locke emphasized was derived exclusively from "self-ownership"—and provided no ground for obligations or morality of any kind. In other words, the Founders could not escape the inevitable forces of modernity—the American Founding was radically modern.[27]

We will examine later how Jaffa came to reject this particular theory, as well how he explored and developed Strauss's other major themes. For now, it is sufficient to mention that in 1944, Jaffa's life was forever changed. Over the next seven years, he attended nineteen courses taught by Strauss, in New York and then Chicago. In addition to classes at the New School, Jaffa would often spend Saturdays at Strauss's home in Riverdale, just north of Manhattan. He would bring his violin, and he frequently entertained Strauss and his wife with a musical performance. It was evident to Strauss in these early years that part of Jaffa's soul was still attracted to art. Although he never relinquished the love of literature (especially Shakespeare) that he developed at Yale, Jaffa had to make a decision about whether to continue with the time and energy his musical practice required. Many of Jaffa's students recall the story he would tell about the fateful day. Visiting Strauss one afternoon, Jaffa had obviously left behind his violin case. Noticing this, Strauss smiled knowingly as if to say that, in the struggle between music and political philosophy, "I won."

With this choice made, Jaffa pursued a PhD under Strauss's direction, which he completed in 1949, and was awarded his doctorate, with honors, in 1950. Jaffa's dissertation, an examination of Thomas Aquinas's interpretation of Aristotle's *Nicomachean Ethics*, was accepted (with Strauss's recommendation) by the University Chicago Press in 1950 and was published as Jaffa's first book in 1952.

Jaffa taught for a while at Queens College and the City College of New York, then followed his teacher to the Midwest, where Strauss had taken a new appointment at the University of Chicago in 1949 and arranged a position for his protégé. Among other topics, Jaffa taught a course in 1950 on Lincoln, a figure who had captured his attention a few years earlier and would become a central subject of his scholarship for the next six decades. In 1951, Jaffa delivered a guest lecture at St. John's College in Annapolis on "Expediency and Morality in the Lincoln-Douglas Debates." This lecture, the kernel of his *Crisis of the House Divided*, was published in 1957 in *Anchor Review* alongside an excerpt from Vladimir Nabokov's *Lolita*. (Jaffa liked to joke that he made Nabokov famous.) In the interim, however, Jaffa had been hired for a tenure track position at Ohio State University in 1951, where he remained until 1964, becoming friends along the way with the famous Ohio State football coach Woody Hayes. Jaffa did return to Chicago for a year, in 1956–57, when Strauss secured him a visiting fellowship to complete the research for *Crisis of the House Divided*.[28]

The appointment at Ohio State was arranged by his former mentor at Yale and war bureaucracy colleague, Harvey Mansfield, a senior figure in the profession who served for a time as editor of the discipline's official journal, the *American Political Science Review*. Along with another scholar hired by Mansfield, David Spitz, Jaffa was the first Jew to become a professor at Ohio State.[29] Mansfield's son, Harvey, Jr., was himself an impressively intelligent young man who would go on to a distinguished career at Harvard. Jaffa took young Harvey under his wing, and the two developed a lifelong, though sometimes contentious, friendship.

Perhaps inspired with patriotic fervor by the booming economy and the US-Soviet space race, Jaffa was a dynamo of scholarly productivity and intellectual development through the 1950s. Less than a decade after receiving his doctorate, he produced two influential books in different fields (*Thomism* in 1952 and *Crisis* in 1959), published a landmark essay on Shakespeare in 1957, and authored numerous essays and book reviews on natural law, classical philosophy, and American politics. In the midst of all this, he undertook an intensive effort to teach himself ancient Greek, focusing on translating and interpreting Plato's dialogue, *Gorgias*. There are indications that Jaffa planned to publish an essay or even a book on the dialogue, but this was never completed. (In 1954, he wrote to Strauss, "I have greatly increased my stock of notes on the *Gorgias*, but I do not know when I will be able to assemble them into a manuscript.")[30]

In 1963, Jaffa made his first foray into Republican politics, signing up for the presidential campaign of Arizona Senator Barry Goldwater. While contributing to the campaign's efforts in Ohio, Jaffa came to the attention of one of Goldwater's senior advisors, who invited him to San Francisco where the Republican convention was to be held.[31] Jaffa had been a New Deal

Democrat but changed his party registration in 1962, in disgust at what he perceived to be President John Kennedy's shameful behavior in the Bay of Pigs incident. Jaffa accepted the invitation to join Goldwater and his top staff in San Francisco as a kind of political theory and history consultant. It would prove to be a momentous decision.

Goldwater's popularity among rank-and-file Republicans revealed a split in the convention and the party between insurgent conservatives mostly from the South and West and moderate Republicans from the older and more blue-blooded East Coast wing. Jaffa attended the heated debates of the platform committee and was appalled at the abuse being heaped on Goldwater by spokesmen for New York Governor Nelson Rockefeller and Pennsylvania Governor Bill Scranton. "They were talking constantly about extremism this, extremism that. So I wrote a paragraph about 'extremism in defense of liberty is no vice.'" Jaffa recalled that during the previous year, in 1963,

> Martin Luther King in one of his greatest productions, his letter from Birmingham Jail, had a long section on extremism. He went from Moses and Jesus and Thomas Aquinas and Jefferson and Lincoln and at the end, each one was a different kind of extremist. And he said the important thing is not whether we should be extremist, but what kind of extremist we should be.[32]

Jaffa was well acquainted with all these figures, and his internal memo, keying off King's Birmingham speech, was meant to provide the campaign with some historical and philosophical background for responding to the accusations by Scranton and Rockefeller. "I wrote that statement, in part, as a repudiation of the critique of extremism," Jaffa recalled.[33] Goldwater was delighted to see such a forceful answer to the criticisms he had been enduring. For weeks, Scranton, who was challenging Goldwater for the nomination, had been pushing the line that Goldwater was a right-wing radical and a loose cannon. The day before the convention delegates were to vote for the party's nominee (and expected to confirm Goldwater's selection), Scranton's campaign circulated a letter claiming that Goldwater stood for "a whole crazy-quilt collection of absurd and dangerous positions."[34]

Journalist Rick Perlstein's account of the Goldwater campaign, *Before the Storm*, recounts what happened next. Chief speechwriter Karl Hess, "brought in a draft that did exactly what an acceptance speech after a divisive primary was supposed to do: proceed as if there had never been any divisions in the first place." But this was precisely the opposite of what Goldwater's most trusted advisors, his "brain trust," wanted. The draft "was dead on arrival." "Goldwater gave the task of composing a new draft to Harry Jaffa," Perlstein reports. "He was impressed with Jaffa's quick thinking [and the] memorandum Jaffa had written." But when Jaffa circulated a new speech, it caused "a major row among his deputies over one line."

> Jaffa had lifted it directly from his memo; Goldwater had singled it out as his favorite. But half the group thought it was way too incendiary and would be utterly misunderstood. Then Goldwater put the argument to a stop by ordering the offending passage underlined twice. And that was that.[35]

When Jaffa wrote the memorandum, he had never intended those passages for public delivery, and in retrospect he thought it was probably imprudent for Goldwater to vent his frustration in that way. "I'm not making an excuse for myself," Jaffa later said. "I was certainly enthusiastically in favor of it at the time." He had not been on the floor of the convention and did not appreciate the indignant mood of the delegates who felt scorned and belittled by Scranton's remarks. "But the Senator *did*" understand how the delegates felt, Jaffa recalled, "and he knew what he was doing. I don't blame him for his feelings."[36]

Perlstein picks up the story with Goldwater at the rostrum, approaching the peroration of his address:

> The air thickened with expectation; he was drawing to a climax. Now texts were finally distributed to delegates and reporters. "And let our Republicanism, so focused and so dedicated, not be made fuzzy and futile by unthinking and stupid labels," he said, concentrating his face. "Those who do not care for our cause we do not expect to enter our ranks in any case."
>
> Then came the passage he had ordered double-underscored on his reading copy and the copies for the press. "*I would remind you that extremism in the defense of liberty—is—no—vice!*"
>
> He had to wait forty-one seconds before he could continue. He pursed his lips, glanced solemnly down at the text:
>
> "*And let me remind you also—that moderation in the pursuit of justice is no virtue!*"
>
> The roar from the galleries could be heard inside the Goldwater trailer [on the street]....A standing ovation began....Frenzied delegates took hold of the struts holding up ABC's broadcast booth and shook them furiously.[37]

Over the years, various claims have been circulated about where Jaffa "found" those famous lines (in Cicero, for example, according to one common but erroneous report), and there have even been suggestions that others were principally responsible for writing the speech. Of course, the senior campaign staff all made edits and provided input. But there is no question that Jaffa was the principal author. As he pointed out, the language has all the fingerprints of his scholarly specialties. He recalled in an interview years later:

> I stayed up all night. Warren Nutter was with me. He was an economist from the University of Virginia, a specialist in the Russian economy. We talked as I was writing it. All the writing was mine, and you could see the speech does not reflect the preoccupations of a specialist in the Russian economy. I mean Aristotle and Lincoln are spread all over the speech.[38]

Though some Straussians might be satisfied with such "textual" evidence, there is also the more significant fact that Goldwater himself had no doubts about who the author was, as he made clear in several letters to Jaffa after the campaign.[39]

After the convention, when it quickly became clear that Goldwater could not win the election, Jaffa decided he had had enough excitement and enough campaign work. He needed to get back to teaching, especially since he had a new tenured position, in Claremont, California, where he would spend the rest of his life.

In 1964, Harry and Marjorie (with their children, Donald, Philip, and Karen) moved to Claremont, where Harry began teaching at what was then Claremont Men's College, later Claremont McKenna College (CMC). He would also take on a joint appointment at the adjacent graduate school. From here, he would teach, publish, and argue until his retirement in 1989, after which he would continue to teach (outside the classroom), publish, and argue until his death in 2015 at the age of 96. Later chapters will examine the scholarship Jaffa produced in these years, his contributions to shaping the American conservative movement, and his many public debates—always vigorous, sometimes acrimonious, but never trivial. Jaffa took quite literally the Socratic dictum that to have one's errors exposed was a great benefit and that anyone who loved truth should be grateful for correction. Not without reason did William F. Buckley once write, "If you think it is hard arguing with Harry Jaffa, try agreeing with him."[40]

No discussion of Jaffa's teaching career in Claremont would

be complete without some reference to Jaffa's friend, coteacher, and alter ego: Harry Neumann. Less well known, even within academic circles, than other prominent Straussians, Neumann was an erudite scholar of classical and modern thought who taught at adjacent Scripps College, part of the consortium of Claremont colleges. An expert on Nietzsche, Neumann claimed that he had been persuaded by the German philosopher to become a nihilist, contending that there is no cosmic or natural support for justice. For many years, Jaffa and Neumann cotaught a seminar, "Socrates or Nihilism,"—known fondly to generations of students as the "Harry and Harry Show"—in which they took up the arguments for and against natural right.

In a letter to an inquiring student in 1996, Jaffa writes:

> Harry Neumann and I form a team, in which I play good cop and he plays bad cop. You are mistaken in thinking that I play Holmes and he Moriarty. It is he who is the Straussian (Holmes) masked as a nihilist unmasking nihilists masked as Straussians. Of course, I add "Or is he?" His self-proclaimed nihilism gives him standing (like Whittaker Chambers) as a member of the party whose membership he is disclosing.[41]

Readers may recall this reference to Sherlock Holmes and Moriarty from Chapter 1, which quoted extensively from the essay Jaffa wrote for and about his colleague, titled "Neumann or Nihilism." In the essay, Jaffa discusses a scene from Arthur Conan Doyle's *The Final Problem*, in which Holmes famously confronts Moriarty at Reichenbach Falls: "Sherlock Holmes, disguised as Dr. Moriarty, unmasks Dr. Moriarty, disguised as Holmes. Or does he? Each proceeds again to unmask the other." Jaffa playfully draws out the implications for what he and Neumann were attempting to do in their team teaching. "In the end it becomes clear—or does it?—that there is no ultimate identity for either. The only reality is—or are—the masks themselves, as they change continuously into their opposite." Of course, Jaffa did not mean to argue seriously that there is no reality or truth. Rather he wanted his readers and his students to think through the implications of each position. Contrary to some impressions, Jaffa never wanted his arguments simply to be imbibed as dogma.

Neumann himself confirms the overarching moral purpose of his collaboration with Jaffa, in which the two teachers reenact the fundamental arguments of political philosophy: "I became aware of the crucial role of politics partly through arguments with Harry Jaffa and his best students.... Jaffa seems to me to be the real heir of Strauss's defense of politics against scientific or nihilistic devaluation." In the wake of the Enlightenment, Neumann explains, philosophic skepticism became "legitimate"—indeed, doctrinaire—in a way that poses serious problems for moral-political life. "So far as I can determine, the only men seriously grappling with this problem in a philosophic way are Jaffa and his best students."[42] We will attempt to explore in the course of this book what this portentous observation might mean.

In the Spring of 1974, Jaffa devoted a substantial amount of time to thinking about homicide. His interest was theoretical, not practical. Hillsdale College in Michigan invited Jaffa to deliver a series of lectures on crime, punishment, and morality. The dramatic trial of Charles Manson's gruesome murders had ended in 1971, and there was much public discussion in the early '70s of criminal depravity. In addition, the Supreme Court's controversial 1972 decision in *Furman v. Georgia* had severely restricted the death penalty. Jaffa used three representative works—Camus's *The Stranger*, Dostoyevsky's *Crime and Punishment*, and Shakespeare's *Macbeth*—to describe, in reverse chronological order, an arc in the "transformation of western man's moral consciousness."[43]

Though his intellectual focus was usually on the meaning of America, broadly conceived, Jaffa's interests ranged widely, as this example shows. He described a 1975 collection of essays, *Conditions of Freedom*, as the book "that represents nearly the full range of my scholarship, with essays on Aristotle, Shakespeare, the Declaration of Independence, Lincoln and Thoreau, Jefferson, Mark Twain, and Winston Churchill (among others)."[44]

Following up on Jaffa's emphatically *political* approach to classical philosophy (a focus that led to the sobriquet "West Coast Straussian"), several of his graduate students formed a think tank in 1979, the Claremont Institute, to extend what they learned in the classroom into public policy advocacy and other practical applications. Forty years later, the institute is now run by those whom Jaffa called his intellectual grandchildren.

Then there is the matter of his correspondence.

Jaffa himself provides some perspective on his letter writing capacity in his doctoral dissertation, where he discusses "heroic virtue," a level of semidivine achievement almost beyond ordinary human capacity. Aristotle's *Nicomachean Ethics* doesn't mention stamina as a virtue, but if there were a heroic version of it, something beyond what is captured by "indefatigable," this would describe Jaffa's bottomless enthusiasm for sending letters. He produced them, thousands altogether, on almost a daily basis; addressed to friends, enemies, and strangers; newspapers and magazines; the famous and the anonymous; publishers, professors, and prime ministers.

The archive of Jaffa's papers at Hillsdale College requires four filing cabinets just to hold his letters, with more than 650 folders itemizing the various individuals to whom he wrote or who wrote to him (he almost invariably replied to any correspondence he received). And he didn't just write, send, and save his missives. He copied them, distributed them, and—as generations of colleagues, students, and employees of the Claremont Institute will recall—read them aloud, regardless (almost) of whatever else the listener might be doing at the time. These recitations were delivered in person, ideally, but Jaffa had no hesitation doing so over the telephone if necessary. Those close to him might sometimes find themselves subjected to the same oration two or even three times.

Jaffa's letters included formalities such as introductions, invitations, congratulations, thank-you notes, and letters of recommendation as well as condolences, personal advice (sometimes solicited, sometimes not), political commentary, reminiscences, gossip (rarely), predictions, instructions, and demonstrations. The language was often pungent. To Walter Berns, the constitutional scholar and fellow Straussian with whom he had an epic, decades-long feud, he once wrote: "In your present state of mind nothing less than a metaphysical two-by-four across the frontal bone would capture your attention." (Berns gave back as good as he got. To a mutual colleague, he wrote, "At the present time, 3,000 miles separate me from Harry Jaffa, and I'm not interested in diminishing that distance by a single inch.")[45]

The letters are occasionally funny, sometimes poignant or profound, and unfailingly open to (and at times demanding) further debate. Jaffa always wanted to argue, but he never wanted to win by default. In a 1983 letter to Robert Goldwin, a scholar at the American Enterprise Institute (AEI) who had been a political advisor to Gerald Ford, Jaffa reiterated his request to air their differences on the American founding:

> You say that it is the policy of [AEI] to promote the fullest "competition of ideas." But you also say that you cannot discuss our points of difference because you "do not like me." But what in the world do liking or disliking have to do with "competition of ideas," particularly as it relates to such high matters as the principles of political and constitutional right?[46]

The correspondence includes the charming and slightly ridiculous (letters to his grandchildren answering their complaints about his "lecturizing") as well as the sublime (two thank-you notes on 10 Downing Street stationary from the office of Winston Churchill, one with Churchill's handwritten initials). Some letters hint at the extraordinary breadth of his intellectual curiosity and personal interests, and amid the occasionally querulous and the necessarily mundane, one can glimpse the astounding influence of his very long life, including a scholarly career spanning almost seven decades. There are letters of commendation, awards, prizes, and notes of congratulations from senators, presidents (college and nation), Supreme Court justices, and legislative assemblies. These include celebrations or commemorations of his retirement from full-time teaching, his sixty-fifth wedding anniversary, his ninetieth birthday, and the publication of his most notable books. Perhaps most rewarding for the student of political philosophy, there are more than thirty letters from Leo Strauss, some in Strauss's nearly indecipherable handwriting, beginning in 1946 and continuing intermittently up to April of 1973, just months before Strauss's death. In addition, the Leo Strauss archive at the University of Chicago contains fifteen letters *from* Jaffa *to* Strauss that are not preserved in Jaffa's papers at Hillsdale.

Once in a while, Jaffa would use a letter to transmit a scholarly tutorial, at times quite recondite, ranging anywhere from five to twenty-five pages. The topic might include the origins of Western civilization, the theological-political problem, Shakespeare's understanding of human nature, the differences between Plato and Aristotle, or the metaphysical ground of the American founding. Though there are recurrent themes, these lectures-by-mail are never identical and are always tailored to the specific interests of the addressee.

In 1980, for example, Jaffa wrote a long epistle to his friend and benefactor Henry Salvatori. An inventor and philanthropist who was a member of Governor Ronald Reagan's kitchen cabinet, Salvatori was an early investor in Jaffa's enterprises. As a major donor to the Goldwater campaign, he admired Jaffa's work and encouraged him to come out to Claremont. He endowed the Salvatori Center for the Study of Individual Freedom in the Modern World at Claremont McKenna College and provided key financial support for the creation of the Claremont Institute. Salvatori once discussed with Jaffa over the telephone his desire (arising perhaps from his engineering background) to find a nonpartisan basis of the common good that could transcend all political or philosophical differences. Jaffa replied to the 1980 phone call with a letter that gently corrected Salvatori's misplaced confidence in a mechanical solution to politics, tracing this impulse to Hobbes's "geometric" solution to human ethics. ("There is no virtue but what is purely artificial" was Alexander Hamilton's disparaging summary of Hobbes's "absurd and impious doctrine."[47])

Jaffa's letter limns the connections and differences between Hobbes and Karl Marx, and it reminds Salvatori that young people were attracted to their Marxist teachers because utopianism offers a vision, however spurious, of something higher than mere mundane existence. "In a perverse way, they have made themselves the heirs of the Biblical and Classical Tradition, because those who ought to represent that Tradition, have abandoned it." Then he added, "I, for one, however, have not abandoned the Tradition."[48]

A 1989 letter to Charles Lofgren, a fellow professor at Claremont McKenna, describes how the American founders intended the United States "to surpass the old Rome both by its geographical and demographical extent and multiplicity; and by forming the center of a cosmopolitan world in which the liberal arts—the arts of freedom—would flourish as never before." A few tantalizing excerpts:

Ancient Rome had never solved the problem of the relationship between the center and the periphery of the empire. Its history, in brief, was one of the center conquering and incorporating the provinces, and ruling them despotically. But the military conquests which subjected the civilized world to Rome, in the end subjected Rome itself. Caesarism proved the death of republicanism.... Cicero compelled philosophy to do in Rome what it had hitherto done in Athens. But was not Cicero's failure to stem Caesarism symbolic of the failure of classical political philosophy? The question of Cicero's success or failure is inseparable from the question of whether Caesarism and Christianity were not reciprocal aspects of one and the same phenomenon.... Here we touch the deepest dilemmas of the modern man, and the deepest source of controversy over the meaning of the American experiment.[49]

As prodigious as his letter writing output was, the boldness and originality of his formal publications were even more significant. In at least three distinct disciplines, Jaffa produced groundbreaking insights:

- In *Thomism and Aristotelianism: A Study of the Commentary by Thomas Aquinas on the Nicomachean Ethics* (described by the philosopher Alasdair McIntyre as "an unduly neglected minor classic"), Jaffa examined Aquinas in light of what he had learned about reason and revelation from Leo Strauss. Jaffa treated Aquinas not merely as a theological synthesizer elaborating Church doctrines but as a philosopher in his own right. He criticized Aquinas's interpretation and possible modification of Aristotle in the book but later came to appreciate it in light of Aquinas's specific challenges and achievements. After sixty-eight years, *Thomism and*

Aristotelianism is still considered one of the authoritative texts on this topic.[50]

- His comprehensive essay exploring *King Lear*, "The Limits of Politics," which appeared in the *American Political Science Review* in 1957, was among the very first analyses on either side of the Atlantic to treat Shakespeare as a political thinker and philosophical poet of the first rank. Jaffa's essay was reprinted as a chapter in the 1964 book he produced with Allan Bloom, *Shakespeare's Politics*, the first in what is now an ever-growing library of Straussian scholarship on Shakespeare's political and philosophical thought. In addition to *King Lear*, Jaffa wrote penetrating essays on *Macbeth* and *Measure for Measure* as well as a sweeping analysis of Shakespeare's "moral universe." An analysis of Shakespeare's English history plays forms a significant part of *A New Birth of Freedom*.

- Above all, *Crisis of the House Divided* and *A New Birth of Freedom* together represent a profoundly rich and complex analysis not only of Lincoln and the Civil War but what Jaffa saw as the world-historical meaning inherent in the proposition of human equality. The penetrating criticism of American historiography he deployed in *Crisis* shifted the whole study American history and the academic treatment of Lincoln, forcing scholars to acknowledge the intellectual depth of Lincoln's statesmanship and the moral seriousness of the arguments leading to the Civil War. Then, in *New Birth*, he expanded his analysis to a multilayered philosophical excavation, going back to ancient Rome, of the American regime as a compound of theoretical truth and practical wisdom.

In each case, Jaffa went exploring in what was regarded as familiar, even worn out, territory, and he returned with startling discoveries.

Altogether, including coauthored and edited volumes (as well as a collection of essays released posthumously), Jaffa produced more than a dozen books over sixty years:

- *Thomism and Aristotelianism: A Study of the Commentary by Thomas Aquinas on the Nicomachean Ethics*, 1952.
- *In the Name of the People: Speeches and Writings of Lincoln and Douglas in the Ohio Campaign of 1859* (editor, with Robert W. Johannsen), 1959.
- *Crisis of the House Divided: An Interpretation of the Issues in the Lincoln-Douglas Debates*, 1959.
- *Shakespeare's Politics* (Allan Bloom with Harry V. Jaffa), 1964.
- *Equality and Liberty: Theory and Practice in American Politics*, 1965.
- *The Conditions of Freedom: Essays in Political Philosophy*, 1975.
- *How to Think about the American Revolution: A Bicentennial Cerebration*, 1978.
- *Statesmanship: Essays in Honor of Sir Winston S. Churchill* (editor), 1982.
- *American Conservatism and the American Founding*, 1984.
- *Original Intent & the Framers of the Constitution: A Disputed Question*, 1994.
- *Storm Over the Constitution*, 1999.
- *A New Birth of Freedom: Abraham Lincoln and the Coming of the Civil War*, 2000.
- *Crisis of the Strauss Divided: Essays on Leo Strauss and Straussianism, East and West*, 2012.

- *The Rediscovery of America: Essays by Harry V. Jaffa on the New Birth of Politics* (Edward J. Erler and Ken Masugi, editors), 2019.

In addition, through the Claremont Institute and the Henry Salvatori Center at CMC, he produced numerous pamphlets and monographs; authored a syndicated newspaper column; published widely in academic journals; contributed articles and book reviews to *National Review, The American Spectator, Human Events,* and *Modern Age,* among other magazines; submitted countless newspaper op-eds and letters to the editor (which sometimes appeared in print); and wrote the introductions, forewords, and prefaces to numerous books by students and colleagues, including the nine volumes in the *Studies in Statesmanship* series (of which he was the general editor) produced by the Winston S. Churchill Association (of which he was the longtime president).

In his essays and articles for the public, Jaffa made at least three significant contributions to American politics. First, by insisting on the centrality of the Declaration of Independence for understanding American constitutionalism, Jaffa was among the first and most influential writers to challenge the doctrine of judicial positivism and promote a natural law jurisprudence.

Second, in his scholarly and popular writings, and through his many students, Jaffa promoted an explicitly political and practically focused application of classical political philosophy. Leo Strauss, virtually single-handedly, had revived the serious reading of the great authors in the Western canon, treating them as enduringly relevant rather than historical curiosities. But without Jaffa's relentless efforts, this stupendous achievement might have settled into an effete sect of apolitical textualism.

Third, in part through his friendship with (and constant badgering of) William F. Buckley, Jaffa was largely responsible for pulling the modern conservative movement toward a more authentically American and pro-Lincoln stance, away from nostalgia for European throne-and-altar traditionalism or (worse) the old slaveholding South. Richard Brookhiser, the long-time senior editor at *National Review*, notes that Jaffa had "converted" Buckley to "the new birth of freedom promised in the Gettysburg Address." Brookhiser notes, "When I came to read the founders on my own, I saw how right Jaffa was."[51] (For his own part, Jaffa frequently complained that his efforts to shape the magazine and the larger movement it informed had little effect. It remains to be seen what constructive role, if any, the conservative movement will play in the current shake-up of American politics.) In any event, to the degree that ordinary Americans who may have been influenced by Buckley's long career as a columnist and television figure still cherish Lincoln and the founding, that lingering sentiment owes much more to Jaffa than to the Tory and Confederate conservatives he labored to displace.

Though neither Jaffa's first nor last books were about Lincoln, *Crisis* and *New Birth* nevertheless were the anchor points of his scholarship. He often recounted, in print and conversation, the story of coming across a copy of the Lincoln-Douglas debates in a used bookstore near the New School for Social Research in 1946. For several days, he would return each afternoon and read passages while standing in the aisle until he could scrounge up the money to buy the book. Poring over the arguments between the two Illinois politicians on the eve of the Civil War, Jaffa was shocked to find that their debate in all its essentials was identical to the arguments between Socrates and Thrasymachus presented by Plato so memorably in *The Republic* and interpreted by Strauss in that 1945 seminar.

To most people, this discovery would seem like a small detail. Even for a graduate student writing a doctoral thesis on medieval philosophy, it might only have piqued his interest momentarily. What made the discovery meaningful, even exhilarating, for Jaffa was seeing how the "liberation" and "rescue" he experienced in Strauss's classrooms were not merely abstract. Finding Plato's arguments about whether justice is "the interest of the stronger" brought to life in the debates of two nineteenth-century US Senate candidates was proof of everything Strauss had said about the permanent possibility of natural right. On those picked-over shelves in downtown Manhattan, Jaffa believed he had discovered political dynamite at the core of what it means to be an American.

3

LINCOLN, JUSTICE, AND AMERICA

> Jim talked out loud all the time while I was talking to
> myself. He was saying how the first thing he would do
> when he got to a free State he would go to saving up
> money and never spend a single cent, and when he got
> enough he would buy his wife, which was owned on a
> farm close to where Miss Watson lived; and then they
> would both work to buy the two children, and if their
> master wouldn't sell them, they'd get an Ab'litionist to go
> and steal them. It most froze me to hear such talk.... Here
> was this nigger, which I had as good as helped to run
> away, coming right out flat-footed and saying he would
> steal his children—children that belonged to a man
> I didn't even know; a man that hadn't ever
> done me no harm.
>
> — MARK TWAIN, *Huckleberry Finn*

In 1858, the United States was on the brink of civil war. Both North and South claimed to be upholding the Constitution. Each side had valid reasons to support that claim. The Constitution aims "to secure the blessing of liberty." To that end, Article IV, Section 4 states, "The United States shall guarantee to every State in this Union a Republican Form of Government." Moreover, the Fifth

Amendment guarantees that "no person...shall be deprived of life, liberty, or property, without due process of law."

In addition to these provisions, the Constitution in 1858 had other clauses, equally valid and legally enforceable. Article I, Section 2 stated that apportionment for the House of Representatives shall be based on "the whole number of free persons...and...three fifths of all other persons." Article I, Section 9 read: "The Migration or Importation of such Persons as any of the States now existing shall think proper to admit shall not be prohibited by the Congress prior to the Year one thousand eight hundred and eight." And Article IV declared: "No person held to service or labor in one state, under the laws thereof, escaping into another, shall, in consequence of any law or regulation therein, be discharged from such service or labor, but shall be delivered up on claim of the party to whom such service or labor may be due." What do these somewhat obscure clauses mean? They refer, of course, to slavery (though the word is never mentioned). These provisions protecting slavery obviously conflict with those guaranteeing liberty.

In June of 1858 at Springfield, Illinois, Abraham Lincoln gave a speech while debating Stephen Douglas, his rival in the race for US Senate, that tried to make sense of these contradictions. It has come to be known as the House Divided speech. Harry Jaffa argued that it was one of the most important speeches in the world and that it changed the course of history. Jaffa traced a direct connection between what Lincoln said there and the events that made the Civil War inevitable.

More than six hundred thousand Americans were killed in that war, nearly as many as in every other military conflict in American history combined. Many thoughtful Americans have wondered, Was it worth it? When Jaffa published *Crisis of the House Divided* in 1959, the dominant opinion among America's most eminent historians was: No.

More than twenty years after he wrote *Crisis*, Jaffa explained
in a letter some of the background and motivations of the book:

> The central thesis of Revisionist historiography, when I began
> work on the Lincoln-Douglas debates, was that the Civil War was
> an "unnecessary war." It was held to have been unnecessary for
> two reasons. First, because the slavery question, which agitated
> the country, was a moral question. And moral questions were held
> to be incapable of resolution by any rational means. Morality—so
> the historians, like the social scientists, believed—was a matter
> of subjective opinion.... So it was thought that the proper way
> to have dealt with slavery was to abstain from inflaming the pas-
> sions by talking about it, either as an evil or a good thing, while
> somehow working out a compromise. But American politicians
> of the period, Revisionists held, were notably irresponsible, and
> fanned the flames recklessly, to advance their political fortunes. The
> "responsible" politician, par excellence, was Stephen A. Douglas,
> because "popular sovereignty" was a way to stop talking about
> slavery, at least on the national level. And of all those who contin-
> ued to talk about slavery none was more reckless than Abraham
> Lincoln. By insisting, at a moment of high tension, that a decision
> was at hand, whereby the country must become all free, or all
> slave, he insisted upon a policy that could only result in civil war.[1]

The letter is to Walter Berns. Jaffa and Berns were old friends
who had studied together under Leo Strauss. Their friendship in
1981, when this was written, had become strained. Even among
colleagues who agreed, or thought they agreed, on the most
important things, the Civil War remained a source of confusion or division. Jaffa goes on to explain the other reason that
many early twentieth-century historians condemned Lincoln.
"Secondly, however, the Civil War was unnecessary, because
at the moment that Lincoln made the House Divided speech,

the territorial issue, the focal point of the slavery question, was virtually solved." It was solved, supposedly, "because of the policy embodied in Lincoln's rival, and the Revisionists' favorite, Stephen A. Douglas."[2]

Douglas had succeeded in blocking the controversial Lecompton Constitution, an underhanded attempt to ride roughshod over the wishes of the residents of Kansas and bring that territory into the Union as a slave state. Douglas's victory in quashing this attempt proved, in the eyes of many historians, that his doctrine of popular sovereignty, letting the people of each territory decide the slavery question locally, would have settled the issue peacefully and in favor of freedom. Jaffa continues in his letter:

> The fight against Lecompton was led every inch of the way by Stephen A. Douglas.... The virtue of popular sovereignty, as seen by Revisionism, was then two-fold: first, that it did not treat slavery as a moral question; and secondly, that it assured the victory of freedom in the territories. Most Revisionists conceded that this was the proper outcome, not because slavery was wrong, but because such an outcome was in keeping with the trends of the nineteenth century.[3]

Both *Crisis of the House Divided* and the later *A New Birth of Freedom* are challenging books, partly because of the subject matter. Any detailed account of the events surrounding the Civil War encompasses a bewildering array of names and issues: James Buchanan and James Polk, the New Orleans Convention and the Charleston Convention, tariffs and temperance, Henry Clay and Horace Greeley, Beecher's Bibles and Bleeding Kansas, John C. Calhoun and John Brown, Know-Nothings and Copperheads. Yet in their debates of the Senate race of 1858 (a preview of the 1860 presidential campaign between the same two men), Lincoln and Douglas focused on what was widely considered the central controversy: the problem of slavery within a republican form of government.

One of the remarkable features of *Crisis* is how convincingly Jaffa presents the different perspectives on this essential question. After a short introductory section, Jaffa devotes a full 139 pages, covering six chapters, to the rationale for Douglas's position. Here, Jaffa outlines the history of Manifest Destiny, explains the fractious history of the two Missouri Compromises of 1820 (which had sought to partition the federal territories into free and slave sections, divided by the 36°30′ latitude), and draws out the implications of the Fugitive Slave Act. With this background in place, Jaffa shows how Douglas worked to replace the Missouri Compromise, repealed in 1854, with his popular sovereignty solution through the Kansas-Nebraska Act. In digesting this compelling account, one can appreciate why the historical revisionists were so attracted to the doctrine of popular sovereignty. For the same reason, many students find Jaffa's "Case for Douglas" unexpectedly persuasive—a phenomenon confirmed by several professors who teach the book.[4] The notion of "letting the people decide" seems at once reassuringly simple and eminently American.

Jaffa's "Case for Lincoln" is nearly the same length as the Douglas section: 134 pages. Here we see Lincoln lament the overturning of the Missouri Compromise settlement and assail the notorious *Dred Scott* decision, in which the Supreme Court held that Congress had no authority to prohibit slavery in any federal territory. Jaffa shows how Lincoln rebuts Douglas's claim that slavery would be naturally excluded from the Northwest territories by inhospitable soil and climate. Above all, we see Lincoln relentlessly exposing the gross injustice of slavery as an affront to self-government and incompatible with America's founding principles of equal natural rights as proclaimed in the Declaration of Independence.[5]

While Jaffa strives to be scrupulously fair in presenting the positions of each antagonist, Lincoln does get more attention, but in an unexpected way. Set off from both of "The Case for …" sections is the fascinating philosophical heart of the book: two chapters that don't address the 1858 debates at all. In this central part, called "The Political Philosophy of a Young Whig," Jaffa offers probing interpretations of the Lyceum speech of 1838 (in which Lincoln discusses the dangers posed to democratic government by mob rule and ambitious tyrants) and the Temperance Address of 1842 (Lincoln's complex satire exploring several political and theological themes, including moral reform, original sin, and civic friendship).[6]

By virtually all accounts, *Crisis of the House Divided* was considered an impressive achievement (though his acidulous comments on several leading historians did elicit some negative reviews).[7] Jaffa was the first scholar in any field to develop a comprehensive argument for Lincoln as a philosophic statesman who also seemed to embody the role of redeeming prophet. Lincoln, as Jaffa portrayed him, was a messianic figure sent by Providence to guide the American people through their trial by fire, a sacrifice in blood to expunge the sin of slavery and purify this "almost chosen people." The Civil War was both politically unavoidable and philosophically necessary to fulfill the founding's sacred covenant with God and nature, articulated in the ringing truth that all men are created equal. Finding such world-historical, even theological, significance in the Civil War may be considered absurd by many cynical readers today. Even in 1959, elite opinion disdained the idea of America as the "last, best hope" of mankind. Yet Jaffa's motive was not merely patriotic. (His friend William F. Buckley once wrote that Jaffa would have devoted himself to the political history of Lithuania if he thought that's where the truth was to be found.[8]) Jaffa believed he saw something in America that exposed and clarified the deepest questions of political philosophy.

This explains his paradoxical remark, in the preface to the 1982 edition, that *Crisis* is only incidentally about the United States.

Ultimately, Jaffa seems to share with Lincoln a belief in a divine or cosmic purpose at work in the United States, testing "whether this nation *or any nation*" dedicated to the experiment of self-government "can long endure." [Emphasis added.] Thus, Jaffa does not stint in his use of religious imagery. Allowing slavery in the territories, he argues, "would have been no less disastrous for Lincoln than a change in the First Commandment from the singular deity to a plural would have been to a pious Jew or Christian."[9] But Jaffa doesn't merely cast the war in apocalyptic terms. He sees the central protagonist as a Christ-like figure:

> We would now observe that Lincoln's political thought is cast almost wholly in the metaphor of a double perspective, in which the function of his statesmanship is seen either on the analogy of the salvation of Israel from Egypt or the salvation of the world by the Messiah. Lincoln's moral imagination worked in and through a kind of conflation of the symbols of Old and New Testaments. It is, for example, impossible to grasp fully what Lincoln believed he was doing…without seeing it as a performance of a prophetic role in the Old Testament sense. Neither is it possible to understand his conception of his Civil War role without seeing the Messianic idea at work. In discussing "political religion" as presented in the Lyceum speech, we will go beyond the framework of the speech itself to show how it involved Lincoln's whole conception of political salvation and of the role of statesmanship as necessarily agreeing in its higher reaches with the purposes and methods of the divine teacher.[10]

For Jaffa, Lincoln's magnanimity and prophetic statesmanship exceed in nobility and significance even the heroism of Washington. In his analysis of the Lyceum speech, we are somewhat taken aback by the way Lincoln is seen to disparage, even disdain, the founders' love of glory. By stoking the peoples' hatred of Britain, Lincoln seems to say that the leaders of the American Revolution rode the popular passion for liberty mainly in pursuit of their own fame.

Readers who come to *Crisis* already familiar with Jaffa's reputation or later works are sometimes surprised at the reproachful tone toward the alleged secularism and self-interest of Washington, Jefferson, and the founders generally. (The Declaration is "wholly a document of the rationalist tradition"; "there is no trace of reverence in Washington's discussion of the need for reverence."[11]) In this, Jaffa is following what he had learned from Strauss about modernity lowering the horizons of politics. He sees the founders creating a republic of liberty, to be sure, but a liberty aimed at nothing more than comfortable self-preservation. Jaffa does portray Washington as genuinely heroic, a man of courage who risked much to lead his people (but not all the people) in demanding their rights. Yet Washington remains compromised by the theoretical deficiency of the founding. Lincoln would surpass even the father of the country by redeeming the fallen nature of the founding and purifying the idea of equality to achieve "the highest degree of moral self-government."[12]

For some readers, the eschatology in Jaffa's rhetoric and the vast sweep of his arguments can be exhilarating. But others have found the messianic language alarming. One of Jaffa's most persistent and intelligent critics was the Yale political theorist Willmoore Kendall. His 1959 review of *Crisis* in Buckley's *National Review* warned that Jaffa's version of the magnanimous and almost superhuman Lincoln would launch his readers,

and with them the nation, upon a political future the very thought of which is hair-raising: a future made up of an endless series of Abraham Lincolns, each persuaded that he is superior in wisdom and virtue to the Fathers, each prepared to insist that those who oppose this or that new application of the equality standard are denying the possibility of self-government, each ultimately willing to plunge America into civil war rather than concede his point....

[The] Caesarism we all need to fear is the contemporary liberal movement, dedicated like Lincoln to egalitarian reforms sanctioned by mandates emanating from national majorities, a movement which is Lincoln's legitimate offspring. In a word, it would seem that we had best learn to live up to the Framers before we seek to transcend them.[13]

This is probably the critique that Jaffa wrestled with most seriously in subsequent years. In fact, Kendall and Jaffa became frequent and friendly sparring partners. While Jaffa never gave an inch to Kendall's arguments defending secession and the old Confederacy, he seemed to take to heart the charge that he had diminished the founders through his near deification of Lincoln. These disputes with Kendall and other figures from the old Right, the so-called paleoconservatives, are discussed in more detail in Chapter 7.[14]

Let's sum up the major arguments of *Crisis*, which remained for decades the Archimedean point of Jaffa's career. The book sets out to demonstrate three key propositions:

- *Natural right.* The great issues of political philosophy— justice, wisdom, happiness—are not artifacts of a particular time and place. Jaffa found a kind of proof of this in Lincoln's appeal to the "axioms" of a free society and wanted to explore and demonstrate that proof. Above all, Jaffa wanted to challenge the historical relativists by showing that the propositions of the Declaration might be true.

- *Equality* and its implications. The protections for slavery in the positive law of the Constitution revealed that the American regime had to be understood according to the "central idea" of equal natural rights, which alone legitimized the founding's social compact theory. The attempt to deny any rights to black slaves meant there could be no ultimate security for the rights of free whites. The Constitution could not be understood apart from the Declaration.
- The *tension between wisdom and consent.* This could be posed as the problem of people consenting to injustice. As Herman Belz notes in his 1988 essay on the thirtieth anniversary of *Crisis,*

Slavery denied equality and consent, yet it existed in the American republic and was supported in varying degrees by the approval or toleration of public opinion. How to resolve the conflict between slavery and the principles of the American regime became the central issue in politics of the 1850s. The problem from the standpoint of political theory was: How wrong could popular opinion be and still constitute the legitimate foundation for government? ...

Lincoln analyzed the problem of popular government in relation to the eternal antagonism between reason and passion, and he proposed to preserve republican institutions by a reverence for the Constitution and the laws, which he referred to as a "political religion." The essence of Lincoln's teaching, termed "political salvation" by Jaffa, was that "the people ... must be made subject to a discipline in virtue of which they will demand only those things in the name of their own supreme authority that are reasonable; i.e. consistent with the implications of their own equal rights."[15]

Crisis touches on many subsidiary questions, of course, such as why the founders did not immediately abolish slavery as well as the complex matter of states' rights and secession. Jaffa would engage these controversies more fully in scholarly essays and magazine articles as well as in his second Lincoln book. But the core of *Crisis* can fairly be distilled to the three elements listed above. What that synopsis does not reveal is how Jaffa understood his aspirations and intentions for the book over the course of his long subsequent career.

Crisis of the House Divided is probably the only book ever published to have two introductions (1972 and 2008) and two prefaces (1958 and 1982) written by the author over a span of fifty years. Of course, not many books remain in print for half a century while the author is still alive. These additions are not merely perfunctory stamps on the publisher's updated cover; they are provocative mini essays in themselves. It is illuminating, therefore, to reflect on what Jaffa highlights with each republication. For those readers who find it odd to focus so much on this front matter, it is worth noting that Jaffa himself devotes significant attention in Chapter 10 of his book to examining a single word in Lincoln's Temperance Address.[16]

The original preface of four pages, dated October 7, 1958—Jaffa's fortieth birthday—describes *Crisis* as the first of a two-part study. (Some time in the late 1980s or early 90s, Jaffa decided he would need a third volume on Lincoln, which he never completed.) He foreshadows his view of Lincoln as "extraordinarily precocious" and possessed of "a self-control that compelled a supremely ambitious man to be a follower when leadership could be seized only by irresponsibility." He also prefigures the conspicuous religious themes of the book: "The crisis of the war years, with all its agony and possibility of failure was yet in a profound sense less critical" than the debates over the central cause. They differed "as the Passion differed from the Temptation in the Wilderness." The preface concludes with three somewhat formal sentences thanking Leo Strauss, who "was and is my teacher," with additional acknowledgement of his fellow Strauss students, Joseph Cropsey, Allan Bloom, and Martin Diamond.[17]

In 1972, Jaffa wrote a new introduction of eight pages after Doubleday had stopped printing the book and it was adopted by the University of Washington Press. The new opening is notable for the way it connects the book's themes to the turbulent politics of that era, especially the Civil Rights Movement. (Jaffa reprinted this introduction in his 1975 collection of essays, *The Conditions of Freedom*.) He mentions "the vitality of the issues" regarding race and equality and "the changes in American citizenship" that "affect, of necessity, all the citizens and the nature of their citizenship." He also highlights the ideologies of historicism and the fact-value distinction gripping modern social science, then deploys a line he would often repeat in the classroom: Thomas Aquinas and Thomas Jefferson "shared a belief concerning the relationship of political philosophy to political authority that neither shared with, let us say, the last ten presidents of the American Political Science Association."

In contrast to the official docents of his profession, Jaffa sees it as the task of political philosophy to "teach the teachers of legislators, of citizens, of statesman the principles in virtue of which political power becomes political authority." He nicely parallels the Supreme Court's *Dred Scott* decision of 1857 with the 1954 *Brown v. Board of Education* ruling, which outlawed school segregation but *not* on the basis of human equality as a moral-political principle. Rather, the court cited the subjective feelings of black students, relying on "a test devised by a social psychologist." There is palpable disappointment and alarm in his observation that the early Civil Rights Movement "quickly passed over into a revolution of black power." The utopian and intolerant demands of that movement went "far beyond the scope of law" and were even at times "in flat contradiction to the principles of the earlier demands for full equality." Much more than in 1959, Jaffa characterizes his book as the practical application of political philosophy to the "the crisis of the West." The urgency of that crisis, and the relevance of what he learned from Leo Strauss, would become even more evident in the next reprint.

The preface to the 1982 edition runs four dense pages, almost every paragraph of which is interesting in its own right. It is entirely about Strauss, or Straussian political philosophy, and Jaffa even imitates the tone and compactness of his teacher's writing. Jaffa mentions that the book is now with University of Chicago Press, and he remarks on his affiliations with the university where Strauss taught for many years. The most important connection is that "between classical natural right as expounded in Leo Strauss's *Natural Right and History* and the conception of political right that guided Abraham Lincoln in the greatest crisis in American (perhaps world) history." Jaffa doesn't explain what he means by "political right," as distinct from "natural right." He hints, however, at an element that is not especially emphasized in *Crisis* but which will be given greater attention in *A New Birth of Freedom*:

> The classical understanding of natural right always pointed simultaneously in two directions: one, toward the philosopher's understanding of the universal, transpolitical dimension of human experience; the other, toward the political man's understanding of the *particular* experiences of *particular* peoples in *particular* regimes. Classical natural right undertook to guide political men, who need to know what is right here and now, but to guide them in the light of what is just always and everywhere. The problem of natural right is the problem of reconciling the necessary skepticism that accompanies any theoretical enterprise, in which life and death are unimportant episodes in an unending quest, and the

necessary dogmatism that accompanies any practical enterprise, in which life and death set inexorable limits within which decision and action must take place. [Emphases added.]

Whereas in 1972 he sketched the baleful consequences of modern social science for American citizenship, Jaffa now indicts modern philosophy for errors causing almost incalculable damage to civilization itself. "Modern philosophy had tried to escape the dilemmas arising from the discrete requirements of theory and practice." It "was both unreasonably skeptical and unreasonably dogmatic." Through its hubristic, utopian attempts to overcome the permanent limits of human nature, it "laid the foundation of modern atheistic totalitarianism, the most terrible form of tyranny in human existence." To overcome this calamity, Leo Strauss had recovered the wisdom and moderation of classical thought and inaugurated "the only genuinely new political science of the past four hundred years." This new or renewed political science emphasized "practical wisdom—*phronesis* or *prudentia*—[and] pointed towards rhetoric as the principal instrument by which political men might implement political wisdom." Rather than the perfunctory acknowledgement of Strauss we saw in 1959, Jaffa now all but assimilates his book into Strauss's project.[18] *Crisis* "was an attempt at a pioneer study of this new political science." All this is undoubtedly driven by what Jaffa viewed as the growing distortion or misrepresentation of Strauss's legacy, a concern that had led to several public arguments with his fellow Straussians since the death of their mentor in 1973.

Jaffa concludes the preface with some oblique reflections on his own method. *Crisis* is "in the form of a disputed question, itself a form of the Socratic dialogue." It therefore "unites elements of history and of poetry." Evoking his earlier discussion of natural right, which joins theory and practice while respecting their independence, he notes that according to Aristotle, history is concerned with particulars, as poetry is with universals. The relationship between history and poetry in the American political tradition may be indicated by saying that if Lincoln had not existed, we would have to invent him. Existing as he did, however, involves showing the elements of art in his life, as well as those of chance.

The person showing us those elements, of course, is Jaffa, which would imply that history, poetry, art, and chance are all at work in the dramatic presentation of *Crisis*. He then concludes with a subtle comparison of Lincoln's "dialectical victory" over Douglas and Socrates's defeat of the sophist Thrasymachus. The connection he sees between the 1858 debates and Book I of *The Republic* is not just about the meaning of justice, though it surely includes that, but it also points to questions about reason, writing, and the dramatist's art. "The art of the dialogue," Jaffa writes, with some ambiguity as to whose dialogue he means, "consists in part in producing a surface which appears, as in history, to be governed by chance."[19]

Finally, in the introduction to the fiftieth anniversary edition, dated August 29, 2008, we find Jaffa just shy of his ninetieth birthday. Twenty-six years have elapsed since the last reprinting, a much longer period than between any of the previous editions. He notes that equality, "the proposition that unites the Gettysburg Address and the Declaration of Independence," has remained "the theme of my life and work...and of the books (especially *A New Birth of Freedom*) that have succeeded *Crisis* over the years." He again mentions *Natural Right and History* and Strauss's refutation of historicism but now appears much more circumspect. "The existence of a timeless reality" is only "an assumption of Socratic philosophy," although an assumption that "can and does withstand the most serious and competent skeptical analysis." While the claim of the dogmatic historicist to know the truth of historicism is self-contradictory, Jaffa explains, this "does not of itself establish a rational foundation for law and ethics." Though it is "fashionable" to suppose this realization leads to nihilism, it "also points toward the direction of the classics." *Also?* It seems that Jaffa is suggesting either option is viable.

The surprisingly tentative tone continues:

> According to Strauss, the classics were abandoned but were never refuted. Among so called Straussians there is a division as to whether he actually believed that modern philosophy had not refuted the classics, and whether Strauss's assertion was real or merely exoteric. But there can be no doubt that Strauss regarded Lincoln's statesmanship, as revealed in *Crisis*, although prudential in the last degree, as perfectly Aristotelian.
>
> To repeat, Strauss's refutation of historicism *can lead to a blind nihilism*, and for many, including many Straussians, it has done so. [Emphasis added.]

The first paragraph appears to propose a convoluted and highly qualified response to a quite serious challenge. Jaffa follows this by again suggesting that nihilism may be a plausible intellectual stance in our time. Has the professor, now surpassing four score and seven years, lost his famous vigor and confidence? This possibility seems to be reenforced by several paragraphs of reminiscing, in which Jaffa relates, through personal anecdotes, the background to Strauss's *Natural Right and History*. In the beginning of that book, Strauss quotes the Declaration of Independence, then adds the following:

> The nation dedicated to this proposition has now become, no doubt partly as a consequence of this dedication, the most powerful and prosperous of the nations of the earth. Does this nation in its maturity still cherish the faith in which it

was conceived and raised? Does it still hold those "truths to
be self-evident"?

Jaffa mentions that it was he who transcribed Strauss's lecture
notes into the first chapters of *Natural Right and History*, published
in 1953. He then describes more generally Strauss's familiarity
with and support of his work on Lincoln. Specifically, in the
midfifties, while in Chicago for his fellowship, Jaffa delivered a
series of lectures on the Lincoln-Douglas debates that formed
the basis of *Crisis*. "Strauss attended the first of these lectures,
and read the manuscript of the others."

All this may seem to be no more than the vanity of an old
man seeking to position himself as the *primus inter pares* of the
Straussian clan. Yet one may also suspect a deeper purpose at
work. Jaffa explicitly challenges the idea that Strauss "remained
at heart a European scholar" who "lacked interest in America."
This is not intended to wrap Strauss in an American flag (whatever
narrow purpose that might serve). Rather, to the degree that the
defense of natural right in the modern world is made possible by
Strauss's recovery of classical philosophy, then the true meaning of Strauss's thought cannot be a matter of either political or
intellectual indifference. Jaffa believes he understood his teacher's
true intention and that he, and we, can therefore find assurance
"that the mission of Socrates, the Founders, Lincoln, Strauss will
not perish from the earth."

The preface concludes with an anecdote. While in Claremont,
where he taught for three semesters (and held informal summer
seminars) after retiring from Chicago, Strauss had praised *Crisis*
to one of Jaffa's students and added that "Professor Jaffa and I
are the only ones who understand it." Without explaining this
enigmatic statement, Jaffa adds,

> I conclude by expressing my regret that Strauss did not live to
> see *A New Birth of Freedom*, which is the sequel to *Crisis*, and a

far more intricate and complicated work, which would have challenged Strauss in the way he best liked to be challenged.

With this, however, we have overshot the mark of examining Jaffa's first Lincoln book. We must turn now to the sequel.

When *A New Birth of Freedom* finally appeared in 2000, virtually all the reviewers agreed that the much-anticipated volume was indeed a bravura performance. A similar consensus prevailed in noting the great span of time that had elapsed since 1959. Jaffa deftly anticipated this with an observation that combined, rather typically, self-promotion, witticism, and allusive erudition. Forty years, he noted in his preface, "corresponds closely to the distance in time that separated Plato's *Republic* from his *Laws*." Several reviewers, including Charles Kesler, have offered thoughtful suggestions for what he meant by this.[20] Given his fondness for biblical references, Jaffa might also have recalled the Israelites' forty years in the wilderness, except that he emphatically denied—before, during, and after the publication of *New Birth*—that he had been lost or wandering in any way. All his intervening work had been arrayed toward the same harmonious purpose. *New Birth* was at last delivered unto the promised readers, but according to the author it had not been delayed.

What is the book about?

On one level, Jaffa is simply working his way forward chronologically. As *Crisis* had expounded Lincoln's prewar career in Illinois, this volume shows us Lincoln on the national stage, from 1860 onward. Lincoln's antagonists, and the nature of the debates, change dramatically: Douglas's "don't care" rhetoric is replaced by the arguments of Alexander Stephens and John C. Calhoun, the intellectual founders of the Confederacy, who cared very much to defend slavery as "a positive good." Stephens, as vice president of the Confederacy, authored the infamous "Cornerstone

Speech," declaring "the great truth that the negro is not equal to the white man; that slavery, subordination to the superior race, is his natural and normal condition."[21] But the truly formidable figure is Calhoun, a brilliant writer and orator (and slaveholder) from South Carolina, whose theories of nullification and concurrent majority supported a radical conception of state's rights.

As before, Jaffa devotes considerable space to interpreting the political drama through the speeches of its leading figures. Whereas in *Crisis* Jaffa says he imitated "the disputed question" used by St. Thomas Aquinas in the *Summa Theologica*, the new book "is conceived as a commentary on the Gettysburg Address, the commentary being another of the characteristic forms in which Thomas Aquinas delivered his thoughts to the world."[22] This description, however, is not as straightforward as it may seem. Though Chapter 2 is titled "The Declaration of Independence, the Gettysburg Address, and the Historians," it does not, in fact, present an extended analysis of the Gettysburg Address. Nor do we find a detailed interpretation of that speech anywhere else in the book.

What we *do* find is something that seems far more ambitious. Situating the Civil War, and America itself, within a grand overview of Western civilization, Jaffa traces an arc through political theory and practice in ancient Rome; the rationalism of the Bible; European Christendom, with all its complexities and challenges; the English monarchy seen through Shakespeare's history plays; and the Glorious Revolution of 1688; arriving finally in eighteenth-century Philadelphia. But while the Declaration of Independence is, of course, the star and compass of this voyage, it is not the year 1776 that commands Jaffa's immediate attention. He opens the book with a fascinating and practical question, one that is of the utmost interest today as the United States finds itself in what Angelo Codevilla, among others, describes as "a cold civil war": What went wrong between the years 1800 and 1860?

What went *right* in 1800 was the world's first peaceful transfer of governmental authority, "in which the instruments of political power passed from one set of hands to those of their most uncompromisingly hostile political rivals and opponents because of a free vote." Of course, the partisan differences were intense. Yet when the votes were counted, Jaffa notes,

> the offices were peacefully vacated by the losers and peacefully occupied by those who had prevailed. Nor were any of the defeated incumbents executed, imprisoned, expropriated, or driven into exile, as were the losers in the English civil wars and in the political contests of the Rome of Cicero and Caesar. The defeated Federalists went about their lawful occupations unmolested and for the most part engaged in the same kind of political activity in which their opponents had previously engaged.[23]

As wondrous as this achievement was, it did not last. Six decades later, the Confederate states attempted to dissolve the Union in the wake of Lincoln's election. We are, presumably, interested to know why this happened and suppose that this book will now tell us. But Jaffa disrupts our expectations by first turning back again. The question of 1860 must be preceded, he observes,

> by the question of how the astounding precedent of 1800 itself was established. A break with all previous human history is even more in need of explanation than a break with a precedent of only threescore years. What was it that persuaded or enabled Americans in 1800 to discover in free elections the basis, not merely for choosing a government, but also for choosing a government from one of two bitterly contending parties? More particularly, what enabled them to accept the results of an election in which each of the rival parties charged the other with being subversive of that form of government for which the American Revolution had been fought?[24]

From the perspective of today, and certainly set against the devastation of the Civil War, we are tempted to see the founding era (after the Constitutional Convention) as comparatively peaceful, high-toned, and unified. Yet Jaffa overturns any complacency we may have on this point. In the electoral contest between John Adams's Federalist Party and Thomas Jefferson's Democratic-Republicans, each side accused the other of *subversion*. The indictment of "the Revolution betrayed" is almost a constant in American politics, Jaffa explains, and in the earliest years of the republic, it was not perfectly clear to any of the founders that loyalty would win out over betrayal. "Not until his inaugural address in 1801 would Jefferson see the right of free election as the normal and peaceable fruit of the right of revolution."[25]

All men everywhere are indeed free and equal by nature, but whether free and equal citizens can participate in and abide by democratic elections is another matter entirely. To explore the conditions that make this possible, Jaffa hurtles the reader through an intellectual tour of the Holy Roman Empire, the Magna Carta, Oliver Cromwell, and the divine right of kings. Within the first twenty pages, we can see that this is something very different from Jaffa's first Lincoln book.

New Birth covers an astonishing amount of ground while also revisiting and elaborating from different angles the most crucial points about secession, social compact theory, majority rule, and federalism. Some readers have found it meandering and repetitive. Thomas West, a former student of Jaffa's, observes in his review in *Interpretation* that it is "a big, sprawling" work, containing "what at first appears to be a bewildering variety of tangents." But as West explains, *New Birth* "has a simple logical structure that falls into three parts." In what he takes to be Jaffa's homage to Strauss's famous book, West sees Chapter 1 as devoted to *natural right* and Chapter 2 to *history*. That constitutes the theoretical first part. The second part is more practical, covering Chapters 3–6:

Here Jaffa presents a brilliant analysis of the political scene in America in the late 1850s and at the beginning of Lincoln's presidency. His point throughout is that the Civil War was about slavery in the broadest sense, that is, not just the chattel slavery that affected blacks, but the Southern denial of the right of a people to govern itself through free speech and elections.

Part 3 (the single Chapter 7), returns to theory. Jaffa shows that Calhoun, Lincoln's deepest antagonist, agreed with Lincoln that political justice depends on getting the theory right. But in Calhoun's theory necessity, force, and the inexorable historical process replace the Founders' reason, deliberation, and the natural right of every man to freedom under the law of nature.[26]

It would take too many pages to elaborate every interesting point mentioned by West, which itself only outlines the plan of the book. Rather than plod through a chapter-by-chapter summary of *New Birth*, we can get a more synoptic view of the book by turning to a question that has engaged several commentators: What, if anything, did Jaffa change his mind about over the course of four decades? What did these long years of reflection teach him—about Lincoln, the founding, and the relationship between political theory and practice—that corresponds in some way to the difference between Plato's *Republic* and his *Laws*? According to West (whose opinion on this point is shared by a number of Jaffa's other students), *Crisis* overextended, as it were, Strauss's theoretical critique of modern philosophy, especially the thought of John Locke.

Here it is necessary to take a brief detour and return to the theme, introduced earlier, of esoteric writing.

Sometime in the 1970s and 1980s, Jaffa began to revisit the way he had depicted the American founders in *Crisis of the House Divided*. In particular, he started to think through the following question: If the moral-political world must be taken seriously as the primary phenomenon of human life, and if we must also understand statesmen such as Lincoln as they understood themselves (as he explained in *Crisis*) rather than seeing them merely as reflections of their socioeconomic or intellectual environment (as the historicists taught), what does this mean for the proper study of Washington, Madison, and Jefferson?

Recall that when he wrote *Crisis* in the late 1950s, Jaffa had already absorbed from Strauss the idea that Locke's esoteric teaching regarded mankind as egotistic profit maximizers (a slight twist on the Hobbesian emphasis on fear as the driver of all human action). Jaffa also knew, even from a cursory review of their speeches and letters, that the founders were greatly influenced by Locke. He simply assumed therefore, as did all of Strauss's students *at first*, that Locke had such a hidden teaching—and that this was the true, underlying meaning of the founding.

In *Crisis*, Jaffa vigorously argues for the possibility that what the Declaration affirms about equal natural rights and "the laws of nature and nature's God" might be *true*, a nearly unprecedented position for a scholarly book in 1959. But in Jaffa's understanding, true does not (yet) mean noble. He sees Lincoln's greatness of soul as necessary to bring the founders' seed of utilitarian natural right to its full flowering of transcendent political justice. Later, Jaffa came to regard the founders as genuine statesmen—not merely agents of a deterministic Hobbesianism—who made deliberate moral choices about the kind of regime they were trying to build. He would therefore put great emphasis in his later career on George Washington's famous Farewell Address, which describes religion and morality as indispensable supports for political prosperity. In *Crisis* and other early writings, however, Jaffa is quite disparaging toward this famous speech by the father of the country, dismissing Washington's high-minded advice as a poor attempt to mingle the "oil and water" of "rationalism and religion."[27]

In a 2001 essay titled "Aristotle and Locke in the American Founding," Jaffa explains his change in perspective:

I took for granted that the account of the Hobbesian Locke in Leo Strauss's *Natural Right and History* represented the Locke that informed the American Founding.... Strauss himself never said this [esoteric] Locke was the founders' Locke, but the spell cast by his book led many of us to apply it to the founders. Many former students of Strauss, to this day, regard it as heresy to think that Strauss's chapters on Hobbes and Locke do not constitute the authoritative account of the philosophic foundations of American constitutionalism. When presented with the evidence of Aristotelianism in the founding, they react like the scholastics who refused to look into Galileo's telescope....

Strauss was clear, in *Natural Right and History*, that his was an account of Locke's esoteric teaching, but that Locke's exoteric doctrine was far more conventional, and far more consistent with both traditional morality and traditional (albeit more tolerant) Christianity. Strauss also taught us that the authors of the past—and this certainly included political men no less than philosophers—were to be understood as they understood themselves, before the attempt was made to understand them differently or better. It was, and is, an anachronism to assume that the founders read Locke through the eyes of Strauss![28]

Looking back from 2011, Jaffa remarks that in *Crisis*, "I regarded the founders as condemning slavery from the perspective of a prudent form of modern natural rights." The founders clearly had a conception of universal justice, but it operated within the cramped horizon of modernity. "This, I then held, was transformed by Lincoln into a prudent form of classical Aristotelianism."

Jaffa accepted the ancients-moderns distinction, but (as a first indication of his turn) he thought it had been breached by Lincoln through a kind of providential intervention of supreme statesmanship. This semimiraculous leap from the ancient world to the modern came to be replaced by a nonmiraculous understanding of prudence and statesmanship as permanent features of human experience. "Now I believe that the prudent form of classical Aristotelianism was already present in the founding," Jaffa continues, "and that Lincoln found it there."

> That is because I do not now think that prudence, rightly understood, admits within itself any division between ancients and moderns. I have come to believe that it is of the essence of the pristinely modern persuasion to eliminate prudence, along with morality, from statesmanship and political philosophy.…
>
> While the manifestations of prudence are as many as the circumstances in which prudent action is possible, the virtue itself remains one and the same. This is why regarding Aristotle and Locke as representing opposing and contradictory philosophic doctrines is mistaken. The assumption that there is such a difference is the nerve of the difference between Eastern and Western Straussians.[29]

Indeed, some Straussians regard Jaffa's assimilation of Aristotle and Locke as almost ludicrous. His boldest claim—"had Aristotle been called upon, in the latter half of the 17th century, to write a guide book for constitution makers, he would have written something very closely approximating Locke's *Second Treatise*"— is sometimes mocked for conjuring a chimerical "Lockistotle." But Jaffa stood his ground. If practical virtue is permanent yet circumstances change, why *wouldn't* Aristotle have "recognized instantly those differences from his *Politics* that prudential wisdom required, in the world of Christian monotheism, with all its peculiar dangers of tyranny"?[30] Thus, according to Jaffa, Strauss's distinction between ancients and moderns is a distinction in the *history* of political philosophy but not a distinction within philosophy itself. Natural right, though changeable in its application to different circumstances, is always grounded in "a human condition that, like the human soul, is not located in time or place."[31]

Virtually all Strauss's students agree that his challenging books deployed different methods for different purposes. Therefore, Jaffa argues, Strauss's complete teaching on Locke has to be balanced with what he wrote elsewhere, particularly the essay "Liberal Education and Responsibility" in his 1968 book, *Liberalism Ancient and Modern*. There, Jaffa notes, we find that Locke is cited "repeatedly and with unvarying favor." In that essay, Strauss "speaks of liberal education as the ladder by which we ascend from mass democracy to democracy as originally meant." The emphasis he places on the ennobling effects of liberal education means that Locke's philosophy cannot be viewed simply as uniformly "low." The framers of the American Constitution likewise placed great emphasis on education. "What the founders intended" for liberal education, "and what Strauss understood it to mean to the founders," Jaffa says, "is set forth with magisterial authority in a letter from Jefferson to John Adams in 1813."[32] This letter is a key document for Jaffa, to which we will return below.

Jaffa's change in perspective, or "second sailing," had some far-reaching implications. For example, the rigid distinction between ancients and moderns, which characterized his thinking in *Crisis*, led Jaffa to embrace a somewhat paradoxical view of equality. As mentioned earlier, Jaffa's understanding of the Declaration in *Crisis* emphasized the inherent tension between wisdom and consent. Therefore, as Thomas West explains, Lincoln actually "rejected the Founders' claim that all men are created equal in the decisive sense." In his earlier book (West argues), Jaffa had understood the Lyceum and Temperance addresses to reveal Lincoln, "abstractly considered," as "fully in agreement with Socrates' suggestion that the lawless rule of the wise without the consent of the governed was the best form of government."[33]

All this undergoes a considerable transformation in the second Lincoln book. West continues:

In *A New Birth,* Jaffa rejects his earlier interpretation of America. Lincoln is still presented as a great man, but his greatness now lies in his brilliant exposition and recovery of the founding principles. The amoral portrayal of the founding principles in *Crisis* is replaced by an exposition of compact theory that brings out its insightfulness and richness. In particular, the moral and religious dimension of the Founders' political teaching, having been neglected in *Crisis,* is now fully articulated, with a real increase of accuracy and sophistication. The Founders' (and Locke's) doctrine of the law of nature, the source of men's rights no less than their moral obligations, is now given its due.[34]

Professors Robert Kraynak and Michael Zuckert also pick up on the disjunction between *Crisis* and *New Birth,* but each takes Jaffa's "turn" in a different and interesting direction, opening up some other large questions. Both respectfully critical essays, along with responses by Jaffa, appeared in the Spring 2009 issue of *The Review of Politics.* (Jaffa republished all four pieces in his 2012 book, *Crisis of the Strauss Divided*). The gist of Jaffa's dialogue with Kraynak, who teaches at Colgate University, can be gleaned from their respective titles. Kraynak's essay is titled "The Moral Order in the Western Tradition: Harry Jaffa's Grand Synthesis of Athens, Jerusalem, and Peoria." To this gentle mockery, Jaffa answers with, "Too Good to be True?: A Reply..." Kraynak sees Jaffa as seeking "a philosophically defensible argument for natural right" that unfolds over Jaffa's entire *oeuvre,* extending to some degree beyond the two Lincoln books. Jaffa's continuation, and even fulfillment, of Strauss's challenge to defend the West was his "greatest intellectual ambition." According to Kraynak, Jaffa argued that

the moral order of the West could be vindicated without definitively resolving ultimate theoretical questions and that this practical solution was a fulfillment of Strauss's intention. The problem, I will conclude, is that...Jaffa's vision of moral order rests on a false synthesis of disparate elements that are best left in their original forms.[35]

Jaffa's fight against "value-free positivism and historicism" forms "the basis of his entire intellectual career," which manifests itself in a Manichean division of heroes and villains: the "proponents of natural right (Socrates, Aristotle, Aquinas, Locke, Jefferson, Lincoln, and Shakespeare)" versus "relativists of one kind or another (Thrasymachus, Douglas, Calhoun, revisionist historians such as Carl Becker, and even Supreme Court Justices Rehnquist and Scalia)." *New Birth*, in particular, tries to establish an almost idealized Declaration-based vision of America through a "grandiose convergence theory of classical Greek, Christian, and modern natural rights (with additions from Roman history)." But on closer inspection, this is "a deliberately exaggerated view...a partially true but overstated expression of a public philosophy." Kraynak finds that Jaffa's final position is an impressive attempt but ultimately too "strained" to be plausible. Jaffa's "ingenious but fanciful" public teaching (which Jaffa himself did not fully believe, Kraynak suggests) tries too hard to accommodate the tensions of human life that Strauss thought were irreconcilable. In the end, Jaffa "encourages people to oversimplify the path to moral order and to understate the radical nature of the philosophic and spiritual life."[36]

Jaffa responds by arguing that Kraynak's interpretation is "noteworthy for its sensitivity and accuracy, but it fails to account for a change in the author's perspective from a book written nearly sixty years ago." He concedes that he had earlier overstated the disjunction between ancient and modern prudence. His more mature understanding takes its bearings from Strauss's important 1945 essay "On Classical Political Philosophy." In that essay, Strauss emphasizes the way Plato and Aristotle grounded their philosophic investigations "directly" in the moral opinions of citizens and the sense of justice "intrinsic to prephilosophic political life." What Kraynak calls a strained and exaggerated attempt to force together disparate elements of Western thought, Jaffa sees as locating the permanent ground of the moral phenomena. This prephilosophic awareness of right and wrong, the awareness of "distinctions rooted in the human condition," does indeed separate the heroes who recognize natural right from the villains who deny it. This Jaffa not only admits but trumpets. This same distinction, he argues, is the point of Strauss's break with Martin Heidegger.

> In his quest for the roots of Western philosophy, Heidegger went behind Socratic to pre-Socratic philosophy, where the moral cosmos is dissolved into the chaos out of which our world—whether created or uncreated—emerged. According to Aristotle and Strauss, we must begin our reasoning with what is known to us, prior to philosophy. The political philosopher thus comes to light presiding over the conflicts that arise in prephilosophic political life. The philosophic resolution of these conflicts preserves the prephilosophic distinctions, but preserves them in a form emancipated from the contradictions that caused the conflicts.[37]

Michael Zuckert's essay "Jaffa's *New Birth*: Harry Jaffa at Ninety" is a long meditation on Jaffa's work, parts of which he previewed in other publications. With his wife, Catherine Zuckert, he has written extensively on Strauss and Straussianism, including substantial analyses of Jaffa's scholarship and his place in the Strauss wars.[38] The couple taught for a short while in Claremont in the 1970s and are now on the faculty at Notre Dame. In this essay, Zuckert says of Jaffa that

He has been a giant in the field of political philosophy and a teacher with rare impact on his students. He has also been a controversial and contentious figure, a polemicist of great talent and vigor, impartially attacking friend and foe alike. He has been a figure to reckon with.[39]

Zuckert notes that *New Birth* "contradicts many of the central points" made in *Crisis*, then goes on to offer his own interpretation of Jaffa's suggestive reference to Plato. The *Laws* is "more practical in intention than *Republic*," and whereas the philosophic heart of *Crisis*—"The Political Philosophy of a Young Whig"— has a clear theoretical character, the center of *New Birth* is called "The Mind of Lincoln's Inaugural and the Argument and Action of the Debate that Shaped It." This "evokes Strauss's reading of Plato's *Laws*, for Strauss's book-length interpretation was called *The Argument and Action of Plato's Laws*."[40]

Echoing several other commentators, Zuckert observes that "Strauss was a thinker of dualities [while] Jaffa, on the contrary, is a thinker of unities." He neatly captures this with the line "What Strauss has put asunder Jaffa attempts to join together." Zuckert notes Jaffa's change on Locke and the founders, then brings out what appears to be a real difficulty: Jaffa dramatically elevates the founding in his later book, but we do not see any commensurate lowering of Lincoln, which might seem necessary to balance the equation. In *New Birth*, Jaffa tells us, he took more seriously Lincoln's own professed debt to the founders. "I have never had a feeling politically," Lincoln said, "that did not spring from the sentiments embodied in the Declaration of Independence." But Zuckert argues that this reveals *Crisis* to be "itself a book divided." That book tells us

Follow Lincoln, the higher path, because the Founding was modern, and therefore imperfect and inadequate. Yet Lincoln tells us:

follow the Founders. We are to follow the imperfect Founders as the solution to the imperfection of the Founders.[41]

As if that were not bad enough, *New Birth* provides no resolution to another tension in *Crisis* that becomes unraveled when Jaffa changes his perspective. As we saw Thomas West suggesting earlier, Lincoln seems to vindicate the principle of human equality only by transcending it. A regime based on equality seems to require (at least occasionally) the statesmanship of great men. In *Crisis*, according to Zuckert, Lincoln upheld the principle of equality but only by "affirming the deeper truth of human *inequality*." Lincoln represented for Jaffa a "peak of moral virtue"; he was a man "beyond concern for honor and power." But this means that the "*theoretical* truth" of the human condition is that there are great differences in "virtue or excellence"; at the same time, "the *practical* or *political* truth is equality."[42] [Emphases added.] This seems to work, but only as long as we accept Lincoln as a savior whose excellence surpassed even Washington's. If, however, as *New Birth* argues, the founding was not so degraded after all—perhaps not even in need of a savior—the depiction of Lincoln as a world-historical messiah figure becomes problematic. Again, if the founding comes up, must not Lincoln come down?

* * *

Some readers who are not well acquainted with Jaffa's two books may feel a bit lost by these labyrinthine arguments. The discussions in the following chapters—on Aristotle and Shakespeare, reason and revelation, statesmanship and magnanimity—will illuminate some of these questions from a different perspective. Jaffa's wide-ranging response to Zuckert will also be clarified at various points in later chapters as the rebuttal raises themes that persist through all of his work. But before concluding this chapter, we need to consider one more commentary, which will lead us into the next major subject in Jaffa's scholarship.

In a 1999 essay, Charles Kesler saw the same difficulty noted by Zuckert regarding Lincoln's exalted status in *Crisis*. Kesler was a longtime colleague of Jaffa's at Claremont McKenna. He wrote about Jaffa for *National Review* when he was a graduate student of Harvey Mansfield, Jr. at Harvard in the late 1970s and was regarded by Jaffa as something of a protégé. (Notwithstanding their friendship, Kesler—as the long-time editor of the *Claremont Review of Books*—more than once provoked Jaffa's annoyance and even exasperation by declining to publish some of his writing in the *CRB*.)

Like Zuckert, Kesler expresses some doubt about the attempt in *Crisis* to affirm human equality as a "political truth" while simultaneously upholding a "theoretical truth" acknowledging Lincoln's radically unequal greatness:

> This result may itself seem either too good to be true—a "*political truth*" is hardly the whole truth—or too true to be good, insofar as it appears to sideline all human virtue that fell short of the godlike. But Jaffa's point was that it was impossible to do justice to human equality and to human inequality at the same time in politics.[43]

As Kesler rightly asks, "What became of Lincoln's greatness in Jaffa's new estimation?" Jaffa seemed to concede that Lincoln was "less original but more profound than he had originally thought." This choice of words is apt.[44] Though Kesler does not make the connection explicit, it captures the shift in how Jaffa presents Lincoln's providential roles. In *Crisis*, Jaffa saw Lincoln's magnanimity as a "conflation of the symbols of Old and New Testaments," encompassing both "a prophetic role in the Old Testament sense" as well as "the Messianic idea." In Jaffa's later work, however, we no longer see this need for Lincoln to be all things: to recover classical prudence within a strictly modern regime—to represent both the Old Covenant and the New. Jaffa's enhanced appreciation for the founding, particularly the classical roots of the Declaration of Independence, leads him to see that the Word was already there, "in the beginning." Thus, Jaffa's later writings no longer speak of Lincoln as a Christ-like redeemer. (*New Birth* never uses the words *messiah* or *savior* in reference to Lincoln. He becomes rather the consummate "political science professor."[45]) The "less original but more profound" version of Lincoln now calls the American people back to their "ancient faith." Thus American statesmanship becomes more consistent with the well-established Judaic, Islamic, and Christian tradition: the tradition, as Kesler describes it, "arising from Alfarabi and Maimonides, of understanding prophecy as the supreme form of rational and philosophic legislation."[46]

Recognizing that "he had been wrong in arguing that Lincoln's understanding of natural rights transformed and transcended that of the Founders," Jaffa was moved to reconsider the philosophical depth of the revolutionary fathers, Kesler argues. In particular, Jaffa came to understand in a new way how they addressed "a problem immanent in Western civilization."

> For Jaffa, the 'new birth of freedom' signifies more now than the nation's rebaptism in its Aristotelianized 'political religion.' While definitely including the nation's re-dedication to the principles of the Revolution, Lincoln's 'new birth of freedom' means also America's baptism in fire, so to speak, as the model regime and exemplary empire of the modern world—as the best regime not as understood by the ancients nor by the Church but of civilization formed by the confluence of both faith and reason.[47]

It is within this much broader perspective, within that "civilization formed by the confluence of faith and reason," that Jaffa "labors to reconstruct American conservatism along Lincolnian lines." This is why he rejected the various schools of conservatism based on Burke, Hayek, and Tocqueville, which contended for authoritative status on the pages of *National Review* and elsewhere. For Jaffa, these thinkers don't fully grasp the deepest roots of the regime. In particular, Kesler argues, he found them "insufficiently attentive to the challenging demands of Aristotle's approach to natural and political right, which Jaffa has, for more than four decades, sought to apply to, or elicit from, America."[48]

To Aristotle, then, we must now turn.

4

THE PHILOSOPHER AND THE POET: ARISTOTLE AND SHAKESPEARE

In the final paragraph of his review of Jaffa's 1975 collection of essays, *The Conditions of Freedom*, Joseph Sobran writes:

> The heart of the book is a long exposition of Aristotle's *Politics*, which it would be futile to summarize here beyond saying that it richly explains the difference between the *polis* and what we call the "state." And that it will leave any attentive reader well-armed against both totalitarian and anarchist. It is this understanding of the *polis* that informs nearly every article in the book, and makes Jaffa so rewarding to read even when—as in his study of *King Lear*—his political insights are inappropriate to his specific subject matter. For it is almost the test of such insights that they survive their misapplication.[1]

The first part of this chapter will examine Jaffa's understanding of Aristotle, which Sobran rightly says informs all of *The Conditions of Freedom*—indeed every book Jaffa wrote. In the second half of this chapter, we will consider whether Jaffa's political interpretation of Shakespeare is in fact "inappropriate." In the book's collection of essays, "The Limits of Politics" is the title of Chapter 2 (Jaffa's groundbreaking analysis of *King Lear*) and is placed directly after his Aristotle essay, "What is Politics?" This perhaps provides some justification for what may seem to be an odd or arbitrary pairing of Aristotle and Shakespeare in the present chapter. In addition to a further connection that must be left for the end, we may note the following: dividing Jaffa's scholarship into the practical and the speculative, Lincoln and the crisis of the Union would exemplify the former. Given the vast scope of the latter, however, it seems proper to call on *two* teachers, representing the great categories of philosophy and poetry. Jaffa, having no time for second-raters, chose as his guides *the* philosopher and *the* poet. And as surprising at it may seem (especially in the case of Shakespeare), what Jaffa learned from these two speculative thinkers has direct bearing on what he saw as the crisis of our time.

* * *

In a letter to Sobran, whose review of *Conditions of Freedom* had been published in *National Review,* Jaffa notes that his first close analysis of Aristotle did not focus on the *Politics* but rather the *Nicomachean Ethics*, which was the basis, via Thomas Aquinas's commentary, of his doctoral dissertation. Starting from the time of his first encounter with Leo Strauss in 1944, Jaffa states, "I lived with that book for five years when I was writing *Thomism and Aristotelianism*. It has shaped my outlook on the world more, I think, than any other."[2] *Thomism* was completed in 1951. Writing for the *New York Times* sixty years later (!), Jaffa warmly reviewed a new 2011 translation by Robert Bartlett and Susan Collins. "Where the 'Ethics' stands among the greatest of all great books perhaps no one can say," Jaffa wrote. "That Aristotle's text, which explores the basis of the best way of human life, belongs on any list of such books is indisputable."³

Though he never repudiated *Thomism and Aristotelianism*—and it remains a respected work of scholarship to this day—Jaffa later came to see its analysis as immature and his criticisms of Thomas Aquinas as somewhat unwarranted. In 1969, the Catholic priest and political theorist Charles N. R. McCoy wrote to Jaffa to say that he had performed "a very naive examination of the status of the separate intellect in Thomas and Aristotle." Jaffa wrote back: "I undertook that study nearly a quarter century ago, and I too have some suspicions as to the naivete of the author."⁴ What he meant by "naivete" was his failure to see that Aquinas's apparently erroneous interpretations (or misrepresentations) were in fact prudent attempts to accommodate Aristotle to church doctrine. In a formulation he repeated often to students and colleagues, Jaffa had originally "thought it was Thomas's intention to make Aristotle safe for Christianity." He later came to believe that St. Thomas wanted to "make Christianity safe for Aristotle." In other words, according to Jaffa, when Aquinas writes that all humans—even apostates and nonbelievers—possess the ability to reason and thus participate in the eternal law, "the eternal law being the law of God's government of the universe," he is implying more than he can openly say. The logic of Thomas's argument suggests that since every normal human possesses reason, it would "certainly seem to entitle them to an equal possibility to participate in civil government. This would mean, for example, that Jews or Infidels, no less than Christians, had that right." Such an inference, implied in the premises, "is one that Thomas did not make and would no doubt have denied." Aquinas would have denied it, Jaffa argues, "for the same reason that Lincoln in 1858 denied any intention to make voters or jurors of Negroes or of permitting them to marry whites."⁵

What is noteworthy here is the way Jaffa's mature interpretation of Aquinas relies on the textual algebra he had learned from Strauss. According to Strauss, when reading any profound theoretical writer, one must add together the historical circumstances plus the writer's implied or suggestive statements in order to sum up his intentions. Taking into account popular prejudice and the threat of persecution, along with the writer's own sensible caution, it becomes not only appropriate but *necessary* to consider the unstated inferences of the arguments. This is the principle of esoteric writing, previously discussed.

In his later reappraisal of Aquinas as a more authentic Aristotelian than he earlier believed, Jaffa would apply this principle of esoteric writing, trying to discern the presence of arguments that would have been risky to proclaim under a theocratic regime. If we can assume Aquinas was capable of transcending the prejudices of medieval public opinion, it is reasonable to infer what "the mighty monk" may have been suggesting—and might have said openly under more favorable circumstances. Aquinas, Jaffa argues,

> was engaged in a great effort to bring reason (as distinct from unreasoning prejudice) into Christian doctrine. The benefits that might eventually accrue to Jews or Infidels from that effort were not something that he could prudently bring to the attention of inquisitors hunting for heretics to burn. This comparison illuminates the fact that at different times and places religious prejudice and racial prejudice are among the most powerful obstacles to reason that prudence must circumvent. Prudence counsels caution and indirection in the face of such obstacles, but compromises do not of themselves imply a lack of principle.[6]

Among those familiar with Straussian hermeneutics, it is not especially difficult to accept this theory about St. Thomas's discrete silence on Jews and infidels. What is surprising, even among those who accept Straussian esotericism, is how Jaffa claims that Aquinas was compelled to be circumspect *"for the same reason* that Lincoln in 1858 denied any intention to make voters or jurors of Negroes." [Emphasis added.] Strauss's esotericism certainly explains how the rare specimen of a truly philosophic writer interested in effecting political change might seek to bend public opinion without breaking his own neck. But nothing in Strauss's book *Persecution and the Art of Writing* had applied this principle to politicians. Esotericism, as presented in *Persecution*, has generally been understood by most of Strauss's students as a way for philosophers to protect themselves from politics, to isolate theory from practice, as it were. But in Jaffa's hands, it becomes a *practical* tool that might be employed by any prudent man or woman in pursuit of political goals. Aquinas, Jaffa claims, had to be mindful of the intolerant orthodoxy of his day *for the same reason* that Lincoln guarded his speech. "To have explicitly endorsed direct participation by Negroes in government in Illinois in 1858—to a public with overpowering racial prejudice, a public very imperfectly committed to the principles of the Declaration," Jaffa explains—"would have destroyed Lincoln as a leader of the free soil movement."[7] The significance of the discovery of esoteric writing (presuming it is true) is that it offers a concrete mechanism whereby—in defiance of historicist dogma—ideas and principles, including those of Aristotle and other ancient writers, might survive and continue to instruct discerning readers through every age and in every political community, even indirectly.[8]

We have now mentioned several times the Aristotelian virtue of prudence, which is a concept of absolutely vital importance for Jaffa. A proper explanation of this term is therefore in order, especially given how misunderstood it is today.

Readers of a certain age may recall the old *Saturday Night Live* skits in which Dana Carvey, portraying President George Bush,

Sr., would wimpishly exclaim, "Wouldn't be prudent!" Even those who haven't seen the episodes can figure out that what is being mocked here is a certain cautious, cost-benefit analysis that would appeal to modern social scientists. ("We assign a 'prudence score' to political decision points by calculating the ratio…") This is certainly *not* what Aristotle, or Jaffa, meant.

Book VI of the *Nicomachean Ethics* describes prudence as that comprehensive *practical wisdom* that directs all the moral virtues (Aristotle enumerates eleven altogether) to their proper ends. In the scholarly tradition, it is often defined as "right reason directed to action." What does a person's ambition or generosity hope to achieve? It cannot be aimless and still be a virtue. A destitute widow, for example, who sends her limited funds to a bogus televangelist is not exercising prudence and therefore is not exercising charity. Prudence supplies the overarching purpose that allows a virtuous man to know how and when to exercise his moral habits. A courageous man, for example, is bold *when appropriate*. Yet it is not the habit of conquering fear, by itself, that supplies this understanding. Courage can be distinguished from recklessness, on the one hand, and timidity, on the other, only when some judgment or discernment is present.

Though not quantifiable, prudence is nevertheless empirical in the sense of being grounded in what Jaffa calls "the reality of a purposeful universe."[9] There is always a right course of action. What is right, however, depends entirely on what the circumstances require. Thus, there can be no inflexible rules that tell us beforehand what we ought to do. The morally correct action is what the prudent person would do in that situation. However unsatisfying this may seem, Aristotle insists that there can be no other answer. We should not understand this to mean that moral choice is merely subjective or arbitrary. It can't be emphasized often enough that Aristotle's moral virtues are enduring reflections of human nature and find objective confirmation in our common-sense experience.

In his Rosary College lecture, Jaffa remarks

> Aristotle says at the beginning of the Seventh Book of the *Politics* that the man who was a perfect coward, who was frightened by anything, and...so intemperate that in order to get food or sex he would sacrifice anyone or anything for his immediate appetite, would be a miserable human being. I think we do have rational knowledge of the highest degree of certitude as to the value of the basic moral virtues for a good life.[10]

The bad effects of greed or vindictiveness on our souls are as real and predictable as the bad effects of smoking on our lungs. Thus, the practically wise or prudent person "is one who understands what happiness is, and why the virtues are good. He alone knows that they are good, because he alone *knows* the end for the sake of which they are good."[11]

To regard prudence merely as caution or amoral risk aversion misses the mark because under some circumstances what is required may be stupendous daring or even heroic sacrifice. Practical wisdom encompasses the entire range of possible human action and is therefore the guiding principle of the most comprehensive human community, the political regime. Prudence is the virtue par excellence of the statesman and "reaches its peak when it obtains the common good."[12]

The modern disregard for prudence may, on the one hand, reject any notion of a "right" course of action. But it may also take the form of an artificially strict or simplistic standard, applied to ourselves or (more commonly) to others. This absolutist stance, which is closer to Immanuel Kant than Aristotle, takes no account of the limited information and limited freedom of action that always constrain any course of conduct. A striking example of this misunderstanding can be seen in Justice Roger Taney's opinion in *Dred Scott*. Taney's ruling claimed, wrongly, that the Declaration's phrase "all men" did not include blacks and that the founders believed blacks possessed no natural rights protected by the Constitution. Jaffa writes

> According to Taney, if the Founding Fathers, as moral men, had believed what they said, they would have abolished slavery. Taney seems to have assumed that moral men were those who acted in accordance with Kant's categorical imperative. As good Kantians they would have acted solely on the basis of their judgment that slavery was wrong, paying no attention whatever to consider- ations of prudence. Taney failed to notice that the Declaration itself rejected Kant when it appealed to the dictates of prudence.

Yet as Jaffa points out, "Taney knew perfectly well that in 1776 or 1787 no American government had the power to abolish slavery throughout the United States."[13] In fact, responding to Taney's obtuse Kantian error, Jaffa crafted one his most memorable observations: "It was not wonderful that a nation of slavehold- ers—and all thirteen states were slave states in 1776—had not abolished slavery. What was wonderful," Jaffa explained, "was that a nation of slaveholders had declared that all men are created equal, and thereby had made the ultimate abolition of slavery a moral necessity."[14]

Be that as it may, our contemporary neglect or misunder- standing of prudence is connected to (or perhaps the result of) our progressive and historicist blinders. The inability to judge the statesmanship of the past on its own terms makes it that much more difficult to appreciate or cultivate statesmanship in our own time. This distorted view of history is not confined to liber- als. In *Crisis of the House Divided*, Jaffa wrote that the historians of 1950s "believed that slavery would not go into the territories because it did not go there, and they implied that the men of the 1850's should have known as much." Similarly, one finds today more than a few young people, on both left and right, who seem to think the victory of the West in the Cold War was bound to happen because it did happen. But the confluence of economic and political forces that seem so clear in retrospect today were by no means evident in the 1970s and 80s.

In his essay "On the Necessity of a Scholarship of the Politics of Freedom," Jaffa argues that a deterministic view of history renders us incapable of judging what is "wise or foolish, noble or base, brave or cowardly." Winston Churchill, as "a writer no less than a maker of history," never made this error. He understood, "as few who have either written or made history have done, the difference between wisdom *in* and wisdom *after* the event.... Because human beings are free, there is genuine indeterminacy" in all political events, even those that seem, after the fact, inevitable. "No one can be certain that a wise action will have a good result," Jaffa argues.[15] Therefore, prudence "is also a virtue that may on occasion tell us that success is impossible, and that noble failure is the only rational alternative."[16]

* * *

Colleen Sheehan, a Claremont PhD who taught political philosophy at Villanova, has remarked that "Aristotle appears on every page of Jaffa's work, even when his name does not."[17] This judgment is hard to dispute and is all the more remarkable given how often Aristotle's name *does* appear in Jaffa's work. A decade after his book on the *Ethics*, he turned his attention to producing a close interpretation of the *Politics*. Strauss had asked Jaffa to write the Aristotle chapter for his *History of Political Philosophy*, a collection of essays by a variety of Strauss's students and colleagues sketching the major figures of Western thought coedited with Joseph Cropsey.[18] Jaffa's prodigious sixty-five-page essay became the second chapter of the book, following Strauss's own slightly shorter essay on Plato.[19]

In a 1963 memo to his department chairman at Ohio State, Jaffa writes

> Despite its comparative brevity this essay represents more, and more difficult labor, than *Crisis of the House Divided*. I believe it was justified however because the *Politics* is not only historically the first methodical book on the subject of politics, but remains the gateway to every subsequent attempt to write philosophically or scientifically on the subject. For every later attempt in the western world has been an attempt either to apply, to amplify, to modify, or to reject Aristotle. In this sense every later attempt has been a reaction to the *Politics* and no one can judge a reaction who does not know the action.[20]

Jaffa's essay does not appear in the third edition of the Strauss-Cropsey *History* (the one now widely available in paperback) and has been replaced with a new Aristotle chapter written by Carnes Lord.[21] But as noted above, Jaffa reprinted the essay in his 1975 *Conditions of Freedom* with the title "What is Politics?"

In Jaffa's long summary and interpretation of the *Politics*, we can discern five broad themes that inform all of his work in political philosophy. The emphasis here is on the broad principles rather than the specific examples that would have been relevant to Aristotle's Greek contemporaries. Jaffa often described the *Ethics* as "a perfect book." The descriptions of individual virtue and the distinctions between distributive and commutative justice, for example, are applicable in all times and places. The *Politics*, however, must be read with an eye to how its underlying lessons can be adapted by...well, prudence, for different historical circumstances.

Roughly approximating the order in which they appear in Aristotle's text, and Jaffa's essay, the major themes outlined here are: 1) The form of the city, from genesis to *telos*; 2) Nature plus art; 3) Unity in compound; 4) The best regime and its approximations; and 5) The politics of the soul: piety and philosophy. Most of the following is drawn from Jaffa's long essay first published in the Strauss-Cropsey *History* volume. In some cases, however, other writings by Jaffa are quoted when they offer a lucid or insightful remark.

FROM GENESIS TO TELOS

Many of his students recall that when teaching the *Nicomachean Ethics*, a significant part of the semester would often go by before Jaffa finished explicating the opening sentence.[22] A line near the beginning of the *Politics* is almost as significant for understanding the whole of that work:

> The city comes into being for the sake of life, but it continues for the sake of the good life.

Aristotle's use of "city" (*polis*) is sometimes translated as "state," but Jaffa presents an extended argument to show this is misleading. The polis—the political community, or regime—makes no distinction between state and society. The polis is comprehensive and "includes or assimilates within its own end or purpose every other form of community."[23] Above all, there is no distinction between government and religion. Each city is "closed" by virtue of having its own gods, and every citizen owes allegiance to those communal gods. The city, or regime, is the church, and piety is a public duty.

The polis originates as a collection of families who come together for the sake of safety or survival. It provides the necessities that individual families and villages cannot secure on their own. Its *end*, however, is not mere survival but the comprehensive human good: happiness. The Greek term for end, *telos*, is the root of *teleological*, an explanation or analysis of goals and purposes. The political regime, Jaffa explains in an entry he wrote for the *International Encyclopedia of Social Science*, "is the comprehensive form of human association, and its purposes ascend from the necessary conditions of human existence" to the higher end of "formation of good character in the citizens." The polis is not a collection of atomized individuals but a true partnership in pursuit of the good life. Civic friendship, therefore, is essential. Jaffa explains: "Friendship, writes Aristotle, seems to hold political communities together more than does justice, and legislators seem to care for it more than for justice." Therefore, "the ultimate sanctions for justice are not the penalties that can be exacted in the law courts but ostracism, formal or informal, from that fellowship in which alone the good citizen feels he can lead the good life."[24]

In his genetic account of the city (that is, explaining how the city originates), Aristotle devotes considerable attention to the family or household. The comprehensiveness of the polis subsumes but does not destroy the lesser communities. The polis, for Aristotle, depends on (and certainly does not replace) the family. "The distinctions which give structure to the family—between husband and wife, father and children—are the foundation of morality within the polis," writes Jaffa.[25] On this point, the modern assault on the integrity of the family that began in the 1960s and 70s, and especially the moral arguments for "sexual liberation," concerned Jaffa greatly. He was particularly alarmed by the radical gay-rights agenda, which he believed would undermine nature as the ground of all morality. "Human nature," Jaffa explains in a 1982 essay, "is partitioned into men and women," and it is these differences "which instruct us in the reality of the whole of nature." All judgments about sexual conduct must flow from this. "The prohibitions upon incest and upon sodomy are not primitive superstitions: Reason and nature tell us that without these prohibitions the structure of the family, and of authority within the family, would collapse."[26]

Two arguments in this early section of the *Politics,* which sound especially odd to modern ears, should be clarified. The first deals with the apparently inverted respect Aristotle accords to war as compared to commerce and finance. While barter and trade are acceptable, Aristotle condemns as "contrary to nature" the commodification of money itself (as in usury). Without getting into the details of Aristotle's subtle discussion, we can note that the two "branches of acquisition" by which societies subsist are rooted in either war or trade. Between them, Jaffa notes, Aristotle condemns trade (at least in its extreme form) as worse than war. This surprising judgment is rooted in Aristotle's emphasis on the importance of virtue for happiness, which is the goal of the city. Ancient Athens recognized debt and credit, which meant that wealth was not limited by the possession of physical capital and real estate.[27] Jaffa suggests that the pursuit of money for its own sake is the more dangerous form of acquisition because it fuels an unchecked gratification of "the desires of the body." And "man, alone among the animals," is capable of infinite desires. "Whether or not this explains Aristotle's judgment," says Jaffa, "it is clear that nature has established limits for human life no less than she has done for the other animals, however much she has left it in the hands of men to enforce those limits."[28] A significant revision of this Aristotelian view was one aspect of the modern revolt against the classics.

The second point to clarify concerns the controversial and (according to Jaffa) frequently misunderstood remarks by Aristotle concerning slavery. Slavery, of course, was a fact of life in the ancient world and generally accepted as a given by most classical authors. Inhabitants of conquered cities were enslaved as a matter of course. Aristotle invests some effort in explaining the difference between such conventional slavery (the justice of which Aristotle seems to question) and what he called the "natural" slave: an individual incapable of being a full citizen. "Perhaps the simplest explanation of what Aristotle means by natural slavery," states Jaffa, is "a man with a mentality like that of a child, who cannot perceive that it is sometimes good to take bitter medicine." Such a person, perhaps born with severe mental impairment or afflicted with Alzheimer's disease, "must be ruled like a child, for his own good." For Aristotle, who defined human beings as "the rational animal," such an individual cannot be considered a complete person. This does not necessarily mean such a life is not worth living (although in Aristotle's society, the killing of "defective" infants was common). But such a person, explains Jaffa, "is not a grown man, although he may have the body of one. He is a part, not a whole, and he may become part of a whole only as he belongs to another," who must supervise and direct his actions.[29] In making this distinction between natural and unnatural slavery, Aristotle seems—at the least—to bring into considerable doubt the justice of enslaving rational men and women through conquest.

NATURE PLUS ART

Because the city can be explained through a genetic account of its origins and also through a teleological account of its end, Aristotle might appear to give conflicting accounts of whether a political community exists by nature or by human art and contrivance. In fact, both are true, depending on what is being examined. In an early review of a book on the medieval theologian Marsilius of Padua, Jaffa writes

Aristotle, in the *Nicomachean Ethics*, says that man is more naturally conjugal than political, since the household is prior to and
more necessary than the city (1162a 15). And this, taken unqualifiedly, would flatly contradict the first chapter of the *Politics*, where
he says that the city is prior in nature to the household and the
individual (1253a 20). Yet it becomes clear from the two contexts
that Aristotle means in the one case that the city is naturally prior
to the household in order of perfection, that is, qua final cause;
and in the other that the household is prior to the city in order
of generation, that is, qua efficient and material cause.[30]

(Since Jaffa mentions the terms here, we should clarify Aristotle's doctrine of causation, which is commonly explained with
reference to the building of a house. The wood and stone constitute the "material" cause. The work of the carpenters and masons
represents the "efficient" cause. The architect's blueprints are the
"formal" cause. All this is for the sake of providing a place to live
for a person or family, which constitutes the "final" cause. In
some cases, chance or random events may represent an additional
cause of how things come to be.[31])

That man is by nature a "political animal" is one of Aristotle's
more famous observations. This means that for Aristotle, and
Jaffa, political life is not a necessary evil, reflecting imperfect
human nature, but rather a *good* for man.[32] A healthy political
regime is the field in which moral virtue—and to some degree
even intellectual virtue—can flourish.

Nevertheless, unlike an acorn growing into an oak tree, the
political community does not spring up automatically; some
individual or group of individuals must act as founders, establishing the polis. In one of Aristotle's subtle and carefully worded
statements, he says that the political community exists *according*
to nature but not *by* nature. An act of founding is necessary to
effectuate man's natural potential; art or practical wisdom must

complete nature. Jaffa often quoted Aristotle's statement that the man who first united men into the political community—the first founder of a city—"was the greatest of benefactors." (Literally, "the greatest cause of good things.")

This distinction between *according to* and *by* nature leads to some questions about how exactly Aristotle understood nature (*physis*) and the ways in which he departs from his teacher Plato. In comparison with the extreme skepticism and antirationalism of modern (and postmodern) philosophy, Jaffa sees little significant difference between the teachings of Plato and Aristotle. Yet on some points there are important distinctions. Aristotle's understanding of the naturalness of the city, and indeed man's relationship to nature in general, reaches into obscure metaphysical questions that we can only touch on here.

An entire book could be written, and many have been written, attempting to understand Plato's doctrine of the Ideas as separate, self-subsisting forms (namely, that there exists, in some real sense, a perfect "idea" of *man*, or *dog*, or *justice*). What interests us here is how this bears on Jaffa's interpretation of Aristotle. For Plato, the Ideas, as objects of theoretical inquiry, are the most true and real beings. "These," Jaffa explains, "always transcend—thus in some sense differ from or contradict—the things of which we have sensible experience. Reality, for Plato, is thus ineluctably paradoxical. Aristotle denies this." To simplify greatly, Aristotle does not see ultimate reality and truth as somehow "beyond" our ordinary experience, accessible only through abstract conjecture or "speech." What is most real is present physically in the here and now. Plato sees all tangible objects, such as men or dogs, as so many imperfect copies of the pure Idea. For Aristotle, the "idea of man," says Jaffa, "is *in* each man, and is ultimately identical with the activity in virtue of which human beings generate human beings and not dogs or horses."[33] [Emphasis added.]

Aristotle certainly does not deny that theoretical categories are helpful and even necessary for understanding politics or anything else. But for him, it is the objects of theory that are abstract and thus less real than what we find readily accessible in nature. Aristotle's famous emphasis on the practical over the theoretical has its roots in this metaphysical point. We will examine a particular example of this in a moment in the way Jaffa sees Plato and Aristotle differing on the question of natural right.

UNITY IN COMPOUND

The polis, to repeat, is the comprehensive community that encompasses all the lesser communities, including the household. It must not, however, attempt to obliterate or replace them. To make the city too much of a unity would destroy the very ends the political community exists to secure.

A political regime, therefore, is properly understood as a compound or complex unity. Plato's tendency to interpret the world through the abstract Ideas leads him to collapse too many important distinctions. This makes the city "too much of a unity." "Aristotle," Jaffa argues, "will not sacrifice heterogeneity to homogeneity, nor homogeneity to heterogeneity."[34] This is the root of the objections laid out in Book II of the *Politics* against Plato's *Republic*. As an entirely utopian construct for the perfectly just regime, it "is an impractical scheme and can no more guide the legislator than the idea of the good can guide the weaver, carpenter, or doctor." Instead, "Aristotle maintains that we have in nature a standard that is both practical and objective."[35] Nature shows that there is a natural end for man, happiness, but also there are a multiplicity of other good things, which may vary for different beings (even perhaps within the same species) and may also differ according to circumstance. Aristotle, ever the seeker of the mean, rejects the superficial egalitarianism that treats all goods as subjective, yet he also avoids the theoretician's error that overlooks the variety obvious to our senses.

The problem of viewing politics too abstractly, and therefore imposing too much unity, was not confined to Plato. One of the most interesting parts of Jaffa's Aristotle essay concerns a character named Hippodamus, whom Aristotle criticizes rather vigorously and even uncharacteristically mocks for his appearance. (Hippodamus, we are told, had long hair, wore too much jewelry, and went about in the same cheap clothes in summer and winter.) Hippodamus was most famous for invariably dividing all political phenomena into groups of three. In doing so, Jaffa writes, he showed himself to be "a theorist in the modern sense,"

> i.e. one who approached politics as an abstract problem in design, without regard for the problems that statesmen as practical men faced. He was also like certain twentieth century political scientists in his attempt to assimilate the science of politics to a mathematically oriented natural science. Hippodamus' scheme has a certain resemblance to Plato's in that it appears to be an attempt to impose mathematical harmony upon the *polis*....He thought that jurors should not give simple verdicts of guilty or not guilty....Finally, Hippodamus proposed a law which would honor anyone who discovered anything new for the advantage of the *polis*.[36]

Jaffa notes throughout the rest of the essay the various ways in which Aristotle himself uses tripartite divisions, almost promiscuously so, yet he does not explain why these are justified and Hippodamus's three-way divisions are not. "This repeated division into three is made clear in Harry V. Jaffa's analysis...although he does not make its significance explicit," observes Aristotle scholar Michael Davis.[37] Davis sees Hippodamus's desire to impose a uniform template on political categories as connected to his proposal for eliminating simple guilty or not-guilty jury verdicts.

(The Athenian practice was to render a single verdict on all the counts in the indictment without separating them.) This reform, Davis argues, "would ultimately undermine the very notion of a general rule," which in turn would undermine trials entirely. "If law cannot be general it cannot be, and without law there is no polis." This points to what Davis sees as the larger lesson of Book II of the *Politics*: the "problematic status of political self-knowledge." Aristotle's own tripartitions are meant ironically to "disclose the incomplete rationality of the polis," he argues.[38] At the end of the chapter, Davis expands on this notion of political life as irrational and goes so far as to say that "the polis is a bit like a drunken man—it is goal directed, but in a very obscure way." The study of politics is "a bit like the science of drunkenness."[39]

Jaffa's critique of Hippodamus proceeds along other lines and points to a different overall interpretation of the *Politics*. People may be, and often are, irrational. But Jaffa would deny that *political life,* as such, is inherently irrational. Such a view leans too much toward the Platonic error of judging every regime against an abstract and therefore impractical ideal of pure reason. For Jaffa, the realm of statesmanship and practical wisdom has its own integrity and coherence.

If the irrationality of political life makes the science of politics like the study of drunkenness, as Davis suggests, this would mean—to play out the metaphor—that a political regime can only aspire to *continence.* The virtue of continence or abstemiousness is a second-best virtue embraced by a person of weak moral fiber who cannot risk imbibing at all. By contrast, as Jaffa explains in *Thomism and Aristotelianism,* the man of well-developed moral character is *moderate,* meaning he can drink (or indulge other pleasures) without becoming a danger to himself.[40] A morally virtuous man is protected, as it were, by his good character. He has greater freedom of action and can take more risks than a man of weaker character. This is likewise true of political communities. "In a republic, the sobriety of the citizens replaces the force of authority as the principal source of order," claims Jaffa.[41] This higher estimation of political life means that a reasonably healthy regime can and should aim for moderation, not merely continence, which gives it greater freedom to act. This will become clearer if we now turn to how Jaffa understands the question of inventions and innovation.

In discussing Hippodamus's proposal for jury verdicts, Jaffa surprises the reader slightly with a neutral, even sympathetic, account. Just a few sentences earlier in the same paragraph, Jaffa had reminded the reader of Aristotle's attitude to city planning: his "characteristic" solution was to mix two desirable goals (in this case, comfort and security). With this example freshly in mind, it is hard to avoid the impression that Jaffa rather approves of Hippodamus's idea for a similar mixture allowing "qualified verdicts finding guilt on some counts but not others." Hippodamus, Jaffa observes without demurral, believed that "finding a man guilty or not guilty, when the juror believed him to be guilty of some things but not of others in the indictment, forced the juror to commit perjury."[42]

But the recommendation by Hippodamus that receives the most attention from Jaffa, a proposal he describes as "attractive but unsafe," would reward inventions or "advantageous novelties." He then offers a quite interesting commentary on political innovation:

> This leads to another, broader question, and it is the fundamental question raised by Hippodamus: is politics an art or science like the other arts or sciences, in which each new discovery is rightly incorporated into the practice of the art or science? Aristotle's reply is that politics is not like medicine or gymnastics, in which every alteration from traditional practice, in the light of better knowledge, is rightly acceptable.[43]

Jaffa understands the danger of innovation at least partly in light of the pedagogic and character-forming authority of tradition. "The law has no power to persuade other than that derived from custom or habit," he observes, "and these are formed only over a long period of time. Changing laws weakens their power." (Notably, however, the more deficient the regime is in terms of moral education and virtue, the more dependent it is on custom.) Of course, the ancient does not, by itself, provide any standards for distinguishing good traditions from bad ones. And sometimes it is necessary to change the laws, as Aristotle himself insists. If no political order is ever to change, "why write the *Politics*?" Jaffa reasonably asks.

> The possibility of improvement in the political order is in fact two-fold first, because of the progress of general intelligence (including progress in the arts and sciences) from primitive man; and second, because of the necessity of every law to be framed in general terms, while the actions governed by law are always particulars. Experience must always reveal ways in which the laws might be better framed, and therefore how they might be improved.[44]

So where is the danger? It consists in the failure to *balance* change with continuity. We ought not to assume (as many modern people are inclined to do) that accepting changes in law means we can readily dispense with the fundamental principles or constitution of the regime. "To use a modern instance," Jaffa asks, "would we here in the United States today accept proposals for changes in the Bill of Rights in the same spirit as changes in the exemptions in the income tax?" Furthermore, doesn't it matter whether a constitutional convention is conducted "under the presiding genius of a George Washington, or by anyone anywhere? These things make a difference in politics that they do not make in the practice of the other arts."[45]

As Jaffa describes the faults of Hippodamus, the error of his tripartite divisions seems to lie principally in their artificiality. The long-haired admirer of novelty had divided the city into farmers, artisans, and warriors arbitrarily for the sake "mathematical harmony." The division ignores economic realities and fails to account for how the competing interests of the three classes will play out. Hippodamus's scheme "reveals confusion after confusion."[46] Not innovation as such but innovation for its own sake is dangerous. (In a healthy and well-constructed regime, incidentally, innovations are less necessary but easier to adopt.) Likewise, divisions into three should be judged on their merits. They are dubious only when imposed merely for the sake of mathematical harmony.[47]

It is important to note that Jaffa is certainly not trying to rehabilitate this rather comical character that Aristotle criticizes. He agrees with the consensus view that Hippodamus lacked prudence. In fact, Jaffa would later heap his greatest scorn on the American Political Science Association's Leo Strauss Award by calling it a "Hippodamus Award." But part of Aristotle's prudence is to show when change *is* necessary and how political triangulation can be done properly. Hippodamus represents a deeply erroneous approach to moral-practical life. Yet, while a geometrician makes a poor political scientist, Jaffa also insists that we must avoid the opposite error. We do not want a regime constructed entirely of right angles, as it were, but neither do we hold up as a political standard a drunk who cannot walk a straight line.

THE BEST REGIME AND ITS APPROXIMATIONS

The criticisms of Plato and Hippodamus (along with some other theoretical and practical models) comprise much of the second book of Aristotle's *Politics*. The next section is widely regarded as the most interesting as well as the intellectual heart of Aristotle's political philosophy. "Book III," Jaffa says, "supplies us with the science of the *polis* and the leading feature of that science: an adequate inquiry in the principles of regimes." Now, when Aristotle "begins to present his own doctrine,"

> he appears not as an external observer but as someone within the polis. The conflicts of opinions with which we are immediately confronted are no longer the conflicts between observers of political life, they are the conflicts among participants, among men who differ as to how the burdens and advantages of political life should be divided and shared. What is most significant about Aristotle's method in Book III is not so much that it is analytical in the sense indicated, but that it draws philosophic conclusions from the opinions of men who are neither philosophers nor legislators, but men who are contending for political advantages in political life.[48]

In this section, Aristotle will sketch his own version of the best regime, or rather, a few different versions of the best regime, with varying levels of achievability. Importantly, none of Aristotle's models is altogether impossible. But the pinnacle of all practical regimes, the monarchical rule of an entirely virtuous and wise individual, depends on such an unlikely combination of circumstances, including luck, that Aristotle sets it aside with little elaboration. We must note that Aristotle's criticism of Plato's utopianism does not mean he rejects the idea of an enduring standard. The two Socratic philosophers are in complete agreement about judging politics (indeed, all human things) by what is highest and most virtuous. In this, both ancient thinkers differ from the moderns who rejected the teleological "politics of virtue" in favor of the efficient pursuit of individual passions and bodily needs. (Here, incidentally, is the origin of the modern "right to privacy.")

Aristotle stakes out the theme of Book III by raising the question of each regime's *arche,* its governing principle or claim to political legitimacy. (Jaffa uses the rather awkward word "hypothesis.") What are the different ruling authorities or legitimating principles that might define a polis? "The claimants are," according to Jaffa, "the many, the rich, the good, the one best of all, and the tyrant." Although the standard remains the rule of the best and most virtuous, Aristotle recognizes that nearly every regime, in practice, will capture only part of complete political excellence. He therefore investigates "the different forms that justice takes when conditions make the predominant factor...something other than virtue."[49]

The constant difficulty (which points to the arbitrating and guiding role played by the political philosopher) is that every form of partial justice tends to inflate its claims. Wealth and freedom are both necessary for the political community. Yet commercial interests tend to make the excessive claim that wealth is the sole aim of the regime, while democratic elements are inclined to reject any constraints on freedom. The founder or legislator must be on guard against this, both in the beginning and while maintaining or preserving the regime, though even careful founders sometimes err. This happened with Sparta, Jaffa explains. Elevating military strength and martial prowess above all other considerations, the legislator committed an "intellectual error" and "mistook a part of virtue for the whole of virtue."[50] Spartan men, obsessed with an exaggerated manliness, ceded rule of their city to the women.

As a general rule, Aristotle views "democracy and oligarchy as the two regimes which in practice dominate political struggles" over how to distribute honors and offices. Therefore, Jaffa explains, Aristotle focuses on these two claims to legitimacy. The various combinations merging the claims of the many and the claims of the rich constitute the best generally available option: a mixture he calls "polity." From "the erroneous but complementary opinions" of the partisans of democracy on the one hand and of oligarchy on the other, "Aristotle compounds the true opinion which is the basis of his own doctrine concerning distributive justice."[51]

Still, all the claims, including aristocracy and kingship, have some merit (even, surprisingly, tyranny in its premodern form, which if nothing else is superior to anarchy). "Each regime is *just*," Jaffa explains, "insofar as it is rightly constituted, insofar as it secures the common good." [Emphasis in the original.] And if "fortune permits" those rare circumstances "where human excellence dominates civic excellence, there is the best regime."[52] These different approximations or versions of justice bring us now to the key concept of natural right in the *Politics*.

> In classical political philosophy "natural right" refers to the objective rightness of the right things, whether the virtue of a soul, the correctness of an action, or the excellence of a regime. Thus Aristotle says in *Politics* (1323a29–33) that no one would call a man happy who was completely lacking in courage, temperance, justice, or wisdom.... Even though chance may occasionally prevent good actions from having their normal consequences, so that sometimes cowards fare better than brave men, courage is still objectively better than cowardice. The virtues and actions that contribute to the good life, and the activities intrinsic to the good life, are naturally right.[53]

Aristotle's understanding of natural right differs from Plato's and differs also from the later doctrine of natural *law*, both in its Christian and modern scientific forms. To take the latter first, Aristotle's natural right is emphatically *prudential* rather than rule based. The correctness of an action does indeed have an objective basis in nature, but no rule can invariably determine beforehand what is correct regardless of circumstances. Whether rushing into a burning building to save a stranger constitutes an act of bravery or suicide depends on a judgment made by a brave and prudent person in the moment.[54]

Because the correct understanding of what is required by natural right is inseparable from prudence, Aristotle says (in a famously challenging section of the *Nicomachean Ethics*) that natural right is part of political right. "Of the just in the political sense, one part is natural, the other, conventional." For example, virtually every society recognizes murder as objectively wrong, but the rules of evidence and the penalties will vary by positive or conventional standards. Some people, Aristotle continues, infer that since what is natural is the same everywhere, "just as fire burns both here and in Persia," then natural justice must have the same universal, unchanging quality. This is true, but only "in a sense." For Aristotle, "there is in fact something that is [just] by nature, though it is altogether changeable."[55]

This apparently confusing account becomes clearer if we recall from the discussion above that, in any given situation, Aristotle insists that there *is* a right and a wrong choice, but only prudence can determine, based on the circumstances, what justice (or courage or moderation) requires. Because such judgments almost invariably involve other people, Aristotle says that natural right is included within, or is part of, political right. The comprehensive human community, the regime, is a mixture of both natural and conventional justice. (Natural justice tells us we can't use our cars to hurt or endanger other people, but conventional justice defines whether we drive on the left- or right-hand side of the road.)

One way to look at this Aristotelian argument is as a critique of utopianism: pure natural right, a regime of perfect justice, is not achievable for most societies—probably any society—and the attempt to implement perfect justice would in fact lead to tyranny. In a somewhat paradoxical way, then, for Aristotle pure natural right is unjust because it is essentially unobtainable. Just as prudence determines the right course of action for an individual in the here and now, political right is the statesman-like determination of what is best for a given regime under the circumstances.[56]

With this principle in view, we can now see Aristotle's difference with Plato, which is somewhat more subtle than the earlier discussion about natural *law* versus natural *right*. Because Plato sees the Ideas, including the Idea of justice, as subsisting perfectly somewhere beyond our perception, the possibility of justice in any particular political regime is inherently problematic. Pure natural right, or perfect justice, seems to be practically impossible. Plato and Aristotle agree on this. But for Plato, natural right is the standard, and political right is the subordinate, imperfect imitation. Political justice, like reality itself, is somewhat paradoxical for Plato, as noted earlier, because there is always a disjunction between anything we perceive in the sensible world and its perfect essence or Idea.[57] For Aristotle, however, perfection or completion (*entelechia*) is best understood as the fulfillment of a natural, inherent purpose in the real world, whether that purpose be the strength of an oak tree, the happiness of a human being, or the common good of a political community.

To bring this somewhat complicated matter to a conclusion, one of Jaffa's students, Edward Erler, offers a useful and concise summation.[58] As Erler explains,

> Plato never answered the question whether natural right could ever become political right. That question was answered by Aristotle. There was no essential disproportion, Aristotle maintained, between the requirements of natural right and the demands of politics. What allowed natural right to become a part of political right was prudence or practical wisdom. Even though theoretical

wisdom is superior, prudence acts independently and rules the sphere of politics, or what Strauss called "the sphere of all human things as such."[59]

PIETY AND PHILOSOPHY

We conclude this overview of Jaffa's understanding of Aristotle by touching on philosophy and the limits of politics.

No city in the ancient world recognized liberty of conscience. Nor does Aristotle carve out any space for freedom of religion, a phrase that would have been incoherent in classical Athens. Piety, once again, was considered a public duty, and it concerned virtually every aspect of life. As Jaffa notes, "according to Aristotle, whatever the law does not command, it forbids. This is perfectly consistent with the idea of law in the Mosaic polity, which is another example of the ancient city."[60] Nevertheless, the first premises for the eventual recognition of what he calls "the metaphysical freedom of the human mind" were laid here, in the example of Socrates (who was executed for his incessant questioning of every opinion, even the most sacred) as well as Aristotle's distinction between theoretical and practical wisdom.

In the letter to Father Charles McCoy referenced earlier, Jaffa writes,

> You cite me as calling the contemplative life "self-regarding," and say that this is "flagrantly to contradict the explicit teaching of Aristotle." You would have been right in your objection, if I had actually written what you attribute to me. In fact, I wrote that "the activity of wisdom," not the contemplative life, is self-regarding.... The activity of wisdom, according to Aristotle, considered in and of itself, is self-regarding, in the same sense as the activity of God. Of course, a man who thinks of divine things is thinking of something "other" than himself, from the point of

view of ordinary human life.... But in another sense it is in accord with what is best in him, because there is something both divine and immortal in him.[61]

In the *Politics*, there is no limitation on government based on a distinction between state and society or a "right to privacy." Aristotle nevertheless sees that the good life pursued by the political community would become destructive if it attempted to displace all other goods, such as those found in the family. "To extend practical activity"—that is, the practical activity of the statesman or legislator—beyond a certain limit, Jaffa argues, is "to turn it from good to evil."

> For example, it is good to be brave and strong, for the weak and cowardly cannot preserve their freedom, and the unfree cannot live good lives. But those who are strong and free, and whose strength and freedom are unchallenged, cannot utilize either their strength or freedom in action. To go into action to dominate others, merely to exercise one's freedom of action and one's bravery, is a perversion of virtue; this was the defect of the Spartan regime. Virtuous activity cannot then be truly practical except as it serves an end which is itself not practical, an activity which is good solely with reference to itself, an activity to which there are no limits because its increase does not extend it beyond itself, an activity which is thus wholly self-contained.[62]

This activity of course is philosophy. Unlike the acquisition of wealth or bodily pleasure, the pursuit of wisdom is not corrupted by being unlimited. The human intellect seems to participate, somehow, in the eternal and divine, and thus the contemplation of truth is "the same as the activity of God, or thought thinking itself. It is the only absolutely self-contained, self-sufficient activity in the universe." The political community can secure the conditions for, but cannot itself supply, this highest good. Political life points beyond itself. Therefore, Jaffa says, "political rulers must have the spirit and practice of philosophy, which means love of wisdom, as distinct from wisdom itself." That is, prudent men in government will appreciate the value and nobility of theoretical wisdom and even be open to its insights without becoming philosophers themselves.[63]

This raises a subtle point about the connection between practical and theoretical virtue. In *Thomism and Aristotelianism*, Jaffa makes some unexpected statements about the limited horizon of moral virtue, which comes to light in the peak of moral excellence—a virtue Aristotle calls magnanimity. The magnanimous man believes he is the highest human type; and indeed he is when "viewed within the dimension of morality." Yet the more comprehensive view of human perfection goes beyond even the surpassing greatness of the magnanimous or "great-souled" individual. From this perspective, "the magnanimous man's world is in one respect at least like the world of a child" inasmuch as his actions are guided "only" by moral habituation and not by the highest wisdom, which is theoretical. Now, the magnanimous man *may* "be something more than magnanimous"—that is, philosophic. But in that case, he has transcended the excellence of moral virtue as such. Because this theme will be elaborated below, we add only one further point: the confident dutifulness of moral gentlemen, which is essential to decent politics, requires a certain discretion or responsibility by the philosopher. Encouraging these gentlemen's openness to philosophy must not lead to unreasonable expectations about what might come of that openness.[64]

Returning to his long Aristotle essay, Jaffa picks up on this same theme, by noting

> The final problem of the *Politics* is the problem of establishing clearly that distinction within true virtue itself which throughout

the *Politics* remained almost invisible: the distinction between the virtue of action—moral virtue plus practical wisdom—and the virtue of thought—theoretical wisdom. And corresponding to these two virtues are the two activities of the active and of the contemplative life.[65]

Pure contemplation, the *activity* that imitates "thought thinking itself," is incompatible with the active demands of civic responsibility. But this activity is not simply identical with the philosopher as a human being, who always lives in some political community and even depends on it. (Socrates, incidentally, served in the Athenian military.) By providing for the separate integrity of theoretical and practical excellence, Jaffa argues, Aristotle denies the "necessary antagonism between philosophy and political life [that] Plato envisaged." This is in part because theoretical wisdom "itself issues no commands." Contemplation of eternal truth has, as it were, no political ambitions. Yet this does not result in a derogation of political life. By recognizing the only human activity that is properly unlimited, Aristotle's conception of philosophic wisdom can indicate the "boundaries to every other activity[,] in virtue of which every other activity becomes good." It is in this sense that practical life "culminates in the recognition of the activity of wisdom as its final cause."[66]

There is a limit to political life in Aristotle. It is found, however, not in the private pleasures of the body but in the sublime aspirations of the soul.

* * *

"Every subject's duty is the King's,
but every subject's soul is his own."

—*Henry V*

Shakespeare was not just a political philosopher but a Socratic one. At least Jaffa makes a strong case for that proposition. Moreover, as we indicated at the beginning, the plays are not merely beautiful and cathartic diversions (though they certainly are that). For Jaffa, they contain abiding wisdom that is very much relevant to our own time.

Though Jaffa's understanding of Shakespeare turns considerably on the playwright's connections with classical thought, Shakespeare was not in fact an Aristotelian. Jaffa indicates repeatedly that Shakespeare must be seen as a Platonist. This is not a surprising view among Straussians (nor indeed Shakespeare scholars in general), but we will need to explore what exactly it meant for Jaffa. For now, we simply note that despite many intimations of Platonic themes, Shakespeare never mentions Plato by name. He does make two references to Aristotle in his plays (per Martin Spevack's *The Harvard Concordance to Shakespeare*). One, in *The Taming of the Shrew*, is by Tranio, the servant to young Lucentio who is soon to be enrolled as a university student. Tranio praises his master's desire to "suck the sweets of sweet philosophy." Yet he advises him not to get so caught up in "Aristotle's checks [moral precepts]" that he becomes a Stoic and forgets "pleasure ta'en." The second occurs in *Troilus and Cressida*, set during the Trojan War, when Hector says Paris and Troilus have "glozed" like "young men, whom Aristotle thought unfit to hear moral philosophy." Since the Trojan War occurred nearly a millennium before Aristotle was born, Jaffa was fond of pointing out the anachronism of finding the *Nicomachean Ethics* in Hector's library. But this "slip" by Shakespeare merely confirms a point Jaffa would insist upon more than once: that the authors of great works of art—whether dramas, dialogues, or eulogies—are not bound by history.[67]

Shakespeare's central theme, in Jaffa's estimation, is the investigation of whether and how classical wisdom may operate in a world radically transformed by both Christianity and the reaction against Christianity initiated by Machiavelli. To make sense of that very large subject, we can divide Jaffa's writings on Shakespeare into five topics, the choice of five being only somewhat arbitrary: 1) Machiavellian modernity; 2) Marriage and the mean; 3) Monarchy, succession, and divine right; 4) The tragedy and comedy of politics; and 5) Philosophic poetry.

In order to understand Jaffa's interpretation of Shakespeare, however, it is essential to appreciate the political situation—the political problem, as Jaffa saw it—confronting the great poet. (This will also make clear why the first half of this chapter focused on ancient Greek philosophy.) A somewhat detailed but instructive historical analysis, from Jaffa's essay "The American Founding as the Best Regime," will prepare us for the analysis of Shakespeare:

> Ancient man obeyed the laws because they were of divine, not human origin. If a city was defeated in war, that meant its gods were defeated by stronger gods, and men might, without any sense of disloyalty, transfer their allegiance to the gods of their masters....
>
> Rome's conquest of the ancient world ended the civic life of the independent polis. The gods of the conquered cities continued a shadowy existence for some time. When, however, everyone might become a Roman citizen, there was in principle but one authority for law. The gods who had been the many authors of the many laws of the many cities flickered out and died. There was only one city, which was no longer an ancient city, but the empire of the world. But by the logic of the ancient city—which to this point dominated the consciousness of civilized mankind—a single source of law implied a single God....
>
> The establishment of Christianity in the Roman empire obeyed the logic of the ancient city, in that membership in the political

association carried the implied requirement of acknowledgment of, and obedience to, the God of that empire. . . . But the Christian empire made belief central to fidelity, and heresy assumed an unprecedented gravity as an offense against the good order not merely of civil society, but of the world. . . . The decline and fall of the ancient empire replaced centralized Roman administration with the most decentralized, and most lawless, of regimes: feudalism. . . . [This] created a problem that went unsolved in the Christian West for a millennium and a half. That problem was how to discover a source of law for particular political communities within the larger framework of the cosmopolis of the city of God.[68]

With that, the stage is set (so to speak) for Shakespeare.

MACHIAVELLIAN MODERNITY

In a wide-ranging essay titled "The Unity of Tragedy, Comedy, and History: An Interpretation of the Shakespearean Universe," which he contributed to a 1981 volume edited by John Alvis and Thomas West, *Shakespeare as a Political Thinker*, Jaffa begins by explaining the title of his contribution. In Plato's dialogue *Symposium*, Socrates prophesies the coming of a poet who could master both tragedy and comedy. This would have been paradoxical in the Athens of that time. "Tragedies were not written by comic poets, and comedies were not written by tragic poets," notes Jaffa.

> Indeed, we do not know, to this day, of any great poet who has written both tragedy and comedy. That is to say, we do not know of any such poet except William Shakespeare. Shakespeare is the greatest—perhaps he is the only—poet to have practiced the art referred to by Socrates at the end of the *Symposium*.[69]

Jaffa suggests that the "single art" that unites both comedy and tragedy is not unlike the art that characterizes "Socratic conversation or dialogue." The "moral universe" constructed by Shakespeare, which Jaffa is about to explicate, bears some resemblance, we infer, to the philosophic cosmos of Plato's dialogues.

The fact that in ancient Athens comedians were always distinguished from tragedians might lead us to think that comedies and tragedies are separate genres and that Shakespeare simply possessed a genius capacious enough to encompass both. Jaffa argues, however, that the apparent difference is misleading, for "in Shakespeare, the causes of laughter, and the causes of tears, are never far removed from each other." In fact, in Shakespeare almost "every comedy could have become a tragedy, and nearly every tragedy has that in it which points towards a non-tragic possibility." Jaffa goes on to explain that the "typical Shakespearean comedy is a tragedy that does not happen, a tragedy prevented from happening by the improbable presence within the play of a wise man or wise woman." [70] This dramatic device of fortuitous philosophic intervention is where Machiavelli enters the scene, an unexpected appearance from stage left that would surprise many traditional Shakespeare scholars. [71]

From his teacher Leo Strauss, Jaffa learned that the modern project inaugurated by the great Florentine author of *The Prince* was, "from the very beginning," the attempt "to be absolutely sovereign, to become the master and owner of nature, to conquer chance." [72] For Machiavelli, the virtuous happiness aimed for by the classical polis, for Plato no less than for Aristotle, was unrealistic and unreasonable. Significantly (even crucially), Machiavelli believed the advent of Christianity made this problem worse: by directing our attention and hopes toward the life hereafter, Christianity inhibited the genuinely needful improvements to our security and comfort. By rejecting the classical and Christian preoccupation with virtue and focusing on the "effective truth" of real-world politics, Machiavelli proposed to bring *Fortuna*, or chance, under our control for the relief of man's estate. Shakespeare's genius displays itself, Jaffa explains, "within a context created by both Platonism and Christianity" and of equal importance "in a context created by the Machiavellian critique of Christianity."[73]

Here we can see the significance of the dramatic "wise interventions" (that is, conquering chance) in the plays. Alternating between their presence and absence, or success and failure, Shakespeare presents to us vividly instructive lessons in either comedy or tragedy. This is hardly the only key to interpreting the plays, to be sure, and this device of "conquering fortune" is not used at all in the history plays.

The cultural and political context *in which* Shakespeare wrote, of course, does not limit the artistic range of *what* he wrote, nor does it limit the settings of the plays, which reach from Egypt to Scotland and from the mythic past of Homer to the new commercial republicanism emerging in cities such as Venice. "Shakespeare's plays, taken as a whole," says Jaffa, "provide us with what we might call a history of [Western] civilization." In a letter to his student Angelo Codevilla in 1970, he writes,

> I might mention that I am currently giving a seminar on Shakespeare's *Measure for Measure*, which I have decided tentatively is Shakespeare's *Laws* just as the *Tempest* is Shakespeare's *Republic*.... The affinity of *Measure for Measure* and *Merchant of Venice* is that both are concerned with the problem of the conflict between Old and New Testament.... [In] both cases there is a representative of classical wisdom attempting to find a ground which will produce harmony out of the divergent principles of the two revealed doctrines.

Jaffa was particularly fond of *Measure for Measure*, which he describes as "a fascinating play in which the wise ruler, who alone knows the truth, never says anything except lies to his subjects. Whether they are Machiavellian or Socratic lies is one of the problems of interpretation."[74] In another letter (to Harvey Mansfield), Jaffa describes *Measure for Measure* as "Shakespeare's version of Machiavelli's *Prince*."[75] A closer look at that play then is warranted.

MARRIAGE AND THE MEAN

Jaffa provides an extended analysis of *Measure for Measure* (set in Vienna around Shakespeare's own time) in an essay titled "Chastity as a Political Principle." This play is a comedy, albeit a dark one, and as with most of Shakespeare's comedies, the humorous aspects—and of course the implausible interventions—are found in the convoluted plot. Jaffa's essay offers a useful summary:

> *Measure for Measure* begins with the Duke, Vincentio, delegating his authority to one Angelo, with the learned Escalus as his second-in-command. The Duke's leaving-taking is done quickly. Neither Angelo nor Escalus is given any definite information as to where the Duke will go.... In fact, the Duke travels a very short distance, to a monastery not far from the city. There he asks to be fitted with a monk's habit [and] will return to Vienna to go undetected among the people and their rulers.... [His] purpose in pretending to go away is to leave the government in the hands of those who will enforce the laws that he himself has long neglected to enforce.[76]

Fourteen years of laxity by the Duke's misrule have allowed lechery and fornication to run rampant. All the major characters are unmarried. Monasteries and convents at one extreme, and whorehouses at the other, seem to be the only alternatives. Rather than clean up the city himself, the Duke delegates this task, fearing that excessive sternness following his long permissiveness would make him seem tyrannical. (Jaffa notes the resemblance to Machiavelli's account in *The Prince* of Remirro de Orco, another proxy sent by a ruler who wanted his city set in order but also to keep his own hands clean.)

Jaffa's summary continues with the deputized Angelo imposing the new legal severity:

> The houses of prostitution are "plucked down," [and] there are "pretty orders" for "heading and hanging." The brunt of the new regime however falls upon a young gentleman named Claudio, who is apprehended, and sentenced to death, for getting with child the young woman, Juliet, to whom he is betrothed but not married. Claudio's sister, Isabella, who is about to enter the nunnery of the Order of St. Clare as a novice, is summoned from the gates of the nunnery, to plead for her brother's life with the Deputy, Angelo, who has sentenced him. Isabella goes to Angelo, and asks for mercy for Claudio, and for his pardon. Her petition is rejected but, unknown to her, she makes a deep impression upon the apparently unrelenting judge, and is told to return. When she does return, the dialogue takes an unexpected turn, and she is offered her brother's pardon, on the condition that she give up her virginity to the judge. Angelo leaves her with this harsh choice, and gives her until the next day to answer.[77]

That's probably complicated enough for those not familiar with the work.[78] It is sufficient to add that the play moves toward an apparently happy ending through a series of improbable Shakespearean devices, including a far-fetched identity swap known as "the bed trick." By these means, the wise Duke saves Claudio's life, Isabella's honor, and his own reputation. In the final scene, Duke Vincentio has arranged several happy (or at least suitable) marriages that seem to tie up all the plot lines but as Jaffa shows leave only a Gordian knot of interpretative difficulties.

The city had been split between lawless brothels and cloistered nunneries with no virtuous mean of healthy citizenship. Marriage, specifically marriage under law, "represents that middle ground between the prostitute and the saint." The importance of marriage is straightforward enough, as we shall see in a moment. Yet matrimony also serves as a metaphor for the way every political community forms a complex whole, in which different classes and interests must be combined and balanced by a wise legislator. At an even higher level, Jaffa's commentary points us to metaphysical concepts such as the union of form and matter in all natural beings. Ultimately, our attention is drawn to man's place in the cosmos. Humans are the creatures who combine an earthly body with a divine soul, a highly unpredictable compound that has the potential for both comedy and tragedy.[79]

All of these underlying themes brought out by Jaffa are being explored by Shakespeare himself, sometimes very subtly. What makes these questions worthy of Shakespeare's genius, and the reason Jaffa labors over his interpretation, is that political-philosophical compounds (like marriages) are rarely perfect. The prudent combination of what Lincoln called "strange, discordant, and even hostile elements" is one of the great challenges of political philosophy, not least in the discretion which must often be exercised. Marriage itself has its own complications. It is both a sacred and civil union. Does it therefore compete with those religious orders in which nuns marry themselves to God? The Duke's first stop after absconding from the city is a monastery, where he obtains his disguise as a friar, an apparently common enough sight not to draw suspicion. Jaffa suggests that perhaps all this Christian asceticism "is but suppressed lust." One reason for Angelo's harshness, he implies, is to cure the city of this "secret tyranny within it" while simultaneously curing the "dissoluteness." This is the meaning of the play's title, he explains: "The extremes will cure each other, 'measure for measure,' to re-establish the mean. In so doing, the city will be re-founded."[80]

"The Duke, in his disguise, plays the role of Providence," writes Jaffa. He is "a practical example of what Machiavelli in *The Prince* meant by the conquest of fortune or chance." But it is precisely the improbability of these interventions that leads us to wonder about Shakespeare's ambiguous message. Indeed, ambiguities abound. The Duke's machinations, conducted "in disguise," resemble Providence inasmuch as they presume an almost divine omniscience. Yet Jaffa also reminds us that the Duke wants to understand. One reason, perhaps the main one, for the whole ruse is so that he can learn what is really going on his city and discover the "true nature" of his subjects. Moreover, the interventions entail several morally dubious scenarios. (In addition to the bed trick, there is a plotline for another identity switch involving decapitated heads.) The implication is that these Machiavellian means are justified by the moral ends, above all the reinvigoration of marriage. As Jaffa notes, "We accept the bed-trick because we know that the Duke can prevent its miscarriage." The Duke also manages to sidestep the reputation for tyranny through his deception, yet "his actual means are not for that reason less outside the bounds of morality. Because of his indirect and invisible government, however, they seem to be moral."[81]

The morality of the Duke's objectives finds its ground in the argument made by Aristotle discussed earlier. The city, Jaffa reminds us, "must be a collection of families in order to be a collection of citizens. Angelo's harsh understanding of law, "which seems absurd to us in its severity, compels us to remember what lies at the root of the idea of law."

Aristotle, in the first book of the *Politics*, characterizes the political community as a collection of families. Except as it is a collection of families, it does not become a collection of citizens. A citizen is not an "individual."... He is the representative of a family, if not the head of a family. And all members of families have genders. It is this that makes the polity a complex, and not a homogeneous entity....Sexual promiscuity can thus be seen as striking at the very root of the idea of paternal power—of patriotism—and hence at the ground of authority. To derive authority from paternity, paternity itself must not be unlawful.[82]

Locating political power in paternal authority, however, presents its own problems, which brings us to the next topic.

MONARCHY AND SUCCESSION

Duke Vincentio was compelled to use subterfuge and a bit of tyranny to mediate between debauchery and asceticism. Other tensions are harder to resolve, even within the artistic freedom of a play.

It is no discredit to Shakespeare that he was unable to solve every problem he perceived. He saw further than almost anyone in recognizing the significance of the Renaissance, especially the revolution in politics and science. Jaffa argues that the new age of modern liberalism and commercial republicanism is already visible to Shakespeare and is portrayed, in its incipient stages, in the Venetian plays, *Othello* and *Merchant of Venice*. History, Shakespeare can see, is about to take a major turn to address the difficulty that began more than a millennium earlier with the birth of Christianity. "It is from the ashes of Caesarism," Jaffa writes, "that the phoenix of Christian empire arises, the empire in which this-wordly rule is subordinated to the rule of another world." The tension between pagan and Christian conceptions of virtue and citizenship, especially the meaning and import of honor, is seen above all in Shakespeare's "understanding of the perplexity befalling human affairs when men's duties as husbands, fathers, and citizens are interpenetrated with their duties as citizens of the city of God."[83]

As briefly examined in Jaffa's historical analysis above, two interconnected dilemmas had for centuries beset Europe. The first was the contest for power and allegiance between the secular authorities of this world and the ecclesiastical authorities of the world to come, the battle between princes and priests. Along a separate axis was the recurring problem of succession: monarchical government could find no principle by which to combine (consistently) legitimacy and competence. These intersect with the conundrum of the divine right of kings, the claim of hereditary authority originating with the Father in heaven.

Like Machiavelli, Shakespeare was acutely aware of this problem of Christianized politics (which is not, of course, the same as calling *Christianity* a problem). But the poet seemed more ambivalent about Machiavelli's solution: a ruthless realpolitik intended to rescue governing authority from the dual temptations of "pious cruelty" and mushy meekness. Because both temptations misunderstand the proper use of power, Christian politics, as Machiavelli saw it, leads to endless chaos and conflict. What Jaffa saw and appreciated in Shakespeare was (in part) a brilliant and poignant search for a different answer. "Machiavelli's critique of Christianity is I believe incorporated by Shakespeare," Jaffa wrote in a 1999 letter to Harvey Mansfield. "In Shakespeare however it is in the service of a more enlightened and tolerant Christianity, such as that presided at the American founding."[84]

In *A New Birth of Freedom*, Jaffa observes, "The divine right of kings, in the comprehensive sense of the right to rule others without their consent, predominated within Western civilization until the American Revolution." To have endured so long, the doctrine must have "had a plausibility not easily visible today."

The best way to understand "the origin and nature of a doctrine that held such power over mind and imagination" is Shakespeare's English histories.

> Although Shakespeare presents us with such monarchy in all its human failings, there does not, on the horizon of the plays, appear to be any alternative theory of political obligation. That is to say, although the divine right of kings is never a sufficient title to rule, it appears always to be a necessary one. And Shakespeare's English histories present us with an almost unbroken spectacle of civil war.[85]

And where there is war and the prospect of power, tyranny follows like a shadow. In Aristotle, tyranny is acknowledged matter-of-factly as one possible regime, ranked, to be sure, at the bottom of Aristotle's classifications. In the *Politics*, one even finds some sensible advice for how to make a tyrannical regime gentler (pitched to the tyrant's self-interest as a way to make his own position less perilous). In Shakespeare's English plays, however, tyranny looms much larger, spanning the range from the guilt-ridden Macbeth to the connoisseur of cruelty, Richard III. Throughout all the plays on British monarchy, Jaffa says, the rightful claim to the crown "is always being contested, and there is no peaceful way of deciding the contest. The king's peace is an illusion," and there is "little if any relief from the violent alternations of tyranny and anarchy."[86]

However partial the claims of the democrats and the oligarchs presented in the *Politics*, Aristotle sees in each (as well as in other partial claims) elements of justice that can be refined and elevated through intelligent mixing. But the doctrine of the divine right of kings smothers every alternative even as it consumes its own champions in endless strife. The rightful heir to the crown was often weak or thoughtless, yet there was "no constitutional way of getting rid of an anointed king...except usurpation and murder." A moral-political justification for tyrannicide, Jaffa notes, "might have operated at least as an aspect or surrogate of the right of revolution," except that any challenge to absolute monarchy became "an instrument to enable popes to bring emperors or kings to heel."[87]

Largely through this Shakespearean education, Jaffa argues, Lincoln was led to equate the despotic rule of kings over subjects with the despotism of masters over slaves—"the same old serpent" whose motto is "You work, I eat." If Lincoln was right (as Jaffa surely believed), the feudalism that reigned from the fall of the Roman Empire to the first stirring of popular sovereignty in the seventeenth century represented a political and moral nadir of Western civilization, unmatched until the murderous ideologies of the twentieth century. This was the grim state of political life in medieval Europe that drove the early modern thinkers to conclude that the only virtue in politics is to appear virtuous and that legitimacy is no more than a word. This sentiment is represented most vividly in Shakespeare by Falstaff's ignoble sermon in *Henry IV, Part I.*

> Can honor set a leg? No. Or an arm? No. Or take away the grief
> of a wound? No. Honor hath no skill in surgery, then? No. What
> is honor? A word. What is in that word "honor"? What is that
> "honor"? Air.

"Falstaff's catechism on honor," says Jaffa, "is the very embodiment, not only of Hobbesianism—of modern nationalism and hedonism—but of the bourgeois preference for self-preservation over any antique virtue."[88] Observations like that have led some scholars to accuse Jaffa of overinterpreting Shakespeare. And this brings us to a complicated point in Jaffa's thinking that can only be touched upon briefly.

Shakespeare's history of the world centered on Rome. And

he understood, according to Jaffa, that "the commercial regime taking form before his eyes would in time become democratic and republican. The Venetian plays present us the principles and nature of bourgeois democracy." But this cycle begins in *Coriolanus* (discussed in Chapter 1, in which a proud general refuses to court the mob), which "shows Roman republicanism in its birth and growth. *Julius Caesar* shows its demise." Yet demise seems too weak a word for the striking historical analysis Jaffa suggests next. The death of Caesar, and with him Roman republicanism (as depicted in *Antony and Cleopatra*), marks "not only the end of the ancient political world,"

> it marks no less the end of modernity as well. For the end of the ancient world and the end of the modern world have this in common: they are accompanied by the prospect of the universal homogenous world state, in which political life, properly so called, will be at an end. The pursuit of private pleasure, without public spirit, is the mark of the bourgeois, properly so called. But it also the mark of communist man.[89]

This statement seems astounding. The "universal homogenous state" is a term from radical modern philosophy. It is surprising, to say the least, to see such an ideological label applied to Shakespearean drama. Yet Jaffa seems to insist on the point. With the elimination of all rivals by Caesar, "there is no anti-Rome." Yet this also means "there can be no Rome." The world empire is too much of a unity. Notwithstanding its size (or perhaps *because* of its size), it sacrifices heterogeneity for homogeneity. "There are no conflicting claims to rule within Rome, as between freedom and equality, or honor and virtue." And as the sole power in the West, there is no contest between Rome and any other regime "as to which city should rule."[90]

To ensure there is no mistake, Jaffa reiterates this point, recalling the work of his student John Marini on modern bureaucracy. "Now that the world is ruled in the name of Caesar by a triumvirate," he writes, "the government of men has in substance been replaced by the administration of things. The new era will call forth the cold-blooded, calculating administrator."[91]

This connection that Jaffa sees between the modern threat of bureaucratic world government and "the end of politics" dramatized in *Julius Caesar* and *Antony and Cleopatra* turns on what may be called "the metaphysics of marriage." The family in republican Rome, according to Jaffa, meant "the perpetuation of a particular family within a particular regime." The world state is precisely *not* a particular regime. It erases the competing claims to rule and along with them erases the arguments over conventional morality that led to the original discovery of natural right.

> Marriage in a homogenous world state must differ according to this difference. Depriving the family of its political nature will require an art to replace that of nature.[92]

What "art" can replace nature? This is one of the great questions in political philosophy. Several of the early modern thinkers, especially Bacon and Descartes, proclaimed it to be science. Later, with Hegel and Marx, it becomes history. (In Marx's communist utopia, incidentally, the family disappears altogether because it serves no purpose.) As either science or history—or both—this "art" would conquer chance, dispense with virtue, and see honor fade into air. But can it succeed? Should it? In Jaffa's view, Shakespeare probes this question deeply but makes us work to discover any answers.

In the world of the plays, the "heroic political passion founded in the family," which characterized republican Rome, dissolves with the advent of Caesarism. The attempt to reinstate the republican family (and thus republicanism itself) "becomes the task of the philosophic statesman, represented by Duke Vincentio" in *Measure for Measure*. "Could Vincentio have succeeded, through his wise interventions, to restore a republic of virtuous families—and the very form of the comedy tells us that he could not—the Roman cycle might have been reinstituted." But the "art" by which the Duke undertakes this attempt is a slippery business.[93]

Vincentio, the "duke of dark corners," is one of the most omniscient and omnipotent characters in Shakespeare. The other is the classically educated intellectual Prospero (in *The Tempest*), whose rule of Milan was usurped by his brother and who subsequently reigns over an island utopia only through illusions. "We are struck," says Jaffa, "by the fact that Prospero's studies of the liberal arts unmanned him for the government of Milan."[94] Vincentio and Prospero are the closest Shakespeare comes to portraying philosopher kings. Neither can rule openly and successfully. Both plays are comedies.

Here we arrive at perhaps the most striking proof of Shakespeare's Platonism, for not only does Shakespeare withhold the possibility of a philosopher king, he declines even to show us any main character who is fully magnanimous.[95] There are some secondary characters (often women)—Cordelia, Volumnia, Portia—who seem very close to perfection. Coriolanus and Lear are two of Shakespeare's most honorable protagonists, but both are tragically flawed. Even the English histories portray "a line of political men—notably Henry IV and Henry V—who are partly Machiavellian, and partly Christian.... They are certainly not great souled."[96] Natural right never seems to become political right.

"In the end," Jaffa says, Shakespeare teaches that "the political world in all its amazing variety, is ineluctably tragic."

> There is no harmonious resolution of all conflicts, except in comedy. Prospero's island is, so to speak, the divine comedy of this world, which anticipates that absolute rule of the wise which

is possible only in speech, and fully legitimate only in the world to come.[97]

But Jaffa does not mean for us to weep. Shakespeare, he argues, does not follow Machiavelli in blaming "Christianity for the absence of Plutarchian heroism from the world." "If saintliness and heroism seem to be in ineluctable tension with each other, the conflict between the two seems to breed characters of surpassing interest." The ancient heroes, such as Coriolanus,

> were no more proof against self-contradiction, by virtue of their single-minded devotion to political virtue, than were Hamlet or Henry of Monmouth, because of the ambiguities wrought into their souls by Christianity. And one might even say that what the latter have lost in political virtue to ambiguity, is more than compensated by the light they shed upon the rich complexity of the human condition.[98]

Jaffa sees the human condition displayed in all its complexity by Shakespeare's genius as part of the same cosmos depicted in Plato's dialogues and in the speeches of Lincoln. It is no more absurd, therefore, to see the danger of modern bureaucracy prefigured in *Antony and Cleopatra* than it was for the American founders to evoke ancient Rome in the architecture of their Constitution and the designs of their buildings. Shakespeare's archetypic regimes reflect enduring possibilities transcending "boundaries of time or space." "The very possibility," says Jaffa, that Shakespeare's historical pageant "can be made the object of contemplation, as he has made it, indicates that we are in some sense free to accept or reject our historic fate."[99]

The tragedies and comedies are mirrors, and what transposes the one to the other is not, in the end, wise intervention, which succeeds only when most implausible. Nor is it even chance. The ambiguity and indeterminacy of the plays is a tribute to human freedom, which is elevated and enlarged by Shakespeare's depiction of its highest and lowest possibilities. "We need not repeat in action the history of Rome," says Jaffa,

> after we have partaken of it, with our passions no less than our understanding, thanks to the genius of the philosopher who is also the supreme poet.... We are enabled to enjoy the tragic catharsis, as we contemplate the greatness inherent in the shortcoming.[100]

THE PHILOSOPHIC POET (OR, ALL THE WORLD'S A STAGE)

We might almost conclude at this point that Shakespeare's tribute to human freedom remains that of a technician whose virtuosity follows the human drama whither it may go, indifferent to the effect he has on the souls of his audience. Jaffa insists, to the contrary, that "Shakespeare's deepest intention [is] to be the poet-philosopher of the English-speaking peoples, the teacher of its citizens, statesmen, and legislators." A teacher, of course, is more than a mere performer. And Shakespeare's most urgent teaching, Jaffa claims, is to display "the reality of a moral universe that is inexorable in its demands."[101]

As mentioned earlier, when Jaffa delivered a series of lectures at Hillsdale College on the topic of crime and punishment in the early 1970s, he took as his texts *Macbeth*, Dostoyevsky's *Crime and Punishment*, and Camus's *The Stranger*. The three works were presented as a descending moral arc, tracing the decline of the West from the soul-wrenching crisis experienced by Macbeth to the revolutionary immorality of Dostoyevsky's Raskolnikov and finally to the anesthetized nihilism of Camus' Meursault. Jaffa challenged the historicist literary criticism then becoming dominant in academia that viewed Shakespeare as simply a creature of his socioeconomic position. In *Macbeth*, Jaffa saw that "Shakespeare's preoccupation is not that of a poet living in an aristocratic age; it is the preoccupation of a moralist who would display human actions on that scale on which alone they can be said to be fully intelligible."[102]

In his classic book *Thoughts on Machiavelli*, Leo Strauss makes the brilliant observation that Machiavelli corrupts his readers by making them unwittingly part of his blasphemous conspiracy. He "compels the reader to think the blasphemy by himself and thus to become Machiavelli's accomplice."[103] It is unclear whether Jaffa had his teacher's book in mind when he delivered his lectures at Hillsdale. Yet he surely makes an apposite observation when he notes that Shakespeare "presented the moral phenomena in such a way that those who respond to his art must, in some way or another, become better human beings."[104]

Given the importance of Rome in Shakespeare's moral universe, let us conclude this section with Jaffa's poignant observation on Shakespeare's greatest Roman:

> We would not give to Coriolanus the wisdom that would have averted his tragedy. But neither do we wish to repeat that tragedy in our own lives. Shakespeare thus teaches us to moderate our own expectations to the level that Coriolanus did not level his. For Coriolanus is no longer necessary to us. We have something infinitely greater: the art and wisdom of William Shakespeare.[105]

Space does not permit a complete investigation of Jaffa's many insightful commentaries on Shakespearean themes. We have omitted, regretfully, any discussion of the towering influence of the Roman matron—embodied by Coriolanus's mother, Volumnia, one of the most impressive characters in all of Shakespeare; the deep ambivalence of Henry V's speeches at Agincourt; the Platonic parallels in *The Tempest* (Shakespeare's most autobiographical play); and the full philosophic interplay of nature, justice, and truth in *King Lear*.

Nevertheless, several key elements have been identified to clarify Jaffa's understanding of both Aristotle and Shakespeare. From Aristotle Jaffa learned that the political community has both a genetic account—the city is formed for the sake of survival—as well as a final, or teleological, account—that is, it exists for the sake of happiness and living well. Man is a political animal, and so the city supports man's natural disposition, yet an act of founding is necessary (and praiseworthy). And while the city is a comprehensive whole, including all lesser communities, it is a heterogeneous unity and does not seek to replace or destroy the family. Shakespeare does not make the origins of regimes a major theme. But Jaffa argues that Shakespeare agrees with Aristotle in regarding the family as the indispensable and irreplaceable component of healthy political life.

Jaffa explores important differences between Plato and Aristotle, which seem to be rooted in whether the Ideas, as objects of contemplation, are most true and real or whether the natural world we perceive with our senses gives us the most authentic account of reality. This in turn raises questions about the integrity and independence of moral-political wisdom and whether political right includes natural right (as Aristotle holds) or whether politics, judged against a philosophic standard, is inherently irrational and somewhat absurd, ever falling short of complete justice. Jaffa sees Shakespeare as a Platonist in this regard.

For our edification, both Aristotle and Shakespeare display catalogues and rankings of the regimes—Aristotle being, as expected, more straightforward and practical, while Shakespeare deploys his dramatic genius to instruct us indirectly through the excitement and inspiration of tragic catharsis and comic relief. The scenes of chaos and conflict portrayed in the English history plays reveal the political quicksand of the divine right of kings. These prepare us for the new age of commercial republicanism appearing on the horizon of Shakespeare's century.

Yet for all his insight and foresight, Shakespeare does not reach the far shore. He could not, as Jaffa understands him, fully conceive of the empire of liberty that would emerge in the American colonies of the new world. Shakespeare's greatest political plays grapple with two apparently irreconcilable imperatives. In *Measure for Measure*, one interpretative key comes "from the seventh chapter of *The Prince*," writes Jaffa. The other key is the title, taken "from the seventh chapter of the Gospel according to St. Matthew." The play begins with "a Machiavellian scheme to bring good government to a bad city." It ends with "a scene of reconciliation and harmony, of charity and forgiveness…almost as if an earthly city had been transformed into a heavenly one."[106] That is, the ending *is* desirable, yet it is a contrivance of the poet's art. The play, Jaffa reminds us, is a "problem" comedy. As with Plato's dialogues, the reader must think through for himself the limits and lessons of the greatest dramas.

The two essays from which this chapter was principally drawn were titled by Jaffa "The Nature of Politics" and "The Limits of Politics." The first is ostensibly on Aristotle and the second on Shakespeare. Yet, as we have seen, Aristotle sees in the contemplative life both the highest end and the natural limit of the political community, while Shakespeare sees in the nature of politics the field for the most memorable displays of depravity, greatness, anguish, and love.

Both the philosopher and the poet would seem to agree, as would Jaffa, with the Roman writer Terence: *Homo sum, humani nihil a me alienum puto.* ("I am a man, nothing human is alien to me.")

5

REASON, REVELATION, AND THE THEOLOGICAL-POLITICAL PROBLEM

"**G**od is dead," Friedrich Nietzsche declared in 1884.
That message came too late for Lincoln, who was assassinated in 1865. The Great Emancipator generally was considered a master of speaking to the American people in the idiom most familiar and most dear to them: the King James Bible. The speech that crowned his many biblical quotations and allusions surely was the Second Inaugural Address (delivered just weeks before his death). It is, by general acclamation, the most profound reflection ever penned by an American on the question of divine justice.

> The Almighty has His own purposes. Woe unto the world because of offences! for it must needs be that offences come; but woe to that man by whom the offence cometh! If we shall suppose that American Slavery is one of those offences which, in the providence of God, must needs come, but which, having continued through

His appointed time, He now wills to remove, and that He gives
to both North and South, this terrible war, as the woe due to
those by whom the offence came, shall we discern therein any
departure from those divine attributes which the believers in a
Living God always ascribe to Him? Fondly do we hope, fervently
do we pray, that this mighty scourge of war may speedily pass
away. Yet, if God wills that it continue, until all the wealth piled
by the bond-man's two hundred and fifty years of unrequited
toil shall be sunk, and until every drop of blood drawn with the
lash, shall be paid by another drawn with the sword, as was said
three thousand years ago, so still it must be said "the judgments
of the Lord, are true and righteous altogether."

Harry Jaffa didn't get Nietzsche's memo either. Actually,
it might be more accurate to say that in Jaffa's case, he got the
memo and tore it up. Exactly one hundred years after the German
philosopher published that statement in *Thus Spoke Zarathustra*,
Jaffa argued that God was certainly more alive than Nietzsche.
In 1984, Jaffa reviewed a collection of essays by Leo Strauss
edited by Thomas Pangle. While he would certainly disavow any
comparison of his own writing to Lincoln's magisterial Second
Inaugural, that essay, appearing in the *Claremont Review of Books*,
contains some of Jaffa's most interesting reflections on the Bible
and political philosophy. Before entering those deep waters, a bit
of background is necessary.

* * *

In the central section of *Crisis of the House Divided*, Jaffa presents
a structural outline of Lincoln's 1842 Temperance Address in
bullet point format, noting its various sections and subsections.
It may be useful to do something similar here with regard to
Jaffa's history of religion in Western civilization. To grasp Jaffa's

understanding of America and especially his perspective on the crisis of the West, we must account for what is deeply radical about the American experiment in liberty and the equally radical *rejection* of that experiment. "Radical" derives from the Latin *radix*, which means going to the roots. In the case of America, those roots can be traced to the philosophic tradition originating with Socrates and Plato and to the Bible.

The following outline will be helpful to understand Jaffa's writings and arguments in the next chapters. These arguments take various twists and turns, both philosophically and chronologically, which can make it hard to keep the broader themes in view. This outline will give the reader at least a sense of Jaffa's broader perspective. In a way, the opening line of the Declaration of Independence, "When in the course of human events," encourages us to look at the American Revolution as Jaffa did—as a turning point in world history. The events implicitly contemplated by the Declaration began in ancient Jerusalem and classical Athens, with questions about faith and reason, man's place in the universe, and the nature of the human soul. From these roots, Jaffa cultivates a surprisingly consistent story of the political and theological developments underlying Western civilization generally and America specifically. The most refined presentation of this story can be found in Chapter 2 of *A New Birth of Freedom*, but additions, elaborations, and some small variations are found throughout Jaffa's writings.

OUTLINE OF JAFFA'S THEOLOGICAL-POLITICAL HISTORY

The Soul: the highest ends of mankind point beyond politics

- The human soul points to something transcendent, and the highest human ends present two alternatives: the life of skeptical philosophy or the life of obedient piety.
  - For the Greeks, this meant the tension between philosophy on the

one hand, and on the other, the poets who narrated the stories of the gods and enforced conventional morality and civic piety.

The Ancient City: the fulfillment of the highest ends requires politics

- Politics is required for both skeptical philosophy and obedient piety.
  - ▫ In the ancient world, Jerusalem was one city among many. Uniquely, the Hebrew God was singular, mysterious, and omnipotent. He ruled over not only the Jews but the whole world. This theological "potency," however, remained inert as long as the Hebrews neither conquered nor proselytized.
  - ▫ All ancient cities (including Jerusalem) were closed societies where civil and religious obedience were identical. All law was divine law. Every city had its own god, or—most often—gods.
  - ▫ In the fifth century BC, Socrates discovered political philosophy, which points to nature as a standard for justice (i.e., natural right).
    - The Socratic tradition holds that the radical skepticism of philosophic inquiry will always be in conflict with the conventions of any political regime.
    - But Socrates was also a defender of prephilosophic morality and piety against the Sophists, who insisted that all politics is merely rhetoric and that all justice is artificial or conventional.

The Universal City: Christianity's universalism transforms the Western understanding of political life

- After Julius Caesar, the Roman Empire becomes cosmopolitan, "the universal city."
- Three centuries later, Christianity becomes the universal religion. (Rome as the world city almost necessitated this.)
  - ▫ The unique, omnipotent, and providential God of the Hebrews joins with the Roman empire to affect a world-historical change in human consciousness.

- The collapse of Rome leaves one God but many regimes. Civil and religious authority become separated (i.e., divine and civil law are no longer the same).
- The problem of dual allegiance between kings and popes emerges. Also, sectarian conflict develops between Catholics who oppress Protestants, and vice versa.
  - The doctrine of the divine right of kings attempts to reconnect civil and divine authority but never finds a way to combine legitimacy with competence.
    - This is the central theme of Shakespeare's history plays.
  - Centuries of religious warfare plague Europe.

Ancient v. Modern: modern philosophy rejects both classical virtue and Christian piety in an attempt to overcome the problems of the universal city

- Seventeenth-century philosophers—especially Spinoza, Hobbes, Bacon, and Descartes (building on Machiavelli)—launch the modern project. They seek a scientific basis of politics. They remove the soul from public concern and focus on the passions and needs of the body.
  - Leo Strauss emphasizes this break, which rejects both biblical faith and Socratic philosophy. He sees modern philosophy as a utopian faith in the mastery of the material world (technology) with "dogmatic skepticism" about any transcendent ends.
  - Scientific laws and institutions supposedly will eliminate the conflict between theory and practice and between wisdom and consent. Thus,
    - There is no need for virtue or morality (i.e., no need for religion).
    - There is no need for prudent rhetoric (esotericism is forgotten).

The American City: the principles of religious liberty and limited government in the American Revolution offer a new solution

- Eighteenth-century American statesmen (not philosophers) craft a different political solution that draws together various elements: ancient and modern, theoretical and practical.
- America can be seen as a kind of apotheosis of Rome and Jerusalem combined.
  - The founders institute the separation of church and state (see Jefferson's Virginia Bill for Religious Freedom).
    - This solves the problem of dual allegiance: no religious test for office, and no official orthodoxy or persecution of heresy.
    - Instead, there is a nonsectarian, rational theology: "the laws of nature and Nature's God."
    - The founding is not Hobbesian and not based in passion. The founders do not deny man's higher ends. (The Declaration's "safety and happiness" evokes Aristotle).
    - Absence of coercion liberates "true Christianity" for the first time (numerous sermons throughout America preach this lesson).
    - Rejection of persecution also grants freedom to philosophy.
    - This elimination of religious coercion closely parallels the elimination of artificial class distinctions, which allows for "true aristocracy" to emerge.
      - Political equality and religious liberty both attempt to replace conventional injustice ("accident and force") with natural right ("deliberation and choice").
      - The medieval class system (including the divine right of kings) on the one hand, and theocratic oppression on the other, both stood in the way of human excellence.
      - Equal opportunity liberates *moral* virtue.
      - Freedom of conscience liberates *intellectual* virtue.

The Restoration of Politics: the American founding is a political achievement of statesmanship and prudence rather than theory

- America, as a real-world regime founded by practical statesmen, is not merely a chapter in the history of political philosophy; it is not fully explained by the theoretical account of modernity. Among other things, religion—especially Christianity—continues to play an important role.
- Thus prudence is still necessary.
- Moderate—not utopian—expectations from politics in America recognize that passions and prejudice remain. Thus, the tension between philosophy and politics remains, along with the need for rhetoric.
  - America does embrace a sensible, moderate idea of enlightenment; the universal truths of the Declaration are true always and everywhere.
    - However, government based on equal natural rights is not feasible in all times and places. Paleoconservatives and traditionalists—and skeptics of "spreading democracy"—are correct that some cultures are not prepared for self-government. (The Declaration of Independence affirms this by referring to "merciless savages" and "barbarous ages.")
  - Because neither human nature nor the nature of politics has changed, Lincoln practices esoteric speech for "exactly the same" reasons as Thomas Aquinas. Popular morality relies on religion but can be corrupted.

The Collapse of the Soul: modern philosophy invades America, and the American regime descends into positivism, atheism, and nihilism

- Strauss shows how the modern project of Spinoza, Hobbes, etc. becomes radicalized through successive "waves" of European philosophers—Rousseau, Kant, Hegel, Nietzsche, Heidegger—ending in positivism, atheism, and nihilism.

- This increasingly radical European philosophy migrates to America and merges with domestic elements in the Progressive Movement.
- Even before the Progressives, there was the historicism of Calhoun, "the Marx of the master class."
- America experiences increasing alienation from the Declaration and the Constitution with Progressivism, the New Deal, and the cultural revolution of the 1960s.
- Both left and right (e.g., legal positivists, libertarians, neoconfederates) come to reject classical rationalism, the theology of the Declaration, and natural right.

The last point, roughly speaking, is the situation that both Strauss and Jaffa saw as the crisis of the West.[1] Jaffa was perhaps less shaken than the German-born Strauss by the collapse of Weimar Germany and the descent of European philosophy into the antiliberalism of Nietzsche and Heidegger. Jaffa, especially through his deep study of Lincoln, seemed to have a more hopeful outlook derived from the principles of the American founding, which he (along with Strauss) defended as noble and just. Jaffa believed those principles were worth articulating and, if possible, perpetuating. That effort alone would have been quite enough to keep him busy as a scholar and a patriot. Yet from his earliest publications to the very end of his career, there seemed to be something else at work. The deeper he looked, the more Jaffa was fascinated by what he saw as a kind of world-historical story revealing itself in the moral-political drama of the American Revolution and the Civil War.

Jaffa was by no means a historicist in the sense of believing that "all vital human communication is sealed within its own time and place," as he described it in one essay.[2] He did, however, see a pattern or logic in the unfolding of Western civilization. The United States was a reenactment or fulfillment of republican Rome and at the same time a "New Jerusalem." Jefferson's principles solved a political dilemma that had plagued Europe for more than a thousand years, even as the Constitution contained an ancient contradiction that would set brother against brother and leave six hundred thousand dead. Something vital about the human condition, yet seemingly beyond human will and control, seemed to be at work in the nation's soul.

Jaffa does not explain this fully in any one place, but there are traces of it in almost all of his writings. It is part history, part philosophy, and part poetry—both rational and mysterious—combining necessity, accident, providence, and deliberation. The "argument and action" of America as the universal nation made flesh in the character of its almost chosen people revealed somehow a unique insight into nature, into the whole, and into first philosophy. In trying to assemble the pieces, it is hard to know whether to describe what Jaffa is pointing to as theory, myth, or prophetic vision.

Consider *A New Birth of Freedom*, which contains numerous references to America's providential destiny. In Chapter 4, Jaffa expounds on Lincoln's 1861 speech in Trenton, New Jersey, claiming that "the burden of world history was bound up with" saving the Union. In the Trenton speech, Lincoln describes America as God's "almost chosen people," and Jaffa highlights the obvious allusions to the biblical story of Exodus. Lincoln's qualification of America as *almost* chosen "does not reflect any reservations as to the providential character of American history but only Lincoln's care in not seeming in any way to contradict the Bible." Jaffa continues:

> The comparison of the emergence of the American people from the "Egypt" of the inequality of Europe's ancient regimes to the republican equality of the promised land, was something of a commonplace in the years when Lincoln was growing up. We might say that the story of the children of Israel and the story

of the American Revolution combine into one symbolic form, representing in the end a universal experience, the story, not of Israel or of America, but of mankind in its mortal travail and its immortal destiny.[3]

Chapter 2 of *New Birth*, titled "The Declaration of Independence, the Gettysburg Address, and the Historians," is in certain respects an extended eighty-page treatment of this theme. After exposing in the first chapter the near-fatal flaw at the heart of the American founding—why the world's first free elections in 1800 were followed just sixty years later by a Civil War—Jaffa nevertheless identifies the United States as a kind of theological and political culmination of Western civilization. Beginning with ancient Rome and the emergence of Christianity, Jaffa takes the reader through an account of feudal Europe, medieval writings on monarchy, and the English conflicts over royal legitimacy. He describes a series of "revolutions in human consciousness" as part of a historical process leading to the final Revolution of 1776. The American founding, Jaffa asserts, was the result of a succession of philosophical and political awakenings building to an awareness of "the divine right or rights with which each individual has been endowed by his Creator." From this realization, the American founders were led to see that "governments have no lawful powers except those granted to them by the governed." This new plane of political enlightenment replaced "the prevailing opinion" that had ruled the Christian West "for more than a millennium and a half."[4]

In his explanation of how the Christianized Roman Empire created a crisis in political authority unknown to Plato and Aristotle, Jaffa contends that there was "something of a providential inevitability in the process by which, once citizenship and law had been universalized, the one God would become the God of the one city." This meant that "the worship of this God would become the only form of worship sanctioned by such a city." Further, "once Christianity was established as the sole religion of the universal (catholic) empire, all the kingdoms of this world were seen as depending upon that other kingdom for their legitimacy." Christ may have promised his followers salvation in another world, but his Gospel upended the dominions of this one. Nor was this an accident, Jaffa argues. He describes the emergence of an awareness or insight shared by "Aquinas, Dante, Shakespeare, and numerous others" that "held that the secular history of Rome reflected God's providential order no less than the sacred history of the Jews." As part of the "necessary" fulfillment of "God's purposes," this historical process required "that Caesar preside at the birth of a universal empire if mankind were to be offered salvation by a universal Savior." The pre-Roman ancient world, "the world of Plato's *Republic* and Aristotle's *Politics*, could not have been a vessel for the reception of the Gospel of Jesus Christ."[5]

The second chapter of *New Birth* concludes with an emphatic reaffirmation of this divine purpose at work in history. Jaffa quotes from a 1910 speech by the prominent Catholic writer and New York politician William Bourke Cockran discussing the religious origins of American liberty:

> It took less than four centuries to convert pagan temples into Christian churches, but it took eighteen centuries for the religious beliefs of Christians to bear fruit in political institutions of freedom.... Here on this soil Christianity has finally borne these, its capital and inevitable fruits. Here the spiritual equality of all men taught by Jesus Christ on Lake Galilee is embodied in a government based upon the political equality of all men.

Jaffa uses Cockran's speech to restate his own argument, which encapsulates the teaching of the whole section: "the doctrine of the Declaration of Independence is alone fully consistent with the 'inevitable' result of the Gospels."[6] As he put it in a 1989 letter, America is a "New Rome," where the principle of political equality, "reflecting the spiritual equality of mankind in Judeo-Christian monotheism, would not only animate the regime, but make it the center of hope to all mankind and of promise to all the world."[7]

Now, it is one thing for an observant Catholic to see the hand of God at work in securing America's manifold blessings. (And certainly Lincoln, as we have seen, made several references to God exacting His justice—both merciful and vengeful—upon the American people.) Yet it is something else again for a Straussian political philosopher to argue so assiduously for an apparently deterministic view of human affairs. Jaffa's statements about the historical process are unmistakably redolent of G. F. Hegel's philosophy of history. An authoritative textbook on political philosophy offers this description of Hegel's *Rechtsstaat*, the rational and final State: "the sun has set; the long day of the mind is ending; humanity has reached its old age which is also its flowering; history is finished."[8] This description, by Pierre Hassner, is not meant to evoke joy or admiration. That is why both Strauss and Jaffa indicted Hegel as the thinker most responsible for substituting history and historical relativism in place of nature and natural right. Nor can we dismiss Jaffa's arguments here as a result of declining mental powers. He may have been eighty-two when *New Birth* was published, but many similar statements can be found throughout his writings, both before and after this book appeared.

In an essay published in *Interpretation* in 2006, Jaffa observed that in the ancient city, people "commonly recognized each other as members of the same family, or clan, or tribe, or city, or nation" rather than as fellow human beings. This was the "ordinary experience of mankind" until "the task of connecting the universal God with a particular regime" could be completed. Such a consummation, however, "would have to await the realization that mankind had been endowed by their Creator with certain unalienable rights." Only with the American founding did history finally reach the "precise point in the long human story at which accident and force was replaced by reflection and choice."[9]

In his 2012 book, *Crisis of the Strauss Divided*, Jaffa asserts that Locke's *Letter Concerning Toleration* "represented the fulfillment of the doctrine set in motion by Jesus." Jesus was speaking, Jaffa explains, "not as an Israelite under the government of David or Solomon…but in a conquered province of the Roman empire, a way station to the modern state." Rome was a way station because it lacked certain essential features that "made that republic a prey to Caesarism." The historical development that would complete what was begun with Jesus's declaration, the struggle in which Rome was merely one stage, "was finally accomplished by the American Founding, rightly understood."[10]

Looking backward from *New Birth*, in 1996 Jaffa described Christianity as the conclusion of "a process of some centuries" that "replaced the polytheism of a pluralistic political world. This change represented the greatest of all historic changes in that human consciousness of the human condition within which the political problem presents itself." The subsequent conflict between civil and religious liberty "went on almost without intermission" until Jefferson and Lincoln created "perfect agreement between the Gospel and the principles of human equality in the Declaration."[11] A 1982 essay titled "The American Regime and the Only Greater Institution" reveals language very similar to what we see two decades later in *New Birth*.

America's uniqueness has always been derived from its peculiar mission in exemplifying a regime founded upon the doctrine of the universality of human rights. America's assertion of the unity of the human race, with respect to [universal] rights, has often been

compared to Israel's assertion of the unity of God....In sacred
history, the particular becomes universal, in the transformation of
the Old Testament promise by the New Testament. In the political
order presided over by the United States, the universal rights of
man become for the first time, the ground or basis of a particular
regime. As the particular becomes universal in the sacred order,
the universal becomes particular in the political order. We might
even say...that with the American Founding the *logos*, the "word
fitly spoken" became incarnate in an actual regime.[12]

We can go back even further to find Jaffa making explicit
claims about America's divine mission and historical destiny.
His 1959 *Crisis of the House Divided* contains striking passages
identifying America as a second Israel being led out of the wilderness by the prophet Lincoln. (We may recall as well the passages
from Jaffa's 1980 lecture on Shakespeare, discussed in the previous chapter, where the modern commercial society prefigured
in the *Merchant of Venice* is said to be "destined from the outset"
in Machiavelli's critique of Christianity.)

These statements cannot be dismissed merely as metaphorical rhetoric. Jaffa seems to say repeatedly and directly that the
United States, and the principles of equal rights and liberty of
conscience, are the culmination of a historical process. There is
in the history of the West "an inherent compulsion of reason,"
as he calls it in yet another essay, which can be seen working
itself out, in some necessary way, over several millennia.[13] The
consistency of his affirmations of historical determinism does not
make Jaffa's assertions any less problematic. A bad argument is
not validated by repetition. Indeed, in the preface to *New Birth*,
Jaffa acknowledges openly that many readers will be puzzled
by his conception of history. He describes his book as a commentary on Lincoln's *logos*, which must be understood within
the larger "drama" in which it took place. *New Birth*, he says, is

a commentary on speeches and deeds in "a historical process" leading to the war. Then he observes

> It may be objected that history is not poetry and that I have confused them. To this I would reply, as I think Lincoln would reply—or rather, as Lincoln in effect did reply—the place of the necessity in great poetry imposed by the artist may be occupied by a providential order in history, revealed in the speeches of the tragic hero.[14]

So, does this make Jaffa a Hegelian? He would not have been shocked by the suggestion. On the contrary, he publicly invited that characterization on at least one occasion. During a lecture and discussion with a large audience at Rosary College in December of 1980, Jaffa gave his argument about Christianity transforming the ancient city.[15] The new relationship instituted between man and God, he explained, confounded the understanding of citizenship found in the classical world. Then Jaffa told the audience, "I leave it to you to decide whether the intervention of Christianity is a matter of history, necessity, or divine intervention.... I'm leaving it to you, whether or not my interpretation is really Hegelian." The discussion continued for some time, and Jaffa never made any attempt to explain that his interpretation is *not* Hegelian. Again, this was not a momentary lapse. Jaffa published the transcript of the event, first in the *Claremont Review of Books* and then in his 1984 collection of essays, *American Conservatism and the American Founding*. On neither occasion did he find any need to qualify this remark with a footnote or reveal his intentions.

This is all very strange, of course.

As already mentioned, both Strauss and Jaffa held Hegel responsible—if not entirely, at least primarily—for the false and debilitating doctrine that all human thoughts and actions are bound to specific historical epochs. Indeed, even in the second chapter of *New Birth*, where Jaffa repeatedly sees a providential thread connecting Jesus's promises to Jefferson's proclamations, there are other pages that *attack* John C. Calhoun for endorsing "Hegel's belief that history is the unfolding of the mind of God." Yet history as the unfolding of God's plan would appear to be Jaffa's view as well *except* that Calhoun's progressivism depended, Jaffa says, on "the conquest of nature by modern science." This is a crucial distinction. Like Karl Marx, who would develop a supposedly scientific version of Hegel under the name of dialectical materialism, Calhoun believed he had found a scientific formula for understanding which "superior races" were favored by history. Both men were committed to "a science based on materialism and materialistic determinism."[16] (For obvious reasons, Jaffa was fond of quoting Richard Hofstadter's observation that Calhoun was "the Marx of the master class.")

Whatever the basis of Jaffa's own quasi-Hegelian account of historical development (and he seemed to keep that intentionally vague), it was definitely *not* grounded in any form of modern science. Moreover, Jaffa's Hegelianism seemed to include the unusual idea that history had taken a wrong turn, as it were. That is not how it is supposed to work. The essence of Hegel's theory of history, for both Calhoun and Marx, meant *progress*. To stretch the metaphor even further, Jaffa seemed to suggest that history had split onto two paths. One followed the theoretical implications of Hegel's historicism (we will turn to that in a moment). The other road, which we might call a *prudent* version of historical destiny, led to the American founding. Calvin Coolidge, the only president born on July 4, observed: "If all men are created equal, that is final.... No advance, no progress can be made beyond these propositions." Although the terrible compromises with slavery would have to be resolved later, Jaffa suggests that the founders' statesmanship brought together all the elements needed for the best regime practically possible in the modern world. Importantly, this was "not the best regime of Plato or Aristotle, and not the best regime according to the Bible." American constitutionalism was a novel solution to new conditions; it sought "a peaceful and civilized resolution" of these different conceptions of the best way of life.[17]

If this account of Jaffa's project is accurate, his fragmentary but frequent references to a Hegelian interpretation of America may not have been intended altogether literally but to serve primarily heuristic or instructive purposes. In the professional lingo of political philosophers, this was (in part) a Socratic *elenchus*— a contrarian position intended mainly to challenge a common opinion. In fact, we might even speculate that Jaffa's approach was both clever and complicated by serving several useful purposes:

- By making a strong case for American democracy, not Prussian statism, as the endpoint of history, Jaffa undermined the authority of Hegel and his disciples, particularly Calhoun and Marx and their "scientific" historicism. The American regime is "rational" in its own way but a product of prudence, not modern science. This aspect (the elenchus) was directed to real and ersatz intellectuals.
- At the same time, Jaffa wanted to appropriate and redirect the popular faith in "progress," which was so prevalent in the twentieth century as to be almost unquestioned. Indeed, the American spirit of optimism has always had a tendency to get a bit carried away. ("No one believed in the idea of progress more firmly than Jefferson," Jaffa wrote in 1987.)[18] If people were going to believe that God or historical destiny had ordained the modern world *in any case*, Jaffa wanted it to be the American version of modernity. Of course, he also carried on at the same time relentless criticisms

of both historicism as an ideology and the Progressive
Movement, both of which represented the bad side of
progress. His rhetorical campaign had several fronts.

- Jaffa identified not late twentieth-century America but
the founders and Lincoln as the peaks. First, the framers
established the principles of the best regime. Then
Lincoln cleansed the nation of the stain of slavery and
rededicated it to the principle of equality. But in Jaffa's
narrative, it's generally downhill after that. This aspect
emphasized a healthy respect for the best American
traditions. And it subtly undermined the idea that
progress is still ongoing, which challenged complacent
"presentism." In the Jaffa story, progress stopped, as it
were, with the achievements of our greatest statesmen.
To fulfill our historical or providential destiny, we must
emulate and advance the work of our forefathers.

- The idea of decline since Lincoln and the founders
introduces some tricky currents. Our present problems,
by Jaffa's own account, derive mostly from modern
philosophy's increasing radicalization of…Hegel's
historicism. Jaffa navigates this rather deftly. The
American founders, as prudent and practical statesmen,
were generally insulated from the intellectual
degradation of European thought. But Lincoln *was* a
philosophic thinker and *did* respond to the philosophical
challenges emanating primarily from Germany. This
is why it was so important for Jaffa to show that
Lincoln's defense of natural right came *after* historical
consciousness had already arrived in America, via the
"ingenious sophisms" of John C. Calhoun. America
becomes, in a way, a battleground between good and bad
versions of progress. (One might describe it as God and
prudence versus history and science.)[19]

- Finally, and perhaps most positively, adopting the grandiose rhetoric of historical destiny and divine providence—a new Israel *and* a modern Rome!—allowed Jaffa to advocate the principles of the founding with an almost unrestrained enthusiasm. For those of a more sophisticated bent, Jaffa's talk of America as the best regime (even in theory) went too far. More than a few East Coast Straussians found it embarrassing. The average American citizen, however, is not so dainty with his patriotism. Jaffa wanted to tap into that boisterous pride and offer the most comprehensive defense of the founding possible. In his 1980 Rosary College talk, shortly after Ronald Reagan's election, Jaffa was discussing his efforts to educate and elevate the Moral Majority (a "family values" organization with considerable influence in the Republican Party at that time). One student rather sarcastically asked Jaffa, "Oh, so you intend to teach Aristotle to the Moral Majority?" To which Jaffa immediately replied, "That's it." It is important to mention here that however bombastic his language might appear, the substance of Jaffa's political philosophy and history lessons generally upheld quite rigorous standards. His public and popular essays explaining social compact theory, Jefferson's statements on religious liberty, or Locke's doctrine of property rights tended to be just as precise and careful as what he taught in the classroom.

One immediate objection to all this is that it explains too much. (An old but somewhat unjust joke among Straussians is that their favorite academic journal, *Interpretation*, should be called *Over-Interpretation*.) After all, Jaffa is not widely known as a Hegelian, quasi or otherwise. So how clever could he have been to construct this elaborate scheme if no one noticed? But perhaps it was not meant to be ostentatious. First, Jaffa was not inventing the idea of America's providential destiny. As noted above, a belief in America's messianic mission was commonplace in Lincoln's time. Nor did it end in the nineteenth century. Scholars such as Louis Hartz, Bernard Bailyn, Gordon Wood, and others have written about American exceptionalism as an enduring theme in the nation's history. Jaffa was merely adapting this preexisting belief to his own purposes. Secondly, the most significant element that Jaffa added *was* noticed. His bold declaration that the principles of the founding represented "the best regime" drew notice and comment from such notable scholars as Herman Belz, Allen Guelzo, Robert Kraynak, and Michael Zuckert among others (not counting Jaffa's own students who have pursued this theme extensively).

This is notable because while the idea of the best regime may seem very similar to Hegel's final and rational state, it actually represents Jaffa's strongest modification of Hegel—in the direction of Aristotle, not surprisingly. As Jaffa explains early in *New Birth*, nineteenth-century historicism "rejected Aristotle's best regime for the same reason that it had rejected natural rights—because it represented a nonhistorical judgment concerning the human condition."[20] In addition to his more famous conjoining of Aristotle with John Locke, it seems that Jaffa also tried to link Aristotle's bloodline to Hegel. (Arranging beneficial marriages, as discussed in the previous chapter, is an essential task of the philosophic statesman.)

There is another, perhaps discomfiting, question that must be asked. If these speculations are accurate, does that mean Jaffa regarded the idea of God's intervention in human history as *just* a story, a useful myth? It is hard to say for certain. Like many thousands before him, he was frankly astonished when he reflected on "the miracle at Philadelphia": the near-impossible odds of so much talent and virtue assembled in one place at one time, willing and able—with both the resources and opportunity—to found a vast new nation on new principles. "[A] generation of political men, unsurpassed by any of Plutarch's heroes" is the phrase he used in a letter to Norman Podhoretz.[21] (And yet, Lincoln, by himself—self-educated in the backwoods of Kentucky—impressed Jaffa almost as much as all the founders together.) If a "personal faith statement" could be made by combining Plato's idea of the good, Aristotle's thought-thinking-itself, and the cosmic justice of the "laws of nature and nature's God," then Jaffa was a believer.

It is certainly safe to say that he firmly rejected the reductionism and materialism of modern science. In fact, he insisted quite seriously that the human soul, especially what Aristotle called the active (or agent) intellect, was a miracle that neither science nor philosophy could explain and which "participates in a reality that transcends all time and change."[22] For Jaffa, as for Aristotle, belief in the existence of the soul and its connection to eternity may require a leap of faith, yet there is nothing untoward about that. In fact, it is the dogmatic rejection of the soul and of God that requires a much greater and blinder leap. Jaffa was fond of quoting Strauss's observation that the only way to disprove the existence of an omnipotent creator God would be to demonstrate "that all fundamental questions have been answered in a perfectly satisfactory way, in other words that there exists what we call the absolute and final philosophic system." But, adds Strauss, "I regard the existence of such a system as at least as improbable as the truth of the Bible." Moreover—and this is key—"the improbability of the truth of the Bible is a contention of the Bible whereas the improbability of the truth of the perfect philosophic system creates a serious difficulty for that system."[23]

Jaffa hammered this point like a blacksmith. The denial of revelation by modern philosophy was based not on proof but on a groundless faith in materialistic science. This presumption did, however, succeed in spreading a shallow, self-absorbed hedonism through the whole of modern society. Moreover, the conceit of a perfect and final philosophical system would justify the goal (very much still alive) of unrestrained government of the whole world, which Jaffa describes as "universal tyranny, the death of Western civilization."[24] Thus, the most urgent task of political philosophy in the face of this crisis is to repudiate—branch and, especially, root—the doctrines of modern radicalism, which were for Jaffa nothing but a series of sophistical errors. The conclusion of an essay Jaffa wrote in 1990 is eloquent on this point:

> Today we are faced with an unprecedented threat to the survival of biblical religion, of autonomous human reason, and to the form and substance of political freedom. It is important to understand why the threat to one of these is also the threat to all. It is above all important to understand why this threat is, above all, an internal one, mining and sapping our ancient faith, both in God and in ourselves. The decline of the West is the paramount reality facing us today. Perhaps our most immediate danger comes from the historical pessimism of those who counsel us that this is inevitable and that nothing can be done by taking thought. But this danger is itself a danger only if we believe it.... As we enter this third century of the Constitution, let us renew our ancient faith.[25]

In one revealing letter, Jaffa claims that he made this challenge his life's mission within a few years of meeting Strauss, when he was no older than thirty.[26] Whether he knew at the time that he had made a sixty-six-year commitment, we cannot say. In all likelihood, he would have wished for another sixty-six years to keep up the fight. In any event, from Strauss and from his preliminary studies of America, Jaffa learned that the "metaphysical freedom of the mind...as Jefferson rightly declared, is the ground of all moral freedom, and hence of civil and religious liberty." The Declaration, Jaffa realized, could not be recovered if it were not understood. Thus, he had to explain why the "constitution-alism of our founding is inseparable from its moral realism and its natural theology."[27]

The moral realism of the founding includes the rather strin-gent ethical requirements necessary for a regime of equal natural rights. Before individuals can participate in governing society, they must be capable of governing themselves. Republican citi-zens must exercise restraint, industry, and self-respect in order to be responsible, first for themselves and then for their families and communities. Related to this, citizens need to understand and defend their rights while also respecting the rights of others. This requires a level of education much greater than what was necessary for serfs under feudalism. Such an education is partly intellectual (from books and classroom instruction) and partly moral and practical (from good habits inculcated in homes, churches, neighborhoods). To emphasize this point, Jaffa was fond of quoting Washington's Farewell Address, which he saw as a clear echo of Aristotle's *Nicomachean Ethics*:

> There is no truth more thoroughly established than that there exists in the economy and course of nature, an indissoluble union between virtue and happiness, between duty and advantage...and the propitious smiles of Heaven, can never be expected on a nation that disregards the eternal rules of order and right, which Heaven itself has ordained.

Such rules ordained by Heaven can be understood by every rational person who makes the effort to study them. In the words of an influential and widely circulated sermon delivered by the Reverend Samuel Cooper in 1780,

> We want not, indeed, a special revelation from heaven to teach us that men are born equal and free; that no man has a natural claim of dominion over his neighbours, nor one nation any such

claim upon another; and that as government is only the administration of the affairs of a number of men combined for their
own security and happiness, such a society have a right freely
to determine by whom and in what manner their own affairs
shall be administered. These are the plain dictates of that reason
and common sense with which the common parent of men has
informed the human bosom.[28]

Because God endowed man with reason, the Bible agrees
with "the plain dictates" of common-sense morality. This natural
theology of the Declaration of Independence does not require "a
special revelation," and therefore sectarian disputes and strictly
theological arguments have no place in American politics (though
they are given free rein in private life). The principle of religious
liberty is the long-awaited solution to the bloody doctrinal conflicts of Europe. In fact, security for freedom of conscience is so
central to the founders' conception of self-government that Jaffa
identifies the provision in Article VI of the Constitution—which
declares "no religious Test shall ever be required as a Qualification to any Office or public Trust"—to be "unamendable" (along
with the republican guarantee clause in Article IV).[29]
Religious liberty allowed Christians in America to worship
God as a free act of personal devotion and love rather than through
compulsion or fear of punishment. In an important sense, as
many ministers in the founding era argued, this allowed authentic
Christianity to flourish for the first time in the modern world.
It also got sectarian differences out of the way, so to speak,
of encouraging the moral virtues needed for self-government.
"The churches could not support morality together were they
to quarrel politically over dogma," Jaffa observed in his Rosary
College lecture. By removing theological disputes from politics,
churches could "cooperate in a role which makes a democratic
politics possible."[30]

This same freedom of conscience also applies, not incidentally, to the intellectual freedom of Socratic inquiry. The founding limited the ends of government, Jaffa liked to say, but it did not lower the ends of man, whether those ends are to be found in piety or philosophy.

∗   ∗   ∗

In different ways and to different degrees, Jaffa worried that in contemporary America each of these preconditions for republican liberty had succumbed to the perennial dangers of laziness, self-indulgence, and indifference—greatly exacerbated by the corrosive influences of modern philosophy.

Though the armies of the Confederacy, Nazi Germany, and the Soviet Union were each vanquished in due course, the ideologies of racial politics and Marxism lived on, perhaps stronger than ever. This is the meaning of Strauss's oft-quoted remark about "a nation defeated on the battlefield and, as it were, annihilated as a political being" that nevertheless "deprived its conqueror of the most sublime fruit of victory, by imposing on him the yoke of its own thought."[31] Though they are disparate in significant ways, Jaffa argued that the doctrines of Calhoun, Marx, and Hitler were alike in their rejection of human equality and natural right. The destructive and inhuman ideologies of the nineteenth and twentieth centuries were the endpoint of the "real" Hegel. *That* historicism, when fully radicalized, terminated not in the best but the worst possible regimes.

This is where many of the original or standard Straussian accounts of the history of political philosophy end. Strauss's *Natural Right and History* offered a profound diagnosis of the crisis of the West but provided no clear remedy or guidance for the *recovery* of natural right. Several of Strauss's students took this as confirmation of their preference to remain immured in the study of ancient texts. Political philosophy is a theoretical enterprise, they held, not primarily concerned with the practical and grubby work of coalition building and campaign slogans. In Jaffa's view, however, this attitude threatened to turn philosophy into mere dilettantism. When taken to an extreme, Jaffa considered this attitude an almost criminal betrayal of Strauss's conviction that (in Jaffa's words) "radical modernity is the enemy equally of autonomous reason and biblical revelation."[32] Several of his fellow Straussians, he thought, did not take the first part of that danger any more seriously than the second part.

"Political philosophy, in one sense, became necessary only when 'sophistry' undermined the gentleman's unsophisticated attachment to his gentlemanship," Jaffa wrote in 1984. "False theories," he continued,

> against which gentlemen as gentlemen had no defense, made necessary political philosophy. Modern philosophy had denied the gentlemen—and the citizens whom the gentlemen ruled by consent and right of nature—access to the self-understanding of their own gentlemanship. This, in part, is what Strauss meant by saying that modern man had dug a cave beneath the "natural" cave, and that what he was trying to do was to make possible a return to that original cave. His work can therefore be understood, at least in one of its fundamental aspects, as a refutation of all those false modern theories that prevent gentlemen from exercising the authority that is rightfully theirs.[33]

What, then, are those false modern theories?

According to the version Jaffa learned from Strauss, modern philosophy, over the course of several hundred years, underwent a kind of unfolding of the internal logic bound up in its original premises, premises which were in essence a rejection of classical rationalism and moderation. This unravelling was in fact a great unreasoning. Martin Heidegger represented the utmost extreme of this radicalization, which drove him to the madness of embracing "the inner truth and greatness" of National Socialism. (Heidegger, according to a dark joke by Jaffa, was the only man who ever became a Nazi on principle.) Yet the seeds of the twentieth century's inhumanity are to be found three centuries earlier, in the denial that nature, including human nature, has any inherent structure or form outside of our will.

For Hobbes and the other founders of the new politics and psychology, the main antagonist is Aristotle, whose account of the metaphysical freedom of the mind, as noted above, is "the ground of all moral freedom, and hence of civil and religious liberty." For Jaffa, modernity's apparently technical or theoretical errors are not abstract quibbles within the ivory tower of academia. They are a direct cause of our current crisis. This comes out clearly in his wide-ranging Rosary College lecture, where he acknowledges that modern technology has brought great benefits to human life. Within a "limited sphere," Jaffa argues, science should properly be seen as a boon to human safety and happiness. But it cannot provide any wisdom about "the problem of human choice." Therefore, if "you accept the deterministic metaphysics and try to found a method on that, I think you are bound ultimately to end with nihilism in philosophy and with totalitarianism in politics."

Jaffa saw two parts to the modern project. First, a dogmatic skepticism that "denies that we do have, or can have, any genuine knowledge of the external world." This was the "precursor of modern scientific positivism, which regards all knowledge as essentially hypothetical and experimental." According to this doctrine, Jaffa explains, "we know only what we make. In constructing a world from hypotheses, we ourselves are the source of all creativity: there is neither need nor room for God."[34] "According to Hobbes," Jaffa states, "sense perception is not an apprehension of anything outside ourselves."

Sense perception—and all thought is generated from sense perception—is purely subjective. Human consciousness is a black box
receiving signals from the outside, but it must interpret those
signals altogether within itself. For Hobbes, the only metaphysical reality is bodies in motion. Psychological reality is a form of
physical reality. Our sense organs record reactions to the bodies
that impinge upon them, the way billiard balls communicate their
motions to each other when they strike each other.[35]

Paradoxically, this dogmatic skepticism led to an equally dogmatic faith in the absolute authority of science because in principle
the motion of every "billiard ball" can be mathematically calcu-
lated. (Here is the germ of that "complete system" Strauss warned
against.) The power of mathematical science, which emerged
in the late Renaissance, produced fantastic advances in optics,
engineering, astronomy, and other fields. This greatly impressed
Hobbes, Descartes, and their allies, and as Jaffa explains, a great
venture was launched to "make nature the universal slave, so that
men can become tyrants in principle without becoming tyrants in
fact." In other words, scientific technology would "enable them to
live lives unrestrained by moral principle without injuring each
other." Thus, the "greatest of the illusions of modern man" held
that human nature is centered on the passions. Jaffa describes
this as the view "that men are rational only when they pursue
bodily self-preservation in preference to any other goal."[36]

It is necessary to interject a brief caveat. Jaffa understood
perfectly well the legitimate concerns that motivated these early
modern philosophers. While he sometimes used simplistic or
Manichean language to make his rhetorical points, he had learned
from Strauss that these men were profound thinkers with sophisticated teachings. Thus, in a letter to his friend Henry Salvatori,
Jaffa offers a more tempered view of the challenge faced by
Hobbes. Though overly impressed by the promise of scientific

advances, Hobbes (taking a cue from his predecessor, Machiavelli) was trying to ameliorate the pious cruelty exhibited by Christian princes, who were often far too willing to use political power to enforce religious conformity. Hobbes, Jaffa explained,

> believed that it was best to substitute the self-preservation of the body in this world for the salvation of the soul in the next. This idea of Hobbes, seen as a prudent modification of the excesses of Christian politics, has much to commend it; at its best (largely under the tutelage of John Locke) it led to the doctrine of the separation of church and state, and to the doctrine of limited government enshrined in the American Declaration of Independence and the United States Constitution. At its worst, however, it led to Marxism-Leninism, and to the re-creation of theological politics under the form of ideological politics.[37]

Despite the understandable, perhaps even reasonable, concerns that had motivated Hobbes and the other early moderns, their strategies were nevertheless highly questionable, and the long-term *results*, Jaffa thought, were undeniably disastrous. In the most general terms, the "aim or purpose of radical modernity," according to Jaffa, "is the elimination of skepticism from human life, the transcendence of the opposition between reason and revelation by the abolition of both."[38]

It may not be clear what Jaffa means by the "elimination of skepticism." Modern science prides itself in taking nothing on trust. All its knowledge is based on rigorous standards of evidence, demonstration, and proof. Except, according to Jaffa, it isn't. Like every (false) belief in a complete system of perfect knowledge, the materialistic dogma—according to which everything in the world can be accounted for through the laws of physics—necessarily exempts the free will of the scientist who postulates this theory. The scientist, Jaffa argues, "cannot at once insist upon the superior truthfulness of his account of the mind, while admitting that what he says is itself subject to the determinism which is his axiomatic premise."[39]

This doctrine of scientific positivism, according to which there is no valid knowledge beyond the quantifiable or testable, is related to *legal* positivism, which insists that judges cannot consider anything outside the bare text of the law. That may sound like a good idea, but Jaffa objected to both versions because they can't work; he regarded all positivism as simply incoherent. (We will delve into the legal question in Chapter 7.) There are always assumptions at work about, for instance, the validity of the very activity we are engaged in and the nature of the subject we are examining. Or even that we exist. One of Jaffa's favorite stories for demonstrating this incoherence comes from a debate he had with a well-known professor who was an editor at *National Review*:

> On one occasion I crossed swords with Ernest van den Haag, that resolute and unflinching advocate of scientific positivism. Our dispute had its origins at a Philadelphia Society meeting, when I was lecturing on "We hold these truths to be self-evident...." Van den Haag stood up and declared "There are no self-evident truths...." I then asked him, "Is it not self-evident to you that you are not a dog?" He replied, "No." I then said, "Don't you know that you are not a dog?" He again replied, "No." I concluded the dialogue by saying "If you don't know that you are not a dog, maybe you don't know that I am not a fire hydrant."

When Jaffa told this story in person, he would share the twist at the end that he omitted from most published versions: "If you don't know that you are not a dog, maybe you don't know that I am not a fire hydrant, *so please keep your distance!*"

As that example shows, every deterministic theory begins with the untenable contradiction of exempting the person who propounds it. From there, it descends into the equally untenable contradiction of defending scientific rationalism, or scientism, while abandoning reason. Strauss elaborates this point in an essay titled "Relativism," which Jaffa reprinted in *Crisis of the Strauss Divided*. According to the dogmatic premises of modern science, Strauss writes, "nothing prevents us from assuming that the world has come into being out of nothing and through nothing." The impossibility of such causeless events in nature (setting aside the idea of an omnipotent creator God) had always been considered the ultimate absurdity in classical philosophy. For Plato and Aristotle, all rational inquiry has to begin with the premise that the universe is coherent, governed by intelligible cause and effect. But, Strauss continues, once modern science rejects that metaphysical premise, "all coherence is gone." Modern materialist and positivist science "is characterized by the abandonment of reason." In an ironic twist, Strauss notes that while many modern scientists lament the persistence of "unscientific" superstitions, they have only their own doctrines to blame because the populist rejection of dogmatic scientism "is the reasonable reply to the flight of science from reason."[40]

Now, this project by Strauss and Jaffa of criticizing modern sophistries is one thing. Proposing an alternative account of the world that is demonstrably true, or at least more evidently true, is a bit harder. Jaffa is not well-known for this, but his writings include long and careful explanations of the nature of reality and the operations of the human mind. He doesn't simply dismiss the assumptions of modern skepticism but offers serious accounts of ontology and epistemology, although not all in one place. A 1972 essay titled "The Conditions of Freedom" (published in his book by the same name) is an inquiry into the question of personal identity. His 1989 lecture "The Reichstag is Still Burning" examines several key premises of modern psychology. A fairly accessible treatment of the most important issues can be found by returning to his Rosary College lecture, where he provides a clear exposition worth quoting at some length.

At this point in the question and answer session, Jaffa is explaining that while Aristotle was a good empirical scientist (in the best and oldest sense), he—Aristotle—also knew that human reason would never master all the mysteries of the whole, the cosmos. Therefore, Jaffa asserts, "Aristotle teaches revelation as much as any Christian theologian—in his own way." Jaffa then presents his argument for why he considers the human soul a miracle. "If you read the treatise *On the Soul* everything comes down in the end to the problem of the agent intellect, which absolutely cannot be explained. You want me to give you a brief rundown?" For an extemporaneous "rundown," it is surprisingly coherent.

> How does Aristotle explain sense perception? Let's take sight, which is the most interesting and the most noble of the senses. In order for seeing to take place, there must be a visible object and an eye capable of seeing things. But in order for the eye which is capable of seeing to actually see, there must be a third thing, light. Now, for thinking to take place, there must be an object capable of being understood, an intelligible, and there must be a mind capable of thinking it. But there has to be a third thing. If I say "light," I'm using a metaphor. Often when we are trying to understand something, there will be a certain moment ("now I see it") when we do understand it. Sometimes we say that we have seen the light. What we mean, however, is that the object of our understanding has been there all the time, but it somehow became "uncovered" (that is what apocalypse, or revelation, means). But who uncovered it, or who turned on the light? How were we transformed from potential seers into actual seers? I do not want to refer to the many stories of revelation within the sacred tradition as mere stories for children; only to point out that

the mystery underlying reason is a genuine mystery. Within that mystery lies the mystery of human freedom. Now from Aristotle's point of view, I think there is no necessary conflict between reason and revelation—if you get down to the real question, which is how thinking takes place. There is the tradition of reason and the tradition of revelation, but I think the problem with revelation is as much in reason itself—it has its own problem within its own structured framework. That's the problem of the active intellect. Where does it happen? Why does it happen? How can I *will* to know? Here I am; I want to know something; but I still don't know it. And then, all of a sudden, "Yes, now I see it." Why?[41]

Jaffa was an iconoclast in many ways, not least because he thought Aristotle might have something intelligent to say about the structure of being and the working of the human mind. Other scholars, especially other Straussians, share Jaffa's keen interest in the *Ethics* and the *Politics*. But fewer seem seriously interested in Aristotle's metaphysics or psychology. Even the East Coast textualists, who enjoy *analyzing* Aristotle's other works, appear reluctant to treat them as empirical observations that might still be valid. They are investigated as arguments in a text but not as descriptions of reality.

Continuing with Jaffa's lecture remarks, he notes that Aristotle's *Metaphysics* includes some discussion of inductive reasoning, then paraphrases the argument:

For example, I say that I understand that this is a chair. When I say that this is a chair, that means two different things. First is the positive or affirmative statement that this particular object is a chair. But implicit in this is the proposition that if this was the only chair in the world I wouldn't be able to make such a statement. This is a particular object constructed in such a way so as to support the body in a semi-recumbent posture. But there are an infinite number of possible ways in which that can be done. That object over there is also a chair; it doesn't look like this one at all. But I perceive something in common between them. Now how is it that my mind makes the jump from the particular to the universal? It's because, on the basis of a series of comparisons, I see with the eye of my mind an *eidos* or *species*, a form which is common to all possible chairs, and in virtue of which they are chairs. And yet this form lacks all the characteristics in virtue of which any particular chair is not merely possible, but actual, and hence a "this." For the form of the chair is at once something that is *like* every possible chair, and yet *different* from any actual chair. This experience of likeness and of difference underlies what I call the miracle of the common noun, which is truly the most miraculous of all possible human experiences. For it is the essential experience which makes language—and hence man—possible.[42]

This is one iteration of the famous "miracle of the common noun" speech that Jaffa memorably impressed on all his students.

These excerpts, though substantial, do not capture all the details of Jaffa's disparate teachings on these matters, which are spread over many years and many books, essays, and lectures. Because he considered the rule of law and constitutionalism to be inseparable from questions of human reason and justice, even his writings on judicial interpretation have substantial theoretical elements. Jaffa's 1994 book, *Original Intent and the Framers of the Constitution*, contains fascinating digressions on poetry and piety, Machiavelli and Rousseau, Judah Halevi and Alexander Kojève, Aristophanes and Spinoza, prophecy and metaphysics. The brief summaries presented here do, however, capture the essential points.

But what purpose does it all serve?

We have quoted Jaffa saying that the theoretical errors of modern philosophy lead directly to political tyranny and moral degradation. Yet we have no more than hinted at what Jaffa means and what he thought his "project" might accomplish.

Modern philosophy's descent into unreason has dragged us into that metaphorical subterranean pit. Historicism, positivism, atheism, and other ideologies create a kind of blindness that prevents us even from understanding the basic moral phenomena of "the natural cave." Many citizens have been, to a greater or lesser degree, educated (Jaffa might say indoctrinated) in such a way that they are quite ready to suspend belief in their own ordinary experiences, common sense, and even basic biology. Under these conditions, it is exceedingly difficult to challenge the claims to expertise that legitimize government by administrative fiat. The basic concepts of citizenship, sovereignty, equal rights, and consent are barely understood. Civic education is vitally needed to repair that. But what Jaffa learned from Strauss is that even deeper currents of political philosophy are at work. We are in the grip of an unquestioned and unthinking faith in science— really, scientism—that distorts our understanding of reality itself and threatens "the metaphysical freedom of the human mind." Those doctrines have burrowed deeply in the consciousness of all modern human beings. Any large-scale procedure attempting to extract them would require a careful combination of theory and practice as well as luck.

The way out of the pit is thus not so simple. The arguments summarized above do in fact provide a refutation of various sophistries and errors. Yet that is not sufficient. Jaffa frankly acknowledges that while Strauss "did not accept the decline of the West fatalistically, [that] does not mean he was an optimist."[43] In his studies of the great medieval Islamic and Jewish philosophers, Strauss had learned how "reason might be employed to defend faith." This reference to faith is meant to be understood in the broadest sense as "a defense of morality—and, therewith, of the cause of mankind at large." The great Islamic scholars called this exercise of philosophic responsibility *kalam*. Jaffa further believed, unlike most Straussians, that this defense of faith and morality is "ultimately indistinguishable in Strauss's mind from the practice of political philosophy, as he wished to revive that practice." However, "Strauss's project is far more difficult" than the challenge faced in the Middle Ages, for "in our time, there is no traditional piety which can form the moral substratum for any such *kalam*." Modernity has relentlessly promoted a "prejudice against traditional piety [which] is equally a prejudice against traditional moral philosophy, and the reason which informed it." In our time, "religious fundamentalism tends to be anti-rational; but what we might call contemporary academic philosophical fundamentalism is equally so!"[44] In other words, radical skepticism has wiped out so many healthy opinions, customs, and habits that political philosophy has very little to work with.

If Strauss was not an optimist, Jaffa hastened to clarify that he was not a pessimist either. In part, this was because Strauss did not believe that modernity had altered human nature. Moreover, to the degree that the modern project originated in and devolved into gross errors, it could never succeed completely. In Jaffa's words,

> Strauss was convinced that the deepest reason in modernity for wanting to conquer nature was a mistaken reason, for he was convinced that even if the technical means for dispensing with virtue were perfected (e.g., if the doctor could always cure you of the consequences of your intemperance), the result would be a combination of boredom and fanaticism, but it would not be happiness.[45]

This is a good explanation for why modern utopianism will never be just or will always require propaganda and force. But that is merely to say that tyranny is tyrannical. It is not really much of a solution. Strauss struck a more optimistic or at least

brave note when he turned to the phenomenon of statesmanship (and wrote wonderfully stirring words about "guns blazing
and flags flying" in defense of "noble failure"). The next chapter
discusses the great admiration both Strauss and Jaffa had for
Winston Churchill. In Churchill, Strauss recognized—somewhat
to his amazement—the classical phenomenon of *megalopsuchia*,
greatness of soul. This awareness of what Churchill represented,
Jaffa claimed, "touches the profoundest level of Strauss's theoretical understanding."[46] The recovery of statesmanship and moral
virtue, then, is as important to Jaffa's project as the theoretical
matters discussed in this chapter. Theoretical clarity must come
first, however, partly because thought always precedes action
but also because the moral gentleman who exercises authority
in every good regime cannot be free to act until he is liberated,
with the help of political philosophy, from debilitating sophistries
he is not equipped to refute.

✳   ✳   ✳

One more topic of the greatest urgency remains. It answers this
question: if Jaffa, with the help of Aristotle, can refute the theoretical errors of modern philosophy, and if magnanimous political actors like Lincoln and Churchill can display the pinnacle of
moral excellence, what is the reason for all of Jaffa's insistent talk
about restoring the authority of the Bible? In one essay he writes,
"The consummation and transformation of philosophy—love
of wisdom—into wisdom itself, were it to succeed, would put
an end to both Socratic skepticism and biblical faith."[47] That's
an odd statement. Is the Bible really opposed to wisdom? More
curiously, if Socratic skepticism is the same as philosophy, then
why would the consummation (i.e., the success) of philosophy
"put an end" to philosophy? What does Jaffa mean?

The Bible is of course the root of Judeo-Christian morality, which Jaffa was keenly interested in buttressing. Yet it commands nothing like the near-universal familiarity and respect it had in Lincoln's day. If college students today read any of Lincoln's speeches, they are highly unlikely even to notice the many biblical allusions. So does Jaffa think that a revival of interest in sacred scripture today would merely be helpful to encourage moral rectitude? Well, of course it is effective for that, as recognized by George Washington along with most people of common sense. Yet, without discounting in any way the Bible as the fundamental moral code of Western civilization, Jaffa wanted to show its necessity beyond any ethical teaching. The God of the Bible is an *ontological* challenge to the threat of universal tyranny.

Unlike the polytheistic religions of ancient Greece, consecrated by the Athenian poets, Judaism and Christianity present philosophy with something entirely different. Human intellect can consider whether the God of the Bible is *reasonable* by examining His laws and commandments. (The god of the Aztecs, who was glorified or appeased by continuous human sacrifices, would fail such a test.) But disproving God's *existence* is another matter.

Jaffa made a very strenuous argument—and kicked off a long argument with his fellow Straussian Thomas Pangle—over this precise point. It began in the *Claremont Review of Books* in 1984 with Jaffa's critique of an introductory essay written by Pangle for a collection of Leo Strauss essays that Strauss intended to publish but was unable to complete before his death. Jaffa's book review was followed by a rebuttal from Pangle and a surrebuttal by Jaffa. The dispute even flashed up again years later in the pages of *National Review*.

Pangle states in his Introduction to the book *Studies in Platonic Political Philosophy* that

> Strauss absolutely denied that the theological-political problem
> was a problem that arose only with the advent of monotheism

or of the biblical religions and the "holy" God....What is most essential in the quarrel between Plato and the Bible is already present in the quarrel between Plato and the poets.[48]

Jaffa emphatically disagreed with that. "In a series of writings," he says in his review, "Strauss demonstrated the internal integrity of the Bible, not as a book among books, but as a perfect product of perfect piety." It must be viewed from an entirely different perspective because the Bible "is not addressed to unbelievers." It was conceived not as a work of human art but a product of divine revelation. It is therefore "perfectly intelligible, but not as poetry."

> To attribute to Strauss—as Pangle does—the view that the Bible is a species of poetry—no different from Greek poetry in the most essential respect—is profoundly mistaken.
>
> The ultimate conflict or tension between the Biblical and the philosophic meanings of wisdom is what Strauss meant by "the theological-political problem."

Jaffa then alludes to a famous statement by Strauss about the respective claims of piety versus philosophy. One should not assume that "because you cannot tell which of two mountains, whose peaks are shrouded in mist, is the higher, that you cannot tell the difference between a mountain and a mole hill!"[49]

Political philosophy in Athens had directed its civic responsibilities to providing a more rational alternative to the quarreling Olympian divinities, who were not ideal models for personal ethics or political justice. The philosophers' contribution toward enhancing natural right consisted of supplying younger, openminded Athenian men a rational teaching about the order of nature (such as the Socratic doctrine of the Ideas). The God of the Bible, however, is immune to such rational "improvement."

As Jaffa explains:

> The story of Genesis is the story of what God has made and done for man, and why fear of the Lord and not wonder is the beginning of wisdom. God has made what He has made, and done what He has done. It is no more possible for man to fathom this than to fathom God Himself.
>
> The issue between Plato and the poets is, to repeat, the issue between the ideas and gods who fight among themselves. The issue between Plato and the Bible is that between the ideas and the One God. The God of the Bible not only is One, but is unknowable precisely because He is One.... The uniqueness and separateness of the Biblical God excludes the possibility of philosophic knowledge of God. Knowledge of God must therefore, to repeat, consist of knowledge of God's ways, of His speeches and deeds, as they are set forth in the Bible.[50]

What does all this mean on a practical level for Jaffa's attempt to steer America away from its postmodern pathologies?

Pulling together various threads already discussed, we recall that biblical religion seems to be essential for popular morality. Yet for Jaffa it was perhaps even more important that the God of the Bible, "who moves in a dark cloud" and "who shall be what He shall be," provides the only irrefutable challenge to the hubris of unchecked rationalism or deranged philosophy.

Socratic philosophy alone cannot stop the universal tyranny of the world state. Partly this is because there are never many Socratic philosophers around. Moreover, the vast majority of those educated in "philosophy" today are part of the problem. Mainly, however, philosophy *by its nature* is ill-equipped for such a fight. Pure rationalism is good at puncturing popular prejudices and superstitions. It is not so good at dealing with attempts to construct a comprehensive scientific or logical system, projects which are, in fact, distortions or exaggerations of rationalism itself.

What Professor Arthur Melzer has called the hyperrationalism of modern philosophy began with the attempt to mathematize politics and ended with the Marxist science of dialectical materialism.[51] Something in addition to Socratic inquiry is required to meet this challenge.

Strauss hinted at this in his discussion of Alfarabi when he comments on a startling claim made by the Islamic philosopher. According to Alfarabi, Plato saw in the trial and execution of Socrates the deficiency of purely rational inquiry. Plato's own (improved) teaching about political philosophy, according to Alfarabi, recognizes that Socratic skepticism must be combined with "the way of Thrasymachus"—that is the need for coercion or force, which may include, if it is effective, punitive rhetoric. (Socrates's limitations "in speech" are revealed by the way Plato mostly confines the dialogues to private and generally friendly conversations.)[52]

Jaffa transmutes Strauss's ambiguous comments into his own typically pungent style by saying, "Philosophers must be taught—sometimes even by chastisement—how to act in a responsible manner." Or, as he put it somewhat less bluntly, "Strauss never believed that men could be governed by speeches alone, or that the art of rhetoric could ever be separated from the art of war."[53]

Biblical faith supplies what pure rationalism cannot. Jaffa clarifies this in his follow-up *CRB* essay:

> It is precisely by the attempt of modern philosophy to transcend the difference between Revelation and Reason that the West is above all endangered, for *if the contention could be maintained that there is no mystery to justify the belief in God, it would follow that there was no ground to doubt that philosophy had been transformed into wisdom.* To believe that philosophy had been transformed into wisdom leads necessarily to the unqualified claim of wisdom to rule: the claim of the universal tyrant. In the face of this challenge of radical modernity, the fate of Socratic philosophy and of the

Bible are linked in both their separateness and their combination. [Emphasis added.][54]

Before concluding this chapter, we need to address what seems to be a problematic conflict between Jaffa's two versions of God. There is the radically unknowable God of the Old Testament, who is not bound by anything and whose will cannot be fathomed by man. But then there is the Declaration's self-evident "laws of Nature and Nature's God." In the natural theology of the founders, God endows man with reason to discern what is right and good. If, however, man can figure out what is just and noble through the rational study of nature, this would seem to eliminate any need for revelation. Why do we need God's law if we can understand nature's law? Jaffa is certainly aware of this tension. In fact, he points to it in at least two places.

In an important but little-known 1960 essay called "The Case Against Political Theory" (republished in *Equality and Liberty* in 1965), Jaffa notes that if we can understand God through the permanent distinction between good and evil, He would be bound, as it were, by his own moral edicts. "He would not be omnipotent. [He] would not be the God of Israel." If the natural theology of the Declaration is true, and if "the essence of God could be known to be forever unchanging, then God would be subject to the intelligible necessity of his nature.... There would be no radical need of man for God."[55]

Similarly, in a fascinating but generally overlooked passage of *Crisis of the House Divided*, Jaffa notes that Lincoln's subtle exploration of theological questions in his Temperance Speech points to this same dilemma between a "philosophic" God bound by the laws of the cosmos and a providential God bound only by his promises. "The relation of moral virtue to revelation on the one hand and to unassisted reason on the other," Jaffa observes, "is the deepest problem of Lincoln's Temperance Address." A lengthy footnote offers hope of some resolution, but after drawing out the inferences of Lincoln's arguments, it concludes that in the end, "the force of the opposition of the two conceptions of deity recurs in full."[56]

The best explanation for what Jaffa intends may be a point that Leo Strauss asserts explicitly. But by following the ins and outs of Jaffa's fragmentary discussions, we may come to appreciate it from a different perspective and in a deeper way. The political and intellectual freedom of man depends absolutely on Athens and Jerusalem remaining in permanent tension. Though Jaffa insisted that they are united against modern philosophy by what we may call their moral and metaphysical realism, both insist on the ultimate mystery of the cosmos and insist that this mystery cannot be overcome. The "two conceptions of deity" in Lincoln's speech may be practically compatible, but perhaps they must remain ultimately irreconcilable. The conquest of revelation by reason or of reason by revelation would mean the end of what Strauss called "the secret vitality of the west."[57]

This may shed some light on Jaffa's apparently strange statement, discussed earlier. Here is the sentence quoted above, along with the remainder of the passage.

> The consummation and transformation of philosophy—love of wisdom—into wisdom itself, were it to succeed, would put an end to both Socratic skepticism and biblical faith. For in such a case, there would be nothing left either for inquiry or for faith. Strauss's critique of modern philosophy showed the impossibility of this enterprise more than any intellectual event of our times. His demonstration that the self-destruction of reason ends in nihilism proved the superiority both of Socratic skepticism and of biblical faith to the modern attempts to supersede them.[58]

Whether this completely solves the tension of Jaffa's two conceptions of God is difficult to say. In any event, the matter cannot be investigated any further here.

In the next chapter, we consider the equally serious but more dramatic—and perhaps more engaging—questions of war and heroism; of blood, toil, tears, and sweat.

6

STATESMANSHIP, TYRANNY, AND FREEDOM

The Weimar Republic was weak.... On the whole it presented
the sorry spectacle of justice without a sword or of justice
unable to use the sword.... The weakness of the Weimar
Republic made certain its speedy destruction.

—LEO STRAUSS

Great men are the ambassadors of Providence sent
to reveal to their fellow men their unknown selves.

—CALVIN COOLIDGE

It seems natural that the theoretical subject matter of the previous chapter should transition to the practical focus of this one. This division of theory and practice is a common distinction in ordinary language as well as in political philosophy. In fact, Jaffa once remarked to his friend Joseph Cropsey, "Almost everything I have written, in the last thirty-five years, has been informed, in one way or another, by the distinction between moral and intellectual virtue."[1] Nevertheless, there is some ambiguity in this dichotomy, which can be seen in several documents from the American founding. Consider a letter Thomas Jefferson wrote in June of 1826.

Near the end of his life, at the age of eighty-three, Jefferson wrote to Roger Weightman, the mayor of Washington, DC, expressing his regret that poor health would prevent him from attending the upcoming celebration of Independence Day in the nation's capital. This was, as far as we know, the last letter Jefferson wrote in his own hand. He died less than two weeks later, on the Fourth of July, fifty years to the day after the signing of the Declaration of Independence. (Five hundred miles away, in Quincy, Massachusetts, John Adams died on the same day, a coincidence much remarked on at the time and taken as a sign of God's blessing on the infant republic.)

Jefferson's colorful letter disparages the "monkish ignorance and superstition" that impeded mankind's "exercise of reason and freedom of opinion." But thanks in part to the example of American independence, "all eyes are opened, or opening to the rights of man." The political achievement of the citizens of the United States, "the choice we made," helped to reveal "the palpable truth that the mass of mankind has not been born, with saddles on their backs, nor a favored few booted and spurred, ready to ride them legitimately, by the grace of God." [2] The language Jefferson uses here is consistent with the Declaration's affirmation of the natural rights of all human beings as a self-evident truth. Likewise, in *Notes on the State of Virginia,* Jefferson observed that "the *error* seems not sufficiently eradicated, that the operations of the mind, as well as the acts of the body, are subjects to the coercion of the laws. But our rulers can have authority over such natural rights only as we have submitted to them." [Emphasis added.] For Jefferson, politics begins with understanding the world as it truly is, yet our moral and political experiences also give us theoretical insights we would not otherwise have. We will come back to this as an important point in Jaffa's own understanding of practical wisdom.

Today, even if one could get a political theorist or social scientist to stipulate to Jefferson's empirical claims about men and horses, he or she would insist that no ethical prescription, no "ought," could be derived from them. That all human beings are neither beasts nor gods tells us nothing about how we should act. Jefferson and his compatriots, however, made no such distinction between their moral assertions and their ontological claims about the nature of the world.

The Declaration establishes a kind of syllogism. The major premise is the self-evident truth of equal natural rights; the minor premise is the list of the king's "abuses and usurpations" against those rights. The conclusion that follows is that "these United Colonies are, and of Right ought to be Free and Independent States." (Of course, a political syllogism—reflecting the world of choice, not necessity—is not a logical syllogism.) None of the Declaration's signers in the Continental Congress had the "benefit" of a modern university education, and thus they were serenely unaware that by proceeding this way they were violating the fact-value distinction.

Jaffa likewise failed to respect the distinctions and orthodoxies of his academic discipline. Professor Kraynak, in his 2009 essay on Jaffa's career (discussed in Chapter 3), characterizes his theory of the founding as "an ingenious but fanciful" mixing of "a theoretical argument about human dignity" with "a practical argument derived from Socratic skepticism." This, Kraynak argues, leads Jaffa to erroneously and somewhat comically lump together all the "heroes" of natural right—Socrates, Aristotle, Aquinas, Locke, Jefferson, Lincoln, and Shakespeare—taking the spirit of *e pluribus unum* too far, presumably. Yet rather than being chastened, Jaffa happily appropriates this charge. In his reply to Kraynak, he notes that conventional scholarship, "under the domination of historicism, regards differences of time and place as fundamental." Rejecting this view, Jaffa recalls and reaffirms the world he discovered decades earlier in Leo Strauss's classroom: a "realm of principle that had no time or place...from which there was a view of the human condition which embraced all times and all places." In Jaffa's hall, Aristotle sits with Shake-speare and winces not.[3]

The point of these remarks is not to deny that there is (as Jaffa himself insisted) a distinction between theoretical and practical wisdom, particularly when viewed from the perspective of politi-cal philosophy. Rather, it is to clarify Jaffa's starting point for political science. With Strauss, he insisted on examining political things from the perspective of the citizen, from prephilosophic political opinion, which does not separate the moral and ontologi-cal understanding of human concerns. "According to Aristotle and Strauss, we must begin our reasoning with what is known to us, prior to philosophy."[4] In fact, Jaffa goes so far as to say in one essay that Strauss's purpose was "a return, not so much to classical political philosophy as such, but 'to the fundamental experiences from which it is derived.'"[5]

*   *   *

The political science that informs American constitutionalism, Jaffa held, represents a coherent moral-political framework. At the analytical level, of course, it is necessary to understand each of its several elements individually. The bundle of interconnected concepts comprising equality, consent, and social compact might be said to form the core of the political theory of the founding.[6] This nexus was central to Jaffa's disputes with the paleoconserva-tives and neoconservatives and to some degree with his fellow Straussians. These controversies will be taken up in detail in the next chapter.

Of almost equal importance for Jaffa is the separation of church and state. This has already been discussed in some detail. Yet there is one significant point to clarify, which is especially relevant to the practical focus of this chapter. In his 1987 essay "The American Founding as the Best Regime," Jaffa writes:

The unprecedented character of the American Founding is that it provided for the coexistence of the claims of reason and of revelation in all their forms, without requiring or permitting any political decisions concerning them. It refused to make unassisted human reason the arbiter of the claims of revelation, and it refused to make revelation the judge of the claims of reason. It is the first regime in Western civilization to do this, and for that reason it is, in its principles or speech (leaving aside the question of its practice or deeds), the best regime.[7]

When conscience is at last liberated from government interference, then by right neither kings nor bureaucrats may punish heresy or define apostasy. All believers (and even nonbelievers) are protected from secular oppression. But this liberation also works in the other direction. When politics ceases to be a vehicle for the highest aspirations of the soul, millenarian expectations are vastly diminished. Jefferson's defense of religious liberty constitutes a great barrier to utopianism. Separation of church and state means that government is divested of both the *power* to arbitrate theological disputes as well as the *purpose* of fulfilling our deepest spiritual longings. Heaven may or may not await us in a life to come, but according to the American founders, it will not be found in this one.

If we simply left the matter there, it might seem that Machiavelli and Hobbes have the last laugh: forget about the soul, let politics concern itself with the needs of the body. This, of course, is not Jaffa's position. He agreed with Strauss's suggestion that the United States may be "the only country in the world which was founded in explicit opposition to Machiavellian principles."[8] Machiavelli banished the soul from the concern of "princes" and radically curtailed the horizon of moral virtue. The founders, on the other hand, were clear that self-government cannot succeed without citizens who are responsible, spirited, and moderate. As Jaffa explains:

[The] virtue of the American Founding rests not only upon its defusing of the tension between reason and revelation, but upon their fundamental agreement on a moral code which can guide human life both privately and publicly. This moral code is the work both of "Nature's God"—reason—and the "Creator"—revelation. Religious freedom properly understood is a principle which emancipates political life not only from sectarian religious conflict, but from the far profounder conflict between reason and revelation. Indeed, it makes reason and revelation—for the first time—open friends and allies on the political level. For they are, to repeat, agreed upon the nature and role of morality in the good society.[9]

This might appear straightforward, yet it does not quite capture everything that needs to be said. Especially in this context of freedom of conscience, the precise nature and role of moral virtue requires a more careful explanation. Jaffa often said that the American founding lowered the ends of government but that it did not lower the ends of human life. Republicanism depends on a citizenry with sound ethical habits, yet it also implies a certain *limitation* on morality. What does that mean?

Aristotle instructs us that the political community comes into existence for the sake of life but continues for the sake of the good life, namely happiness. The regime points beyond itself to something higher: the contemplative life of philosophy. For Aristotle, this was the most excellent possible activity of the soul. The somewhat mundane quality of the Greeks' pagan gods (though, importantly, supplying supernatural support for the moral-political life of the city) did not pose a serious intellectual challenge to philosophy. The God of the Bible, however—as the One, separate, and unknowable Creator of the universe—represented something entirely different. Unlike the pagan deities cavorting on Mount Olympus, the omnipotent and mysterious God of the Hebrews could not be dismissed or refuted by philosophy. The monotheistic faiths based on the Bible, therefore, must be considered a second possibility for man's spiritual aspirations.

Strauss argued that neither of these alternatives, reason or revelation, presents an absolute, unquestionable case for itself. Philosophy, no less than piety, seems to require a leap of faith. Therefore, the best way of life involves a choice, and this choice is ultimately a moral not an intellectual one. What is essential is that both alternatives offer the possibility of fulfilling the human longing for wisdom or truth, and both transcend the realm of political and practical wisdom. Neither philosophy nor piety, strictly speaking, is comprehended within the moral life of the modern citizen.

With this context, we are now in a position to clarify Jaffa's arguments discussed in Chapter 4 about the magnanimous man who is "only" moral. Though Jaffa came to a higher appreciation of Thomas Aquinas, he never repudiated what he said about Aristotle and moral virtue in his first book. (His statements in *Thomism and Aristotelianism* pale in comparison with an even more shocking statement by Leo Strauss, referring to moral men who are not philosophers as "mutilated human beings." We will turn to that in a moment.) Jaffa's apparent derogation of moral virtue is consistent with statements he makes elsewhere. For example, in a letter to Joseph Cropsey, Jaffa refers to the "absurd elevation of morality beyond its proper sphere" in the writings of Immanuel Kant.[10]

The rigid, elaborate ethical system constructed by Kant, largely around the principle of the "categorical imperative," attempted to do away with any individual judgment. In particular, Kant wanted to displace the Aristotelian understanding of natural right, which relied on prudence to determine the proper action in any particular circumstance. Now, it may be a mistake to replace flexibility with rigidity, but why does this constitute an "absurd elevation of morality beyond its proper sphere"?

Let's consider the reference to Kant in context by quoting the whole paragraph from Jaffa's letter:

> It is precisely because of the denial of the possibility of theoretical wisdom, in the classical sense, by modern philosophy, that we have the egregious extremes represented by Kant and popular Machiavellianism. Kant, by denying the possibility of philosophical wisdom, of knowledge of things in themselves, made morality an end in itself. As such an end, it could never be "useful." This absurd elevation of morality beyond its proper sphere led in the end to the complete depreciation of morality, because of its separation of morality from happiness, and therewith of morality from political life. It led to that relativism with which we are now afflicted.

In other words, Kant makes morality nothing more or less than a duty, unconnected to any conception of individual human well-being, especially happiness. If this still seems a bit convoluted, Jaffa's point will become clearer in a moment.

Consider what is widely regarded as one of Leo Strauss's most extreme or disturbing statements. A philosopher, he says, "is devoted to the pursuit of something which is absolutely higher in dignity than any human things," that is "the unchangeable truth." Therefore, if the pursuit of the eternal truth is "the ultimate end of man, justice and moral virtue in general can be fully legitimated only by the fact that they are required for the sake of that ultimate end." "From this point of view," Strauss continues, "the man who is merely just or moral without being a philosopher appears as a mutilated human being."[11]

Shadia Drury, author of *The Political Ideas of Leo Strauss* (1988), cites this remark in a letter to Jaffa as evidence of Strauss's alleged contempt for common decency and virtue. Jaffa's response was later published in the journal *Political Theory*. Strauss's remark, said Jaffa, was a "simply true" statement and perfectly reasonable when read in its context and in light of Strauss's other observations about philosophy and morality. "With the exception of Kant," Jaffa explains, "there has never, so far as I know, been anyone who has maintained that morality can stand entirely or simply on its own foundation." The dignity of moral life, therefore,

> can be seen to derive, at least in part, from its service to an end that transcends morality. And Kant's attempt to make morality an end in itself is disastrous. Consider that [Kant's] "rational being" of "good will" must tell a would-be murderer the truth about where he might find his intended victim! Now that is a mutilated human being![12]

Jaffa cites a passage from Strauss's essay "The Mutual Influence of Theology and Philosophy," which notes that the Bible and Greek philosophy share a broad agreement "regarding both morality and the *insufficiency of morality*." [Emphasis added.] This insufficiency concerns the two alternatives of piety or philosophy, which point beyond political life to the purely intellectual or spiritual realm. The disagreement between Jerusalem and Athens, Strauss says, "concerns the 'X' which completes morality." For classical philosophy, Strauss continues, "that 'X' is *theoria* or contemplation, and the biblical completion we may call, I think, without creating any misleading understanding, piety, the need for divine redemption, obedient love."

Why morality is therefore "insufficient" Jaffa now makes evident:

> Is it not clear that from the point of view of the man who "loves his God, with all his heart, and with all his mind, and with all his might," the merely moral man must appear a defective human being? The pious man thinks that in obeying the moral law he is obeying and honoring God. To him, a man who in obeying the

moral law merely dignifies himself must appear as less than fully human. Whether from the perspective of Reason or of Revelation, it is the capacity of the human soul to transcend time and participate in eternity that is the ultimate cause of that soul's dignity. Morality is thus elevated, not depreciated, by its link with transcendence. Morality cut off from transcendence sinks into Kantian absurdity.[13]

This is a crucial point. Strauss does indeed, like Aristotle, place moral virtue below intellectual virtue. Jaffa complained that some of his fellow Straussians seemed to understand this too simplistically and therefore regarded the sphere of politics and practical wisdom as vulgar, undeserving of any sustained interest by a true philosopher. Socrates may have begun his inquiries by questioning the "opinions of the marketplace," but this was (supposedly) merely a stepping-stone to higher pursuits. Jaffa took nearly the opposite view. In the same letter to Cropsey, he remarks, "By making morality solely a matter of duty, and without regard for consequences, Kant abolished the role of prudence, and divorced morality from utility or happiness." But morality "should serve happiness," and this end, this *summum bonum*, "must possess a transcendent and trans-moral component." Moreover—and this is key—there is an essential "kinship" that links happiness, as the highest good of man, with the highest achievements or excellence of man.

The moral-political realm is necessary, even—or rather, especially—for the philosopher, Jaffa insists, to understand both the low and the high. Socratic inquiry begins by examining the conventional or unreflective opinions of the particular regime, the cave. But the political philosopher is also interested in human excellence. The peak of moral virtue, the phenomenon of *megalopsuchia*, reveals "that strength of soul—of a Lincoln or of a Churchill—by which evil is confronted, and by which evil is made to reveal itself as what it truly is."

Not only is such greatness sometimes the cause of the actual triumph over evil (although never necessarily so), but the spectacle it affords is, as Strauss says in his eulogy of Churchill, "one of the greatest lessons which men can learn at any time." [Such] moral phenomena are in the end of final importance because of the access they provide to metaphysical reality: "seeing things as they are."[14]

So far from denigrating morality and statesmanship, Strauss's whole project turned on their primacy for political philosophy. Jaffa asserts that Strauss inaugurated "the only genuinely new political science of the past four hundred years"—that is to say, since (and in opposition to) Machiavelli. That claim is from the 1981 preface to *Crisis* discussed in Chapter 3. Jaffa describes this new (or perhaps renewed) political science as "more modest in its goals than the political science it offers to replace. It would vindicate moderation—and the moral virtues generally." And it "would have at its heart the study of the speeches and deeds of statesmen."[15]

In that spirit, let us turn (at last) to some specific, practical problems that confront the American regime and political life more generally. We will look at four examples of "the speeches and deeds of statesmen" that were of particular interest to Jaffa and to which he devoted significant attention. Each has a focus on a particular challenge or set of circumstances and yet points to enduring questions of the human condition.

LINCOLN'S LYCEUM SPEECH (THE PROBLEM OF FACTIONS)

In his essay on Aristotle's *Politics*, Jaffa explains that Book V, the longest in the *Politics*, is focused on how regimes change or decay. Paraphrasing and summarizing Aristotle's analysis, Jaffa relates how problems arise when some citizens believe they are not getting "their fair share." The people may experience a "sense of oppression" from the wealthy few, or conversely the elites may feel dishonored by "those they deem their inferiors." In general, "expropriation," "insolence," and other types of abuse or injury can lead to forgetting or rejecting "what is just" and potentially instigate *metabole*, revolution.[16] This analysis is similar to what Madison (writing as Publius) describes in *Federalist No. 10* as the problem of faction: "a number of citizens whether amounting to a majority or minority of the whole, who are united and actuated by some common impulse of passion, or of interest, adverse to the rights of other citizens." In simple terms, the most basic cause of political unrest is when some (or many) citizens place their self-interest or self-regard above the common good. Jaffa sees an especially subtle and incisive treatment of this theme in Lincoln's 1838 speech "The Perpetuation of Our Political Institutions," often referred to simply as the Lyceum Address. (The venue for the speech was the Young Men's Lyceum in Springfield, Illinois.)[17]

Lincoln, astonishingly, was only twenty-eight when he delivered this profound analysis of how self-government is threatened by lawless mobs and demagogic tyrants, apparently separate dangers that are in fact intertwined. Jaffa's examination of the Lyceum speech in *Crisis* is followed by an equally close interpretation of the 1842 Temperance Address, which together take up eighty pages and comprise the book's central section, "The Political Philosophy of a Young Whig." The latter speech will be discussed below.

Commenting on how the two are related, Jaffa notes that in neither oration does Lincoln

> present the problem of slavery in the leading position it occupies in the Second Inaugural. Rather does he see the difficulty of free government in the broader context of the eternal problem created by the power of evil passions—of which slavery is but a particular manifestation—over mankind.... The central topic of both is the same, but the first emphasizes the political side, the second the

moral. For Lincoln, the question of the "capability of a people to govern themselves" was always twofold: it referred both to the viability of popular political institutions and to their moral basis in the individual men who must make those institutions work.[18]

The Lyceum speech warns that mob rule is hazardous enough in itself but if left unchecked leads to an even greater danger. Lincoln begins by noting how bands of citizens, outraged at first by a few appalling crimes, took the law into their own hands. But while such actions might initially have been motivated by a thirst for justice, they quickly turned to mere bloodlust:

> Thus went on this process of hanging, from gamblers to negroes, from negroes to white citizens, and from these to strangers; till, dead men were seen literally dangling from the boughs of trees upon every road side; and in numbers almost sufficient, to rival the native Spanish moss of the country, as a drapery of the forest.[19]

Such arbitrary killings, of course, present a great menace for any innocent person who might find himself in the wrong place and time. Yet much worse is when citizens, despairing for their safety and security in the face of such lawlessness, lose faith in democratic government. Under these circumstances, Lincoln warns, "men of sufficient talent and ambition will not be wanting to seize the opportunity, strike the blow, and overturn that fair fabric, which for the last half century, has been the fondest hope, of the lovers of freedom, throughout the world."

Like many readers of the speech, the critic Edmund Wilson assumed that "Lincoln has projected himself into the role against which he is warning."[20] The discussion in Chapter 3 already touched on Jaffa's complex views about Lincoln, equality, and the founders. We must return to that theme briefly to clarify a point and then bring out the practical lessons. As Jaffa notes in his commentary on the speech: "Mobs and tyrants are reciprocals, the former easily becoming the armies of the latter. The mobs of the French Revolution became the armies of Napoleon."[21] To these challenges there is only one solution, proclaims Lincoln, in one of his most famous rhetorical expositions:

> Let reverence for the laws, be breathed by every American mother, to the lisping babe, that prattles on her lap—let it be taught in schools, in seminaries, and in colleges; let it be written in Primers, spelling books, and in Almanacs;—let it be preached from the pulpit, proclaimed in legislative halls, and enforced in courts of justice. And, in short, let it become the political religion of the nation.

In his long analysis of this speech in *Crisis*, Jaffa still viewed Lincoln as a messianic figure guiding the nation through the tribulation of war to atone for the sin of slavery. America's great experiment in self-government had to be vindicated through the intervention of a great-souled leader who placed his superior virtue in the cause of equality. Jaffa's interpretation of the Lyceum speech therefore places considerable emphasis on contrasting Lincoln with the most famous destroyers of republics, "commencing demagogues, and ending tyrants": Alexander, Caesar, and Napoleon. Whereas Lincoln matches these "wolves" in cunning, he exceeds them in justice—becoming a shepherd who drives the wolves from his flock. Lincoln's goal was to save America from other men with Lincoln's talent and ambition but without his virtue. The mechanism whereby this savior rescues his people is a *political religion*: "an engrafting of the passion of revealed religion upon the body of secular political rationalism."[22]

As Jaffa's estimation of the founding improves over the course of his career, the need for a savior diminishes, and Jaffa's rhetoric about patriotic citizenship becomes more *political* and less *reli-*

gious. Of course, he continues to see Lincoln as an extraordinary statesman who transcends Caesar and Napoleon by his refusal to succumb to either of the demagogic temptations available to him. On the one hand, Lincoln easily could have stoked the fanaticism of the abolitionists, who would have destroyed the Union to vindicate the purity of their principles, and ridden to power on the adulation generated by William Lloyd Garrison's influential abolitionist newspaper. On the other hand, Lincoln was a better rhetorician than Stephen Douglas, and had he abandoned his principles might well have displaced "the little giant" at the head of the popular sovereignty cause, which would have permitted the Union to become all-slave rather than impose any moral limit on majoritarianism.

In his later writings, Jaffa regularly invokes the Lyceum Address, and he retains from his analysis in *Crisis* the key theme of tyranny arising from unchecked populism, when men forget the moral ground of their freedom. Thus, in *A New Birth of Freedom*, Jaffa says,

> Lincoln stressed the necessity of obeying even bad laws while working for their repeal or reform, because disobedience to bad laws engenders a habit of lawlessness that easily turns into mob rule. And when law cannot protect persons and property, men will turn away from the rule of law to despotism for their security.... [This concern] was substantially the same as the one that animated those who called for the Constitutional Convention of 1787.[23]

The problem of mob violence is of course highly relevant in contemporary American politics. Throughout much of 2020, protests by the Black Lives Matters (BLM) movement in cities across the United States frequently descended into, or merged with, violent riots led by the anarcho-communist entity Antifa.

The lines between the two were often hard to discern. Of course, these incidents were quite different from the epidemic of lynchings that occurred in 1830s Illinois. Yet Lincoln's warnings are no less prescient. As Jaffa notes, the "entire speech is a defense of the rule of law from all forms of arbitrary rule."[24]

The purpose of the BLM protests, according to its defenders, was to combat racial injustice or "systemic racism." This may indeed have been the motivation for many participants. But it does not preclude the possibility that such rallying cries were, for some, an ad hoc cover for seeking power or prestige. Most likely, the crowds represented a complex mixture of idealism, cynicism, trendiness, and self-delusion. "Even the mob that killed [the abolitionist editor Elijah] Lovejoy might have felt it was defending the Constitution," Jaffa observes. We will return to the problem of "true believers" in a moment. Here, we note only that racial politics in the United States—which have never disappeared, but simply flipped positions—always seek to add a moral component to a self-interested one. In Calhoun's notorious defense of the South's peculiar institution in the 1830s, the greed of the slaveowners conveniently disappears behind the "positive good" that slavery supposedly conferred on the slaves themselves. "It is no accident that the Civil Rights Movement, ever since the passage of the great Civil Rights Acts of 1964 and 1965, has been based almost entirely upon the idea of group as opposed to individual rights," Jaffa wrote in *New Birth*. "As a theoretical concept, 'black power' is no different from the 'white power' espoused by Calhoun."[25]

In a letter to the *Los Angeles Times*, Jaffa claimed that the US Commission on Civil Rights under President Jimmy Carter "was little more than an organization for securing preferred status in the marketplace for its constituent groups. Never has the idea of equal justice under law been subject to more cynical perversion." And in a paper prepared for a conference in 1996, Jaffa stated,

Like the "poverty industry" and its huge bureaucracy that thrives on poverty, there is a "civil rights industry." It too has its own bureaucracy, both governmental and non-governmental, with thousands of well-paying jobs, and with enormous patronage and profits. It lives and prospers by continuing to discover "racism," a concept which has become as pervasive, elusive, and multifaceted as original sin. The civil rights bureaucracy is particularly adept at discovering racism where it also discovers deep pockets.[26]

The only solution, he claimed in his *Los Angeles Times* letter, is for the nation to rededicate itself to the principles of the Declaration: "each individual American citizen, whatever his color, ethnic origin, or religion, should be judged—in the market place and elsewhere—on his merits as an individual." *How* such rededication is to be accomplished, how bad opinions mingled with bad motives may be changed into good ones, is the great challenge of democratic government that Lincoln's Lyceum Address grapples with.

Even in his first Lincoln book, Jaffa recognizes that Lincoln's prophetic role of bringing the American people to a higher faith in equality could supply only part of what is necessary to make constitutionalism work. As we will discuss in the section below on the 1842 Temperance Address, republican government always combines elements of passion, faith, and reason. Lincoln sought to establish a political religion that would instill a reverence for our constitutional "temple of liberty" (the only religious establishment Jefferson would favor, perhaps). Like a catechism to be memorized first and examined later, it should extend even to the "lisping babe." Yet Lincoln concludes the same speech by insisting that only "cold, calculating, unimpassioned reason" can preserve the republic. Jaffa cites *Federalist No. 49* to remind us that reverence for the laws "would not be necessary were men able to be governed by the voice of enlightened reason alone."

There is an eternal "antagonism" and "irreconcilability" in human nature between passion and reason and thus a tension in both individual and political self-government. (One is reminded here of the persistent anti-utopianism that runs through of all of Jaffa's work.) We may observe, he notes, that there cannot be "reverence without reason" or "reason without reverence." Neither is "politically true or viable without the other."[27]

JEFFERSON'S ARISTOI LETTER (THE PROBLEM OF WISDOM)

If the Lyceum Address showed how anarchy and lawlessness threaten republican liberty, this section might be said to focus on a nearly opposite problem: an excess of legalistic authority, or rather, illegitimate claims to authority. This is not the despotism of the populist demagogue but a tyranny of a different sort. Jaffa's understanding of this problem turns on the proper meaning of aristocracy in a republic of natural rights.

In the modern world, the interrelated concepts of equality, consent, and social compact form the core of legitimate government in large part because of the peculiar problem created by Christianity and the crisis in political obligation arising from the end of the ancient city. For the classics, however, the permanent problem of political life centered on the question of how to approximate, in practice, the theoretical standard of the rule of the wise. This question does not disappear in America—indeed, it remains central. But it takes on a different dimension. Jaffa nearly always discussed this issue with reference to Thomas Jefferson's "aristoi" letter.

Between the rancorous election of 1800 and the day they both died, on the nation's fiftieth Independence Day, Thomas Jefferson and John Adams repaired an old but broken friendship. During this time, they exchanged some of the most erudite correspondence in the English language. The letter Jaffa found most significant is surely the one written by Jefferson to Adams on October 28, 1813. Intermingled with commentary on Pythagorean philosophy (with passages from Theognis written out in ancient Greek, along with Jefferson's own translations), there is a memorable discussion of what the author of the Declaration of Independence did *not* mean by equality.

> For I agree with you that there is a natural aristocracy among men. The grounds of this are virtue and talents.... There is also an artificial aristocracy founded on wealth and birth, without either virtue or talents; for with these it would belong to the first class. The natural aristocracy I consider as the most precious gift of nature for the instruction, the trusts, and government of society. And indeed it would have been inconsistent in creation to have formed man for the social state, and not to have provided virtue and wisdom enough to manage the concerns of the society. May we not even say that that form of government is the best which provides the most effectually for a pure selection of these natural *aristoi* into the offices of government? The artificial aristocracy is a mischievous ingredient in government, and provision should be made to prevent its ascendancy.... I think the best remedy is exactly that provided by all our constitutions, to leave to the citizens the free election and separation of the *aristoi* from the pseudo-*aristoi*, of the wheat from the chaff.[28]

Jaffa was especially fond of these passages because of the clear connection they establish with classical thought. For that very reason, Strauss directly quotes these same lines in the center of his essay "On Classical Political Philosophy," which Jaffa regarded as having "unsurpassed authority in the Strauss canon."[29]

The *aristoi* letter was written toward the end of Jefferson's life. But the distinction between natural and artificial (or legitimate and illegitimate) aristocracy had concerned him since his younger days as a hot-headed revolutionary. "The rule of kings and priests, whose claims were without merit, aroused Jefferson's greatest indignation," Jaffa writes in his 2009 response to Professor Kraynak. "Divine right monarchy, supporting and supported by a class system of inherited wealth and birth, constituted the negation of aristocracy, as understood by classical political philosophy no less than by Jefferson."[30] As with Jefferson, we find that this a persistent theme Jaffa returns to often. More than twenty years earlier, in his crucial essay "Equality, Liberty, Wisdom, Morality and Consent in the Idea of Political Freedom," Jaffa argued that the founders were entirely consistent with the classical philosophers about who should rule:

> Is not government, like all the arts by which human life is benefited, itself benefited by being conducted by the wise and the good? Is it not best conducted, in the words of the 10th *Federalist*, by those whose "wisdom may best discern the true interests of their country …[?]" Is not the fact that man is the rational animal reason to place in authority—to use one of Locke's favorite phrases—"the rational and industrious?" The answer to all these questions is of course an emphatic affirmative.[31]

Jaffa repeatedly quoted this and other passages demonstrating the founders' attachment to classical virtue, moral education, and natural hierarchy—not to mention their pledge in the Declaration of their lives, fortunes, and sacred honor. Nevertheless, he found himself arguing almost constantly against the idea that equal natural rights must mean egalitarian levelling. But as he explains in his response to Kraynak, "there is no impediment to the rule of the *aristoi* arising from the equality proclaimed in the Declaration of Independence." Lincoln states in his debate with Douglas at Alton that the founders "did not mean to declare all men equal *in all respects.* They did not mean to say all were equal in color, size, intellect, moral developments, or social capacity." In fact, they "defined with tolerable distinctness, in what respects they did consider all men created equal"—namely, "equal in 'certain inalienable rights, among which are life, liberty, and the pursuit of happiness.'" [Emphasis Lincoln's.][32]

It is this political equality, Jaffa explains, that "becomes the means whereby the people may distinguish the pseudo-aristoi from the real ones."

> The non-aristoi, who in the Jeffersonian republic will have full participation in the electoral process, will have the same interest in choosing real aristocrats to govern, as the layman has in choosing real doctors rather than quacks. For Jefferson, as for Strauss, the means for preventing quacks from taking over the government was education.

Such a classical education—of the kind Jefferson painstakingly planned for the University of Virginia, of which he was the proud founder—"would assist the people in a democracy to recognize their true representatives, and defeat the plots of the scoundrels posing as aristocrats."[33] Unfortunately, this intention for liberal education failed to achieve its intended purpose. On the contrary, higher education today seems dedicated to precisely the opposite goal.

Previous chapters have discussed in some detail the modern administrative state and its baleful effects on republican liberty and self-government. What is noteworthy in the present context is how closely it tracks with Jaffa's more extended analysis of how pseudo-aristocracy can merge with pseudo-philosophy. Here we must note a pivotal distinction between the superior knowledge of representatives freely chosen by the people and those who assert their own superiority as a claim to rule. (Consider the difference between submitting to the advice of a doctor you have chosen, versus having your medical decisions made by healthcare experts appointed by others.) The bureaucratic government implemented by progressivism stakes its legitimacy on a form of specialized expertise derived from professional academic training in the social sciences. This is essentially a claim to the direct and unfettered rule of wisdom.

The absolute rule of the wise *seems* to be the argument made by the classical philosophers (such, at least, is what some Straussians claim). Yet, as Jaffa points out, Strauss himself appears to undercut this argument. In *Natural Right and History*, he writes:

> The few wise cannot rule the many unwise by force [and] the ability of the wise to persuade the unwise is extremely limited.... Therefore it is extremely unlikely that the conditions required for the rule of the wise will ever be met.[34]

Jaffa quotes this passage in a letter to Shadia Drury and adds in his own name that the "absolute rule of the wise is then a theoretical premise, necessary for our understanding of the problem of wise or just rule, but in no sense a practical conclusion." Further, he notes, Strauss warns against those who would assert this claim. Quoting again from *Natural Right and History*: "What is more likely to happen is that an unwise man, appealing to the natural right of wisdom and catering to the lowest desires of the many, will persuade the multitude of his right." For that reason, writes Strauss, tyranny is in fact the more likely outcome. "This being the case, the natural right of the wise must be questioned, and the indispensable requirement for wisdom must be qualified by the requirement for consent." Therefore, Jaffa concludes—with a line he repeated often to his students—"anyone who advances the claims of wisdom as a ground for ruling must be an unwise adventurer, discredited in advance by the fact that he has advanced such claims." From this perspective, the expertise invoked by those who seek to replace consent and the rule of law with administrative fiat is illegitimate in every way.[35]

The "virtue and talents" that belong to the natural aristocracy certainly include *practical* wisdom. But this quality serves rather than overrides consent, for as Jefferson's letter notes, it is by the citizens' "free election" that the "separation of the *aristoi* from the pseudo-*aristoi*" will be accomplished. It is not the theoretical or abstract learning of intellectuals, and certainly not technical expertise, that characterize this class of upright, responsible citizens, who are (we now perceive) those self-same moral gentlemen who Aristotle said must form the rulers of any decent regime.[36] A final word, then, is in order, before moving on to the next section, about how to cultivate this class of laudable men and women.

No regime can depend, in any regular way, on the rare philosophic statesman such as Lincoln who does not crave honor but "who prefers even to the voice of his country-men the approving voice heard only by himself, 'Well done, thou good and faithful servant.'"[37] Even a figure as great as Washington was extremely conscious of personal slights and welcomed the esteem of his compatriots. Jaffa notes that "Washington and Jefferson might have stood high in the service of King George III, as Moses might have continued to do in the service of Pharaoh." Instead, they took enormous risks for the cause of independence. If a republic cannot depend on a Lincoln every generation, it must at least have at some decent intervals statesmen who rise above the class of moral gentlemen who possess civic virtue. Yet for such supremely competent individuals, who could succeed in almost any endeavor, the rewards of public service are uncertain while the costs are often incalculable.

> All the weary experience of the past is against such men; the boundlessness of the infamy which surrounds the prospect of failure on their lonely pinnacles of largely unshared responsibility is unimaginably terrible. They…must bear the reproaches of those who yearn for the fleshpots of Egypt or watch the summer soldiers depart as winter closes over Valley Forge.

The man who joins these ranks, Jaffa adds, "alone knows what it is to affirm its value while all the alternatives he has rejected crowd around him, beckoning him from the uncharted voyage to the easier, safer, and conventional paths."[38]

Consider then, the lawless destruction and defilement of our national monuments and statues that occurred through the tumultuous year of 2020. The full implications of this assault on American civic piety and the feckless response of our political leaders have yet to be reckoned. For those pained by these dishonors, it is perhaps some consolation to recall Aristotle's observation in the *Ethics* that common men of low virtue express contempt at random.[39] Or consider the remark of H. H. Asquith who, when asked why the dislike of Churchill was so general, replied, "It is the envy with which mediocrity always views genius."[40] Yet there seems to be little hope for cultivating heroism in a world ruled overwhelmingly by Falstaff's catechism: "What is honor? A word.…What is that 'honor'? Air."

The belief in the natural *aristoi*, Jaffa says, unites Jefferson and Strauss, Locke and Aristotle. Finding such moral gentlemen and potential statesmen, he adds, "providing for their education, and discovering the ways and means in particular circumstances to maximize their influence, is the task of political philosophy, whether in the ancient or modern world."[41] Yet this well-nigh impossible task will lose even a glimmer of hope unless the American people reverse the attempt to obliterate the nation's history and make clear that sacred honor is not held in contempt.

LINCOLN'S TEMPERANCE ADDRESS (THE PROBLEM OF FANATICISM)

The occasion of this 1842 speech, delivered in the Second Presbyterian Church of Springfield, Illinois, was the 110th anniversary of George Washington's birth (February 22). The date was significant for the audience, largely made up of reformed alcoholics and members of the Washingtonian Society, a relatively new organization that sought to encourage sobriety through a greater emphasis on moral encouragement and comradery. "Like the Lyceum speech, the Temperance Address had its occasion in contemporary political developments," Jaffa observes. "When Lincoln delivered it, it would have been difficult to say whether temperance or slavery would be the dominating vote producing question of the years just ahead."[42]

Lincoln's address is complex and artfully composed, even more so than the Lyceum Address; Jaffa calls it a "literary masterpiece." With unexpected turns, surprising and even puzzling assertions, and theoretical subtlety alternating with heavy irony, the speech defies easy summation. The chapter devoted to it in *Crisis* states, "Lincoln discoursed on a theme that had taxed the wisest heads of Athens and Jerusalem.... [Its] real subject is the difference between the wrong and right way of effecting *any* moral reform in society."[43] Many commentators have noted how the speech weaves together insights on temptation, religious orthodoxy, persuasion versus condemnation, and the differences and similarities between compassion, tolerance, and friendship. Indeed, the proper understanding of these last three ideas captures what Lincoln (at least in Jaffa's estimation) held to be the speech's most important lesson. In addition, there are profound philosophical and theological inquiries into human nature, the metaphysics of cause and effect, necessity and choice, and even that greatest of all questions: What is God? If that were not enough, Jaffa's interpretation is as intricate and wide-ranging as the speech itself.[44] We can do no more here than touch briefly on one or two key themes.

This section will focus on one broad issue that, again, has practical relevance today. The Lyceum Address, recall, warns about populist or majoritarian movements that disregard the rule of law and the common good (and thereby open the door to demagogic tyrants). Jefferson's letter on aristocracy addresses false claims to wisdom and the importance of moral gentlemen. The Temperance Address adds to this list of dangers a different kind of lawlessness, not from the anarchy of mobs but the fanaticism of zealots.

What made the Washingtonian Society distinctive was that it rejected what Lincoln called the "thundering tones of anathema and denunciation," by which drunks had previously been condemned as irredeemable sinners worthy only of contempt and ostracism. Jaffa describes this as "the Pharisaical Christianity of the old school."[45] Of course, some "morally abominable" acts *do* deserve unremitting censure. But drunkenness is not in this category. Moral reform in a democracy turns on the ability to distinguish what can never be acceptable in decent society from the flawed (but not evil) missteps of an erring brother. The latter requires not denunciation but encouragement and persuasion.

This might not at first appear to be a great difficulty, but as Jaffa points out in his interpretation, there can be a strange moral inversion between the failings of certain sinners and the sanctimonious condemnation of those who are not tempted by *that* sin. Some self-appointed reformers, Jaffa observes, may "derive pleasure not so much from the sense of their own salvation as from that of the damnation of others." Here we come to the central difficulty. Self-government requires a fairly high level of moral probity, which Lincoln and the founders generally thought depended on religious faith. But this very necessity, Jaffa argues, may give rise to "the most dangerous of all political types":

the ascetic reformer whose underlying motivation is perverted sensuality. It is the Angelo of Shakespeare's *Measure for Measure* [who] insists upon creating a new Jerusalem upon earth, if necessary by removing from the world all who cannot live by their criterion of saintliness.... It is an illicit passion, masked by an intellectual error as a passion for justice. The pleasure that such men derive from the odor of their own sanctity, while it may make them proof against ordinary vices, also makes them capable of extraordinary crimes.[46]

It is the zealots who preen themselves on castigating sins of the flesh who are not only sinners themselves but perhaps the greater sinners, for real temperance "is far more a virtue of the appetites of the mind than of those of the body," Jaffa observes. Temperance "has more to do with the control of one's thoughts, or the expression of those thoughts, than with the control of one's thirst."[47] The fanatical "ascetic reformer" is, then, the greater threat to republican government because patriotism depends on "civic friendship." Only with such friendship can "human beings who do not know each other" come to see "in each other sharers in a common heritage." Aristotle, Jaffa reminds us, "wisely says that friendship is better than justice, and that legislators attempt to provide for it even more than they do justice." For this reason, the recognition of our common human nature "means recognition of its defects—or limitations—as well as its capacity to transcend those limitations by virtue and friendship."[48]

As with the problem of lawless mobs, many readers may recognize this phenomenon of righteous zealots, hurling "anathema and denunciation," against those who do not meet the latest criteria of saintliness. Of course, today's irredeemable sins are those phobias and -*isms* at the heart of identity politics. Jaffa saw this coming in an essay he wrote about the early outbursts of political correctness in the late 1980s and early 90s:

"Racism" is the generic term for...any opinions not considered politically correct. To point out the contradiction in these demands—or indeed of any demands made by the politically correct—is to bring on the accusations of "logism," which means the use of reason, a vice held characteristic of "Eurocentrism."

In the vocabulary of political correctness, "racism" has nothing to do with what once was called race prejudice—an unreasonable depreciation of other human beings because of their race, color, or ethnic origin. The charge of "racism" is made by the very people demanding racial quotas, race norming, and segregated racial and ethnic centers.[49]

If Jaffa seems prescient with these words written in 1991 (just replace *logism* with *privilege*), consider how he ends this chapter of *Crisis*, published in 1959. The nineteenth century, he observes, would come to be "gripped by the idea of progress." This "dangerous delusion" assumed "the upward direction of social change was assured" and (quoting a line from Shakespeare by which Macbeth justifies his wicked plans) "would ever trammel up the consequences of evil means." In the Temperance Address, Jaffa concludes, we see "a diagnosis of the totalitarian impulse within the heart of modern egalitarianism of surpassing brilliance."[50]

This impulse, glimpsed in Lincoln's prescient analysis, lies at the heart of the current struggle over Western civilization and brings us to the final section of this chapter.

CHURCHILLIAN MAGNANIMITY
(MODERN IDEOLOGY AND THE PRESENT CRISIS)

Both Jaffa and Leo Strauss regarded Winston Churchill as the greatest statesman of the twentieth century. Churchill's supreme enemy, Adolf Hitler, would then be the greatest tyrant of the century. Yet the spirit of "modern egalitarianism" is nearly opposite of the threat posed by Hitler's Germany. What could be more antithetical to the egalitarian spirit than the imperialism and militarism of the Aryan state and the horrors of the concentration camps in which supposedly inferior races and other undesirables were exterminated? Whether this difference is more apparent than real, we will consider in a moment.

Churchill identified the Nazi menace early on and never wavered in excoriating that "power, which spurns Christian ethics, which cheers its onward course by a barbarous paganism, which vaunts the spirit of aggression and conquest." Not only aggressive but also wicked, Nazism "derives strength and perverted pleasure from persecution, and uses, as we have seen, with pitiless brutality the threat of murderous force."[51]

History has not been kind to the experts, the diplomats, and the social scientists who denied or downplayed the Nazi peril. Jaffa observes that in the 1930s, when "Winston Churchill called Hitler 'that bad man,' the sophisticates in the universities fell out of their chairs laughing at him for failing to realize that he had, without knowing it, committed a 'value judgment.'"[52] Yet even getting the English-speaking peoples to see Hitler's iniquity was only part of his great effort, for Churchill also needed to bring into effect that concerted action necessary to defeat the German military machine. As with the crisis in the United States in 1860, Churchill seemed to believe that the confrontation with Hitler meant Europe would become either all free or all slave.

It was not merely the clarity of his insight or the power of his rhetoric but also his ruthless determination that Jaffa considered essential to Churchill's greatness. Writing in the *CRB* in 2001, he argued that Churchill, almost alone at first, understood that "Hitler could not be appeased."

> He was a bloodthirsty tyrant who had to be overthrown from within, or defeated from without. By continually making conces-

sions in the interest of peace, the appeasers only made the war, when it came, more difficult and costly. The imbecility of the democracies in dealing with Hitler was rooted in their inability to see his regime for what it was. There was no diplomatic solution to the problem presented by Hitler.... The problem of Hitler could be resolved only by the destruction of Hitler.[53]

Statesmanship entails a hard-to-define mixture of intransigence and prudence. Or rather, the prudence of the statesman includes knowing when to be intransigent and when to seek accommodation or even appeasement (which may be the right option in some cases). In classical political philosophy, the statesman concerns himself with the common good of the political community, which encompasses all other communities. The political man par excellence therefore seeks the greatest of all practical goods. And because practical wisdom, or prudence, includes and directs all the moral virtues, the highest form of statesmanship achieves a crowning excellence: Aristotle's megalopsuchia. In the modern world, this form of moral excellence is still essential, yet any statesman today also faces additional complications.

The possibility that magnanimous statesmanship could still be possible in the modern world was a matter of the utmost significance for Jaffa. The young Churchill himself had some doubts on this score. In the 1920s, while Martin Heidegger was laboring to produce his magnum opus, *Being and Time*, Winston Churchill was exploring a similar theme, though with a very different temperament. In several essays, which he assembled in a volume called *Thoughts and Adventures*, Churchill predicted some of the most salient features of our current state, including mankind's recently acquired ability (thanks to technology) to destroy itself:

> Mankind has never been in this position before. Without having improved appreciably in virtue or enjoying wiser guidance, it has got into its hands for the first time the tools by which it can

unfailingly accomplish its own extermination.... Death stands at attention, obedient, expectant, ready to serve, ready to shear away the peoples *en masse*; ready, if called on, to pulverize, without hope of repair, what is left of civilization.[54]

But the destructive capacities of modern technology are not limited to the physical world. The spiritual dimension, the effect on what used to be called virtue, is perhaps even more significant.

In barbarous times superior martial virtues—physical strength, courage, skill, discipline—were required to secure such a supremacy; and in the hard evolution of mankind the best and fittest stocks came to the fore. But no such saving guarantee exists today. There is no reason why a base, degenerate, immoral race should not make an enemy far above them in quality, the prostrate subject of their caprice or tyranny, simply because they happened to be possessed at a given moment of some new death-dealing or terror-working process and were ruthless in its employment. The liberties of men are no longer to be guarded by their natural qualities, but by their dodges; and superior virtue and valour may fall an easy prey to the latest diabolical trick.[55]

The most oppressive feature of our time is the way "our affairs [are] increasingly being settled by mass processes." The individual seems lost amid vast, impersonal forces of modern life. "We have long seen the old family business, where the master was in direct personal touch with his workmen, swept out of existence or absorbed by powerful companies, which in their turn are swallowed by mammoth trusts." He notes that newspapers (we can substitute social media) "do an immense amount of thinking for the average man and woman. In fact they supply them with such a continuous stream of standardized opinion...that there is neither the need nor the leisure for personal reflection." Anticipating the radical left's new infatuation with defacing, destroying, or removing statues and monuments, Churchill asks, "Can modern communities do without great men?" In general, he notes, we "see a restlessness around us. . . . There is a sense of vacancy and of fatuity, of incompleteness."[56]

Jaffa discusses these observations in a 1975 lecture "Can There Be Another Winston Churchill?" (published in his 1981 book, *Statesmanship*). He seems to share Churchill's apprehension that "individuals are increasingly submerged by the giant scale upon which modern life is increasingly organized," characterized by "mass communications, large corporations, the standardization of production and consumption." In this, Jaffa argues, Churchill agrees with Lincoln and the American founders, who also opposed the egalitarian homogenization of society. Yet Churchill's own adventures, as it were, contradicted his thoughts. As Jaffa observes, his "willfulness, his stubbornness, his refusal to take counsel against his own sense of the fitness of things—his preference, so to speak, to being shamed before the world rather than to be ashamed of himself—in the end served him better than he knew." When the confrontation with Germany became inevitable in 1940, Churchill "was the only man the country would trust to see it through."[57]

In a letter that Leo Strauss wrote to his friend Karl Löwith immediately after World War II, Strauss says, "I know from my experience how incomprehensible and foreign Aristotle's concept of *megalopsuchia* was to me originally and that *now* I not only theoretically but also practically approve of it." Jaffa regarded this as an astounding statement by itself. Perhaps even more remarkable, Strauss goes on to say, "A man like Churchill proves that the possibility of *megalopsuchia* exists today *exactly* as it did in the 5th century B.C."[58] Somewhat in the spirit of Jefferson's 1826 letter, Strauss seemed to believe that the political world can provide access to or confirmation of theoretical insights that are not available in books. For Jaffa, this further confirmed that Strauss's distinction between ancients and moderns was a distinction in the *history* of political philosophy and not within philosophy itself, still less a distinction within the nature of politics or human nature.

In a 1984 essay, Jaffa writes that Strauss "knew that…the great-souled man was not only possible but actual." This recognition of "Churchill as the embodiment of *megalopsuchia*" is decisively important, "theoretically no less than practically." Within the anti-Machiavellian political science that Strauss launched and Jaffa carried forward, men like Lincoln and Churchill are "decisive for establishing the importance of the moral and political phenomena as the theoretical, no less than the practical, ground of philosophic wisdom." Again, Jaffa insists that political philosophy must begin with the perspective of the citizen, with the anti-deterministic and anti-historicist recognition that, as Strauss remarked "there are phenomena which are simply irreducible to their conditions."[59]

In one of his first close examinations of a classical text, while the rubble of World War II was still smoldering, Strauss embarked on a study of Xenophon's compact and neglected dialogue *Hiero, or Tyrannicus* (typically called *On Tyranny* in English; the dual title is Xenophon's.) In the introduction to his interpretative essay, published in 1948, Strauss remarks that modern tyranny poses a threat unknown to the ancients. Seeking not merely the rule of men but the "conquest of nature," including human nature, modern tyranny threatens to become "what no earlier tyranny ever became: perpetual and universal."[60] This ambition is related to or even derives from "an essential difference between the tyranny analyzed by the classics and that of our age." Modern tyranny "has at its disposal 'technology' as well as 'ideologies,'" and this "appalling" complication impels us, Strauss explains, to understand in a fresh way "the elementary and unobtrusive conditions of human freedom."[61] This lesson that Jaffa learned from his teacher led him to conclude that Churchill "was the supreme enemy of Hitler because in the decisive respects he was not touched by modern philosophy."[62]

Untouched by modern philosophy, however, certainly does not mean oblivious to theoretical insights, nor does it mean unthinking or unthoughtful. In his remarks about the two men he regarded as the greatest statesmen of the modern world, Jaffa again returns to his subtle and ambiguous distinction between practical and intellectual wisdom. In a letter to a friend in 1975, Jaffa explains, "I think that the contemplative life is better than the active life; but this proposition is reflected in the lives of the great men of action no less than in the great thinkers." His models of statesmanship, Lincoln and Churchill, "were great men of action, yet they were also far more, and more deeply, contemplative than many (or most, or all) of the supposed thinkers of their times." Indeed, we should not assume "that they would have been more contemplative had they not followed paths of action. Action may have stimulated them to think more deeply than they might otherwise have done."[63]

Even more than his teacher's remarkable letter to Löwith in 1946, Jaffa was influenced by—and frequently quoted from—the eulogy to Churchill that Strauss delivered in class in 1965, the day after the British statesman's death.[64] (Jaffa reprints the remarks in their entirety as the epigraph to his *Statesmanship* book.) Because of the intrinsic worth of this statement by Strauss and its great importance to Jaffa, we quote the eulogy in full:

> The death of Churchill is a healthy reminder to academic students of political science of their limitations, the limitations of their craft.
>
> The tyrant stood at the pinnacle of his power. The contrast between the indomitable and magnanimous statesman and the

insane tyrant—this spectacle in its clear simplicity was one of the greatest lessons which men can learn, at any time.

No less enlightening is the lesson conveyed by Churchill's failure which is too great to be called tragedy. I mean the fact that Churchill's heroic action on behalf of human freedom against Hitler only contributed, through no fault of Churchill's, to increase the threat to freedom which is posed by Stalin or his successors. Churchill did the utmost that a man could do to counter that threat—publicly and most visibly in Greece and in Fulton, Missouri. Not a whit less important than his deeds and speeches are his writings, above all his *Marlborough*—the greatest historical work written in our century, an inexhaustible mine of political wisdom and understanding, which should be required reading for every student of political science.

The death of Churchill reminds us of the limitations of our craft, and therewith of our duty. We have no higher duty, and no more pressing duty, than to remind ourselves and our students, of political greatness, human greatness, of the peaks of human excellence. For we are supposed to train ourselves and others in seeing things as they are, and this means above all in seeing their greatness and their misery, their excellence and their vileness, their nobility and their baseness, and therefore never to mistake mediocrity, however brilliant, for true greatness. In our age this duty demands of us in the first place that we liberate ourselves from the supposition that value statements cannot be factual statements.[65]

As an expression of political insight, Jaffa regarded this statement as rivaling the Declaration of Independence and the Gettysburg Address in its compact wisdom. In his exchange with Pangle in the *CRB*, Jaffa provides an almost line-by-line exegesis of this eulogy. In particular, he sees the allusions to failure and tragedy, and the references to "the limitation of our craft," as reminders that the "ground of the moral and political life is the distinction between noble failure and base success." The "spectacle" of Churchill, in which Strauss finds such a great lesson, "teaches how to act: that we should not submit to evil."[66]

This belief or faith in our freedom of action, however, is rejected by the modern scientific project: the technical mastery of those physical laws that govern all material objects and which would subsume human conduct within a mechanistic order. Here we come to that other "threat to freedom" Strauss mentions in his eulogy, the one "posed by Stalin or his successors" and described by Marx as dialectical materialism. In 1965, when Churchill died, that threat was very great. Today, the Soviet Union is gone, but the deepest roots of its ideology are perhaps as strong as ever.

Among the "successors" to Stalin, Strauss certainly had in mind the powerful French bureaucrat and influential neo-Hegelian intellectual Alexandre Kojève. Strauss and Kojève carried on a remarkable correspondence from the early 1930s through the mid-60s. Many of their most interesting exchanges centered on Strauss's interpretation of Xenophon's *On Tyranny*. Jaffa remarks that this debate on natural right and history "may very well be the greatest intellectual confrontation of the last century, at least."[67]

Strauss's debate with Kojève focused on the latter's aspiration for implementing Hegel's vision of a world state, which he did not hesitate to describe as a tyranny. On the surface, this would seem to have little in common with the Nazi ambition for a thousand-year Reich. Yet Jaffa (who was hardly alone in this opinion) saw the two great totalitarian regimes of the twentieth century as mirror images. Churchill's democratic statesmanship, not to mention American constitutionalism, stood equally opposed to race struggle and class struggle; both attempt to replace nature with history. As threats to the survival of liberal democracy, Jaffa saw no significant difference "between the paths marked out by Hegel (and Marx and Kojève), and those of Nietzsche and Heidegger."[68]

What is the relevance of all that to our present crisis?

Today, American politics seems to be consumed with a new variant on the old obsession with race. Yet that movement is allied with and at least partly driven by a deeper theoretical project that rejects constitutionalism and that, Jaffa argues, would "turn over the application of power to a highly trained bureaucracy." Such an elite "would bring scientific method to bear upon the problems of society. Science and democracy would march in lockstep."[69] This attempt to complete the modern conquest of nature and chance implies something very much like Kojève's final progressive utopia. Extended, as it logically must be, to all of humanity, this would become the world-homogenous state.

By definition, the final world state means the end of politics (because there is nothing left to argue about) and the end of moral virtue (because we would have no unfulfilled desires). In that dystopia, wisdom and consent merge, and rational administration takes the place of deliberation and habit. There is a single claim to rule and a single regime. By removing any conflicting accounts or claims about justice, the openness to (or even awareness of) natural right disappears. The distinction between nature and convention disappears. Everyone will look different but think alike. Philosophy becomes superfluous and then subversive and finally impossible. When wisdom has in principle been achieved, there is no whole beyond the whole embodied in the global order. The world homogenous state is the cosmos; it is everything that exists at the level of human comprehension and significance. Natural science may continue to find new details about the physical world and may even gild the lily of comfortable self-preservation. But there is nothing that will alter the meaning or purpose of human life. Moral virtue and intellectual virtue are eclipsed in the same way and for the same reason.

Where does that vision stand today? Despite the defeat of the Soviet Union, we seem in some ways closer to this condition than when Churchill died in 1965. Yet Jaffa did not think we were helpless in the face of this threat. In his 1990 essay "The American Founding as Best Regime," he returns to the argument that "we are faced with an unprecedented threat to the survival of biblical religion, of autonomous human reason, and to the form and substance of political freedom." These are not separate problems; "the threat to one of these is also the threat to all. It is above all important to understand why this threat is, above all, an internal one, mining and sapping our ancient faith, both in God and in ourselves."[70]

That was written in 1990. One is forced to wonder whether Jaffa's warnings fell not merely on the deaf but also the blind and the dumb. The intervening thirty years have seen no surcease in the mining and sapping of our civic piety. Perhaps the only rational course now is to give in.

That certainly was the advice many rational men offered to Churchill in May of 1940, when Hitler dominated the continent of Europe and Britain's doom seemed certain. Appeasement or accommodation appeared to be the only sane choice. In response to that suggestion, Churchill declared during the war cabinet meeting of May 28, "I am convinced that every man of you would rise up and tear me down from my place if I were for one moment to contemplate parley or surrender." "If this long island story of ours is to end," Churchill continued, "let it end only when each of us lies choking in his own blood upon the ground."[71]

One reason Jaffa loved Strauss's eulogy of Churchill is because it drew a theoretical lesson from Churchill's stubborn trust in the possibility of victory, even in the face of apparently certain defeat. And if stubborn resistance failed, noble defeat would be preferable to ignoble surrender. In the introduction to the 1981 *Statesmanship* book he edited, Jaffa writes that "there is no metaphysical necessity dooming us to the loss of our freedom."

> At the root of the decline of Churchill's influence and Churchill's reputation in today's world are certain false but dominant opinions concerning the nature of man. These opinions are more congenial to and compatible with totalitarian tyranny than with constitutional freedom. The dominant modes in present-day scholarship in history, politics, and the social sciences are rooted in a belief that man's metaphysical freedom is a delusion.... From the denial of man's metaphysical freedom to the denial of any right to moral or political freedom, is but a short step.[72]

The defense of that metaphysical freedom draws inspiration from statesmen such as Churchill, hurling defiance across the English Channel. But few of us are, like Churchill, immune to the sophistries and confusions sown by modern skepticism. It may be that political philosophy has yet some role to play in supporting the determination of those moral gentlemen whose fortitude is weakened by doubt and uncertainty. In his "Best Regime" essay quoted above, Jaffa writes that the decline of the West "is the paramount reality facing us today." The most "immediate danger," however, "comes from the historical pessimism of those who counsel us that this is inevitable and that nothing can be done by taking thought." Despair, however, is not merely a sin but also an intellectual error. Fatalism, Jaffa continues, "is itself a danger only if we believe it." This moral weakness, therefore, can find a remedy in the intellectual refutation of the false "superstition." Our pessimism, both moral and intellectual, can be dispelled, and "with it, the unreasoning fears that it breeds."[73]

The courageous action demanded by our present crisis depends on prudence, for we must certainly know what end or purpose we hope to achieve through courageous action. Yet the very meaning of prudence presupposes that neither success nor failure is guaranteed. "Because human beings are free, there is a genuine indeterminacy in the nature of things," Jaffa argues. "No one can be certain that a wise action will have a good result," and even a brave action may fail, "as Aristotle long ago observed—but that is no excuse to play the coward."[74]

This chapter on political practice points, then, back to the discussion of theory. "Because we know we can think, we know we can think about right and wrong, good and evil," Jaffa wrote in his retirement speech from Claremont McKenna College. "We can understand what are our rights, and what are our duties. Understanding this, we understand that the fate of our civilization is yet in our hands, because it is in our minds."[75]

7

QUARRELS: NEOCONS AND PALEOCONS, THE STRAUSS WARS, ORIGINAL INTENT

The classics were fully aware of the essential weakness of
the mind of the individual. Hence their teaching about the
philosophic life is a teaching about friendship: the philosopher is as philosopher in need of friends....Friendship
is bound to lead to, or to consist in, the cultivation and
perpetuation of common prejudices by a closely knit
group of kindred spirits. It is therefore incompatible with
the idea of philosophy. The philosopher must leave the
closed and charmed circle of the "initiated" if he intends
to remain a philosopher. He must go out to the market place; the conflict with the political men cannot be
avoided. And this conflict by itself, to say nothing of its
cause or its effect, is a political action.

—LEO STRAUSS, *On Tyranny*

Even some of Jaffa's friends sometimes grew impatient with
what Thomas Pangle called his "ceaseless *logomachy*" (war of
words). But Jaffa's position was that verbal combat is usually
preferable to the other kind. Jaw-jaw, observed Churchill, is better than war-war.[1]

The whole point of the American experiment in liberty was to determine if mankind could replace bullets with ballots. Our constitutional polity, based on a voluntary social compact, presupposes the possibility of civic friendship. It presupposes that citizens will fight *for* each other rather than *with* each other. This is only possible, however, when the differences of opinion settled through elections are grounded in a deeper agreement. *E Pluribus Unum*, Jaffa wrote in a 1980 essay, refers "less obviously, but more profoundly, to the moral unity that underlies the moral diversity" of a pluralistic society. "By virtue of this moral unity, the American people are 'one nation, under God.' It is the antecedent moral unity that makes the political unity possible."[2] Jaffa often compared the task of political philosophy to the art of medicine and seemed to think that America was dying, in part from a steady diet of epicurean self-indulgence and nihilism. The restorative lay in the American people's understanding of and devotion to the "constitutionalism of our founding [that] is inseparable from its moral realism and its natural theology."[3]

Setting aside the issue of constitutional jurisprudence, most of Jaffa's battles, which are hardly settled today, can be divided into two camps. On the one hand are those self-described conservatives who want morality without nature. This faction comprises that significant portion of the right that disdains Enlightenment rationalism, even to the point of rejecting the Declaration of Independence and natural rights. Jaffa's second major front was directed against those Straussians who want nature without morality. They regard the Declaration as mere rhetoric, at best a vulgar "half-truth" that reflected and encouraged the levelling doctrines of modernity. The founders' prudence and rationalism, Jaffa thought, requires a defense from stolid traditionalists who have no use for natural rights theory *and* from the cloud-dwelling scholars who disdain political life "on the ground."

The traditionalist or paleoconservative wing of conservatism, which has its geographic and intellectual roots in the South, generally consists of freedom-loving patriots who cherish America and defend its moral-religious heritage, cultural integrity, and distinctive way of life. Today, their arguments can be found in publications such as *Chronicles* and *The Imaginative Conservative*. This group understands that moral standards, strong communities, and especially revealed faith are among the "great pillars of human happiness" and the "firmest props of the duties of men and citizens," as George Washington observed in his Farewell Address. Like Washington, Jaffa respected and cherished these "dispositions and habits" and even expressed deep respect for tradition.[4]

Yet in the same speech, Washington averred that public opinion should be "enlightened." This indicates both the possibility and the necessity of a rational faculty accessible to all intelligent beings. The paleoconservatives, however, have little interest in—and often actively oppose—any rational account or political theory of the founding, enlightened or otherwise. They prefer American nationalism on the grounds that we ought to love our country simply because it is ours. This is a healthy disposition, but not fully adequate. As an important side note, the paleoconservative resistance to equality and the Declaration (as dangerous abstractions) often manifests itself less as an aversion to Jefferson and more as a deep antipathy to Lincoln. Garry Wills—whose 1978 *Inventing America* and 1992 *Lincoln at Gettysburg* were excoriated by Jaffa—claimed that the Gettysburg Address was a "giant swindle" because Lincoln's emphasis on human equality amounted to "a startling new interpretation" of the founding.[5]

Jaffa argued that the paleoconservatives and traditionalists could not supply a theoretical defense of the regime because they are, in a certain sense, "pre-Socratic." While he completely agreed that every decent society needs an authoritative tradition, Jaffa had learned from Socrates that not all traditions are equal.

Not only are many ancient practices barbaric, but the traditions themselves often conflict. That is why, in the fifth century BC, Socrates first articulated the principle of natural right in response to the inadequacy of conventionalism and positivism. Today's paleoconservatives have never really absorbed this lesson. When confronted by people who adhere to different authoritative customs or different values, the defenders of tradition and convention have no objective ground on which to settle disputes, which leaves only recourse to force. This is the crisis into which the United States is now descending.

Even conservatives who don't consider themselves opposed to the Declaration of Independence tend to be (Jaffa thought) ignorant of or alienated from its principles, along with the principles of the founding generally. Therefore, this problem regarding the ground of political justice afflicts the whole conservative establishment. His attempt to remedy this defect and prevent the crisis we now face was arguably the entire purpose of his political project.

The Straussians, immersed in classical philosophy, understand perfectly well the shortcomings of conventionalism. They defend with great erudition and subtlety the philosophic discovery of natural right. But for many of them, this is a merely abstract theorizing and textual analysis. They interpret the permanent tension between philosophy and the city to mean that the philosopher always transcends citizenship, standing above the crude moral-political disputes of the city. Jaffa thought this politically sterile conception of natural right provides no support for the patriotic spirit of actual citizens. Of course, philosophy as such need not be political: metaphysics, mathematics, and natural science can be—and indeed are—worthy pursuits. Yet Strauss clearly eschewed these subjects, and his students claim that they are following their teacher's interest in *political* philosophy.

Specific examples of these arguments will be discussed below. For the moment we note that both camps undermine what Jaffa regarded as the necessary conditions of republican government.

When separated from nature, conventional justice lacks any permanent foundation. On the other hand, when separated from the moral concerns of the citizen, nature (or the philosophic study of nature) becomes barren. Jaffa put these points starkly in a letter to his student Paul Basinski. The Eastern Straussians, he wrote, think that moral virtue "is for fools" and that "the purpose of philosophy is to enable them to look down with contempt upon both politics and morality." On the other hand, the establishment conservatives "differ mainly in that they regard the conventions of morality to which they are attached (which might include slavery or Jim Crow or dumping on Jews) as sufficiently justified merely because they prefer them." Irrationally opposed to reason, they "detest the idea of a rational standard by which their prejudices might be judged."[6]

The last section of this chapter addresses the jurisprudence of legal positivism. In Jaffa's mind, this doctrine disastrously combines the failures of *both* the paleo-conventionalists and the apolitical academics.

The purpose of this book is not to present a hagiography of Jaffa nor to suggest that he was right about everything. It is important to note, therefore, that both of these broad disputes represent areas in which Jaffa changed his mind. His confrontation with the paleoconservatives—above all with Willmoore Kendall (whom Jaffa respected and liked)—led him to a deeper appreciation of how natural right must always be adapted to a particular regime, to a people with a particular character.[7]

His disputes with his fellow Straussians represent a different sort of change in his thinking. In that case, it was Jaffa's own internal doubts that prompted his "second sailing," leading him to depart from the original form of orthodox Straussianism (which he helped to develop) and leave behind many of his former colleagues. Several of them, Jaffa thought, also changed their positions but did so by embracing an even more radical form of the errors Jaffa wanted to correct.

Jaffa's most intense battles mostly occurred from the late 1970s through the 1980s, although intermittent sniper fire continued into the 1990s and even past 2000. These debates played an important role in determining the character of the conservative movement and indirectly the policy positions and rhetoric of the Republican Party. As Charles Kesler noted in *National Review* in 1979, "Conservatism presupposes that there is something worth conserving—but we can hardly know what to conserve without knowing what America is and what it stands for."[8]

Until the 1970s, Southern traditionalism was not quite the *only* form of self-conscious American conservatism, but it was the dominant strain. Thus, the disputes that Jaffa helped instigate had far-reaching effects. Of course, neither the movement nor the party went altogether in the direction Jaffa wanted. Hedonism and nihilism "are no more dominant among liberals than among conservatives," Jaffa wrote in a letter to AEI President Chris DeMuth in 1998. "Here is the cancer eating out the substance of western civilization. And, in the most important respect, AEI (like Heritage) is part of the problem, not of the solution."[9] Still, a good case might be made that things could have been worse. After Jaffa encouraged Buckley to move away from his early sympathies with the Southern nostalgia wing (a predilection he inherited from Kendall, his professor at Yale), Jaffa mostly complained that conservatism was *unprincipled* rather than committed to *bad* principles. Without his efforts, however, the movement might have remained in thrall to the egregious loyalties of neo-Confederatism and the medieval confessional state.

In any event, many of the specific policy issues—and, even more so, the specific individuals—are now mostly of antiquarian interest. The names of Walter Berns, Allan Bloom, Mel Bradford, Martin Diamond, Willmoore Kendall, Russell Kirk, Irving Kristol, and Garry Wills are still reasonably well-known today, at least among well-read conservatives. Younger readers, however, may have only vague notions of what positions any of those names represent. We will try to focus, therefore, on the principles rather than the personalities. In any event, space permits only a few representative selections. (Those interested in feuds, gossip, tales of academic intrigue, and professional backstabbing may consult the extensive Jaffa archives at Hillsdale, although there is much less of this than one might expect given Jaffa's reputation for irascibility.)

Incidentally, these fights didn't *always* consist of Jaffa alone, *contra mundum*. Many prominent conservatives argued with each other, independently of any quarrels with Jaffa. Still, he was if not perpetually then at least preponderantly in the thick of things, often mounting remonstrations in several directions at once. More than a few times, his colleagues and students recalled the joke about the figurative Irishman who enters a bar to find a ferocious brawl under way. "Is this a private fight," he asks the bartender, "or can anyone join in?"

LIBERALS AND EX-LIBERALS

Jaffa criticized the left all the time but rarely found it worth-while to argue with liberals.[10] In a letter to Stephen Balch (one of the founders of the National Association of Scholars), he wrote that we are "involved in a death struggle with the radical Left to control our universities." This fight had to be won, but Jaffa did not think most liberals could be persuaded. What was necessary and frequently difficult was to rally the right to the battle. "Our enemies are filled with moral zeal. They are filled with contempt—not altogether unreasonably—for those who have no other conviction than the conviction that one ought never to have convictions."[11] Still, in some cases Jaffa found it worthwhile to engage with a prominent intellectual or academic colleague on the left.

Some of these colloquies were in deadly earnest. In the early 1970s, Claremont McKenna College published an essay in its internal newsletter, *Res Publica*, that Jaffa saw as an explicit justification for Marxist guerilla insurrection written by, of all people, a professor of Christian ethics and the dean of the School of Theology in Claremont. The essay by Joseph Hough, according to Jaffa,

> was essentially an adaptation to the exigencies of liberation theology of Herbert Marcuse's *Repressive Tolerance*. Its thesis was that liberals should not be afraid of being considered illiberal, when it was necessary to adopt the rough methods sometimes required to bring about social change. When Hough published these sentiments, the utility of the bombings and the burnings in bringing about "liberation" in Claremont was fresh in everyone's minds. The true role of the churches [the essay argued] was that of a "social action ministry" which required "group decision and mobilization" of "cadres" of the committed.

According to Hough, Jaffa argued, "true liberalism...was to be found in resolute action, otherwise known as revolution." The newsletter refused to print Jaffa's rebuttal, so—as was his practice—he simply included it in his next collection of essays, in this case, *The Conditions of Freedom*. What was especially shocking to Jaffa was how eager the college seemed to reaffirm its limp response to the campus violence of just a few years earlier, when it had refused "to defend civil liberty, while submitting to gangsterism."[12]

More often, when Jaffa engaged directly with the left, it was to mock the mushy tolerance of someone who, as the poet Robert Frost said, is too broadminded to take his own side in an argument. An essay called "Looking at Mr. Goodlyfe" exposed what Jaffa regarded as the vacuous lessons of his colleague Steven Smith in a course called "Theories of the Good Life."[13] The course was featured in a 1979 article for another CMC publication, *Current*, in which Smith describes his teaching style as "values clarification" in a "personalized learning environment." He goes on to describe the therapeutic origins of the course in his own "personal crisis," which caused him to "cast about" for the meaning of life and to teach the course "not because I knew what the good life is, but because I needed to know."[14]

At this point in our study, the reader may already anticipate the glee and vigor with which Jaffa demolishes this piñata of liberal pieties. "Let me now disavow any wish or desire to intrude upon Professor Smith's privacy," Jaffa remarks. But since Smith himself mentioned it, Jaffa feels free to observe how it has "become almost obligatory, in some departments, to have had a 'personal crisis.'" Indeed, there are places "in which a young scholar would not even be considered for tenure unless he presented affidavits from three psychologists that he had had an 'existential' or 'identity' crisis." Jaffa goes on, as one might expect, to contrast Smith's nonjudgmental "facilitation" with the clear precepts by which Aristotle instructed his readers concerning virtue, friendship, and happiness.

Jaffa is having some sport here, but there is a serious reason why, as he says, "a busy scholar" such as himself would "waste such heavy ammunition upon something so trite and shallow" as this PR puff piece. Partly, he wishes to expose the fact that CMC claims to create future leaders and avers that if this is the education they are receiving, "then clearly our public life is doomed." What really bothers him is that the college where he works and which he even loves "lacks seriousness about the most serious things in the world." He then offers an apologia for his determination to challenge and improve, to the degree he can, Claremont McKenna, which may seem "too small and too insignificant" to change the world.

But political philosophy, like charity, also has its domestic duties. Socrates went about the streets of Athens, admonishing and exhorting his fellow Athenians, not because they were Athenians, but because they were his neighbors.... To subject the opinions of Americans—and even Claremonters—to the same kind of critique to which Socrates subjected the opinions of Athenians [seems] to lower the dignity of the discipline. But I think I am right and even Socratic in my procedure, and I shall persevere. If I cannot equal Socrates in other respects, I hope I shall not equal him in this respect either: that my critique comes too late.

Those are two of Jaffa's colleagues, but where are the public intellectuals mentioned earlier? Garry Wills, mentioned above, initially followed the political inclinations of his teacher, Willmoore Kendall, even writing for *National Review*, but later abandoned Kendall's conservative views. His 1978 book, *Inventing America*, certainly followed Kendall in attempting to read natural-rights individualism out of the founding. Wills, who had become at this point a quasi-liberal, tried to recast Jefferson as a communitarian whose thinking was dominated by the Scottish Enlightenment. The book made a big splash and was effusively praised across the political spectrum.

Jaffa argued that the author's political shift was more apparent than real because Wills's repugnance for classical rationalism revealed an "inner consistency between the Right and the Left."[15] He eviscerated the book in a long and devastating review, criticizing it for tendentious scholarship and declaring that it "should never have been published."[16]

Wills hates the very idea that the United States was born out a dedication to liberty and justice. For him, the belief that our political arrangements are in some particular sense in accordance with universal principles of natural right, breeds only a sense of self-righteousness, and makes us a danger to ourselves and others.[17]

Following Rousseau, Wills saw "rationalism" as the root of political evil, which helped to explain the praise of the book from such divergent sources. "The Rousseauian denigration of reason," Jaffa wrote, "is the core of nineteenth century romanticism, both in its Left phases (e.g. anarchism, syndicalism, socialism, communism), and its Right phases (e.g. monarchism, clericalism, feudalism, slavery)." It is on the basis of this shared commitment to romanticism that Wills rejected the natural rights philosophy of the Declaration and the Gettysburg Address, claiming that Lincoln "invented" a "fallacious myth about our origins as a nation."[18]

When Wills updated his arguments with his 1992 *Lincoln at Gettysburg*, Jaffa gave it only a brief review in *CRB* and later observed sardonically that Wills "received a Pulitzer Prize [for] repeating the 'giant swindle' charge of his old Yale professor," Willmoore Kendall. "Wills, however, in deference to his latter day left-wing constituency, called it a good swindle!"[19]

Whereas Wills had started as a conservative and moved to the Left, Jaffa's most prominent dispute in this arena was with a man famous for being a former liberal: Irving Kristol. Yet his fight with Kristol, the "godfather of the neoconservatives," turned on Jaffa's contention that Kristol—in moving to the right to launch a patriotic defense of America—had missed what most needed conserving.[20]

In his 1978 *How to Think About the American Revolution: A Bicentennial Cerebration*—which contains his principal skirmishes with Wills, Kristol, Mel Bradford, George Carey, Martin Diamond, and Willmoore Kendall—Jaffa notes that "Professor Irving Kristol has gained something of a national reputation in recent years as a spokesman for American conservatism." "No one," Jaffa continued, "it would seem, could be more orthodox in his regard for the wisdom of the founding fathers." It is with some dismay then that Jaffa discovers Kristol's actual writings on the founding to be similar in key respects to that of Richard Hofstadter, the scion of liberal historiography whom he vitu-

perates in *Crisis of the House Divided*. Hofstadter held that the
founders' political science had been rendered obsolete by history,
whereas Kristol purports to salvage the "practice" of the founding from its theoretical rhetoric. Jaffa sees this as "symptomatic"
of conservatism's "underlying agreement with the liberalism it
purports to attack."[21]

Though Jaffa's critique of Kristol was published in 1978, the
fusillade was first delivered in person during a legendary panel
discussion at the 1975 annual meeting of the American Political
Science Association (APSA). Kristol, then a professor at NYU,
was both the chairman and a discussant for a session with the
deceptively bland title "On American Political Thought." In its
typical fashion, the APSA had assigned this panel, with some of
the profession's most controversial and well-known scholars,
to an unusually small meeting room in the convention hotel,
the San Francisco Hilton. The audience was overflowing into
the hallway when Jaffa and Kristol waged a heated debate about
the meaning and significance of the founding.[22] Although the
program lists Jaffa's paper title as "Nullification Reconsidered:
Calhoun versus Madison, 1828–1832," the actual presentation was
a wide-ranging analysis of the American political tradition, with
stinging critiques of some of its most prominent interpreters.
In addition to Kristol, Jaffa launched several broadsides against
Martin Diamond, whom Jaffa had invited to the panel but who
had not (Jaffa thought) shown up. According to several of Jaffa's
students who were there, however, Diamond *did* attend, standing in the back of the room until the panel concluded and then
exiting quickly.[23]

What was Jaffa's complaint, exactly?

As mentioned in Chapter 3, the neoconservatives were liberals
who had moved rightward in response to the violent ideology of
the New Left in the late 1960s and early 70s. Some were trained
as social scientists and thought political questions could usefully

be examined with greater empirical rigor. Both of these considerations may have led to a certain wariness about "theory." Whether or not such considerations informed Kristol's thinking, here is what he said in a widely distributed Distinguished Lecture, part of a series commemorating the upcoming Bicentennial of the United States organized by the American Enterprise Institute:

> To begin at the beginning, the American Revolution was successful in that those who led it were able, in later years, to look back in tranquility at what they had wrought and to say that it was good. This was a revolution which, unlike all subsequent revolutions, did not devour its children: the men who made the revolution were the men who went on to create the new political order, who then held the highest elected positions in this order, and who all died in bed....Alone among the revolutions of modernity, the American Revolution did not give rise to the pathetic myth of "the revolution betrayed." It spawned no literature of disillusionment; it left behind no grand hopes frustrated, no grand expectations unsatisfied, no grand illusions shattered. Indeed, in one important respect the American Revolution was so successful as to be almost self-defeating: it turned the attention of thinking men away from politics, which now seemed utterly unproblematic, so that political theory lost its vigor, and even the political thought of the Founding Fathers was not seriously studied. This intellectual sloth, engendered by success, rendered us incompetent to explain this successful revolution to the world, and even to ourselves. The American political tradition became an inarticulate tradition.[24]

This is an extremely bold, even astounding, series of statements, and Jaffa did not shrink from responding with equal boldness. In the published version of his essay, Jaffa writes, "If there is any amnesia in this story of America after the Revolution, it is Professor Kristol's omission of the Civil War from their perspective in which he views the American past." The two wars constitute "the first and last acts of a single drama"; indeed they "comprehend the action of a tremendous world-historical tragedy." Jaffa observes that "in no other sequence of political events of which I know, did history and poetry so closely resemble each other. I would certainly agree with Professor Kristol that the outcome of the American Revolution was a success." That success, however, was not "the prosaic comedy of Professor Kristol's imagination." Rather, the "successful outcome resembled in the end far more that which we find at the end of Macbeth or Hamlet, when Scotland and Denmark are restored to political health by the pity and terror of a tragic consummation."[25]

In a later essay, reprising this debate, Jaffa deflates Kristol's portrayal of America's "tranquil" history with a quip as sharp as a needle. Regarding the claim that "the Founding Fathers all died in bed," he notes that one "of those who did so was Alexander Hamilton. The former Secretary of the Treasury died in bed after being shot by the Vice President of the United States."[26] The politically motivated 1804 duel between Hamilton and Aaron Burr was a notable example of violent conflict in the years after the Revolution. Yet this incident was merely one daub of red on the riotous canvas of the young nation. As Jaffa points out, the "tranquility" that followed the ratification of the Constitution in 1789 included near-constant accusations and counteraccusations of treason and subversion. To name just the most dramatic controversies: the Alien and Sedition Act of 1798, the Virginia and Kentucky Resolutions of 1798–99, the intensely bitter election of 1800, the Nullification Crisis of 1832, the violent struggle over slavery in the territories throughout the 1850s, the secession of eleven southern states in 1860–61, and finally the outbreak of the Civil War itself in April of 1861. Warming to his theme, Jaffa says of Kristol's "inarticulate" allegation, "One knows not whether to laugh or weep at the imagined spectacle of Madison, Jefferson,

Adams, Franklin, and Washington, sitting around a table, at a loss to know what to say to each other!"[27]

Despite Jaffa's vigorous criticisms at the APSA meeting, Kristol reaffirmed his thesis—that American history is devoid of political and intellectual controversy—in a 1989 essay, "The Character of the American Political Order."

> [The] American people seem never to have been torn by conflicting interpretations of the American political tradition, though scholars may be. Even our very bloody Civil War had surprisingly little effect on the course of American history. If one were to write an American history textbook with the chapter on the Civil War dropped out, to be replaced by a single sentence to the effect that slavery was abolished by constitutional amendment in 1865, very little in subsequent chapters as now written, would need revision.... A textbook on American intellectual history could safely ignore the Civil War, were it not for the fact that one feels it to be almost sacrilegious that so much suffering should be so barren of consequence. The Civil War was and is a most memorable event—but not any kind of turning point in American history.[28]

Presumably, the reader who has made it this far does not require lengthy quotations from Jaffa to infer his response to this stunning assertion. It is sufficient to note the rhetorical question with which Jaffa concludes his 2010 retrospective on this debate: "What can be the fate of a conservatism nurtured on such a doctrine?"[29]

These excerpts from Kristol's writings raise an interesting point about Jaffa's fights. Because he was so cantankerous and sometimes did go overboard with his rhetoric, people assume that he may have exaggerated or distorted his opponents' positions. But Jaffa was punctilious about always providing direct and often extensive quotations from adversaries (even as early as 1959, with his 130-page treatment of Stephen Douglas in *Crisis*). Thus, it sometimes comes as a surprise when readers actually see these statements by his antagonists, which quite often are just as startling as Jaffa claimed. We will review a few more examples below.

PALEOCONSERVATIVES

Contrary to Professor Jaffa, it is my view that the Declaration of Independence is not very revolutionary at all. Nor the Revolution itself. Nor the Constitution. Only Mr. Lincoln and those who gave him support, both in his day and in the following century. And the moralistic, verbally disguised instrument which Lincoln invented may indeed be the most revolutionary force in the modern world: a pure gnostic force.

—M. E. BRADFORD, "The Heresy of Equality: A Reply to Harry Jaffa"

In his two Lincoln books, Jaffa argued that the meaning of the Civil War is inseparable from the meaning of America, especially with regard to the principles of equality, consent, federalism, and union. In their own way (and unlike Irving Kristol), many of the paleoconservatives agree.

One important clarification is necessary here. Grouping together different figures under one broad label does not mean that they were identical or interchangeable. Russell Kirk, the author of the influential *The Conservative Mind*, was a genteel technophobe from Michigan, who, as Jaffa acknowledged, "never directly espoused the cause of the Old South, or of Jim Crow." Still, along with lionizing John Adams as the most sober of the founders, Kirk "often and loudly praised Calhoun" and even wrote for *The Southern Partisan*, which according to Jaffa in 1996, was still "fanatically devoted to the Confederacy and openly espousing the cause of slavery."[30] M. E. (Mel) Bradford, a proud Texan, was probably the most vocal defender of the Confederacy. Despite this, he and Jaffa were friends, and Jaffa publicly endorsed Bradford's unsuccessful nomination to chair the National Endowment for the Humanities in 1981. Willmoore Kendall's arguments with Jaffa were the most theoretical, and though he was also a Southerner, Kendall was not especially attached to any romantic notions about "the Lost Cause." Despite these differences among paleoconservatives, however, Lincoln and the natural equality of the Declaration remained at the heart of their disputes with Jaffa.

The arguments for and against the claims of Southern secession often devolve into extremely minute analyses of particular events. We are, of course, more interested in the larger issues at stake. But these analyses can be hard to separate when we try to understand the speeches and deeds of statesmen: political principles appear in, and are understood through, political actions. It is necessary, therefore, to revisit some of the historical questions discussed in Chapter 3. Happily, one vignette can serve to clarify the key points.

By the time he was in his eighties, Jaffa could distill the essence of his arguments into a few paragraphs. A year after *A New Birth of Freedom* was released, an opportunity arose to present a concentrated version of the key points elaborated in various places throughout the thousands of pages comprising his books and essays.

Enter Jack Kemp, a football star turned prominent Republican politician, nominee for vice president of the United States, and a one-time presidential candidate (as well as Lincoln aficionado). In 2001, Kemp had become engaged in a public spat, played out on the pages of *National Review*, with *NR* editor Joe Sobran about the Civil War. In the 1970s and 80s, Sobran, though an inveterate traditionalist, had warmly reviewed several of Jaffa's books and seemed persuaded of the arguments. By 2001, however, he had lapsed, as Jaffa would see it, back to the neo-Confederate camp.

Jaffa weighed in on the "uncivil war" between Kemp and Sobran in an essay for the *CRB*. Sobran had quoted several statements by Lincoln that seemed to show him as less of an advocate for the rights of black people than commonly supposed. Jaffa writes:

> Many of the passages Sobran cites, including the one quoted above, were subjected to exhaustive analysis in my 1959 book *Crisis of the House Divided: An Interpretation of the Issues in the Lincoln-Douglas Debates*, a book Sobran once knew well, and once spoke of with great approval. In it I explained that Douglas's strategy was to identify Lincoln with abolitionists, the most radical, and radically unpopular, of those in the antislavery coalition. Lincoln's disavowal of abolitionism was absolutely necessary to his political survival in the climate of opinion of Illinois voters in the 1850s. To have failed to make such disavowals would simply have disqualified him as a political leader of the antislavery cause. Sobran knows this, and his present use of these quotations is simply disingenuous.[31]

Sobran repeats the claim that the South had a *constitutional* (rather than *revolutionary*) right to secede and that it was Lincoln who (in Sobran's words) "launched a bloody war against the South, violating the Constitution he'd sworn to uphold." Jaffa's *New Birth* addresses this claim in some detail. The Southern claim, however, could be reduced to a simple formulation that Jaffa renders thus: "the idea of secession means that those who have lost an election can break up the government rather than abide by its results."

> If minorities can set aside the result of an election, then there is no point in having elections at all. Lincoln's defense of the

Union was therefore a defense of the principle of constitutional majority rule, a principle not recognized anywhere else in the world of that time. Unless the defense of that principle succeeded here, it is not likely that it would ever have succeeded elsewhere. That is what Lincoln meant at Gettysburg when he said that the Civil War was a test whether popular government would perish from the earth.

Jaffa then turns to the inevitable twist on the argument, which alleged that the Southern states "had the same lawful right to de-ratify the Constitution as they had to ratify it. Secession, they said, was neither more nor less than de-ratification." The Union established by the Constitution was, purportedly, no more than "a voluntary contractual agreement among the states. [The South] had the same contractual right, they said, to leave the Union as to join it." Whereas many paleoconservatives see this as an irrefutable argument, Jaffa denies it any legitimacy. By the uncontroverted principle and tradition of contracts, he explains,

> obligations freely undertaken can never be disavowed unilaterally. That the Constitution would by granting a right of secession provide for its own demise—assisted suicide so to speak—is absurd....
>
> What the states reserved was the right of *revolution*, as set forth in the Declaration of Independence. But that is a natural right, under the laws of nature, and not a constitutional right. The seceders were careful not to appeal to the right of revolution, since that would be a right to which their slaves might appeal not less than themselves.

In *New Birth*, Jaffa argued that the need to defend their peculiar institution had driven the Confederates not merely into bad logic and political theory but distorted their practical judgment as well. Insisting on slavery as a positive good made all compromise impossible and led the South to insist on a massive increase in centralized power through a federal slave code, a demand that proved ultimately self-defeating. At the 1860 Democratic National Convention, the South effectively split the party on the rock of this ultimatum. During the platform debate,

> seven states—the same that would secede before Lincoln's inauguration—demanded that the party platform include a slave code for the territories. This was a demand for federal police protection for any slave owner who went into any federal territory with his slaves.... This would mean a repudiation of [Stephen] Douglas's doctrine of popular sovereignty, by which the people of each territory would decide for themselves whether to become free or slave. It would also mean the indefinite extension of slavery.

The enormity of this demand seriously undercut the claim that the South was the victim of an overbearing central power impinging on states' rights. The actual implementation of such a far-reaching slave code, enforced by the full national authority of Washington, DC, "would have resulted in the greatest expansion of federal governmental power before the New Deal." Losing all sense of perspective, Jaffa maintains, the South became its own worst political enemy:

> By splitting the Democratic Party they virtually assured the election of Lincoln. Douglas, as the candidate of a united Democratic Party, would almost certainly have been elected—particularly because powerful elements in the Republican Party held him in high regard. Just as Lincoln would raid the Democratic Party of its free-soil element, so Douglas could have raided the Republican Party for those who saw popular sovereignty as a satisfactory compromise of the slavery question.... The one thing that it was

politically impossible for Douglas to do was endorse the demand for federal slave codes.

In the end, Jaffa argues, "it was the secession of the Deep South, not from Lincoln and the Republicans, but from Stephen A. Douglas, that made the Civil War virtually inevitable—and brought about the abolition of slavery."

* * *

Before the Reagan Revolution, the authoritative text for many conservatives was *The Basic Symbols of the American Political Tradition*, edited by Willmoore Kendall and George Carey. The book elaborates on Kendall's thesis that America was "derailed" from its true, organic roots. The nation, they argue,

> moved away from the unique and defining principles and practices central to the political tradition of our founding fathers, those associated with self-government by a virtuous people deliberating under God. In their place, it is contended, we have embraced a new, largely contrived, "tradition" derived from the language of the Declaration of Independence with "equality" and "rights" at its center.... [Lincoln] turned our tradition upside down by linking our beginnings or 'founding' as a united people with the Declaration of Independence.[32]

Jaffa takes aim at this book, and the critics of the Declaration more generally, in his long essay "Equality as a Conservative Principle" in *How to Think about the American Revolution*. He refutes what he sees as the persistent misunderstandings or misrepresentations about the founding, some of which have already been discussed. Here are a few highlights from Jaffa's rebuttal:

- "The Declaration of Independence is the central document of our political tradition, not because of any trick played by Abraham Lincoln, but because it is the most eloquent, as well as the most succinct, statement of political teaching of all the great documents of the period."
- "Kendall and Carey believe that the idea of equality dropped out of sight when the constitution of 1787 came to be written, and that the constitutional morality of the *Federalist Papers* has nothing to do with it. They are dead wrong on both counts. The idea of equality, as expressed in the Declaration, is the key to the morality of 'the laws of nature and of nature's God.'"
- "According to Kendall and Carey, the supreme 'symbol' of the American political tradition is the virtuous people, or the representatives of the virtuous people, deliberating under God. We have no quarrel with this formulation, as far as it goes. We prefer, on the whole, to speak of the principles of the tradition, rather than its symbols."
- "Kendall and Carey, like Douglas, do not see that the people's right to give their consent is itself derived from the equality of *all* men and therefore limits and directs what it is to which they may rightfully consent."[33]

There is another element of *Basic Symbols*, however, that Jaffa does not criticize. Carey and Kendall write, almost in passing, about "the challenge of...the newly arrived immigrant [who] spoke no English and had no experience with anything remotely resembling American political principles." There was a time, the authors note, when "everybody seemed to know what needed to be done" to affect the immigrant's "Americanization." In fact, everyone agreed "that there was such a thing as Americanism."[34]

Jaffa, too, understood this need for assimilation. He quotes, often and with feeling, Lincoln's great Independence Day speech in 1858: those not directly descended from "the Fathers" can nevertheless claim an inheritance through the moral principle of human equality. New Americans "have a right to claim it as though they were blood of the blood, and flesh of the flesh of the men who wrote that Declaration." That bond is "the electric cord in that Declaration that links the hearts of patriotic and liberty-loving men together."[35] Yet we might say that in *Crisis* Jaffa emphasized the electric cord, while later he would come to consider more closely what was implied in the biblical and ancestral connotations of blood and flesh.

The complexities of these historical investigations obscure the most regrettable issue in these debates: Kendall (and to a lesser degree, the others) had one very good argument, which was nearly lost amid several bad ones. The important and necessary part of the paleoconservative message—the emphasis on grounding political life in a particular people with concrete religious and cultural habits—was always entangled with and tainted by the animus toward Lincoln (and, at times, fairly overt apologies for the old Confederacy).

Jaffa had learned from Aristotle that every political community is a complex unity that combines a *form* (a principle of justice, or claim to legitimate rule, based on some aspect of natural right) with particular *matter* (the opinions and customs that create "a people" as a distinct political community). He alludes to this in his "Equality as a Conservative Principle" essay by observing that "Kendall and Carey assume the existence of the people, and never ask what it is, from the viewpoint of the founding fathers, that entitled the American people to consider themselves as sovereign." Having put his finger on the problem, Jaffa says that "the answer to that question, we propose to demonstrate, is equality."[36] And while that concept would remain essential for Jaffa, he is not quite able in this essay, despite an impressive effort, to elaborate a fully satisfactory account.

If equality as a universal principle applies to all men, as Jaffa always insisted, he does not quite explain how the founders made a community of fellow citizens out of *those* men, the actual human beings living in the colonies at that time. "But who are the people?" Jaffa asked in a 1974 essay on compact theory and federalism. "The difficulty in answering this question is the greater because the word itself may take the same form, whether in the singular or the plural."[37] His fully developed answer turned out to be more complicated than he expected, and the four decades he took to write his sequel to *Crisis* can be partly explained by the fact that he needed some time to sort this out. Let's take a moment to clarify that.

When he came across the Lincoln-Douglas debates in that used bookstore in 1946, just after having studied Plato's *Republic* with Strauss, Jaffa was thunderstruck to see Socrates's arguments about natural right reenacted in an 1858 Illinois Senate race. His first Lincoln book, then, marshalled Strauss's criticism of historicism into a stupendous assault on the pettifoggery of American history scholarship, rescuing statesmanship and natural justice as grand, transhistorical principles. But this classically informed reinterpretation of America may have launched *Crisis* too high.

Kendall's critique in *National Review* argued that "Jaffa's Lincoln sees the great task of the 19th century as that of affirming the cherished accomplishment of the fathers by transcending it." That meant seeing "the equality clause as having an allegedly unavoidable meaning with which it was always pregnant, but which the fathers apprehended only dimly." To fulfill the potential for self-government, Jaffa makes Lincoln the "anti-Caesar, himself as indifferent to power and glory as Caesar is avid for it." But by establishing, even glorifying, the precedent of what

Jaffa himself called a messianic savior, Kendall feared that Jaffa would launch his readers,

> and with them the nation, upon a political future the very thought of which is hair raising: a future made up of an endless series of Abraham Lincolns, each persuaded that he is superior in wisdom and virtue to the fathers, each prepared to insist that those who oppose this or that new application of the equality standard are denying the possibility of self-government, each ultimately willing to plunge America into civil war rather than concede his point.[38]

Natural right, the philosophic conception of pure justice, is "dynamite," as Leo Strauss called it, unless and until is embodied as a particular ruling principle, an arche, of a specific regime. The reference here to Strauss is significant. While Kendall was a paleoconservative, he was somewhat unusual in also being an admirer of Strauss (with whom he struck up a friendly correspondence), and his critique here is similar to some points made by the Eastern Straussians, which will be discussed below.

This passage quoted from Kendall's review was mentioned earlier, but its significance for Jaffa's thought can now be appreciated more fully. In reflecting on this and related considerations, Jaffa came to realize that he needed to do a bit more to bring his Americanized political philosophy down from the heavens and into the city.[39]

Jaffa's dilemma in the late 1970s was that he did not have an alternative to the paleoconservative account of America's organic customs and culture. So long as anti-Lincoln nostalgia for southern agrarianism was the only option available, Jaffa found great difficulty in combining the "form" of natural right with a concrete expression of American identity.

A related challenge was how to understand the complex relationship of the Union and the states. A political community, as we recall from Aristotle, is a compound—too much unity destroys the regime. Federalism is a major component—one of the "improvements," in fact—of the founders' political science. Contrary to a frequent but erroneous charge, neither Lincoln nor Jaffa wanted to centralize the United States under an all-powerful national government. Much more than in *Crisis*, Jaffa delves into this question in *A New Birth of Freedom*, where he expresses awe as well as sympathy with James Madison's struggles over this difficult issue.[40]

A significant signpost in Jaffa's journey toward explaining America's compound unity appears in the preface he added to *Crisis* in 1982:

> The classical understanding of natural right always pointed simultaneously in two directions: one, toward the philosopher's understanding of the universal, transpolitical dimension of human experience; the other, toward the political man's understanding of the *particular* experiences of *particular* peoples in *particular* regimes. [Emphasis added.]

The real breakthrough, however, came in his 1987 essay "Equality, Liberty, Wisdom, Morality, and Consent." Jaffa now affirms that a "constitution, a regime, a way of life" cannot merely be "willed" any more than the virtuous habits of "courage, temperance, justice, or wisdom." Without rejecting the idea of "political religion" as a product of philosophic poetry or rhetoric (which featured so prominently in *Crisis*), Jaffa emphasizes that statesmanship must secure the conditions of political freedom through "those institutions of education and of government, by which such principles become the actual ground of the way of life of a people."

> Nor was it a challenge that could be met merely by a recourse to

the principles. Even in the lives of individuals, it is no easy matter to discover the connection between, let us say, good health and healthy habits. Yet even when that knowledge has been gained, it is frequently a matter of greater difficulty to implement the practices that the knowledge would dictate.[41]

Equality remains at the center of the founding's natural theology, but Jaffa now expands the orbit to encompass derivative and related concepts. In particular, the consent of the governed is fundamental not only for "the responsibility of the government to the governed in the political sense, but in the broader sense" of securing and legitimating the ways that wisdom can be "beneficial to the whole community." Civic friendship based on our natural equality and our common humanity complements but does not displace friendship on the "more obvious" ground of "family, clan, nation, or any other form of personal relationship, arising from particular circumstances or shared interests." These "other forms of friendship are naturally more intense and nobler and better than those of mere humanity. Of particular note, Jaffa observes,

> One must also recognize that there is no abstract answer to the question of what constitutes an "equal" share in lawmaking. Although the principle can and must be stated in abstract or universal terms—that all men are created equal—the means of implementing this principle must follow the dictates of prudence, taking into consideration circumstances that are not universal, but particular.[42]

Jaffa is here finding the matter he needed to understand how the "form" of natural right could be embodied in the American regime. This insight was bound up with Jaffa's other intellectual breakthrough that has been discussed: his wide-ranging account of the theological-political problem caused by the destruction of the ancient cities and the rise of a universal faith. As discussed earlier, Christianized politics created a problem for political obligation that Aristotle never confronted. When the opportunity arose, the solution was found in Jefferson's mighty sword of religious liberty, cleaving ecclesiastical and political authority. But the "divided mind" that had torn Europe apart for 1,500 years could not be solved only by partition; a certain unity needed to be restored.

Separation of church and state is a prudent, humane, even necessary step in the modern world. But it presents a new problem that, Jaffa insisted, needed a new solution.

> Nowhere in the *Politics* does Aristotle confront the question of how the citizens will be persuaded to obey the laws, if there are no gods to whom those laws will be ascribed.... The state of nature and the social contract supply that mediation. Aristotle recognizes that particular polities will require particular institutions—that they will be the work of legislators acting in particular circumstances. But if these legislators can no longer crown their work by appealing to the authority of particular gods as the foundation of their laws, they must appeal directly to nature. They must have some way of translating the authority of a universal nature into the ground of particular laws. This, to repeat, is exactly what the doctrine of the state of nature, as we have described it above, accomplished.... Moreover, the idea of the state of nature, by treating civil society as a voluntary association, lays a firmer foundation for the idea of the rule of law than in Aristotle's *Politics*.... [The] rule of law, resulting from the social contract, contains guarantees against despotism, which are not guaranteed by the rule of law as described by Aristotle.[43]

America rescues the promise of ancient republicanism—becomes a new Rome, in fact—by solving at long last the problem created by Roman imperialism. "The Founding Fathers intended that the United States of America would be a new Rome," Jaffa wrote in a letter to a colleague in 1989. "It would have a Capitol and a Senate; its most famous book would be authored by Publius; and its most famous society that of the Cincinnati." But in refounding Rome, the United States "would refound as well the idea of the rule of law—the inner core of the greatness of ancient Rome—upon the idea of human equality. Human equality as the ground of law implied and required the idea of representative government."[44]

Leo Strauss had remarked that nature is older than all traditions. Jaffa's argument for natural right offers a deeper and more solid foundation for republicanism than the most venerable customs. Indeed, he went the paleoconservatives one better by "out-ancienting" the traditionalists. Never mind the Old South or even English common law, Jaffa shows that America traces its roots to the origins of Western civilization—to Rome, and also to Athens and Jerusalem.

EASTERN STRAUSSIANS

"Ransomed? What's that?"

"I don't know. But that's what they do. I've seen it in books; and so of course that's what we've got to do."

"But how can we do it if we don't know what it is?"

"Why, blame it all, we've *got* to do it. Don't I tell you it's in the books? Do you want to go to doing different from what's in the books, and get things all muddled up?"

—MARK TWAIN, *The Adventures of Huckleberry Finn*

Claremont, California, April 1996

The excitement among the graduate students, including the present writer, was palpable. An upcoming conference would feature a *gigantomachia peri tes ousias*—a battle between the gods over the meaning of being.

Charles Kesler, as director of the Henry Salvatori Center at Claremont McKenna College, had organized a major symposium to commemorate the center's twenty-fifth anniversary. Several prominent speakers were expected, including the legendary free-market economist Milton Friedman, who would deliver the dinner keynote address. But what whetted the appetites of the political philosophy students was the participation of Harvey Mansfield from Harvard. He and Jaffa had expressed some intermittent differences in print, and these had become somewhat sharper in recent years. Everyone anticipated the conference would be an occasion for the two influential scholars to air their intra-Straussian disagreements in person. Jaffa's pugilistic instincts, never entirely dormant, were fully energized, and he had encouraged all the aspiring future professors to attend what was sure to be both an intellectual feast and entertaining spectacle.

In the written version of his remarks, reprinted in *The Rediscovery of America*, Jaffa criticized Mansfield for pushing the Hobbesian-Locke understanding of the founding and contrasting this understanding with Aristotle. In a book review published a few years earlier, Mansfield had written that the founders' "fateful conception" of the state of nature "opposed and replaced" the thought of Aristotle, in which "there is no beginning behind or before politics that provides a guide or basis for politics; every beginning of politics is political."[45] In his paper, Jaffa objects both to the supposed opposition between the founders and Aristotle as well as the claim that "in Aristotle there is no beginning behind or before politics." In the *Politics*, Jaffa argues, "The political community is preceded by the family and the village." Moreover, while "the impulse to form a political community is in all men by nature," the formation of an actual regime requires a "founding lawgiver...who forges a political community, usually in circumstances of the greatest difficulty and against great opposition and resistance."[46]

What may appear to be a trivial academic distinction in fact reveals an important difference in how to understand not only Aristotle but natural right and politics in general. In his book review, Mansfield mentions the cycle of regimes, by which all political communities rise and fall. "In every case they fall for accidental causes but also, and especially, for one essential cause: they are all imperfect. They are imperfect because they are partial and partisan." All regimes claim to advance the public good, but "in fact they represent the good of a party," typically oligarchs or democrats. Because of this inherent partisanship, Mansfield continues, "A regime based upon the self-evident half-truth that all men are created equal will eventually founder because of its disregard of the many ways in which men are created unequal."[47]

Unsurprisingly, this last statement in particular did not meet with Jaffa's approval. That humans are in many ways unequal was a common-sense observation that he himself, along with Jefferson and Madison, insisted upon, as discussed in the previous chapter. Yet to regard the *political* equality of all men in their natural rights as a half-truth "is more than a demeaning of the Declaration and the Gettysburg Address," Jaffa argued. "A half-truth is not merely a falsehood, but a deceitful falsehood." In the paper he circulated before the conference, Jaffa elaborated on these objections with his usual forcefulness, arguing that the founders' "new order of the ages" hoped to break out of the "melancholy" cycle of regime change by establishing a nation "based not on partisanship but upon truth." And that truth was emphatically not, Jaffa insisted, Hobbes's "passion of fear," as Mansfield had suggested.[48]

Before a large crowd of faculty and students, Mansfield, in his oral remarks, accused Jaffa of "attacking your friends." "What you do is stand behind the front lines, and point your weapon at the backs of your friends and shoot!" In the course of their vigorous colloquy, Mansfield elaborated on his statements in the book review Jaffa had criticized.

> I didn't say that the doctrine [of equality] was a half-truth, I said that the statement was a half-truth. You're the one who said the equal protection of unequal faculties was inherent from the outset in the doctrine of human equality in the American Founding. So there is a basis for saying that the equality of man is—that "all men are created equal" is—a half-truth, if all men are also created unequal.
>
> What happens, what tends to happen in the American regime is that the state of nature which…was a pre-political basis or foundation for politics, has become a principle of politics in the Aristotelian sense, the ruling principle, a kind of *arche*. So that the state of nature is not understood simply as a basis from which we would prepare to rule, but a basis upon which we would continue to rule.
>
> And this is the argument of Tocqueville's *Democracy in America*, a book which you do not sufficiently appreciate. That book says that we live in the midst of a democratic revolution… [and] the problem today…is to hold down this democratic revolution.[49]

Apart from the merits of the arguments, Jaffa was somewhat offended by the charge that "I have been in the back line and that I have been firing from the rear at the backs of my friends." He insisted that "I've been very straightforward [and] certainly haven't hidden myself."[50]

In a series of letters following up on their exchange, Jaffa questioned whether Tocqueville's critique of equality was as relevant as Mansfield had suggested, given that "the equality feared by Tocqueville was grounded in Rousseau," who had a quite different philosophical framework than the one guiding the

American founders. Nevertheless, Jaffa did agree that "the future of freedom" was very much at risk. The "leveling tendency within any popular government is always present. That is all the more reason why the principle of equality must be rightly understood."[51]

The last letter, in 1999, takes note of some additional writings by Mansfield in the interim and observes:

> As I interpret you, classical philosophy and biblical religion, and even more, the morality common to them, have been dealt a death blow by Machiavelli, and whatever of either deserved to survive does so in one or another of the form of Machiavelli's teaching. From your point of view, if I can penetrate the layers of your onion, neither moral rationalism, grounded in nature, nor biblical morality, are either defensible or desirable. Machiavelli's version of "natural right" was domesticated by Hobbes and Locke, and constitutional formalism becomes the simulacrum of morality. The "effectual truth" of executive power leaves the private citizen free for the unhindered pursuit of property and pleasure.

For Jaffa, by contrast, the permanent distinctions between humans, beasts, and God reflect the "great chain of being" that "is common to Aristotle and the Declaration of Independence."[52]

∗　∗　∗

Jaffa's emphasis on America's classical roots was intended as a rebuttal to many paleoconservatives as well as many Eastern Straussians who seem to regard the founding's rationalism as no more than a degraded offspring of the Enlightenment. For orthodox Eastern Straussians, in fact, the American regime itself is nothing more, really, than an epiphenomenon of modern philosophy.

In his 1977 book, *Political Philosophy and the Issue of Politics*, Joseph Cropsey surprised even some of his colleagues with how forcefully he asserted this claim. The meaning "embedded" in the "great public utterances" that define America's purpose were "infiltrated" such that "the imperfection of our regime" is "identical with the invasion of the regime by thought." What Cropsey means by these elliptical statements in his chapter "The United States as Regime" becomes slightly clearer when he says,

> The founding documents are the premise of a gigantic argument, subsequent propositions in which are the decayed or decaying moments of modern thought....It follows that the United States is the microcosm of modernity, repeating in its regime, on the level of popular consciousness, the major noetic events of the modern world.[53]

This is a more abstruse variation of a remark by Walter Berns, which Jaffa quotes in the appendix to his seminal 1987 essay. Berns had written in an article for *This World* that "the champions of separation [of church and state] in the United States—Madison, Washington, and Jefferson, for example—were not Christians, except perhaps in the most nominal of senses." In fact, he says, "I would go further: the very idea of natural rights is incompatible with Christian doctrine and, by its formulators, was understood to be incompatible." The evidence for this rests on the fact that "Thomas Hobbes and John Locke were enemies of all revealed religions."[54]

By the time Jaffa was fleshing out his more comprehensive understanding of America and world history, he had long since abandoned (if he ever fully believed) the notion that the founders were the unconscious psychic prisoners of an atheistic Hobbesian doctrine they explicitly rejected. In fact, insofar as this view denigrates the founders' practical wisdom and freedom of moral deliberation, Jaffa had come to regard this doctrine as a form of the very historicism Strauss deplored.

The revolutionary idea of reading what the founders actually wrote, examining what they did, and judging them accordingly was a theme taken up by many of Jaffa's students. On the specific question of classical influences, consider an essay by Charles Kesler, "The Founders and the Classics."

> For the founders, instruction in the classics was, to a great extent, the study of living wisdom that happened to have been written centuries ago in different languages. To be sure, some parts of ancient learning had to be rejected or questioned in light of Christian revelation and later discoveries in the sciences; but as guides to logic, rhetoric, ethics, history, politics, poetry, mathematics, and even to some parts of theology, the classical writers remained, if not always authoritative, nonetheless principal authorities in the curriculum of schools and of life....
>
> Pamphlets, newspaper articles, sermons, and political debates of the day [were] strewn with classical quotations and allusions.

More than this, the founders adopted classical ideas and principles into their political theory. Kesler, the editor of a popular annotation of *The Federalist Papers*, closely analyzes the form of republican government articulated by Madison, Hamilton, and John Jay (writing as "Publius," of course). He concludes that "the political theory of the American regime cannot be understood apart from the political science of the classics."[55]

If, in Jaffa's account, the paleoconservatives' patriotic defense of America lacks a rational, theoretical account, the Eastern Straussians see *only* the theoretical dimension. In a letter to Eugene Miller, Jaffa writes, "I am certainly not the only one of Strauss's students to direct his students towards political things, although I am the first to have done so." Yet, he adds, "I do find relatively little interest among the others, and that a diminishing interest, in such political things." The main concern of the Eastern Straussians is becoming "something more akin to metaphysics than to politics. Texts become objects for legerdemain, rather than for the discovery of truth about political things."[56]

The radical separation of philosophy from politics was a theme of Jaffa's *CRB* altercation with Thomas Pangle in 1984–85, based on Pangle's introduction to *Studies in Platonic Political Philosophy*. We have discussed their disagreement on the question of how Strauss viewed biblical revelation, but Jaffa also takes issue with Pangle's claim that morality arises only from "the plastic power of custom." Jaffa concludes that the "reductionism" Pangle invokes "to explain the moral phenomena, when applied to the universe as a whole, can result in nothing but modern nihilism." Interestingly, he does not quote another arresting passage in Pangle's introduction: "All men other than the philosopher, one may say, live lives that are tragic or comic or both." Ordinary men "are in the most important respects deluded boasters, skaters on thin ice who are unwilling or unable to look down for very long at what lies under our feet."[57]

Similarly, in his scorching review of Allan Bloom's *Closing of the American Mind* (1987), Jaffa argues that Bloom disregarded their teacher's admonition to begin with the perspective of the citizen. Taking the morality of the regime seriously had become (at best) a pose for Bloom. Anticipating the theoretical critique of always-imperfect political justice, Bloom encouraged his students simply to jump ahead, as it were, to the stance of philosophic detachment. This, Jaffa argued, entirely missed the point. A joke in his foreword to Neumann's *Liberalism*, comparing Bloom to the once-famous bank robber Willie Sutton, drives this home:

> Bloom's attack on academic relativism, and his concern for the morals of his students is reminiscent of Willie's anxiety for the morals of bank managers. Willie didn't want to go to all the trouble

of breaking open the bank's safe only to find out that the man with the combination had already emptied it.... Bloom's conception of philosophy—or the reason for teaching the Great Books—is that it encourages skeptical doubt—and skeptical inquiry—into the received opinions—the conventional wisdom—of one's society. It encourages us to ask—as Plato's *Republic* does—"Is Justice good?" And if so, "For what?" And if so, "For whom?" But such philosophy presupposes a conventional morality to which the student is attached, and which he is being invited to question. If the only opinion that the student brings into the classroom is the opinion that all morality is a matter of opinion—and that no opinion can be proved superior to any other—then there really is very little to talk about.[58]

More than anything else, perhaps, Jaffa was struck by Bloom's apparent turn away from Strauss and toward Heidegger. In the early 1960s, when the two were close (their collaborative effort, *Shakespeare's Politics*, was published in 1964), Bloom had written that Strauss "single-handedly revived the serious study of ancient political thought." In doing so, Strauss had shown that political philosophy "is not merely an object of historical curiosity but is relevant to our most vital present concerns."[59] Jaffa certainly agreed with that. Yet two decades later, *The Closing of the American Mind* included only a single brief reference to Strauss ("As Leo Strauss put it, the moderns 'built on low but solid ground.'")[60] More striking is how Bloom now described the rediscovery of classical thought. At the end of his long discussion of the decline of the American scholarship and the neglect of any serious concern with the ancients, Bloom omits any reference to Strauss and writes that "it was Heidegger, practically alone, for whom the study of Greek philosophy became truly central, a pressing concern for his meditation on being."[61]

There is a risk at this point of misrepresenting Jaffa's differences with his fellow Straussians. Family squabbles can often be the bitterest, and a dispute over principles may be exacerbated by the occasional personal conflict. Thus, the common ground of Strauss's broader teaching might be missed. The difficulty is that Strauss's thought was subtle and his writing exceedingly precise (though sometimes appearing ambiguous or convoluted). He often obliged the reader to infer his meaning from omissions and hints as well as his notoriously erudite and sometimes puzzling footnotes. Thus, differences in interpreting Strauss's writing often begin as questions of emphasis. Yet these have grown to the point that quite radically different views now separate those who consider themselves his students, reaching today into the third and even fourth generation. Jaffa was candid in acknowledging this: "I do not claim Strauss's authority for the conclusions I draw from them. Other students of Leo Strauss draw very different conclusions—indeed, in some cases, opposite conclusions—from his writings than I have done."[62]

Nevertheless, there do seem to be some key points that distinguish Straussian thought from the more or less uniform doctrines of modern academia. For obvious reasons, there was little or no division among Strauss's students about the meaning of his teaching while he was still alive. The following list of ideas, principles, and themes therefore attempts to capture what virtually all his students seemed to accept before his death in 1973.

- The return to classical political thought is justified because the human condition does not fundamentally change. What Strauss called "the permanent problems" are in key respects the same for us today as they were for the ancient philosophers. The history of Western philosophy is the ongoing attempt to grapple with these enduring questions about (to name a few) justice, friendship, love, honor, wisdom, and happiness. In addition, the permanent problems include theoretical questions about man's place in the cosmos, how we think or know anything, and the meaning of "nature" or "natural." Ancient Greek philosophy remains of particular interest if we accept that Plato, Aristotle, and Xenophon may have reflected on these questions as incisively as anyone before or since. In fact, the freshness and originality of Greek thought—uncluttered by centuries of philosophic schools and systems—preserve the classical writers as sources of perennial interest.

- If there are, in fact, permanent problems—indeed, even if this is only a possibility—then the radical dogmatism of modern philosophy becomes impossible to sustain. In particular, Strauss denied that scientific progress or the unfolding of history have resolved or overcome the enduring questions arising from the human soul. As discussed in several places throughout this book, Strauss rejected and even sought to refute the stultifying doctrines of historicism and positivism, which actually foreclose philosophical inquiry.

- If human beings have—at least in part—an unchanging nature (that is, if man does not make himself) then we must consider whether nature may supply guidance for human life. That is, the just and unjust, the noble and the base, may have some objective ground outside our will. There may be standards in nature by which to judge our opinions about the ends of life and the meaning of human excellence.

- Strauss considered himself a student of Socrates, who was not the first philosopher but rather the first *political* philosopher. Humans always live in some political community, and our inquiries about the most important things always begin with the authoritative opinions of our political order. Thus, in the subjects he addressed and the roles he took within academia, Strauss consistently positioned himself as a teacher in the social sciences, not abstract philosophy.[63] To the degree that his project had a practical bearing, it attempted to rescue political science from the debilitating doctrines of modern philosophy. (Virtually all of Strauss's graduate students went on to teach in departments in political science.)

A Strauss essay simply called "An Epilogue" (the concluding chapter of a 1962 volume of articles by former students, edited by Herbert Storing, titled *Essays on the Scientific Study of Politics*) contrasts classical political science with modern, value-free social science. One scholar who studied with both Bloom and Jaffa has compiled some of its key passages, distilling Strauss's practical, Aristotelian teaching:

1. "Political science is identical with political philosophy."
2. "Human action has principles of its own which are known independently of theoretical science (physics and metaphysics).... The principles of action are the natural ends toward which man is by nature inclined and of which he has by nature some awareness."
3. "The awareness of the principles of action shows itself primarily to a higher degree in public or authoritative speech, particularly in law and legislation, rather than in merely private speech. Hence Aristotelian political science views political things in the perspective of the citizen."
4. "Aristotelian political science necessarily evaluates political things."
5. "Man is a being *sui generis*, with a dignity of its own: man is the rational and political animal." His dignity is based on "his awareness of what he ought to be or how he should live."[64]

At this point, however, we have may have already left neutral ground. Not all of Strauss's students agree that his remarks about practical politics represent his deepest or most esoteric thought, and some seek to separate his thought from Aristotle.[65] Moreover, the scholar who compiled theses quotations is Thomas West, widely regarded as a Western Straussian, whose work has focused on the American political tradition.

The essay in which West reproduces these quotations was paired with another Straussian analysis in a volume titled *Leo Strauss: Political Philosopher and Jewish Thinker* (though several of the contributions don't discuss any specifically Jewish themes). The essay following West's is by Christopher Bruell, of Boston College, and titled "A Return to Classical Philosophy and the Understanding of the American Founding." It is worthy of a brief examination because it strikingly highlights the most "far Eastern" position of Straussian geography.

Bruell begins by noting Strauss's concern with "the crisis of our time" as well as Strauss's belief that modern philosophy had ended in the "self-destruction of reason." Strauss's attempt to recover classical rationalism as a source of political wisdom, Bruell notes, might entice Americans into "holding the guiding principles of the Founding to be simply true." Bruell, however, quickly sets aside such civic interests, for Strauss's apparent political motives are in fact marked by deep ambiguities, and it "is on these ambiguities, then, insofar as they affect the study of the American Founding, that we must concentrate our attention."[66]

Yet Bruell's interest in America is not so much ambiguous as utterly absent. Other than the historian Gordon Wood and Strauss himself, he quotes no Americans, certainly no statesmen from the founding nor any American political documents or speeches. Indeed, despite the title, the essay says literally nothing about any specifically American institution or principle. Bruell treats America as an avatar of modern politics; indeed, the essay might just as easily have focused on France or Britain. As in the passages from Joseph Cropsey quoted above, America is purely a manifestation of modern theory.

From Bruell's perspective, Strauss's defense of democracy, including his strident condemnation of modern political science for failing to recognize tyranny, should be seen as strictly mercenary. Constitutional liberty means only that "we should take advantage of the freedom democracy affords to all to 'cultivate our garden'—that is, to pursue excellence on our own, so far as we are capable of doing so." Strauss's interest in America and the application of his thought to the founding cannot really be taken seriously, says Bruell, because (fainthearted readers beware) the "classical political philosophers were not democrats, and still less liberal democrats."[67]

As noted above, Jaffa saw this attitude as a very curious misapplication of Strauss's ancient-moderns distinction, which was (Jaffa believed) largely a heuristic device to refocus serious attention on classical thought. If the universe and the human mind remain essentially the same, the permanent questions don't change; only our opinions and attitudes do. What *has* changed since the time of Plato and Aristotle is the status of political obligation and the "divine" basis of laws after Christianity became the universal religion of the Western world. "The classical political solutions are strictly speaking only for the ancient city," Jaffa argued. The American founders' social compact theory was a necessary adaptation of the broader principles in order to address "a problem peculiarly that of the Christian West, arising from the conflicting claims of reason and revelation."[68] This is what Jaffa understood by Aristotle's dictum that "natural right is changeable."

Bruell seems to reverse this template. He emphasizes the less-than-shocking truth that Plato and Aristotle were not liberal democrats. Then he devotes the rest of his essay to exploring what Strauss may have discerned in his analysis of modern versus premodern rationalism. The implication seems to be that, for Bruell, political life must always be judged against the inflexible standards of the ancient polis, while the world of theoretical philosophy appears to undergo historical change. However that may be, Jaffa, for his part, insisted that theoretical philosophy always focuses on the same eternal subjects (without ever arriving at any final answers). But in the practical world, the wisdom of classical political science lives on through the statesmanlike application of prudence to changing circumstances.[69]

Jaffa was not the only voice dissenting from this apolitical interpretation of Strauss. Hilail Gildin, for example, the longtime editor of *Interpretation*, wrote piercingly on Strauss's deep and unquestionably moral attachment to Israel.[70] David Lowenthal, whose scholarly interests track closely with Jaffa's, continues to write engagingly about Lincoln's statesmanship and Shakespeare's concern for virtue and honor. The great playwright, in fact, seems to be important to several of these disputes, somewhat in the way Lincoln is central to Jaffa's fights with paleoconservatives. As Paul Cantor observes (without naming names), a key difference turns on whether Shakespearean poetry is little more than a retreat from politics into a "seemingly self-contained play world," which, Cantor argues, prevents a full appreciation of how love, wisdom, friendship, and justice are portrayed by our greatest poet.[71]

To recap a few of these complex points: Since philosophy is always in tension with the life of obedient piety, Eastern Straussians tend to emphasize philosophy as atheistic. To the degree that natural justice can be discovered at all, it consists, they suggest, in the radical superiority and separateness of the philosophic life. Jaffa's undue elevation of the moral-political sphere allegedly suppresses the grave challenge that philosophic skepticism always poses to moral-political opinions. Jaffa's response is that Socratic philosophy is *zetetic*, that is, Socratic skepticism consists not in a fixed disposition of unbelief but in constant (and strenuous) *openness*. Harry Neumann called this the "psychological tension" between the philosopher's "need for unquestioning loyalty (which their ignorance does not really permit them to discredit) and their need to seriously question that loyalty."[72] This is not the doctrinaire scientism and reductionism of modern philosophy.

Atheism, along with positivism and historicism, are the authoritative opinions of our modern cave. Thus, Eastern Straussians cease to be zetetic when they reduce atheism to a dogma. In this vein, consider the epigraph to this chapter, in which Strauss warns against intellectual complacency and the "perpetuation of common prejudices by a closely knit group of kindred spirits." To retain the spirit of zetetic vigilance, Strauss insists that the "philosopher must leave the closed and charmed circle of the 'initiated' if he intends to remain a philosopher." Rather than remain behind a garden wall, he "must go out to the market place; the conflict with the political men cannot be avoided. And this conflict by itself, to say nothing of its cause or its effect, is a political action."[73]

For Jaffa, moral-political life has an inherent dignity and purpose that does not contravene philosophy as the best way of life for a few rare souls. And since even philosophers must live in some community, one function of political philosophy (though hardly the only one) is to provide rational guidance and intellectual clarity in support of good laws and opinions. Such guidance recognizes that the "best regime" remains an enduring theoretical standard "in speech," yet political life always depends on the practical wisdom of moral gentlemen who strive for the best arrangements under the circumstances. It is this sense that Jaffa saw Locke and Aristotle as aiming toward the same end and described America as, in principle, "the best regime" possible *in the modern world.* By liberating and protecting both philosophy and piety and by dignifying the citizen statesmen who seek the common good, America revives classical teleology. As Locke (in Strauss's mature estimation) and certainly the founders believed, human life has natural ends and standards of excellence. To the degree that the United States today has lost its way, Jaffa averred, it is not because of some Hobbesian virus or merely because it is modern but because its foundations in natural right have been rejected and forgotten.

* * *

But perhaps the Eastern Straussians are right. One might even wonder, reasonably, "Was Harry Jaffa actually Strauss's worst student?" He certainly seemed to be the boldest in going his own way and departing from Strauss's reputation for quiet, circumspect erudition. (This latter-day portrayal of Strauss is not entirely accurate, as we will see in a moment.) Jaffa was the first, and to some degree still the only one, to form his own "school." To consider this question of Jaffa's lapsarianism and to conclude this section, we need briefly to consider his unique role in publicly opposing the Leo Strauss dissertation award of the American Political Science Association.

In 1974, the APSA established an annual award for the best PhD dissertation in political philosophy, named to memorialize Strauss, who had died the previous year. "It is important that the Association signalize to the profession in general," the petition stated, "and to graduate students in this field, its recognition of political philosophy as one of the important traditions within the discipline."

Jaffa strenuously objected to this apparently harmless courtesy and lambasted those who had voted for it, leading a number of colleagues to wonder, Is there nothing this quarrelsome man won't fight about? Jaffa's friend Hadley Arkes once remarked to him (about another matter), "Harry, you don't know how to take 'Yes' for an answer!" If the APSA wanted to honor Strauss, what sense did it make for Jaffa to object?

In a letter to the APSA's journal (which the editors declined to publish but which he then circulated himself), Jaffa wrote:

> The motion in favor of the Strauss Award speaks of "the universal recognition of Strauss' exemplary devotion to the philosophic study of politics." In truth, however, there has been no such recognition of Strauss, nor did he ever wish for it. If there can be no universal recognition of the philosophic study of politics, how can there be universal recognition of Strauss' devotion to it? If Strauss ever taught anything, it is the impossibility, not to mention the undesirability, of such universal opinions. Indeed, he was particularly averse to any alleged universal opinion in favor of a philosophic study of politics. Could there be such an opinion, he thought, it might lead to the establishment of the universal tyranny of the universal homogeneous state. That was his contention in his debate with Kojeve in *On Tyranny*.

Jaffa noted that "Leo Strauss was at odds with the mainstream—or perhaps one should say the various mainstreams—of the political science profession throughout his career." And Strauss's contempt "was warmly reciprocated" by the profession.

> On the whole, Strauss enjoyed this adversary relationship. *Solet Aristoteles quaerere pugnam* was the epigraph for his Walgreen Lectures in 1949. And Aristotle himself did not join battle more assiduously than Leo Strauss. How then is an Association consisting overwhelmingly of those whom Strauss attacked, and who attacked him, during his life, to agree on the standards of excellence to be honored in his name?[74]

Years later, Jaffa would take some satisfaction in pointing out that a recent award had been given to a dissertation on Louis

Althusser that was nothing more than "an exercise in intrasectarian Marxist dialectics."[75] This confirmed, in Jaffa's mind, the prescience of his earlier prediction, that the prize would be given for the best drawing of a horse by judges who had "themselves never seen a horse, or did not know that they had ever seen a horse."

Many to whom Jaffa sent his letter were "keen students of the problem of knowledge, so central to the problem of political knowledge, and hence to the question of what is political philosophy." Yet he describes the reaction to his arguments as "sullen silence, punctuated by muttered imprecations." The most charitable explanation Jaffa could offer was "a kind of amnesia" about what Strauss taught.[76]

But here is a puzzling feature of this episode. Why was it Jaffa, of all people, who opposed the award—and nearly alone? He had earned almost singular condemnation among Strauss's first students for soiling the nobility and independence of political philosophy. A 1965 article in *Commentary* had rebuked him for his descent into partisan politics: joining the Goldwater campaign must "surely be beyond reasonable limits."[77] Walter Berns would later write in *National Review* that Jaffa was "a textbook case of someone converting philosophy into ideology, of abusing theoretical teachings for his own practical end."[78]

If this charge were true, one would expect that it would be *Jaffa* who would seize on the opportunity to use such an award for narrow or partisan ends, while the theoretical "purists" would want to keep Strauss's teaching and reputation free from academic horse trading. Yet Jaffa argued that it was *he* who was preserving political philosophy's unique character and, in fact, preserving its integrity from professional bartering. The advocates of the Leo Strauss Award, he claimed, "by proposing to recognize political philosophy by a political process, have subordinated political philosophy to the political process."[79]

The APSA dissertation prize, Jaffa concluded, "was, among other things, a white flag, by those who had grown weary of Strauss's unrelenting contentiousness, and who wanted now to be at peace with the mainstream of the profession." The Straussians who supported the award had, he thought, indicated their unwillingness or inability to uphold Strauss's own example of intransigence. Socratic querulousness, which Strauss imitated in his own antagonistic relations with the academic establishment, would be sacrificed for the sake of official recognition.

The price, however, was a kind of emasculation, certainly a dethroning, of the monarchical role that Socrates and Strauss had accorded to their search for wisdom and justice. The disagreement over this apparently harmless gesture, turned—for Jaffa—on a disagreement about the meaning of political philosophy.

> Strauss' indictment of the "new political science" was above all that it abstracted from the differences between a decent and humane constitutionalism, and the vilest of tyrannies....For Strauss *did* have a practical teaching, and it took the form of a celebration of the virtues, above all, of Anglo-American constitutionalism at its best. The preoccupation, among his students, with the American Founders, with Lincoln, and with Churchill, is a direct reflection of his teaching.
>
> But liberal democracy, Strauss taught, although it may treat many things unequal in themselves, as being politically equal, cannot treat the principles of liberal democracy as being no better or worse than their denial. Yet it was neutrality upon this life and death issue that constituted the heart of the 'new political science.' This is what Strauss meant when he said that the fiddlers did not even know that Rome was burning. Is it not absurd then, for the sake of meliorism and reformism, to have a fiddlers' award in the name of Leo Strauss?"[80]

LEGAL POSITIVISTS

In disquisitions of every kind, there are certain primary
truths, or first principles, upon which all subsequent
reasonings must depend. These contain an internal evidence which, antecedent to all reflection or combination,
commands the assent of the mind.... Of this nature are
the maxims in geometry, that "the whole is greater than
its part; that things equal to the same are equal to one
another; two straight lines cannot enclose a space; and all
right angles are equal to each other." Of the same nature
are these other maxims in ethics and politics, that there
cannot be an effect without a cause; that the means ought
to be proportioned to the end; that every power ought
to be commensurate with its object; that there ought to
be no limitation of a power destined to effect a purpose
which is itself incapable of limitation.

—*Federalist No. 31*

At the risk of overusing the metaphor, Jaffa believed that no major
figures in American public life have fiddled to lesser effect than
those "conservative" judges and their scholarly allies who defend
legal positivism, a strictly procedural and value-neutral account
of constitutional interpretation. Jaffa thought the Constitution
was not fully coherent without reference to the natural law principles underlying it. He often explained that Jefferson and Madison, when establishing the curriculum for the law school at the
University of Virginia (where they sat on the Board of Visitors),
prescribed as the first guide to the principles of the Constitution
"the Declaration of Independence as the fundamental act of Union
of these States." The US Code also includes the Declaration as
the first of the "organic laws" of the United States.[81]

Lacking any proper theory, let alone defense, of the Constitution, the positivists seem to resemble the paleoconservatives discussed earlier. Yet they lack the paleos' patriotic willingness to take a stand on moral issues. In this, they imitate the Eastern Straussians' arid textualism. The consequences, Jaffa thought, speak for themselves. For a century or more, left-wing judges have articulated a concept of a "living constitution" that pursues the common good (however misconceived that may be) *and* poured into this capacious vessel all their policy preferences. In its failure to resist this two-pronged strategy, conservative jurisprudence performs a double act of self-mutilation, cutting off its nose to spite its face and then shooting itself in the foot.

The positivists who reject natural law jurisprudence sometimes warn gravely about the danger of judges imposing their personal preferences. But after decades of almost uninterrupted liberal victories at the Supreme Court, Jaffa's students today find this argument hard to take seriously. Conservative proceduralism and deference to *stare decisis* ("let the decision stand") simply create a ratchet effect. Leftist rulings have been locked into place because change only occurs in one direction, with a few, usually temporary, pauses. As the screw of judicial activism has tightened, many conservative voters and even politicians have come to see the shortcomings of mere proceduralism.

After his two Lincoln books, Jaffa's fame—or notoriety— derives in large part from this fight over jurisprudence and the tremendous volleys he fired at eminent legal figures on the right, including (but not limited to) Edwin Meese, Robert Bork, William Rehnquist, and Antonin Scalia. Jaffa was the first conservative to publicly challenge this reigning legal positivism, beginning in the 1980s. Today, even after Jaffa's passing in 2015, his arguments (and students) continue to shape the debate, which is carried on with the same admixture of heat as well as light. Ken Kersch's 2019 *Conservatives and the Constitution: Imagining Constitutional*

Restoration in the Heyday of American Liberalism makes Jaffa "the pivotal intellectual in the book's story" as "the figure the Left should most fear," in the words of one reviewer.[82]

Jaffa's jeremiads are mostly to be found in his *Original Intent and the Framers of the Constitution* (1994) and *Storm Over the Constitution* (1999). He attributed to his opponents the view that within the law, strictly speaking, there is no right or wrong, just or unjust, only whatever "positive" affirmation the law commands, an argument rejected by no less a figure than Socrates. Jaffa considered this sterile proceduralism as incoherent and self-defeating as every other form of positivism. Given that the Constitution does not define "property," "person," "life," "liberty," or even "law," judges *must* ground the meaning of the text in something. Jaffa was emphatic that what *Federalist No. 31* called the "primary truths, or first principles" of the Constitution are located in the Declaration.

The positivist judges and their defenders claim to be upholders of the "original understanding" of the framers. But Jaffa insisted that they misunderstood and rejected not only the intention of the framers but even their own oath to the Constitution. The oath and the powers of the judiciary granted by Article III are part of the coherent, natural-rights theory elaborated by James Madison and the other framers. The practice of judging is itself legitimate only as an act of republican self-government.

Again, the actual words of Jaffa's antagonists may surprise some readers. Chief Justice William Rehnquist, in a 1976 article for the *Texas Law Review* titled "The Notion of a Living Constitution," comments on "the nature of political value judgments in a democratic society."

If such a society adopts a constitution and incorporates in that constitution safeguards for individual liberty, these safeguards do indeed take on a generalized moral rightness or goodness.

272 • THE SOUL OF POLITICS

They assume a general social acceptance, neither because of any intrinsic worth nor because of any unique origins in someone's idea of natural justice but instead simply because they have been incorporated in a constitution by a people.[83]

At a public lecture in Rome in 1996, Justice Antonin Scalia declared,

> You either agree with democratic theory or you do not. But you cannot have democratic theory and then say, but what about the minority? The minority loses, except to the extent that the majority, in its document of government, has agreed to accord the minority rights.

And again,

> Once you adopt democratic theory...you accept the proposition [that]...if the people...want abortion the state should permit abortion. If the people do not want it, the state should be able to prohibit it.[84]

It should be noted, as Jaffa himself insisted, that Rehnquist, Scalia, and other conservative judges nearly always issued opinions that arrived at the same outcome Jaffa would want. But is that sufficient? What is the effect, in terms of the people's understanding of their Constitution, when the reasoning of Supreme Court decisions is plainly indifferent to the larger purpose of law?

Given Jaffa's fondness for comparing politics to medicine, we might liken these judges to a surgeon who declares, "It is not my business whether the patient lives or dies, I am simply following the procedure." Confronted by a contradiction or ambiguity in the technical manual, such a surgeon (we might call him a medical positivist) would insist that he can't or shouldn't consider whether health and life are better than disease and death. But the people consent to a judge's superior ability to interpret the law for the same reason that a layman consents to treatment by someone trained in the medical arts. As Jaffa notes,

> When we go to the doctor, we subject ourselves to his regimen. We consent to be governed by him, in one of the most important respects in which, during our lives, we subject ourselves to the rule of others. We do so because we think that it is better to be governed by one with medical knowledge than by ourselves, with respect to our health. But we also think that it is essential, that the full extent of the doctor's skill be devoted to our benefit. We want him to be neither negligent nor lackadaisical, because of any indifference towards us.[85]

Jaffa approached these matters from a broad perspective in order to understand and teach the conditions of self-government. Precisely on these grounds, his opponents sometimes tried to have him disbarred from the proceedings, arguing that he was merely a political philosopher and not a lawyer. True, his arguments were sparse in citing specific case law, with the notable exception of course of *Dred Scott v. Sanford*. In that 1857 case, as we recall from the beginning of Chapter 3, the Supreme Court was confronted by explicitly contradictory statements in the Constitution: guarantees for individual rights as well as protections for slavery.

Justice Roger Taney held that that blacks were not people but

> beings of an inferior order, and altogether unfit to associate with the white race, either in social or political relations; and so far inferior, that they had no rights which the white man was bound to respect; and that the negro might justly and lawfully be reduced to slavery for his benefit.[86]

Lincoln forcefully eviscerated Taney's opinion, showing that while the text of the Constitution treated blacks as both persons and property, that ambiguity is reconciled (and really can only be reconciled) in the plain moral and metaphysical reasoning about human equality affirmed unanimously by the founders.

Alluding to these arguments in his First Inaugural, Lincoln adds, not incidentally, an explicit rejection of judicial supremacy:

> The candid citizen must confess that if the policy of the Government upon vital questions affecting the whole people is to be irrevocably fixed by decisions of the Supreme Court, the instant they are made in ordinary litigation between parties in personal actions the people will have ceased to be their own rulers, having to that extent practically resigned their Government into the hands of that eminent tribunal.[87]

The proper interpretation of Taney's opinion in *Dred Scott* was at the root of a long, boisterous exchange with Robert Bork. Jaffa's most interesting and instructive disagreements were with antagonists who fought back, sometimes with equal gusto. Bork, like Walter Berns, was not bashful about responding to Jaffa's criticism. He ended his review of one of Jaffa's books by saying, "Written in dyspeptic prose, *Original Intent and the Framers of the Constitution* is one of the least coherent, least consequential, and most disingenuous pieces of constitutional theorizing on record.... This may sound unduly harsh. I have tried to show that it is only duly harsh."[88] Jaffa was greatly amused, and energized, by this attack.

We should note again that he tried not to take intellectual disagreements personally, though he treated the issues with the utmost seriousness. Nor did he let them get in the way of practical political judgments. As with Mel Bradford's nomination to the National Endowment for the Humanities,

Jaffa supported Bork's 1987 nomination to the Supreme Court and even donated money to the public campaign supporting him.[89] But with this practical accommodation in the bank, so to speak, the two felt free to rain invective on each other for several years—to the edification of readers of *National Review* as well as the magazine *First Things*. Of course, the rancor between Jaffa and Bork was nothing compared to the calumnies directed at the judge during his confirmation hearings, which set the precedent for bitter and openly partisan warfare in Supreme Court appointments.

Jaffa's second book on this topic was aptly titled *Storm Over the Constitution*. Judge Bork (like other legal positivists) wanted to take shelter from the storm of judicial activism in the plain words of the document. But as Jaffa argued, in some key cases, there is nowhere to hide. In the *Dred Scott* case, Bork claimed the court had usurped Congress's authority by deciding for itself the issue of slavery in the territories. But Congress (in a now-familiar evasion of responsibility) had, in Jaffa's memorable analogy, laid the issue at the court's doorstep, rang the bell, and then ran away.[90] Bork claimed that the court had "invented" a right to own slaves. The problem, as Jaffa pointed out, was that the original Constitution, in one of the famous compromises necessary to secure ratification, mentions the ownership of other human beings no less than three times. The contradiction *in the text*, where slaves are described as both people and property, Jaffa insisted, "can be resolved only by recourse to the principles of natural right and natural law."[91]

So far, we have discussed the theoretical and practical shortcomings of positivism. But where is the case for the coherence and feasibility of Jaffa's natural-law view? The answer to that may be found in the jurisprudence of the longest-serving member of the current Supreme Court, Clarence Thomas, the only Justice who cites Harry Jaffa as a major intellectual influence.[92] Thomas's opinions show how such an approach actually works in practice. In the words of John Eastman, a Jaffa student who clerked for Thomas and was for a number of years dean of the Chapman University Law School,

> Thomas's own jurisprudential philosophy is more in line with the principles of our nation's founders, and hence with the Constitution they framed, than any other sitting Justice's is. And while the nation comes slowly to understand that, he will keep laying down markers, like so many breadcrumbs, patiently pursuing his mission to help us all find the way back toward a constitutionalism grounded in the immutable truths of the Declaration of Independence.[93]

Myron Magnet's 2019 *Clarence Thomas and the Lost Constitution* points out that Thomas differs from most of his conservative allies in his attitude toward *stare decisis*. Precedent should indeed guide the lower courts, Thomas believes, but the Supreme Court is bound first and above all by the Constitution, and it should not hesitate to overturn precedents that are wrong. Thomas does not feel indentured to a century of liberal judicial errors. Magnet describes his approach to such prior rulings.

> [Thomas] begins with the plain command of the constitutional text or amendment in question, locates it in all the concrete complexity of its historical context, traces the historical process by which the command got distorted from its original meaning, explains the real world consequences of that distortion, and points out how the court can repair the damage going forward. His goal is a return to the framers' vision, aimed at protecting the liberty he cherishes as dearly as they did.[94]

That last point brings us back to the core of Jaffa's argument. Magnet's book relates how Thomas first came to learn about Jaffa's work when he was chairman of the Equal Employment Opportunity Commission (EEOC). One of Jaffa's students, Ken Masugi, recalls that as an EEOC staff member, he wrote Thomas brief memos "about issues of the day—political, legal, and moral—and how they reflected deeper, abiding questions of political philosophy." One such memo to Thomas mentioned "an essay by John Marini on the administrative state." Masugi relates that Thomas "scrawled on top of it, 'i must see marini!'"[95]

In his autobiography, *My Grandfather's Son*, Justice Thomas notes that instead of "rehashing the usual partisan debates over quotas and civil rights," he was more interested in "substantive questions" that would help him "break free from the mind-numbing effects of the daily grind of running a government agency." "Among other things," Thomas relates, "I led my staffers (especially Ken Masugi and John Marini) in discussions of the natural-law philosophy with which the Declaration of Independence, America's first founding document, is permeated." Masugi and Marini brought the work of Jaffa into these discussions. Thus, Thomas recalls, "we debated at length the implications of natural-law thinking, and speculated on how it might apply to contemporary political discussions."[96]

As John Eastman points out, Thomas is really the only justice who takes seriously what Jefferson, Madison, and Lincoln said about the first principles of the Constitution. In the 1995 *Adarand v. Peña* case, the court held that a strict scrutiny standard must apply to justify any racial classifications by the government. Thomas issued a concurring opinion that stated, in part,

> That these programs may have been motivated, in part, by good intentions cannot provide refuge from the principle that under our Constitution, the government may not make distinctions on the basis of race. As far as the Constitution is concerned, it is irrelevant whether a government's racial classifications are drawn by those who wish to oppress a race or by those who have

a sincere desire to help those thought to be disadvantaged. There can be no doubt that the paternalism that appears to lie at the heart of this program is at war with the principle of inherent equality that underlies and infuses our Constitution. See Declaration of Independence ("We hold these truths to be self-evident, that all men are created equal, that they are endowed by their Creator with certain unalienable Rights, that among these are Life, Liberty, and the pursuit of Happiness").[97]

In *Storm Over the Constitution*, Jaffa elucidates what is implicit in Justice Thomas's opinion in a section called "Aristotle for lawyers." Here he shows that the argument about the "miracle of the common noun" is not only the philosophical basis for comprehending the world but that it also reveals the moral basis of just government. To see every human as equally a member of a "natural kind" is to see that every human is "*homo sapiens*, the rational animal." Because every common noun abstracts from particular qualities of size, shape, color, etc., "we can say that the mind has no color, and therefore that man's humanity has no color. This is the ultimate source of the doctrine that the Constitution is, or of right ought to be, color blind."

"Because the human species has reason, it has freedom, and with it the power of both good and evil, that no other species possesses." This is the foundation of that consent that makes constitutional government possible and justifies the rule of law as both necessary and proper. Such principles, Jaffa concludes, are "neither more nor less than what is meant by the natural law foundation of the Constitution."[98]

8

"THE UNFINISHED AND UNFINISHABLE QUEST"—JAFFA'S LEGACY AND THE FUTURE OF AMERICA

> For this writing is, in part at least, the writing of those
> who see the beacon in the midst of tyranny and learn how
> to find those around them who also yearn for the end
> of tyranny, how to communicate with them, and how to
> teach them, and how to strengthen their souls. But those
> who carry on the works of humanity humbly need to look
> backward towards those beacons, that their fellow men
> may also some day once again see the light. And those
> who hold up those beacons, even if they fall in the battle,
> shall not be forgotten. Their memory shall not perish
> from the earth. For the ground of noble action itself lives
> not in time, but in eternity.
>
> —HARRY JAFFA

At a White House ceremony on November 21, 2019, the Claremont Institute was awarded the National Endowment for the Humanities Medal. Institute President Ryan Williams said, "The medal is more than anything a testament to forty years of teaching and writing about the history and intellectual traditions of the American founding and their application to our politics today."

The White House citation reads, in part,

For championing the Nation's founding principles and enriching American minds. Its publications and public events have deepened our understanding and appreciation of American freedom, democracy, justice, and rule of law.

The mission of the Claremont Institute is "to restore the principles of the American Founding to their rightful, preeminent authority in our national life." A think tank located far away from Washington, D.C., in Upland, California, Claremont was founded in 1979 by a handful of students of the late political philosopher Harry V. Jaffa, whose views continue to shape the institute, its scholars, and its programs....

Following Jaffa, the Claremont Institute champions the view that the promises of liberty and equality before the law are written into the Declaration of Independence and expressed not only in the Founding but, especially, in the Lincoln presidency. Arguing against more historicist interpretations that denigrate the contributions of the Founders as needing constant correction, Claremont scholars such as Thomas G. West and others have sought to vindicate the Founders and show how their legacy has been under attack from more statist philosophies. According to this school of thought, the Progressive Era, especially the administrations of Woodrow Wilson, Franklin Delano Roosevelt, and Lyndon Baines Johnson, introduced many corruptions to American political thought that cry out for reconsideration in light of the Founding principles.

The Claremont Institute is a think tank in the traditional sense of being home to a group of collaborative scholars, about two dozen of them, who write penetrating articles and books on the American Founding, Lincoln, the Civil War, progressivism, the administrative state, and the importance of statesmanship. It is also, however, a training ground for young thinkers and doers, recent college graduates as well as mid-career professionals in media, elective politics, government, and law, who visit as summer fellows and receive "a crash course in American political thought" from the Founders onward.

"Our strategy has always been to teach the teachers and the opinion leaders and the policy makers," says Claremont president Ryan Williams. This effort began in Claremont's first year with the Publius Fellowship, a three-week program of seminars for recent college graduates. Today, Claremont also offers brief fellowships for journalists, law clerks, and even speechwriters, counting more than seven hundred alumni from its programs. The students, Williams says, are "public spirited and want to engage in a career that shapes the national political and intellectual conversation."[1]

Jaffa would have been pleased by the recognition, for himself and his students. But in all likelihood, he would have investigated rigorously the other award recipients, past and present, uncovering their deficiencies to show that no real standards of excellence guided the selections. In terms of the qualifications of those conferring the award, he might have concluded that the honor was merely accidental, as it were. Jaffa both coveted and disdained official recognition, but to some degree he coveted the recognition in order to disdain it. His intent was to demonstrate, *ad oculus*, Aristotle's argument that honor depends on the quality of those doing the honoring. (This is a point he made in some detail in both *Thomism and Aristotelianism* and *Crisis of the House Divided*.)

In a 1978 letter to Robert Horwitz, then a professor at Kenyon College, Jaffa remarks on the untimely death of Martin Diamond, the first fellow Straussian with whom he publicly broke. Jaffa mentions that Horwitz would be chairing a panel devoted to Diamond at the upcoming APSA meeting. "I expect that you intend your panel to be a memorial session rather than a critical one," he notes, "and so you might not want to have me around." He then comments on his own attitude about the worst fate that might await him after death. "Consulting my own ghost, I'm assured that I would much rather be attacked than ignored, and being the subject of a prayer session is not altogether different from being ignored."[2]

Jaffa's ghost was surely gratified to see that on the occasion of his death on January 10, 2015 (and since), he was not ignored. The *New York Times* obituary dwelled at length on his involvement with the Goldwater campaign, although it properly noted that Jaffa saw his role as instrumental to a larger purpose: "I thought of the Goldwater campaign as an attempt to educate the American people and the conservative movement itself, which I hoped to influence."[3] Closer to home, the *Los Angeles Times* quoted several friends and acquaintances, including William Buckley, and observed,

> Jaffa was hailed as a prophet of a brand of American conservatism that could trace its lineage to Lincoln, Thomas Jefferson and earlier proponents of natural law, the idea that human conduct should be guided by a universal standard of justice rather than the arbitrary rules of society.[4]

Jaffa's antagonists on the right marked his achievements respectfully, but with caveats. Harvey Mansfield, writing in *The Weekly Standard*, claimed Jaffa as a friend yet noted that he "was a man of greater zeal than loyalty." Of *Crisis of the House Divided*, he wrote,

> One might think it impossible to exaggerate the importance of this book if Jaffa had not shown us how. In other books he made the

understanding of Lincoln's America the solution to all difficulties, the combination of all good things: democracy and aristocracy, ancients and moderns, prudence and principle, Christians and pagans, philosophy and statesmanship, the good and one's own. The only dualities he left intact were liberal and conservative, Jew and Gentile. These he kept in order to maintain or, more accurately, appease his excess of fighting spirit.[5]

Law & Liberty offered milder observations with a thoughtful essay on Jaffa "by those of us who disagreed with him." Citing primarily his differences with Mel Bradford, the authors questioned Jaffa's "assessments of Aristotle, St. Thomas Aquinas, John C. Calhoun, Abraham Lincoln, and contemporary conservatism, among other concerns." Yet, they added, "the extended debate he and Bradford undertook proves that honest dialogue can take place even when confronting significant areas of disagreement."[6]

The most direct and vehement attacks, which by his own admission Jaffa welcomed more than oblivion, came from the left. *Salon* deplored his "torrent of rancid diatribes," while *Jacobin* magazine wrote,

> Jaffa has received glowing obituaries in outlets both mainstream and right-wing. Against these encomiums, we need to remember what Jaffa really stood for: homophobia, the alliance between self-styled philosophers and religious bigots, and a circumscribed view of freedom that finds racial segregation an acceptable price for national unity.[7]

Of course, most of the remembrances came from admirers and friends. In *National Review*, John Miller wrote that "Jaffa may be the most important conservative political theorist of his generation."[8] The *Journal of the Abraham Lincoln Association* published a long essay by Joseph Fornieri that paid "tribute to the profound, groundbreaking, and transformative legacy of Harry V. Jaffa on Abraham Lincoln scholarship."[9] The *Claremont Review of Books* produced a special issue in which Jaffa's former students shared their reminiscences. William Allen, who then taught at Harvey Mudd College (part of the Claremont consortium), noted Jaffa's belief that he had advanced his teacher's project "more substantially than any other of Strauss's acolytes." That work was "to unlock the door to philosophy through reflection on politics (quite the opposite of the conventional approach of unlocking the doors of politics by reflecting on philosophy)." Hadley Arkes recalled an episode decades earlier when the *New York Times* asked him, "What book would you take with you to the moon if you could take only one?" In explaining his answer of *Crisis of the House Divided*, Arkes says the book

> gives us an account of Lincoln at his highest pitch by taking seriously the substance of Lincoln's thought on the highest questions he had to face as a political man: Jaffa gave us a compelling account of truths that formed the grounds of Lincoln's judgment and his understanding of his political ends. To explain in that way the reasons for Lincoln's mission, and the justification for his acts, is to explain the most important things that give the meaning to Lincoln's life.

Jaffa's inclination to probe and pry open what appeared to others as minor differences led Norman Podhoretz to conclude that for Jaffa, in "the most consequential subjects, everything is at stake. And when everything is at stake, every detail counts." "It is not enough to agree in general," Podhoretz observed, because "the particulars, each and every one of them, have to be got right. An imprecise formulation, a misplaced emphasis, an inadvertent implication can and does lead one astray, not only into intellectual confusion but into dangerous and destructive courses of action."[10]

At the memorial service held at Todd Chapel in Claremont, eulogies were delivered by Jaffa's son Philip as well as Larry Arnn, Edward Erler, Michael Uhlmann, and Thomas West.[11] In addition, Hillsdale College in Michigan, where several of Jaffa's students now teach, organized its own commemoration. College President Larry Arnn, Professors Thomas West and John Grant, and Dean Ronald Pestritto shared their reflections.[12] (Other notable Jaffa students at Hillsdale include Professor Mickey Craig, Vice President Matthew Spalding, and retired professor Will Morrisey.)

Leaving aside the vehemence of his enemies, even his fondest admirers acknowledged that Jaffa inspired exasperation as well as devotion. Michael Uhlmann, a lawyer who earned a PhD under Jaffa and served in several Republican Justice Department positions, sometimes clashed with his teacher over Jaffa's attacks on Justice Antonin Scalia and Attorney General Edwin Meese. Uhlmann recalled in his eulogy his "failures" on "those occasions when I tried to tone down his more acerbic rhetoric. All of us ground our teeth at some of his *ad hominem* excesses." Charles Kesler's review of *A New Birth of Freedom* in the *CRB* memorably described Jaffa as "splenetic and vainglorious."

Aside from his admitted fondness for picking fights, Jaffa could be slow to express professional gratitude, both for the intellectual debts he incurred to other scholars (besides Strauss) as well as those, other than his wife, who labored behind the scenes to support his scholarly efforts. He may have taken too much to heart Aristotle's observation that the magnanimous man enjoys giving benefits but not receiving them.[13]

He also erred in some important political judgments. More than once, Jaffa pinned unreasonable expectations on some bright Republican star to guide the party back to the principles of the founding, only to find in the end that he had invested in a dim bulb. (Admittedly, Jaffa was hardly the lone resident in this land of dashed hopes.) In part because of his enthusiasm for equal opportunity and the promise of the American melting pot, Jaffa initially opposed a landmark 1994 ballot proposition in California, Proposition 187, to curtail public services to illegal immigrants. As with his early support of the 1964 Civil Rights Act, he sometimes underestimated how ideologues exploit popular goodwill and "anti-racism" to undermine legal equality and citizenship. Jaffa even questioned, at first, the creation of the Claremont Institute by his students (Arnn, Christopher Flannery, Peter Schramm, and Thomas Silver). He later came to be an enthusiastic supporter and never missed an opportunity to offer detailed instructions from the back seat about how the institute should be run.

Nevertheless, on the deepest questions and on most significant issues, Jaffa's judgment could be uncanny.

- He saw early on how the Civil Rights Movement (and later the Civil Rights Act itself) had been coopted by the advocates of "black power." And while he never wavered in his attachment to the *principle* of color-blind equality, he came to see the legal and regulatory regime established by the 1964 Civil Rights Act as unworkable. In a 1992 review of Richard Epstein's *Forbidden Grounds: The Case against Employment Discrimination Laws*, Jaffa writes, "Epstein has convinced me...that the abuses of the anti-discrimination laws are so intimately connected with misconceptions in the laws themselves that any benefits from them will always be far outweighed by the harm they do." Therefore, "the steady pressure of self-interest in a free market" is a better method of promoting nondiscrimination.[14] In fact, he might have agreed with Christopher Caldwell's even more far-reaching conclusions in *The Age of Entitlement* (2020) that anti-discrimination laws, as such, simply cannot be squared with the Constitution.

- He warned, in the face of tremendous vituperation, that there was no logical (or decent) limit to the aims of the radical gay rights movement and the sexual liberation agenda more broadly. Some of his friends, such as the law professor George Anastaplo, thought Jaffa was too gleeful in deploying the word "sodomite," yet his serious argument about the consequences of denying nature as the standard of morality have certainly been born out, now that elite opinion has reached the point of defending transgender hormone "therapy" for young children.
- Jaffa sensed that the end of the Cold War merely cut off the exposed weed of Marxism, leaving the roots untouched. "The defeat of communism in the USSR and its satellite empires by no means assures its defeat in the world," he wrote in 1991. "Indeed, the release of the West from its conflict with the East emancipates utopian communism at home from the suspicion of its affinity with an external enemy." Therefore, he predicted, the "struggle for the preservation of Western civilization has entered a new—and perhaps far more deadly and dangerous—phase."[15]
- He always understood the brutal nihilist core of progressive leftism. In his classic 1989 essay, "The Reichstag Is Still Burning," Jaffa explains how the soft relativism of the 1960s—with its apparently easy mixture of tolerance, diversity, and individuality—led directly to today's militant aggressiveness. As liberalism gained power, it came to experience an inevitable tension between tolerance and "the uninhibited cultivation of individuality." In the face of this alternative, the left chose the passionate or willful resolve of the uninhibited self. "Once this step was taken, tolerance appeared as one value or ideal among many, and not intrinsically

superior to its opposite." This meant that "intolerance appeared as a value equal in dignity to tolerance. But it is practically impossible to leave it at the equality of all preferences or choices." Without any permanent standards in God or nature by which to rank our choices, the determination of the will becomes all that is meaningful, and liberalism descends into a "seminary of intolerance."[16]

- From his long study of America's tumultuous history, he was clear-eyed about the dangers of democratic tyranny, the temptation to criminalize political differences, and the possibility of a majoritarian police state. When some conservatives in the 1980s called for dispensing with civil protections such as the exclusionary rule (which prohibited the use of illegally obtained evidence), he was alarmed and wrote to *National Review* publisher William Rusher that "the presumption of innocence...is not a fiction of the bleeding heart liberals." It is "one of the principal marks" by which American legal procedure "is distinguished from a totalitarian system like the U.S.S.R."[17]

- Above all, he saw the hollowness of the contemporary political establishment and that a Potemkin conservatism could never succeed in preserving constitutional self-government. The current fracturing of the republic is a great shock to many (and still not evident to some) but is probably least surprising to Jaffa's students.

A few words on this last point are in order. Regardless of what Jaffa would have thought of today's politics, were he alive today, his students have staked out a distinct political and philosophical position, often referred to simply as the "Claremont" camp or school of thought. This moniker includes of course the Claremont

Institute but also encompasses the scholarship and political outlook of several professors at Hillsdale and a few other colleges
along with miscellaneous writers and public officials who have
studied with Jaffa and his circle.

To understand this perspective, it is helpful to look back to
2012, when Charles Kesler, who had come to Claremont decades
earlier as something of a protégé to Jaffa, published *I Am the
Change: Barack Obama and the Crisis of Liberalism*. The book is a
close examination of Obama's writings and policies in light of
what Kesler sees as the "fatal contradictions" in liberalism as a
governing philosophy. This was the same year that Jaffa, at age
ninety-three, released *Crisis of the Strauss Divided*, a rumination
on his major intellectual concerns. Though not intended as such,
the two books can be viewed as something of a handoff: Jaffa's
retrospective of his career in political philosophy transitions to
Kesler's distillation of key themes in the Claremont analysis of
American politics.[18]

Kesler's book, which explores the antagonism between progressivism and the founding, serves as sequel and prequel to
Jaffa's two prodigious Lincoln books. *Crisis of the House Divided*
and *A New Birth of Freedom* established the Claremont position
on the Civil War and its attendant controversies in rich detail.
But Jaffa came to his serious examination of the founding late
and circuitously. Therefore, while some of his students have
carried forward his Lincoln studies, most have focused either
on developing a deeper understanding of the founding or the
subsequent attempt by the progressives to transcend the principles and institutions of the original Constitution. This work
has generally followed Jaffa's teaching on the interdependence
of political theory and practice. Claremont scholarship on the
founding acknowledges the powerful influence of political philosophy, but it is noteworthy for treating the framers primarily
as prudent statesmen, not theorists, who drew upon numerous

sources, classical and modern (including works in economics, military history, and law), to fashion a republican government suitable to their circumstances. Also cutting across the grain of much American historiography and political science, the Claremont approach to the progressives has emphasized the influence of German historicism and the radicalness of progressive theory, in which political philosophy, nature, and prudence are replaced with social science, history, and administrative expertise.

Kesler's 2012 book used Obama as a lens to refract and illuminate the "crisis of liberalism" and consider whether its deficiencies might herald a possible reinvigoration of the principles of the Declaration. The book notes how the New Left emerged in the 1960s partly as a Romantic reaction against the egoistic individualism of consumerist society. The Vietnam War and the threat of nuclear annihilation (among other factors) had caused the student protestors' faith in progress to waver, yet the movement never faced "the contradictions in its own position," which wanted politics without a state and "visions without leaders." The young radicals "longed for moral truth but had no idea where or how to find it." With liberalism's rejection of both the Bible and natural right, moral truths became "values," which could only be created through an existentialist act of autonomous will. Six decades on, in the Obama presidency, the progressive sprint to the future struggles to stay ahead of the doubts and nihilism that threaten to overtake it. Kesler observes that the "authoritarian streak" in liberalism may yet lead to something "very undemocratic." Nevertheless, he ends on a hopeful note, speculating that liberalism's "coming apart" will allow us to "get back in touch with political, moral, and fiscal reality."[19]

What a difference eight years makes. Kesler's book uses the word "oligarch" only once, and then in reference to the populist critique of the so-called robber barons of the late nineteenth century. This omission is not so much evidence of Kesler's lack of foresight as an indication of how much, and how quickly, the political landscape changed. In the 2020 election, political liberalism—ominously abetted by what seems to be a new private sector Ministry of Information—firmly put down Donald Trump's challenge to its authority. Progressivism muted its doubts, clamped shut its internal contradictions, and assumed undivided command of the regime.

Quite a few of Jaffa's students had supported Donald Trump, though often with caveats and reservations about his self-destructive tendencies. More so than Trump the man, the Claremonsters (as they wryly call themselves) appreciated and gave intellectual legitimacy to the populist revolt against the politically correct contempt of the ruling class. The bipartisan Washington establishment had long been one of Jaffa's targets; he considered most Republicans to be nearly as alienated from the principles of the founding as the Democrats. Previous presidents, particularly Nixon and Reagan, had campaigned against—and to some degree governed over and through—the Beltway blob. The 2016 election, however, was widely seen in Claremont circles as decisive for the fate of American constitutionalism.[20] Yet Trump's victory was at best a reprieve. Even his staunch supporters thought Trump left much undone in his first term, notwithstanding some notable policy accomplishments and a large number of important judicial appointments. Any lasting achievements would take a second term and probably a like-minded successor. But the war against the administrative state was over before it really started.

Remarking on the Claremont Institute's plans under the new Democratic administration of 2021, institute President Ryan Williams said,

> The most urgent question for all American patriots right now—
> from the neighborhood to the city council to state legislatures to
> the halls of Congress to the presidency—is whether and under

292 • THE SOUL OF POLITICS

what conditions we can save America from dissolution and collapse. The modern Left has made their bet and is all-in: the
future of America is a new social "justice" caste system based
on a hierarchy of past oppression, guilt, and endless reparations.
This vision would be a repudiation of the principles of American
justice announced and codified during the Founding and will
guarantee American collapse and misery for untold millions.
The only alternative is the preservation of the American way of
life and the best of Western civilization: Americanism, properly
understood, the equal protection of equal rights.[21]

FOR OURSELVES AND OUR POSTERITY: JAFFA'S PRACTICAL TEACHING

America, Jaffa believed, is in principle the best regime possible
in the modern world. Both the Bible and political philosophy,
however, teach that all human things change and finally pass away.
This is not to say that American's end is imminent, of course.
It would be foolish, however, to assume it will last forever or
that it is immune to radical change. Already we are far from the
original principles and practices of the Constitution. What then
are Jaffa's lessons as we confront what is undeniably a kind of
revolution in the regime?

To the degree that a return to genuine republican government is still possible, Jaffa would urge, again, a rededication to
the self-evident truths of 1776 that underlie and inform the Constitution of 1787. The framers' wise institutions are an enduring
lesson in prudence. Yet that wisdom, and the practical utility of
the institutions, must be judged by the more basic principles of
natural right, outlined in the Declaration. Elections, for example,
are possible only on the basis of commonly shared convictions
about the limits and purposes of free government and as long
as the governing majority respects the rights of the minority.[22]

Digging a bit deeper, it may be that the original institutions
cannot fully be recovered, and America will move to some more

extreme form of federalism or de facto separation.[23] Even then, both the red and blue sections of America will likely embrace a form of liberal democracy, though of course with radically different interpretations of what that means. Most basically, this will include the recognition that all human beings are less than divine but more than animals. Even the creation of a rigidly aristocratic, closed society could not—except by tyrannical means—force the modern mind to unknow the species-equality of mankind, which is triply confirmed by philosophic natural right, the Bible, and the mapping of the human genome. What *will* be hard for many to learn or relearn is that the founder's anti-egalitarian political equality imposes a strenuous standard of moral virtue. Equal natural rights are not for the weak. (Lincoln once spoke of the efforts needed for "rising to equality."[24])

Of course, the principles of equality and republican self-government could become even more widely rejected than they are today. America was not only the first democracy of the New World but is still in some ways emblematic of the best aspirations of modernity. Its failure might point to the collapse of the whole Enlightenment project. The strange dichotomy in our contemporary politics, between racial and ethnic separatism on the one hand and global oligarchy on the other, points to possible disaster in two directions, a collapse into tribalist anarchy or some form of global tyranny indicated by the theories of Hegel and Marx—a universal homogeneous state. In either case, equality would be replaced by a despotism in which everyone "knows his place," either as color or component. The current tech oligarchs would probably welcome a caste system designed to maximize production and consumption.

With authentic political life torn between unnatural tyranny and irrational primitivism, the lessons of Aristotle and Shakespeare might instruct us anew in the conditions of human sociability. From the philosopher and the poet, Jaffa learned—and taught—that every political community is a complex whole. Any prospective founder of a new regime would have to consider both the available "matter" and the achievable "form" most compatible with justice. Statesmen and citizens may need to think through, from the beginning, the questions Jaffa explored about what makes "one people." From there we would need to recall that in any peaceful community larger than the village, a diversity of opinions and variety of interests are only possible with common agreement on first principles.

Perhaps most fundamentally, Jaffa reminds us about the relationship between theory and practice, or between philosophy and politics. The first lesson is that thought precedes action.[25] Any worthwhile undertaking must have some good purpose toward which it aims. Statesmanship and prudent action are always teleological. This is why we reflect on the best regime as a standard by which to determine what can be accomplished, here and now, under these circumstances. Jaffa's long meditations on Aristotle, Shakespeare, Locke, and Strauss discerned an enduring interest in the types of regimes: how they are built, what they require, how they succeed or fail. To disdain theory, or political philosophy, because it is "abstract" is as senseless as rejecting blueprints for the construction of a house as "mere drawings." Of course, when decisive action is called for, someone must declare that discussion and deliberation have ended. But this very formulation means that the deliberation has already occurred. Rational thinking must begin before it can end, when it yields to practical implementation. The alternative can only be chaotic lashing out. No matter how courageous or well-intentioned, thoughtless action rarely brings us any closer to justice. Lincoln and Churchill, to whom Jaffa draws our attention over and over, are instructive not merely for their iron determination but for their foresight and preparation.

The other danger is to confuse politics with rhetoric—or to retreat into books and lose sight of reality. In response to the violent protests that shut down many colleges in the

1960s, Allan Bloom (then teaching at Cornell) describes in *The Closing of the American Mind* one of his "greatest satisfactions as a teacher." Several of his students, who didn't want their philosophy seminar interrupted by the campus occupation, copied down lines from Plato's *Republic* about the madness of crowds and the Athenian assembly and reproduced them on leaflets. With these in hand, the students went down into the quad and handed out their philosophic quotation to the angry (and armed!) demonstrators. Their intent, according to Bloom, was to show that they were "more interested in the book than the revolution."[26]

Jaffa mocked this episode in his review of *Closing*: "It is difficult to imagine what effect—other than inflammatory—Bloom thought this Platonic passage might have had on the rioters." Bloom's misplaced pride in this gesture, Jaffa thought, illustrated that he could not "comment instructively on the relationship between political life and the philosophic life" because he did not "know what political life is."[27] That life is always a mixture of reason and passion, justice and self-interest, persuasion and force. To mistake one for the other, or to fail to see the difference altogether, is feckless and dangerous. (It is hard to know whether this is better or worse than the other vice Jaffa pinned on some Eastern Straussians: the tendency to persist in rummaging through the opinions of the Athenians, heedless of either the relevance or the fate of their own regime.)

Regardless of how the current crisis in America unfolds, any future statesmanship—as the highest form of practical wisdom—must always weigh the preference for reasonable rhetoric against the need for compulsion or force. Militant tribalists, dogmatic ideologues, demagogic sophists—these are only some of the forms of aspiring tyranny and barbarism against which reason has limited effect. Barbarians and tyrants, as such, are not capable of self-government and thus cannot be fellow citizens in a republic without some form of correction and education. But how or even whether such efforts can be attempted must be a determination of prudence.

In his essay "The Reichstag is Still Burning," Jaffa exposed the nihilistic heart of modern philosophy—the unsupported, merely willful conviction that "the only truth is that there is no truth." This apparent open-mindedness is "a two-edged sword."

> As Leo Strauss pointed out, it may at first suggest indifference. But human beings by nature love, and they also hate. By nature, they begin by loving their own. But when they are told that there is no ground for distinguishing their own—or what they love—from the good, they are told that there is no ground for imposing any limits or restraints upon either their loves or their hates. Then the indifference of the dilettante turns quickly into either the adventurism of the scoundrel, or the passionate commitment of the fanatic.[28]

Confronted with scoundrels and fanatics, the contemporary defenders of natural right may yet succeed. History is not determined. As Jaffa was fond of recalling, the "soundness of the soundest predictions must allow for the intervention of human freedom, whether it appears under the guise either of wisdom or of folly." Who, in the spring of 1940, he asked, "could have predicted that Hitler would lose the war? Who—that is to say—except the madman Churchill?"[29]

To have even a chance of success, however, one must deserve it. Whatever else, (to quote the epigraph to this chapter) it is necessary to stand fast, and keep lit the beacons of truth, with the hope that even if they fall in the battle, their defense of the noble shall not be forgotten.[30] Jaffa taught that war is for the sake of peace, yet an honorable peace—a life acceptable to moral gentlemen—may require war. What is by nature most worthy of love is the good, and it is sometimes necessary to fight for what we love.

THE PROBLEM OF THE DIVIDED MIND

Maimonides next put the whole question on the broadest
basis by speaking of the relation of the philosophers and
the *Torah*....As appears from the context, his purpose in
doing this is to present as it were a unitary front
of philosophy and the *Torah* against astrology.[1]

—LEO STRAUSS

My feeling is that today we are somewhere near a termi-
nal process in the history of western civilization—not just
in the history of this republic—in which a dark night of
the soul could very well be the fate of the world if certain
cataclysms with which we are threatened come to pass.[2]

—HARRY JAFFA

*This postscript revisits some of the major themes of the book, in part
by exploring a key concept in Jaffa's work: "the divided mind." This
concept runs like a thread through many of his writings. Consider,
for example, the table of contents to* A New Birth of Freedom.[3] *The
following essay focuses on two principal instances of psychic division,
which are in fact connected: first, the crisis in political obligation following the rise of the Roman Empire, and then a puzzling dualism
in the contemporary left, which may seem to call into question the
fate of Enlightenment liberalism altogether.*

"I say, they can't both be true. Ed just can't make up his mind."

My remark that afternoon, in a friendly conversation after lunch, was directed to Ryan Williams, the president of the Claremont Institute. "Ed" was a reference to Edward Erler, a senior fellow and member of the institute's board of directors.

I was not ordinarily in the habit of questioning the cogency of any observations by Erler. I've known Ed and respected him since I was a graduate student in Claremont. Moreover, he had just been honored the previous evening with the institute's Winston Churchill statesmanship award for his contributions to "the scholarship of the politics of freedom." Yet, I was having a hard time making sense of what he had said in his remarks.

The occasion of my conversation with Ryan was a retreat in North Carolina organized by the institute in November of 2020. The institute arranges such events once or twice a year for the alumni of their various fellowship programs to hear from interesting guest speakers, strategize, network, and reflect.

What puzzled me about Erler's remarks was a contradiction (I thought) in his diagnosis of the threats to the American republic. The presidential election had taken place a week earlier, and while CNN and some other mainstream news outlets had already declared Joe Biden the winner, the results in some key states were still considered by many analysts to be in dispute. For most people at the retreat, however, the tremendous strains on our constitutional system were evident—and worrisome—almost regardless of the election outcome.

In his speech the previous evening, Erler had mentioned Jaffa's warnings about the decline of the republic and the need to rededicate ourselves to the founders' principles. The part that confused me was how Ed seemed to be pointing to two different and contradictory forces at work. On the one hand, his speech identified the main danger as racial separatism, politically correct cancel and censor culture, and the academic sophistry of "white privilege," all of which characterize our new tribalism. On the other hand, he also took aim at the danger of globalist oligarchy using the arguments of Aristotelian political science. Erler described this latter menace in a subsequent essay as

> the ruling class elites in the media, in academia, both political parties in government (where politicians freely make promises to voters but find it easy to evade and ignore), the bureaucracy, the deep state (including the intelligence agencies), corporations, Silicon Valley, and other centers of influence.[4]

Though he spoke eloquently and perceptively, Ed didn't shock anyone by targeting this double threat to American citizenship. Everyone seemed to agree with his analysis, yet I couldn't help but think that Ed—and the rest of us—were of two minds. An oligarchy of forward-looking, meritocratic, cosmopolitan elites is a very different faction (with different interests) than the angry young hordes of race-obsessed militants who, at least rhetorically, adhere to a quasi-Marxism that despises multinational corporations. What kind of alliance is this? Who is using whom? Isn't it a bit schizophrenic to confuse these two very different phenomena? But is the schizophrenia in the analysis or in the political movement itself?

Ed's references to Jaffa got me to thinking about various disconnected remarks scattered through Jaffa's writings as well as the writings of his friend and colleague Harry Neumann. So I went back to Jaffa's and Neumann's books and essays looking for answers.

I discovered that Ed was right to point to both phenomena. Jaffa's work (with some supplementary clarification from Neumann) contained a corollary to his narrative about the theological-political problem that helps us understand how these two factions fit together—or more accurately *don't* fit, despite their tactical allegiance.

Part of what is happening at both ends of the political spectrum today could be described as the return of the ancient gods. We can see elements of this among the mostly young men in the dissident right with their contempt for bourgeois "bug men" and glorification of warrior manliness.[5] What is far more interesting and problematic, however, is the return of ancient piety on the political left, partly because it is so strange and partly because the left now commands virtually every locus of power in American society, public and private. Many commentators have noted the odd alliances, rhetorical contradictions, and confusing motives that make our current political situation so bewildering. We are witnessing, it seems, a deep and very old tension between two conflicting psychological imperatives bursting out into the open. The momentum as well as the contradictions of this schizophrenia seem to be *the* driving force of our regime's current revolution (metabole).

POLYTHEISM AND THE UNITY OF THE ANCIENT MIND

In the beginning were the cities, and gods dwelt among the cities, and they were holy.

That idea, which I discussed at some length in the book, is the starting point for Jaffa's grand theological-political narrative. It is important for understanding Jaffa's project to appreciate the psychology of such closed regimes, such "cities of righteousness." The polis, Jaffa explained, was "a community of blood, of common descent."

> You were an Athenian—a Spartan, or a Cretan, or an Israelite— only because of your father and mother. Citizenship was not a voluntary act. The attachment of each city to its gods, and of its

gods to its city, which we see so clearly in the relationship of God and Israel, defines the fundamental dimension of human political consciousness in ancient cities.[6]

Jaffa is by no means the first to make this observation. In his lectures and writings, Strauss often mentioned the insights into this mindset by the historian Fustel de Coulanges.[7] As Coulanges showed, every ancient citizen recognized that other tribal nations or peoples were part of the physical world. But they were fundamentally *alien*. For that reason, Jaffa explains, the "ultimate sanctions for justice are not the penalties that can be exacted in the law-courts, but *ostracism*, formal or informal, from that fellowship in which alone the good citizen feels he can lead the good life."[8] [Emphasis added.]

I should clarify one point here. Citizenship and piety (or political and religious identity) were united *within each city*. The cities themselves, however, represented a great welter of differing gods and divine laws. And all ancient cities, excepting Jerusalem, were polytheistic, with many strange, arbitrary, and irrational customs, typically celebrated not only by the priests but also the poets of each city. It was precisely this contradictory variety in the traditional laws that led Socrates—in asking "What is justice?"—to propose *nature* as a standard of right. For the citizens, of course (as opposed to philosophers), the obligations of the law were simply accepted as sacred. Foreigners were both alien and profane.

Thus, writes Jaffa,

> to be an Athenian was a far more fundamental fact...than to be a human being. What divided them from all non-Athenians was paramount, what they had in common with each other was in comparison trivial. No appeal to the humanity of barbarians, for example, could be reason for refraining from their enslavement.[9]

This civic wholeness, as it were, led Aristotle (who was familiar with alternatives such as tribes and empires) to regard the city, the polis, as the most natural regime, the cave par excellence, and most representative of our inclinations as a political animal.

INVISIBLE GOVERNMENT

In his somewhat oddly constructed book *Original Intent and the Framers of the Constitution*, Jaffa includes several long and interesting digressions on various topics, including his responses to a series of questions from his friend George Anastaplo. In one such exchange, he is candid about the way political philosophers are the true "legislators" who govern the world, albeit indirectly and behind the scenes by shaping the community's authoritative opinions. This is not the only place Jaffa discusses this phenomenon. In one of his disputes with Harvey Mansfield, he cites John Maynard Keynes's observation that "the world is ruled" by "the ideas of economists and political philosophers."[10] And in his essay on the Bible and political philosophy, he remarks that in both Plato and Aristotle, "one can see the philosophers replacing the poets (and/or the Sophists)...as the source of a noncontradictory moral instruction."[11] Why this is necessary or appropriate we shall see in a moment.

Unlike the Sophists and materialist philosophers who preceded him, Socrates turned to *political* philosophy—to the examination of opinions about human concerns—in part to escape the immoderation of his predecessors. In key respects, Strauss explains, "pre-Socratic philosophy was mad." "To take a simple example," Strauss continues,

> Pre-Socratic philosophy said the whole is one, or they said the whole is infinite. Both are mad statements because, if the whole is one, it would mean, for example: this chair is the whole.... That

doesn't make sense. The very fact that we can speak of the chair within the whole shows [that] it's wrong to say the whole is simply one. And also, if there were an infinite variety of distinctions, then no possibility of any intelligent orientation would exist. It would lead to insanity. Sanity requires a finite number of distinctions.... So Socratic philosophy is emphatically commonsensical.[12]

To the degree that moral-political concerns are more immediate and evident to us, they may actually reveal more about the cosmos than, for example, looking into the heavens. "If human beings are part of the universe," Jaffa explains, "then whatever enables us to understand human beings must thereby enable us better to understand the universe of which they are a part." Approaching philosophy in exactly this way, by examining the principles of his own regime, Jaffa notes that the Declaration of Independence "embodies propositions about God and the universe, propositions that are metaphysical, no less than moral and political."[13]

The correspondence or parallel between political and metaphysical insights is what allows political philosophers to offer assistance in matters where the practical wisdom of moral gentlemen may be insufficient. The paradigmatic case is the Socratic insight into "the many and the one," as mentioned by Strauss above. Socratic philosophers understand that rational politics requires accommodating both the whole and the parts, a balance between unity and diversity.[14] Recall Jaffa's remark from Chapter 4 that, according to Aristotle, a healthy political community must be a compound whole that incorporates both homogeneity and heterogeneity. Socrates's discovery of natural right, or the idea of the Good, was partly an attempt to supplant or regulate the chaotic manyness of the polytheistic gods. As Jaffa says, "within the context of the Platonic dialogues, the gods of the ancient cities, who quarrel among themselves, provide no sure guidance to man." Plato's dialogue on piety, *Euthyphro*, presents the Socratic doctrine of the Ideas "as *the* alternative [to] the fighting gods." This juxtaposition, broadly understood, is not limited to ancient Greece. In our time, Jaffa points out, the polytheistic gods present themselves as "contending values."[15]

Socratic or natural right philosophy attempts to correct both the irrationality of the poets and the madness of the pre-Socratic materialist philosophers. (As we will see, there is a certain parallel to our current situation.) Reason, in the form of political philosophy, must assert itself as a kind of umpire—as the architectonic discipline—because "if there are many separate and equal sciences of human things, then there will be many separate and equally authoritative opinions concerning the human good." Without such rational guidance, Jaffa explains, the regime devolves into too much diversity or too much unity; the contending values "will issue either in 'permissive egalitarianism' or unpermissive totalitarianism."[16]

To emphasize the political implications of these abstract arguments, Jaffa reminds us that a "free society is a fellowship—a unity, or oneness of mind." Of course, it is not necessary (in fact it would be harmful) to have uniformity of opinion on all matters. However, to be fellow citizens, Americans must recognize the truth of equal, natural rights as "the basis of their social and political relationship, within which they can resolve their differences peacefully by debate, discussion, and free elections." For this reason, Aristotle emphasizes the "unanimity (literally, 'oneness of mind')" that characterizes friendship, which is even "greater than justice" because it "draws men towards justice."[17] When such friendship and justice are undermined, healthy politics cannot thrive. "Where the gods of the city are hostile to the virtues," Jaffa writes, "it may be necessary for Socratic philosophy to turn the city towards a purer religion."[18]

PHILOSOPHERS AND GENTLEMEN

To help ensure that the gods—the authoritative myths and traditions of the regimes—reflect sound theory, Socratic philosophers
rule indirectly "through the new breed of Sophists and poets that
results from the philosophers' influence on education—or, as in
the case of Aristotle, through the gentlemen whose education they
will supervise."[19] In this context, "gentlemen" refers to Aristotle's
spoudaios, serious and prudent citizens who take responsibility for
civic affairs. In most decent regimes, it is respectable, upstanding
property owners—not hectoring, shoeless philosophers—who are
best suited to be the acknowledged rulers. Yet these responsible
citizens, exemplars of practical wisdom, may require a certain support only philosophers can supply. Continuing with his response
to Anastaplo, Jaffa writes,

> The gentleman, qua gentleman, does not need reasons for being
> moral. Indeed, the true gentleman tends to regard the giving of
> such reasons as demeaning. In this lies both his strength and his
> weakness. But...gentlemen are nearly defenseless against false
> gods and false theories. Such theories might—and frequently do—
> destroy the ground of virtue in the souls of the non-gentlemen,
> and sometimes even in the souls of the gentlemen. Gentleman-
> ship requires that the gods of the city—and here I use classical
> terminology—look with favor upon these virtues, and those who
> practice them. The rule of gentlemen is *a priori* possible only
> within the cities that look to such gods.[20]

The rule of gentlemen—of free, responsible, prudent citizens—is a fair description of republican government, which fell
into a long dormancy after the fall of Rome. Jaffa argues that the
American founders rescued republicanism from the dungeon of

European feudalism. But before they could do so, they had to overcome the divided mind of political obligation. Chapter 5 discussed how this split occurred when Christianity and the Roman Empire broke the ancient city's "bond between God or the gods and law" and initiated the long battle "between the secular and the sacred, between Popes and Emperors within the Holy Roman empire." As Jaffa explains,

> Political life henceforth was dominated, not by the requirements of laws directing human actions as such, but by the requirements of faith directing men's souls toward eternity. If men's dearest interests were in another world, if the interests which they shared with aliens and enemies were in some sense dearer than those they shared with friends and fellow citizens, then citizenship became problematic in a way unknown to the ancient city.

In other words, a conflict between the universal and the particular arose in a way that did not confront citizens of Athens and Carthage.

> Coercion in matters of faith, coercion unrelated to morality or to disobedience to any laws prescriptive of justice or the common good, was virtually unknown in the ancient city. It was incompatible with the idea of gentlemanship. Now it became central to the political process. Henceforth western man was faced, not with the political problem properly so called, but with the political-theological problem.[21]

Another way of putting this is that patriotism became afflicted with a guilty conscience whenever the Bible, or natural right, or the universal rights of man, conflicted with duty to one's particular regime. Modern liberals make light of this tension, pretending to be citizens of the world. But that slogan is easier to proclaim than to live by. Suppressing the primordial need to belong to a particular community turns out to be not only difficult but dangerous, as I argue below.

The solution devised by the American founders involved, paradoxically, a separation that restored the possibility of unity. Religious liberty removed government from theological disputes and kept sectarians from making converts by force. Moreover, because classical natural right and the Bible agree broadly on the content of morality and its importance, a regime of equality and liberty could promote virtue while respecting the independent claims of both reason and religion. "Perhaps for the time," says Jaffa, "the rule of Christian gentlemen" became possible.[22] And while the Declaration expresses a truth applicable to all, the United States secures the rights only of Americans, a people with unique habits and customs. The universal and the particular are accommodated.

While some of Jaffa's critics found his talk of morality tedious, he considered it a key to the nation's wholeness. In a 1980 essay, he explains that for Aristotle the main effect of legislation "lies essentially in the power of habit, which is 'second nature.' That is why the formation of good habits is the primary task of the law. The moral virtues are good habits." The motto of the United States, *e pluribus unum*, refers in one sense to the union of the states. But, Jaffa argues, "it also refers, less obviously, but more profoundly, to the moral unity that underlies" the regime.

> *By virtue of this moral unity*, the American people are "one nation, under God." it is the antecedent moral unity that makes the political unity possible. Tolerance, for example, is certainly one of the virtues of a free republican people. But tolerance, as itself a moral virtue, cannot be indifferent to moral distinctions.[23] [Emphasis added.]

At one level, all this seems relatively straightforward. (And we are reminded again of why the injustice of slavery struck at the very essence of the regime.) There are, however, some complications. As discussed in Chapter 7, Jaffa needed a long time to figure out how the transcendent truths of the Declaration found concrete expression in "one people."

AUTHORITATIVE TRADITION

The American experiment—and Jaffa was clear that it was an experiment—depended on recovering moral gentlemanship from its long desuetude. This restoration, in turn, depended on the political theory of social compact and the framers' ingenious institutional solutions, especially federalism (that is, the balance between the one and the many). Jaffa writes,

> These wise theories of civil and religious liberty, are necessary conditions of gentlemanship in the modern world, not substitutes for it. But gentlemanship—the qualities necessary for the deserved supremacy of the untheoretical moral virtues within the political community—is possible only within the framework of these theories. In this sense, the emancipation of practice from theory must be a work of theory.[24]

All regimes, even secular ones, have gods or myths that legitimize and compel allegiance to the ruling authority. (What else is history for Marxist regimes, or science for our current technocratic oligarchy?) These of course may be more or less reasonable. The core of Jaffa's teaching on America was that the nonsectarian God of the Declaration of Independence—the author of the laws of nature—represented an unprecedented and judicious marriage of the Bible and philosophic natural right.[25]

The *perpetuation* of the founders' achievement, Jaffa further believed, had to come partly from men of theoretical wisdom. "No regime can survive," he once wrote, "that does not have within it the equivalent of a Sanhedrin, a College of Cardinals, or a Nocturnal Council." These "unidentified philosopher-kings" must "continuously interpret and reinterpret, amidst changing circumstances, the unchanging meaning of the fundamental principles upon which it rests." So important is this function that "without the silent operation of its invisible presence, political authority will fail of its purpose. There must be keepers of the tablets, or there will be no political salvation."[26] The indirect rule of Socratic philosophers mostly functions by shaping or guiding popular piety and common opinions; it relies on preexisting religious traditions and patriotic sentiments. "Plato himself found many of the materials of his art in 'history,' the central historical event being the life and death of Socrates," Jaffa notes. "Without these materials of history there would have been nothing to form into his art."[27] The philosophic legislator identifies and strengthens the best elements in the regime but cannot contrive politically salutary opinions out of nothing.

I think that Jaffa saw his own work, including the artful blending of history and poetry, in this vein.[28] In a letter to Steve Smith, a political philosophy professor at Yale, he observed that his work on Lincoln and America was inspired by an "oft repeated maxim" by Strauss: that a "decent political life is possible only within the framework of an authoritative tradition. Lincoln convinced me—and I think Strauss—that this was no less true, possibly even more true, of a democratic regime than of any other."[29] The American experiment (in its own self-understanding, a test of self-government for *all* mankind) could succeed only as long as the American mind held together. Such unity depended, in turn, on the success of an authoritative tradition. When this arrangement began to dissolve in the acid of radical skepticism, it opened up an even deeper and more worrisome divide.

The dogmas of positivism and historicism—which undermine both morality and reason—have pushed modern politics into the pit beneath the cave, in Strauss's memorable image. "Our institutions, beneficent and prosperous as they may be, subsist only on the inertia of old loyalties and narrow self-interest," Jaffa warned in 1980. They are "unsupported by anything resembling a rational faith, either in divine guidance or philosophic wisdom."[30] He elaborates on this in *A New Birth of Freedom*, where he repeatedly quotes from and discusses Jefferson's ringing statement in the Virginia Statute for Religious Freedom

> that truth is great and will prevail if left to herself; that she is the proper and sufficient antagonist to error, and has nothing to fear from the conflict unless by human interposition disarmed of her natural weapons, free argument and debate; errors ceasing to be dangerous when it is permitted freely to contradict them.

Yet Jaffa's point in several of these references is that truth quite often *is* disarmed, particularly "in our time." Most educated people in the West believe in some vague way in democracy and individual rights, yet they deny that we can "know what is just or unjust, right or wrong, true or false." Jaffa explains that if "there is no truth, or if the truth is beyond the power of the human mind to know, then free argument and debate as means of arriving at the truth are meaningless." The extent of "this challenge to the principle of a free society" is a danger "that neither Jefferson nor Lincoln anticipated."[31]

That is a striking assertion, and it underlines just how radical Strauss and Jaffa understood the crisis of the West to be. The situation confronting political philosophy today is in some ways similar to what Socrates faced when he interrogated the irrationality of the polytheistic gods (or "contending values") celebrated by the poets and also the distorted rationalism of the materialist philosophers. Yet, as Jaffa explains, Socrates could operate on the foundation of morality supported by Athenian laws and habits. Today, modernity's "prejudice against traditional piety is equally a prejudice against traditional moral philosophy, and the reason which informed it."[32] In the pit under the cave, to stretch the metaphor a bit, there is neither sunlight nor soil to sustain natural political life and healthy opinions. After a century of systematic attacks on the founding and distortions of America's history, the "materials of Plato's art," as Jaffa called them, have almost vanished.

Consider that in 1839, the exquisitely educated John Quincy Adams could proclaim matter-of-factly that the laws of nature and of nature's God presuppose "the existence of a God, the moral ruler of the universe, and a rule of right and wrong, of just and unjust, binding upon men, preceding all institutions of human society and government."[33] On almost any American college campus, this statement would now be considered simply laughable. Of course, these same sophisticated thinkers who would mock Adams fail to see that their own intellectual self-confidence rests on nothing but a delusion, which, as I argue below, cannot last.

Jaffa tried to show how thin and unstable such delusions are. "Modern philosophy," he wrote in a letter to Henry Salvatori, "has been a failure."

> It has proved powerful only in destroying reason and revelation as guides of human life, but has put literally nothing in their place. *Nothing* however has proved to be the angriest and most jealous of gods! Nihilism and atheism are the residue of the self-destruction of reason by modern philosophy. And they are the dominant modes of unthinking thought in the West today.

The resulting "metaphysical despair," he argued, will drive young people to "something worse" than Marxism "unless they can be led toward a universe that seems to hold some promise of meaning for their lives."[34] Modern liberalism seeks "to make each human being, as far as possible, a universal tyrant within his own world, commanding all the pleasures possible in that world."[35] But as Jaffa notes elsewhere, the tyrant—among other considerations—cannot have friends; and according to Aristotle, a life without friends is not worth living. The result is a universal ostracism, an existential alienation that so far from being liberating is ultimately unbearable. Here we see the second and more serious "divided mind." But to understand it properly, we need to back up four hundred years.

FALSE IDOLS AND DEAD ENDS

One of Jaffa's persistent criticisms of Eastern Straussians was their tendency to forget that someone is always shaping the opinions of the regimes. If Socratic thinkers disdain that responsibility, it will be seized by less capable or less beneficent mythmakers. Like nature, the cave abhors a vacuum. This difficulty is not resolved merely by having such self-interested theorizers proclaim themselves "philosophers." Because Jaffa had a higher estimation of practical virtue and statesmanship, he cast a jaundiced eye on the privileges due to anyone who claimed this title.[36] Recall his striking statement, in his *CRB* dispute with Thomas Pangle: "Philosophers must be taught—sometimes even by chastisement—how to act in a responsible manner."[37]

Although (as Jaffa saw it) *classical* or *Socratic* political philosophy attempts indirectly to strengthen reason and moderation, there may be other attempts to shape opinion—by ideologues and sophists—that recklessly weaken the people's faith in their gods. This irresponsible undermining of healthy piety "may justly be regarded as a doubtful blessing, if not a curse." When these efforts succeed, the regime is afflicted with irrational or immoral "gods" in the form of unsound and tyrannical theories. Locating this phenomenon in the origins of the modern project, Jaffa argues that

> non-Socratic philosophy—or the influence of such philosophy— may elevate bad faith, cruelty, and selfishness over morality. We see that, above all, in Machiavelli, and the Machiavellians who—with notable exceptions—have dominated the theoretical landscape (and the poetry that has accompanied it) for over 400 years.[38]

Confronted by the political schizophrenia of official Christianity in Europe, the early moderns—to use an extreme metaphor— thought the best cure was a lobotomy. Simply cut away that part of man called "soul" or "virtue," with all its wild expectations about transcendent truth and justice, and focus on what politics can accomplish in the here and now. With the aid of modern science, government could ensure our security and the satisfaction of our material desires (in principle, all of them).

Given the innumerable miseries of European theocracy and the horrors of doctrinal warfare, Jaffa appreciated this groping for *some* solution. But the ambition conceived by Hobbes, Descartes, and others proved to be disastrous, descending finally (although of course indirectly) to the murderous ideologies of the twentieth century and the soft nihilism of our contemporary universities and popular culture. If America offered a prudent political solution to the divided mind, the other path was represented by modern theory, which over four centuries worked out the premises of the original scientific project: skepticism, materialism, and positivism.

The powerful German thinkers Nietzsche and Heidegger recognized that this led finally to a philosophic dead end. But they drew very different conclusions than Strauss and Jaffa had. They too saw the world-historical change in the transformation of the ancient psyche. In their view, however, what Socrates and his students initiated—as the first teachers of natural right and universal Ideas—was a cataclysm in the history of philosophy. Notwithstanding Plato's use, in *The Republic* and *Laws,* of religious poetry and "autochthonous" myths (by which citizens would be taught that their ancestors sprang out of the soil), the notion of cosmopolitan ideas accessible to all human beings took on a life of its own. Nietzsche famously derided Christianity as "Platonism for the masses," referring to the discovery (or invention) of transcendent truths. Heidegger attributed man's existential angst, or "homesickness," to the destruction of authentic piety grounded in a particular community.[39]

NOTHING FROM NOTHING

Jaffa, of course, regarded nihilism and radical skepticism as a *rejection* of Socratic philosophy, as did his friend Harry Neumann, though from a quite different perspective. Neumann, who was born into an Orthodox Jewish family in Germany before emigrating to the US, believed that he had pursued the implications of German nihilism further than either Nietzsche or Heidegger. By taking the inner logic of nihilism to its ultimate (and, he would insist, undeniable) implications, Neumann believed he grasped something in the original Socratic enterprise that was missed by conventional liberal scholars. His colleague's intellectual courage led Jaffa to remark that "I have learned more about the inner relationship between philosophy and politics from Harry Neumann than from anyone else except Leo Strauss." Jaffa goes on to say, "No one living has so ruthlessly uncovered the divided mind—the political schizophrenia—arising from the unconscious (and conscious) nihilism of contemporary liberalism."[40]

For Neumann, true Socratic philosophy requires a difficult—almost impossible—zetetic skepticism that seeks wisdom about the Good but remains persistently open-minded. The true philosopher never knows enough to declare atheism as simply true. Yet virtually all modern philosophy dogmatically avows amoral nihilism, which Neumann regarded as the root of modern liberalism and science. "Nihilism," he argued, "means that nothing has an identity or nature." *Everything* is "subject to radical, random change or obliteration at any moment."

> No divine or natural support exists for the commonsense faith that anything is more than nothing. Nothing is more than what it experiences or what is experienced about it. There is nothing in, behind or above things to make them more than empty experiences (thoughts, perceptions, moods, feelings, etc.), impressions as Hume called them.... Nothing prevents anything from changing or being changed into anything else or into the nothing which everything always is.[41]

This less-than-cheerful doctrine is hard for most enlightened, democratic people to accept, so they try to avoid thinking about the stark consequences. The problem is that when God, nature, and tradition have been relentlessly discredited, nihilism remains the only logical alternative. Yet human beings are not reliably logical. Neumann believed that even Nietzsche and Heidegger had flinched. Their doctrines of the eternal return, or new gods who would disclose Being, were surrenders to the nearly irresistible human need to believe in something.[42]

Neumann readily admitted that he had never—and could never—*prove* the truth of nihilism. So he and Jaffa disputed the great questions, back and forth, year after year. Whether Neumann finally believed in the truth of nihilism or was playing Dr. Moriarty to Jaffa's Sherlock Holmes is not relevant. As teachers, they had the same goal. "The ultimate ground for the refutation of nihilism," Jaffa pointed out, "is moral reality. Whether or not I have in fact refuted nihilism—as I believe I have—Neumann agrees that the only ground upon which it can be refuted—if it is refuted—is on the ground of moral reality."[43]

Because Neumann was interested in exploring nihilistic themes in art and literature (such as the novels of Joseph Conrad and Franz Kafka), his writings help us understand the terror and fanatical hatred that *nothing* can evoke. When the empty myths of the sophisticates are exposed, he observed, "liberalism inspires suicidal boredom or murderous rage in those unable to endure it." Unable to live with their doctrinaire rejection of moral reality, liberals cling to propaganda about progress and science. But when these prove unable to offer any happiness or account of the good life, the "central insight" about nihilism emerges. The innate "moral or political striving" for meaning, which cannot find any fulfillment, leads to a "fanatical determination to hide the truth from oneself." The further this fanaticism proceeds, "the more desperate the resolve to eradicate liberal pluralism becomes." This passionate intensity finally "consciously or unconsciously confuses or destroys politics." Neumann points out that Nietzsche had predicted the emergence of "last men," those timid, consensus-seeking figures described in Chapter 1 as "mole-men." But Neumann insisted that Nietzsche was mistaken, as was Tocqueville, for the same reason. They both failed to recognize that as the falsity of the propaganda becomes apparent, "human passion and its spiritedness will become violent.... The last thing this virulent hatred will produce is last men!"[44]

THE CITY OF LOST SOULS

Because many Americans today, especially the young, cannot tolerate their existential ostracism, we seem to be witnessing the bizarre return of an ancient, closed city—complete with vengeful gods and strictly enforced piety—yet committed to half-believed slogans about liberal "values." It might be called the Holy City of Anti-Racism (though one could also mention identity politics, "wokeness," political correctness, etc.). Not the least of its strange features is the cognitive dissonance between its Enlightenment pretensions—progress, science, human rights, individualism—and its primitive obsessions with racialism, resentment, and revenge. As Neumann remarked presciently about these refugees from the abyss, "Their modern rootlessness makes it impossible to acknowledge their deep need for what they despise as backwardness, superstition or racism."[45]

The unmistakably religious character of this phenomenon has led quite a few commentators to see the "woke" agenda as a perverted form of Christianity. There surely are elements of America's Puritan heritage at work, and comparisons to the Inquisition and witch-burning are not off base. Fewer, however, have tried to explain the intermingled elements of nihilism, reminiscent especially of Nietzsche. Overall, I think too much emphasis on Protestant notions of guilt obscures more than it reveals.

My own view is that this new religiosity is not a bastardized form of Christianity but rather something older, deeper, and simpler: the need to belong to a sacred community with a moral purpose. Scott Atran, a professor of anthropology and psychology, has extensively studied the literature on the psychic need for belonging and purpose and has also done extensive field work to understand the motivations of Islamic jihadists. The most aggressive factions of the punitive left in America bear a striking resemblance to the Muslim martyrs that Atran profiles. Islamic terrorists often know very little about the Koran and have no clear agenda for social reform or political improvement. Atran finds that what attracts young men to jihad is mainly a feeling of "group pride" in "great achievements," "moral simplicity," and a "call to passion and action on humanity's behalf." He cites scholarly research showing that adherents to many different religions profess "a willingness to die for one's god or gods and belief that other religions are responsible for problems in the world."[46]

Altogether, I think what we are witnessing is a longing for the pre-Christian holy city memorably described by Jaffa above—the human need for a close-knit community of comrades devoted to a sacred cause. It is not Christian theology but the tribal ethos of Sparta and Carthage that better captures the left's obsession with racial kinship, which rejects the Golden Rule in favor of the rule of blood and iron. As mentioned above, this phenomenon appears to some degree among young Nietzscheans on the right but is far more pronounced on the other side of the political spectrum, where the expulsion of patriotism, the Bible, and classical rationalism have left only a gaping hole. The divided mind of the postmodern abyss is seeking to become whole, but what has emerged from the attempt so far appears to be a Frankenstein monster.

WHO RULES WHOM?

To return now to the beginning: what about Ed Erler's speech at the Claremont Institute retreat, in which he paired (correctly, it turns out) the threats of oligarchy and identity politics? My brief look into Jaffa's examination of the divided mind does not provide complete answers about what we are witnessing and where it will go. Even apart from the agenda of the Silicon Valley tech moguls, the leftist urge to recreate the ancient city is very confusing, not least to its own devotees. History has never before witnessed the birth of a Holy City of Nihilism. Having wiped out all traditions, these founders seek to build their castle not merely on sand but on air. Yet as far as we know, only God can create a world *ex nihilo*. Beyond snarling at its enemies and enforcing its protean catechism of sacred pieties, it isn't clear what this closed city wants to be. Paul Gottfried has noted the striking absence of any coherent agenda within Antifa.[47] And Charles Kesler has observed that the left's intense feelings about public monuments extends only to tearing down statues; they have no heroes to install on these vacant pedestals.[48] The radicals burn for moral purpose, but beyond some loose rhetoric about social justice and equity, they seem unable to identify any definite goals for their moral passion. Jaffa would have something to offer these confused souls.

I'm still not clear myself whether the tribalists are using the oligarchs or vice-versa. It's always a bad to idea to bet against money and power, of course. Yet in their cultural assumptions and intellectual prejudices (one can't call them rational opinions), these are not two separate phenomena. The real difference seems to be that a small minority of the nihilist left are successfully managing their existential crisis with the narcotic of wealth and privilege. Some of the oligarchs may actually believe in the platitudes of the movements they lavishly fund; some may only be cynically repeating the talking points. In either case, their ability to spend their way out of the abyss is only a short-term answer. It seems likely that they can insulate themselves from the existential dread—which their poorer allies feel so acutely—only as long as the money keeps flowing. Yet this does nothing to calm the resentment and anxiety of those troops on the ground. Moreover, the steps needed for the oligarchs to maintain their privilege will only exacerbate the pain of the empty souls who find no joy in a life limited to consumerism and cubicle labor. I doubt, therefore, that even a global tyranny will ultimately be able to control such a primordial human need, which seems likely only to intensify. Yet some form of a universal homogenous state, similar to what Alexandre Kojève predicted, could still persist for a long time. In any case, my purpose here is not to prognosticate but only to examine some unappreciated features of our current discontents.

NATURE, PRUDENCE, AND THE GOOD

And blessed are those
Whose blood and judgment are so well commingled,
That they are not a pipe for Fortune's finger
To sound what stop she please. Give me that man
That is not passion's slave, and I will wear him
In my heart's core, ay, in my heart of heart.

—HAMLEt, *Act III, Scene ii.*

Let me close by mentioning two points in Jaffa's teaching that may help us navigate our way, intellectually and politically.

First, the Nihilist City cannot succeed, though it may cause great damage before this becomes apparent. Nothing, King Lear reminded his beloved daughter, can come of nothing. There are also some on the right who are enchanted by the allure of "authentic" life in a premodern, homogenous community under a Charlamagne or an Alcibiades. My suggestion to them is not to wait for the collapse of the leftist fantasy but rather to give up now their specious dreams about a mythic past. As I mentioned in the last chapter, mankind cannot turn back the clock on the Socratic discovery of transcendent truth and natural right or the Christian and scientific insights into human equality. Any modern attempt to return to the polytheistic chaos of tribalism would entail not an ascent back to the natural cave but a regression into the subhuman. Rejecting the rule of reason over passion, Jaffa argued, by refusing to "recognize how man's nature is circumscribed within the order of creation" will not bring back a prehistoric or prephilosophic Eden. The attempt will only lead to something "not divine but bestial."[49] As Neumann liked to remind his students, there was no freedom in the mandatory piety of the polis, and romanticized visions of life in the ancient world tend to overlook its stultifying conformity.[50] Are the spirited, piratical young men of the dissident right really so eager for that?

The more important point Jaffa would probably make would be in the form of a question to the social justice warriors: "What will you do with your life when you eliminate all the racists?"[51] Of course, it might be unfair to expect a coherent answer from agitated young radicals. But even among his learned colleagues who study Plato and Aristotle with great seriousness, Jaffa noticed that many Straussians have little to say about the good life for nonphilosophers—that is, nearly everyone.

If the time ever comes when lost and angry young people might be willing to consider—in their desperation—the distilled teaching of a dead Greek, they could turn to Jaffa's writings and find this:

> Since Aristotle, happiness has been defined as the *summum bonum*, that highest good which comprehends all lesser goods, and renders them beneficial to their possessor. One cannot, for example, imagine a happy man, who was a fool, lacking in self-respect, a slave, and without friends. Happiness implies the presence of the other good things, in such manner and proportion, as to contribute to the well-being of their possessor.[52]

To reflect on or even comprehend such ideas—and entertain the possibility that they might be relevant, or even true—presupposes the metaphysical freedom of the human mind. And before a divided mind can become whole, it first must be free. Not incidentally, this requires the peace and leisure necessary to think and act without despotic constraints. That raises in turn the grave question of whether the modern impulse to philosophic and political tyranny (and barbaric anarchy is also a form of tyranny) can permanently suppress human nature or even the human awareness of nature. Jaffa, for his part, believed that "the evidence, supplied by both philosophy and revelation," shows that the human soul irrepressibly "participates in a reality that transcends all time and change."[53]

If this is so, political philosophy remains possible and may still devise republican remedies as yet unknown to preserve or recover a regime of liberty by applying practical wisdom to changing circumstances. We may also call this simply the exercise of prudence, which is now and always the soul of politics.

ACKNOWLEDGMENTS

I cannot adequately express my gratitude to Larry Arnn and Matthew Spalding at Hillsdale College for their generosity and unwavering support. Whether our teacher would be pleased by this effort, I cannot say. He would surely have appreciated the attention, if nothing else. I can only hope this book has done him some credit and justified the trust invested in me by my old friends. Thank you, Larry and Matt.

The staff of Hillsdale's Mossey Library—especially Maurine McCourry, Lori Curtis, and Brendan LaVoie—provided indispensable help to facilitate my extensive use of the Jaffa archives. Two promising young scholars, first Kevin LoTruglio and then Joey Barretta, aided me under the rubric of research assistants. Their energy, dedication, and discernment, however, far exceeded that description. I look forward to watching their careers unfold.

Many friends encouraged this project and read parts or all of the manuscript. I am particularly grateful to Michael Anton, Charles Kesler, Chris Flannery, R. J. Pestritto, Julie Ponzi, Richard Reeb, and especially Rebecca Teti, Ken Masugi, and Eric Wise. I would like to thank each of them properly, as they deserve, by acknowledging the many brilliant suggestions and criticisms they shared. But that would require another book.

Encounter, my excellent publisher, is a model of professionalism—and courage. I am proud to be part of its stable. I am grateful to Ryan Williams at the Claremont Institute for establishing that connection and for generous support while I was getting this book ready for publication.

My mother is not a scholar but rather something better: an American by choice and temperament. Her constant enthusiasm—delighting in any updates even when I had almost nothing to report—meant the world to me.

HARRY V. JAFFA
SELECTED BIBLIOGRAPHY

1949

"War Powers Under the Pact, Scope of Presidential Authority in Event of Attack Discussed." Letter, *New York Times*, April 4, 1949

1952

Thomism and Aristotelianism, A Study of the Commentary by Thomas Aquinas on the Nicomachean Ethics. Chicago: University of Chicago Press, 1952. Reprinted by Greenwood Press, 1979.

Review of Alan Gewirth, *Marsilius of Padua, The Defender of Peace. Social Research*, March 1952.

1953

Review of Max Hamburger, *Morals and Law, The Growth of Aristotle's Legal Theory. American Political Science Review*, June 1953.

1954

Remarks at "The Trial and Death of Socrates." A dramatization by Columbia University in its series "Man's Right to Knowledge and the Free Use Thereof." WOSU, October 6, 1954.

Review of Giorgio Del Vecchio, *Justice: An Historical and Philosophical Essay. The Journal of Criminal Law, Criminology and Political Science* 45, No. 4 (November–December 1954).

1955

Review of John Bowle, *Politics and Opinion in the Nineteenth Century: An Historical Introduction. Annals of American Academy of Political and Social Science* 297 (January 1955).

Review of Kurt Von Fritz, *The Theory of the Mixed Constitution in Antiquity: A Critical Analysis of Polybius' Political Ideas. American Political Science Review*, June 1956.

1957

"Expediency and Morality in the Lincoln-Douglas Debates." *The Anchor Review* 2, (1957).

"In Defense of the Natural Law Thesis." *American Political Science Review*, March 1957. Reprinted in *Equality and Liberty.*

"The Limits of Politics: An Interpretation of *King Lear*, Act I, Scene 1." *American Political Science Review*, September 1957. Reprinted in *Shakespeare's Politics* and *The Conditions of Freedom.*

1958

Review of *Created Equal: The Complete Lincoln Douglas Debates of 1858*, edited by Paul M. Angle. *The New Leader*, August 1958. Reprinted in *The Conditions of Freedom.*

"'Value-Consensus in Democracy': The Issue in the Lincoln-Douglas Debates," *American Political Science Review*, September 1958. Reprinted in *Equality and Liberty.*

1959

In the Name of the People, Speeches and Writings of Lincoln and Douglas in the Ohio Campaign of 1858. Edited with an Introduction by Harry V. Jaffa and Robert W. Johannsen. Columbus: Ohio State University Press, 1959.

Crisis of the House Divided, An Interpretation of the Issues in the Lincoln-Douglas Debates. Garden City, NY: Doubleday and Company, 1959. Republished by University of Washington Press, 1973. Republished by University of Chicago Press, 1982, 2009.

1960

"The Case Against Political Theory." *The Journal of Politics*, May 1960. Reprinted in *Equality and Liberty*.

Reply to Allan Nevins's review of *Crisis of the House Divided*. *The New Leader*, June 20, 1960.

1961

"The Case for a Stronger National Government." In *A Nation of States*, edited by Robert A. Goldwin. Chicago: Rand McNally, 1961.

"Agrarian Virtue and Republican Freedom: An Historical Perspective." In *Goals and Values in Agricultural Policy*. Ames: Iowa State University Press, 1961. Reprinted in *Equality and Liberty*.

"The Nature and Origin of the American Party System." In *Political Parties, U.S.A.*, edited by Robert A. Goldwin. Chicago: Rand McNally, 1961. Reprinted in *Equality and Liberty*.

"The Sovereign Republic: Notes of a Citizen of the United States." Hillsdale College archive.

"Strauss on Political Philosophy." *American Political Science Review*, September 1961.

1962

"Aristotle." In *History of Political Philosophy*, edited by Leo Strauss and Joseph Cropsey. Chicago: Rand McNally, 1962. Reprinted in *The Conditions of Freedom*.

"Letters of a Patriot." Review of *The Letters of Stephen A. Douglas*, edited by Robert W. Johannsen. *Journal of Southern History* 28, No. 2 (May 1962). Reprinted in *The Conditions of Freedom*.

"Patriotism and Morality." Review of Donald W. Riddle, *Congressman Abraham Lincoln*. *Chicago Review*, Summer–Autumn 1962. Reprinted in *Equality and Liberty*.

1963

"Conflicts Within the Idea of the Liberal Tradition," *Comparative Studies in Society and History* 5, No. 3 (April 1963).

1964

Bloom, Allan with Jaffa, Harry V., *Shakespeare's Politics*. New York: Basic Books, 1964. Reprinted, University of Chicago Press, 1982.

"On the Nature of Civil and Religious Liberty." In *The Conservative Papers*, edited by Melvin A. Laird. New York: Doubleday Anchor, 1964. Reprinted in *Equality and Liberty*.

1965

Equality and Liberty: Theory and Practice in American Politics. New York: Oxford University Press, 1965. Republished by the Claremont Institute, 1999.

"Reconstruction, Old and New." Review of Kenneth M. Stammp, *The Era of Reconstruction 1865–1877*. *National Review*, April 20, 1965. Reprinted in *The Conditions of Freedom*.

"Lincoln and the Cause of Freedom." *National Review*, September 21, 1965. Reprinted in *The Conditions of Freedom*.

1966

"The Virtue of a Nation of Cities." In *A Nation of Cities*, edited by Robert A. Goldwin. Chicago: Rand McNally, 1966. Reprinted in *The Conditions of Freedom*.

1968

"Natural Rights." *International Encyclopedia of the Social Sciences*. New York: Macmillan Company, 1968.

"The Limits of Dissent." Review of Abe Fortas, *Concerning Dissent and Civil Disobedience*. *National Review*, September 10, 1968.

1969

"Reflections on Thoreau and Lincoln." In *On Civil Disobedience, Essays Old and New*, edited by Robert A. Goldwin. New York: Rand McNally, 1969. Reprinted in *The Conditions of Freedom*.

1970

"Spokesman for the Political Tradition." Review of Jim G. Lucas, *Agnew, Profile in Conflict. National Review*, October 6, 1970.

"Weathermen and Fort Sumter." *National Review*, December 29, 1970.

"Political Obligation and the American Political Tradition." Prepared for delivery at the 1970 meeting of the American Political Science Association. Reprinted in *The Conditions of Freedom*.

1972

"The Conditions of Freedom." *Claremont Journal of Public Affairs*, Spring 1972. Reprinted in *The Conditions of Freedom*.

"Tom Sawyer: Hero of Middle America." *Interpretation*, Spring 1972. Reprinted in *The Conditions of Freedom*.

"What is Equality?" Prepared for delivery at The Center for Constructive Alternatives, Hillsdale College, September 1972. Reprinted in *The Conditions of Freedom*.

1973

"Partly Federal, Partly National: On the Political Theory of the Civil War." In *A Nation of States*, Revised Edition, edited by Robert A. Goldwin. New York: Rand McNally, 1973. Reprinted in *The Conditions of Freedom*.

"Contra Herndon." Review of Elton Trueblood, *Abraham Lincoln: Theologian of American Anguish. National Review*, March 30, 1973.

"Portrait of a Patriot." Review of Robert W. Johannsen, *Stephen A. Douglas, National Review*, May 25, 1973. Reprinted in *The Conditions of Freedom*.

"The Truth About War." Review of *Young Winston's Wars: The Original Despatches of Winston S. Churchill, War Correspondent 1897–1900*, edited by Frederick Woods. *National Review*, August 3, 1973. Reprinted in *The Conditions of Freedom*.

"Full-Scale versus Large-Scale." Reply to Professor Alexander Bickel. *National Review*, September 28, 1973.

"Amoral America and the Liberal Dilemma." Prepared for a symposium by the Committee for Academic Freedom, Claremont, California, Fall 1973. Reprinted in *The Conditions of Freedom*.

"What About the Dardanelles." Review of Martin Gilbert, *Winston S. Churchill, 1914–1916: The Tests of War* and *Winston S. Churchill: Companion Volume III*, edited by Martin Gilbert. *National Review*, November 23, 1973. Reprinted in *The Conditions of Freedom*.

"Leo Strauss." Memorial address delivered in Claremont, California, November 3, 1973. Published in *National Review*, December 7, 1973. Reprinted in *The Conditions of Freedom*.

1974

"Torpedoing the Lusitania Thesis." *National Review*, March 15, 1974.

"The Sinking of the Lusitania: Bungling, Brutality, or Betrayal?" *Claremont Journal of Public Affairs*, Spring 1974. Reprinted in *Statesmanship: Essays in Honor of Sir Winston Churchill*.

"Camus' *The Stranger*." Lecture prepared for delivery at Hillsdale College, April 1974. Hillsdale College archive.

"Dostoevsky's *Crime and Punishment*." Lecture prepared for delivery at Hillsdale College, April 1974. Hillsdale College archive.

"*Macbeth* and the Moral Universe." Lecture prepared for delivery at Hillsdale College, April 1974. Reprinted in the *Claremont Review of Books*, Winter 2007–2008.

"Equality as a Conservative Principle." Prepared for delivery at the 1974 annual meeting of the American Political Science Association. Reprinted in *How to Think About the American Revolution*.

1975

The Conditions of Freedom: Essays in Political Philosophy. Baltimore: Johns Hopkins University Press, 1975. Reprinted by the Claremont Institute, 2000.

"Time on the Cross Debate: But Not Redeemed." *National Review*, March 28, 1975.

"How to Think About the American Revolution: A Bicentennial Cerebration." Prepared for delivery at the 1975 annual meeting of the American Political Science Association. Reprinted in *How to Think About the American Revolution*.

1976
"Lincoln and the Bicentennial." Editorial. *Lincoln Herald*, Fall 1976.

1977
"The (OKAY) Imperial Presidency." Review of Joseph P. Lash, *Roosevelt and Churchill, 1939–1941: The Partnership that Saved the West. National Review*, February 4, 1977. Reprinted in *Statesmanship: Essays in Honor of Sir Winston Churchill.*

"Equality, Justice, and the American Revolution: A Reply to Bradford's 'The Heresy of Equality.'" *Modern Age*, Spring 1977. Reprinted in *How to Think About the American Revolution.*

"Democracy, Good and Bad." *National Review*, May 13, 1977.

"Political Philosophy and Honor." *Modern Age*, Fall 1977. Reprinted in *How to Think About the American Revolution.*

"On Mano's Jews for Jesus: An Exchange." *National Review*, December 9, 1977.

"A Phoenix from the Ashes: The Death of James Madison's Constitution (Killed by James Madison) and the Birth of Party Government." Prepared for delivery at the 1977 annual meeting of the American Political Science Association. Hillsdale College archive.

1978
How to Think About the American Revolution: A Bicentennial Cerebration. Durham: Carolina Academic Press, 1978. Reprinted by the Claremont Institute, 2001.

"Comment on Professor Lewis S. Feuer's 'The Problems of a Conservative Democrat.'" Prepared for delivery at a conference on the Philosophy of Spinoza, The Jewish Theological Seminary, April 1978. Hillsdale College archive.

"Human Rights and Détente." Column distributed by Public Research, Syndicated, June 23, 1978. Hillsdale College archive.

"What Happened at Camp David?" Column distributed by Public Research, Syndicated, October 21, 1978. Hillsdale College archive.

1979

"Marietta Founders and Scholars Day Speech." Prepared for delivery upon receiving an honorary degree, February 1979.

"Has Reagan Promised Too Much?" August 1980, a syndicated column distributed by Public Research, Syndicated. Hillsdale College archive.

"Looking at Mr. Goodlyfe." *Current*, September 1979. Reprinted in *American Conservatism and the American Founding.*

1980

"Foreword." In Harold W. Rood, *The Kingdoms of the Blind.* Studies in Statesmanship Series, Harry V. Jaffa, general editor. Durham: Carolina Academic Press, 1980.

"Another Look at the Declaration of Independence." *National Review*, July 11, 1980. Reprinted in *American Conservatism and the American Founding.*

1981

Statesmanship: Essays in Honor of Sir Winston Spencer Churchill, edited with contributions by Harry V. Jaffa. Durham: Carolina Academic Press, 1981.

"Chastity as a Political Principle: An Interpretation of Shakespeare's *Measure for Measure.*" In *Shakespeare as Political Thinker*, edited by John Alvis and Thomas G. West. Durham: Carolina Academic Press, 1981.

"The Unity of Comedy, Tragedy, and History: An Interpretation of the Shakespearean Universe." In *Shakespeare as Political Thinker*, edited by John Alvis and Thomas G. West. Durham: Carolina Academic Press, 1981.

"Foreword." In Jeffrey D. Wallin, *By Ships Alone: Churchill and the Dardanelles.* Studies in Statesmanship Series, Harry V. Jaffa, general editor. Durham: Carolina Academic Press, 1981.

"Inventing the Past: Gary Wills' *Inventing America* and the Pathology of Ideological Scholarship." *St. John's Review* 33, No. 1, (Autumn 1981).

"The Wisdom of the People Must Correct the Folly of the Court." Column distributed by Public Research, Syndicated. November 27, 1981. Hillsdale College archive.

"The 1980 Presidential Election: A Watershed in the Making," *Current*, Winter 1981. Reprinted in *American Conservatism and the American Founding.*

"A Conversation with Harry V. Jaffa at Rosary College." *Claremont Review of Books*, December 1981. Reprinted in *American Conservatism and the American Founding.*

"For the Good Government and the Happiness of Mankind: The Moral Majority and the American Founding." Prepared for delivery at Loyola University of Chicago, December 1981. *Reprinted in American Conservatism and the American Founding.*

"Dred Scott and the American Regime." Prepared for delivery at the 1981 annual meeting of the American Political Association. Reprinted in *American Conservatism and the American Founding.*

1982

"Foreword." In Thomas B. Silver, *Coolidge and the Historians.* Studies in Statesmanship Series, Harry V. Jaffa, general editor. Durham: Carolina Academic Press, 1982.

"In Defense of Political Philosophy: A Letter to Walter Berns." *National Review*, January 22, 1982. Reprinted in *American Conservatism and the American Founding.*

"July 4, 1982: The 110th Anniversary of Calvin Coolidge's Birth." Column distributed by Public Research, Syndicated. June 23, 1982. Hillsdale College archive.

"Behavioral Science and the Hinckley Verdict." Column distributed by Public Research, Syndicated, July 15, 1982. Hillsdale College archive.

"The Primary of the Good: Leo Strauss Remembered." *Modern Age* 26, No. 3–4 (Summer/Fall 1982). Reprinted in *American Conservatism and the American Founding.*

"Old Left Right Out or the Whose Ox is Gored School of Constitutional Jurisprudence." Column distributed by Public Research, Syndicated, October 1, 1982. Hillsdale College archive.

"The Declaration and the Draft." Column distributed by Public Research, Syndicated, October 29, 1982. Hillsdale College archive.

"Human Rights and the Crisis of the West." Prepared for delivery at the Tocqueville Forum on Public Policy, Wake Forest University. Reprinted in *American Conservatism and the American Founding*.

1983

"The Doughface Dilemma or The Hidden Slave in the American Enterprise Institute's Bicentennial." *Occasional Paper* Number 5, The Claremont Institute, January 1983. Reprinted in *American Conservatism and the American Founding*.

"The Birthday of Abraham Lincoln." Column distributed by Public Research, Syndicated, February 4, 1983. Hillsdale College archive.

"The Birthday of George Washington." Column distributed by Public Research, Syndicated, February 15, 1983. Hillsdale College archive.

"Marxism 100 Years After the Death of Marx." Column distributed by Public Research, Syndicated, March 4, 1983. Hillsdale College archive.

"Martin Luther King, Jr. Remembered." Column distributed by Public Research, Syndicated, March 22, 1983. Hillsdale College archive.

"On the Education of the Guardians of Freedom." Prepared for delivery at the thirtieth anniversary of the Intercollegiate Studies Institute, September 1983. Published in *Modern Age* 30, No. 2 (Spring 1986).

"The Death of 007." Column distributed by Public Research, Syndicated, September 9, 1983. Hillsdale College archive.

"The Massacre of the Palestinians: What Lessons Can We Learn?" Column distributed by Public Research, Syndicated, October 1, 1983. Hillsdale College archive.

"Municipal Defense Policy: The Latest Attempt at Nullifying the Constitution" Column distributed by Public Research, Syndicated, November 22, 1983. Hillsdale College archive.

"Detente: The Opiate of the Democracies." Column distributed by Public Research, Syndicated, November 29,1983. Hillsdale College archive.

1984

American Conservatism and the American Founding. Durham: Carolina Academic Press, 1984. Reprinted by the Claremont Institute, 2002.

"Foreword." In Francis Canavan, *Freedom of Expression: Purpose as Limit.* Studies in Statesmanship Series, Harry V. Jaffa, general editor. Durham Carolina Academic Press, 1984.

"Abraham Lincoln and Equality." Column distributed by Public Research, Syndicated, February 3, 1984. Hillsdale College archive.

"Marxist-Leninist Committee Criticizes U.S. Imperialism." *The Collage,* February 14, 1984. Hillsdale College archive.

"The Birthday of George Washington." Column distributed by Public Research, Syndicated, February 14, 1984. Hillsdale College archive.

"American Policy in Lebanon: What Next?" Column distributed by Public Research, Syndicated, February 22, 1984. Hillsdale College archive.

Letter to the Editor, "What's So Bad About Being a Marxist-Leninist?" *The Collage,* February 28, 1984. Hillsdale College archive.

"Let's Have a Sanity Clause." Column distributed by Public Research, Syndicated, March 8, 1984. Hillsdale College archive.

"Does the Soviet Union Seek World Domination?" Column distributed by Public Research, Syndicated, May 1, 1984. Hillsdale College archive.

"How to Think About the Olympic Games." Column distributed by Public Research, Syndicated, May 15, 1984. Hillsdale College archive.

"Were the Founding Fathers Christian?" *This World,* Spring/Summer 1984.

"Barry Goldwater's Victory." Column distributed by Public Research, Syndicated, June 28, 1984. Hillsdale College archive.

"Goldwater's Famous 'Gaffe.'" *National Review,* August 10, 1984.

"The Legacy of Leo Strauss." Review of Leo Strauss, *Studies in Platonic Political Philosophy. Claremont Review of Books,* Fall 1984. Reprinted in *Crisis of the Strauss Divided.*

"Leo Strauss's Churchillian Speech and the Question of the Decline of the West." *Teaching Political Science* 12, No. 2 (Winter 1984–1985). Reprinted in *Crisis of the Strauss Divided.*

1985

"The Legacy of Leo Strauss Defended." *Claremont Review of Books*, Spring 1985. Reprinted in *Crisis of the Strauss Divided.*

"Bradford and Jaffa: Once More on Lincoln." *The American Spectator*, June 1985.

"Never Again: The Lessons of the Holocaust." Column distributed by Public Research, Syndicated, June 12, 1985. Hillsdale College archive.

"Israel's Right to Exist." *The Washington Times*, July 8, 1985.

"Democracy Under Siege: Israel and the United States." Column distributed by Public Research, Syndicated, July 11, 1985. Hillsdale College archive.

"Whose Self-Determination." *National Review*, May 31, 1985.

"A Reply to Thomas Pangle." *National Review*, November 29, 1985.

1986

"Abraham Lincoln, Equality, and the Constitution." Column distributed by Public Research, Syndicated, February 5, 1986. Hillsdale College archive.

"Jefferson's Slave Mistress." *The Washington Times*, February 14, 1988.

"Lincoln-Douglas Debated." *National Review*, April 25, 1986.

"Are these Truths Now, Or Have They Ever Been, Self-Evident?" Column distributed by Public Research, Syndicated, June 25, 1987. Hillsdale College archive.

"The Constitution: An Application of Natural Law." *Century Magazine*, July/August 1986.

"Jefferson's Tarnished Legacy." Letter. *The Wall Street Journal*, July 31, 1986.

"The Constitution's Abstract Truths." Letter. *The Wall Street Journal*, September 29, 1986.

"The Case for Taking Hostages." Column distributed by Public Research, Syndicated, November 11, 1986. Hillsdale College archive.

"Equality as a Conservative Principle." *Harvard Journal of Law and Public Policy* 9, No. 1 (Winter 1986).

"Neumann Or Nihilism? The Case for Politics." Prepared for delivery at the 1986 annual meeting of the American Political Science Association. Reprinted in Harry Neumann, *Liberalism.*

1987

"Foreword." In Francis Canavan, *Edmund Burke: Prescription and Providence*, Studies in Statesmanship Series, Harry V. Jaffa, general editor. Durham: Carolina Academic Press, 1987.

"Equality, Liberty, Wisdom, Morality, and Consent in the Idea of Political Freedom." *Interpretation* 15, No. 1 (January 1987). Reprinted in *The Rediscovery of America*.

"What President Regan Ought to Do." Column distributed by Public Research, Syndicated, January 7, 1987.

"From Heidegger to Hitler." Letter. *National Review*, February 3, 1987.

"The Right to Be Queer: A Very Queer Right." *The Proposition*, March 1987. Hillsdale College archive.

"Defenders of the Constitution: Calhoun versus Madison, A Bicentennial Cerebration." Prepared for delivery at the University of Dallas, April 2, 1987. Published in *Constitutionalism in America*, the Bicentennial Project of the University of Dallas, 1987.

"Farewell to Woody Hays." Column distributed by Public Research, Syndicated, March 17, 1987. Hillsdale College archive.

"What Were the 'Original Intentions' of the Framers of the Constitution of the United States?" *University of Puget Sound Law Review* 10, No. 3 (Spring 1987). Reprinted in *Original Intent and the Framers of the Constitution*.

"On the Bicentennial of the Constitution." Commencement address delivered at Ripon College, May 17, 1987. Hillsdale College archive.

"The Disinformation of Mathias Rust." Column distributed by Public Research, Syndicated, June 3, 1987. Hillsdale College archive.

"Save the Constitution: Abolish the Bicentennial Commission!" Column distributed by Public Research, Syndicated, June 24, 1987. Hillsdale College archive.

"Admiral Poindexter: Where the Buck Stopped." Column distributed by Public Research, Syndicated, July 29, 1987. Hillsdale College archive.

"The Constitution is Not a Suicide Pact." Column distributed by Public Research, Syndicated, July 31, 1987. Hillsdale College archive.

"Dear Professor Drury: A Response to 'Leo Strauss' Natural Right Teaching.'" *Political Theory* 15, No. 3 (August 1987). Reprinted in *Crisis of the Strauss Divided.*

"Crisis of the Strauss Divided: The Legacy Reconsidered." *Social Research* 54, No. 3 (Autumn 1987). Reprinted in *Crisis of the Strauss Divided.*

"A Reply to Dinesh D'Souza." *Policy Review* 42 (Fall 1987).

"The American Founding as the Best Regime: The Bonding of Civil and Religious Liberty." Prepared for delivery as a lecture for *Novus Ordo Seclorum*, the Claremont Institute's Bicentennial Series, September 17, 1987. Reprinted in *The Rediscovery of America.*

"Why the Bork Nomination Went Wrong." Column distributed by Public Research, Syndicated, October 23, 1987. Hillsdale College archive.

"The Constitution." Letter. *Commentary*, October 1987.

"A Reply to Walter Berns." Letter. *Commentary*, November 1987.

"Crazy Summitry: Pearl Harbor Anniversary Marred by 'Useful Idiocy.'" *The Proposition*, December 1987. Hillsdale College archive.

"God at the Summit." Column distributed by Public Research, Syndicated, December 5, 1987. Hillsdale College archive.

"The Principle Behind the Constitution." Column distributed by Public Research, Syndicated, December 10, 1987. Hillsdale College archive.

"Useful Idiots, Then and Now." Column distributed by Public Research, Syndicated, December 12, 1987. Hillsdale College archive.

1988

What is Political Science? Or How to Deal with the Lemming (or Gadarene Swine) Instinct. Published as a pamphlet by The Salvatori Center for the Study of Freedom in the Modern World, Claremont McKenna College, 1988. Hillsdale College archive.

"Equality and the Founding." In *The American Founding: Essays on the Formation of the Constitution*, edited by Jackson Barlow, Leonard Levy, and Ken Masugi. New York: Greenwood Press, 1988.

"Foreword." In Kirk Emmert, *Churchill on Empire.* Studies in the Statesmanship Series, Harry V. Jaffa, general editor. Durham: Carolina Academic Press, Fall 1988.

"Trust but Verify: An Open Letter to the U.S. Senate." *The Proposition*, January 1988. Hillsdale College archive.

"Ninth Amendment Curb on Powers of State." Letter. *The Wall Street Journal*, January 28, 1988.

"A Reply to Robert A. Goldwin," *Commentary*, February 1988.

"The Supreme Court Monkeys Around." *National Review*, February 5, 1988.

"Our Chief Justice Says It's All Right to Call Your Mother an Incestuous Whore." *The Proposition*, March 1988. Hillsdale College archive.

"Judge Bork's Mistake." *National Review*, March 4, 1988.

"Old Thinking for New Suckers." Review of Mikhail Gorbachev, *Perestroika: New Thinking for Our Country and the World*. *Claremont Review of Books*, Spring 1988.

"Bork and his Enemies." Letter. *Commentary*, May 1988.

"Humanizing Certitudes and Impoverishing Doubts: A Critique of The Closing of the American Mind." *Interpretation* 16, No. 1 (Fall 1988). Reprinted in *The Rediscovery of America*.

"Judicial Conscience and Natural Rights: A Reply to Professor Ledewitz." *University of Puget Sound Law Review* 11, No. 2 (Winter 1988). Reprinted in *Original Intent and the Framers of the Constitution*.

"Who Killed Cock Robin? A Retrospective on the Bork Nomination and A Reply to 'Jaffa Divides the House' by Roger Stone." Prepared for delivered at the 1988 annual meeting of the American Political Science Association. Reprinted in *Original Intent and the Framers of the Constitution*.

1989

The Reichstag Is Still Burning: The Failure of Higher Education and the Decline of the West: A Valedictory Lecture. Published as a pamphlet by the Claremont Institute, 1989. Republished in *The Rediscovery of America*.

"A Right to Privacy?" *National Review*, March 24, 1989.

"The Artful Dodger." Letter. *National Review*, May 19, 1989.

"The Hour Has Passed." Letter. *National Review*, June 16, 1989.

1990

Homosexuality and the Natural Law. Published as a pamphlet by the Claremont Institute. Hillsdale College archive.

The American Founding as the Best Regime: The Bonding of Civil and Religious Liberty. Published as a pamphlet by the Claremont Institute, 1990. Republished in *The Rediscovery of America*.

"Lincoln's Character Assassins." *National Review*, January 21, 1990.

"Bork Revisited." Letter. *Commentary*. June 1990.

"The Closing of the Conservative Mind." Review of Robert Bork, *The Tempting of America: The Political Seduction of the Law*. *National Review*, July 9, 1990.

"The Anti-Anti-Smoking Brigade." *National Review*, November 15, 1990.

"The End of History Means the End of Freedom." Posted on the website of the Claremont Institute, 1990. Republished in *The Rediscovery of America*.

"Remarks for Churchill's Birthday." November 1990. Hillsdale College archive.

1991

"Foreword." In Harry Neumann, *Liberalism*. Durham: Carolina Academic Press, 1991. Studies in Statesmanship Series, Harry V. Jaffa, general editor.

"Western Civ." Letter. *Commentary*, January 1991.

"Taking Bork to Task." Letter. *National Review*, February 11, 1991.

"Anti-Semitism." Letter. *Commentary*, October 1991.

"Political Philosophy and Political Reality." Published as "The Long Arm of Socialism" on the Claremont Institute website. Hillsdale College archive.

1992

"Of Men, Hogs, and Law." *National Review*, February 3, 1992.

"America and Israel." Letter. *Commentary*, May 1992.

"Required Discrimination." Review of Richard A. Epstein, *Forbidden Grounds*. *The Wall Street Journal*, September 8, 1992.

"As the Tide of Despotism and Tyranny Recedes, the Tide of Anarchy is Rising: Thoughts for Churchill's Birthday, 1992." Hillsdale College archive.

1993

"In Abraham's Bosom." Eulogy of M. E. Bradford. *National Review*, April 12, 1993.

"Socrates Acquitted." *National Review,* November 1, 1993.

"What is Moral." Letter. *Commentary*, November 1993.

"The Effect of Liberty: Thoughts for Churchill's Birthday, 1993." Hillsdale College archive.

1994

Original Intent and the Framers of the Constitution, Washington, D.C.: Regnery Gateway, 1994.

"Leo Strauss, Political Philosophy, and the Bible." In *Leo Strauss: Political Philosopher and Jewish Thinker*, edited by Kenneth L. Deutsch and Walter Nicgorski. Lanham, MD: Rowman and Littlefield, 1994. Republished in *Crisis of the Strauss Divided*.

"Jaffa v. Bork: An Exchange," *National Review*, March 21, 1994.

1995

"Matters of Church and State." *National Review*, March 6, 1995.

"God is Part and Parcel of the Constitution." Letter. *Los Angeles Times*, November 28, 1995.

1996

"Understanding Justice Sutherland as He Understood Himself." With John C. Eastman. Review of Hadley Arkes, *The Return of George Sutherland: Restoring a Jurisprudence of Natural Rights. University of Chicago Law Review* 63, No. 3 (Summer 1996).

"The Party of Lincoln vs. The Party of Bureaucrats." The *Wall Street Journal*, Sept. 12, 1996.

"On the Racism Industry." *Academic Questions* 9, No. 83–85 (1996).

1997

"About Strauss." Letter. *National Review*, March 10, 1997.

"The Speech that Changed the World." *Interpretation* 24, No. 3 (Spring 1997).

1998

"The False Prophets of American Conservatism." Prepared for delivery as a lecture in Claremont, February 1998. Published in *A Moral Enterprise: Politics, Reason, and the Human Good*, edited by Kenneth L. Grasso and Robert P. Hunt. Wilmington: ISI Books, 2002.

"Preferences and the 14th." *National Review*, July 6, 1998.

"Order in the Court." *National Review*, September 28, 1998.

1999

Storm Over the Constitution, Lexington, MD: Lexington Books, 1999.

"The Deepening Crisis." Prepared for delivery at the Claremont Institute Lincoln Day Colloquium, February 1999. Hillsdale College archive.

"Clarifying Strauss." Letter. *National Review*, July 26, 1999.

"The Declaration as Foundation." *National Review*, December 20, 1999.

2000

A New Birth of Freedom: Abraham Lincoln and the Coming of the Civil War. Lanham, MD: Rowman & Littlefield, 2000.

"Why Special Interests (and the Constitution) Are Good for You." *Claremont Review of Books*, digital edition, February 9, 2000.

2001

"Campaign Reform is Unconstitutional, No Matter What McCain May Claim," *Claremont Review of Books*, digital edition, January 2, 2001.

"Thoughts on Lincoln's Birthday." *Claremont Review of Books*, digital edition, January 22, 2001.

"The Peace Process is Dead. Let's Bury It," *Human Events*, May 28, 2001.

"In Re Jack Kemp vs Joe Sobran." *Claremont Review of Books*, digital edition, July 30, 2001.

"Aristotle and Locke in the American Founding." *Claremont Review of Books*, Winter 2001. Reprinted in *The Rediscovery of America*.

"Our Embattled Constitution." Prepared for delivery as Constitution Day lecture, 2001. Hillsdale College archive.

2002

"Abraham Lincoln and the Universal Meaning of the Declaration of Independence." In *The Declaration Of Independence: Origins and Impact.* Edited by Scott Gerber. Washington, DC: CQ Press, 2002.

"Bush's Lincolnian Challenge." *Claremont Review of Books*, digital edition, February 15, 2002.

"Response to Lewis and Sheppard." *Interpretation* 29, No. 3 (Spring 2002).

"'Terminator' IRS Hounded Joe Louis into Poverty." Letter, The *Wall Street Journal*, December 27, 2002.

2003

"L'Envoi to Woody Hayes." *Claremont Review of Books*, digital edition, January 3, 2003.

"Is Diversity Good?" *Claremont Review of Books*, digital edition, January 17, 2003.

"American Conservatism and the Present Crisis." *Claremont Review of Books*, Spring 2003.

"Strauss at 100." *Claremont Review of Books*, digital edition, May 14, 2003. Reprinted in *Crisis of the Strauss Divided*.

2004

"Wages of Sin," *Claremont Review of Books*, Spring 2004.

"Never Before in History." *Claremont Review of Books*, digital edition, July 2, 2004.

"Ignoble Liars and Noble Truth-Tellers." *Claremont Review of Books*, digital edition, August 17, 2004.

"The Logic of the Colorblind Constitution." *Claremont Review of Books*, digital edition, December 6, 2004.

2006

"Original Intent and the American Soul," *Claremont Review of Books*, Winter 2005–2006.

"The Central Idea." *Claremont Review of Books*, digital edition, February 19, 2006.

"Who Owns the Copyright of the Universe." *Claremont Review of Books*, Spring 2006.

"Thomas Aquinas Meets Thomas Jefferson." *Interpretation* 33, No. 2 (Spring 2006). Republished in *The Rediscovery of America*.

"Founding Father." Letter. *Commentary*, August 1996.

2007

"The Disputed Question." *Claremont Review of Books*, Winter 2006–2007.

2008

"New Introduction to *Thomism and Aristotelianism*." January 2008. Hillsdale College archive.

"God Bless America." *The Claremont Review of Books*, Spring 2008.

"Dred Scott Revisited." *Harvard Journal of Law & Public Policy* 31, No. 1 (Winter 2008). Reprinted in *The Rediscovery of America*.

2009

"A Reply to Michael Zuckert's 'Jaffa's New Birth: Harry Jaffa at Ninety.'" *The Review of Politics* 71, No. 2 (Spring 2009).

"Too Good to be True? A Reply to Robert Kraynak's "Moral Order in the Western Tradition: Harry Jaffa's Grand Synthesis of Athens, Jerusalem, and Peoria." *The Review of Politics* 71, No. 2 (Spring 2009).

"An Open Letter." *Claremont Review of Books*, Summer 2009

"Lincoln in Peoria." *Claremont Review of Books*, Fall 2009.

2011

"Aristotle and the Higher Good." Review of *Nicomachean Ethics*. Translated with an Interpretative Essay by Robert C. Bartlett and Susan D. Collins. *New York Times*, July 1, 2011.

2012

Crisis of the Strauss Divided, Lanham, MD: Rowman & Littlefield, 2012.

"Joseph Cropsey, Rest in Peace." *Claremont Review of Books*, digital edition, July 18, 2012.

Published posthumously 2019

The Rediscovery of America: Essays by Harry V. Jaffa on the New Birth of Politics, edited by Edward J. Erler and Ken Masugi. Lanham, MD: Rowman and Littlefield, 2019.

NOTES

The three epigraphs at the beginning of this book are taken from
- Harry V. Jaffa, *A New Birth of Freedom: Abraham Lincoln and the Coming of the Civil War* (Lanham, MD: Rowman & Littlefield, 2000), 5.
- Harry V. Jaffa, *Crisis of the Strauss Divided: Essays on Leo Strauss and Straussianism, East and West* (Lanham, MD: Rowman & Littlefield, 2012), 28.
- Leo Strauss, "Jerusalem and Athens: Some Preliminary Reflections," in *Studies in Platonic Political Philosophy*, ed. Thomas L. Pangle (Chicago: University of Chicago Press, 1983), 147.

The blockquote in "A Note to the Reader" is taken from "The End of History Means the End of Freedom" in *The Rediscovery of America: Essays by Harry V. Jaffa on the New Birth of Politics*, eds. Edward J. Erler and Ken Masugi (Lanham, MD: Rowman & Littlefield, 2019), 117.

CHAPTER 1

1　The Claremont Colleges share contiguous campuses around a central library, forming a university consortium about thirty miles east of Los Angeles. They include Scripps, Pomona, Claremont Men's College (now Claremont McKenna College), Pitzer, and Harvey Mudd College as well as Claremont Graduate University.

2　Harry V. Jaffa, *The Rediscovery of America*, 91. Some of the details in this section are drawn from Professor Ward Elliott's informative first-hand account: http://www1.cmc.edu/pages/faculty/welliott/cmchistory.htm. An interesting retrospective from someone who was an undergraduate student at Pomona at the time can be found at https://www.city-journal.org/html/how-my-friends-and-i-wrecked-pomona-college-14331.html.

3　The exact quotation by Churchill is a bit different: "We seem to be very near the bleak choice between War and Shame. My feeling is that we shall choose Shame, and then have War thrown in." See Richard M. Langworth, "Churchill's words: Choosing between War and Shame—and getting both," posted at https://richardlangworth.com/war-shame.

4　Jaffa, *A New Birth of Freedom*, 501.

5　Letter to Charles Lofgren, February 11, 1989, Hillsdale College archive (henceforth referred to as "archive").

6 Rick Perlstein, *Before the Storm: Barry Goldwater and the Unmaking of the American Consensus* (New York: Nation Books, 2001), 392.

7 Letter to Lewis Lehrman, January 1, 1986, archive.

8 Letter to Jack Kemp, November 1, 1988, archive.

9 Harry V. Jaffa, Foreword to Harry Neumann, *Liberalism* (Durham: Carolina Academic Press 1991), vii.

10 John Marini, *Unmasking the Administrative State: The Crisis of American Politics in the Twenty-First Century* (New York: Encounter Books, 2019), 275.

11 Leo Strauss, *Natural Right and History* (Chicago: University of Chicago Press, 1953), 31–32.

12 "Neumann or Nihilism: The Case for Politics," *Liberalism*, 61–62.

13 *Liberalism*, 62.

14 Harry V. Jaffa, "The Unity of Comedy, Tragedy, and History: An Interpretation of Shakespeare's Universe," in *Shakespeare as Political Thinker*, eds. John Alvis and Thomas G. West (Durham: Carolina Academic Press, 1981), 44–45.

15 *Liberalism*, 70.

16 Harry V. Jaffa, *American Conservatism and the American Founding* (Durham: Carolina Academic Press, 1984), 170.

17 *Liberalism*, 71.

18 *Unmasking the Administrative State*, 8.

19 *Unmasking the Administrative State*, 103.

20 *Liberalism*, 71.

21 Harry V. Jaffa, "'Value-Consensus in Democracy': The Issue in the Lincoln-Douglas Debates," in *Equality and Liberty* (New York: Oxford University Press, 1965), 227.

CHAPTER 2

1 "Psychoanalysis," Jaffa argued, "only offered to restore to each individual the aimless freedom that was the starting point of his trouble." *American Conservatism and the American Founding*, 171.

2 Eulogy to Frances Landau Jaffa, archives. Many of the details in this chapter are taken from this unpublished eulogy.

3 Some helpful and well-timed advice from a mentor during his graduate studies at Yale persuaded Jaffa to be "alert to the mystery of the ways of Providence, which often proceeds by the most inauspicious indirection to accomplish its ends." *Crisis of the Strauss Divided*, 7.

4 *American Conservatism and the American Founding*, 51. John Kayser, Jaffa's first PhD student, recalls that Jaffa "never felt comfortable at a place until he made a few enemies." Communication with the author, November 16, 2020.

5 Letter to Norman Podhoretz, April 10, 1984, archive.

6 Eulogy, archives.

7 Harry V. Jaffa, "Joseph Cropsey, Rest in Peace," *Claremont Review of Books*, July18, 2012, digital exclusive, posted at https://claremontreviewofbooks.com/digital/joseph-cropsey-rest-in-peace/.

8 *Crisis of the Strauss Divided*, 2–3.

9 *Crisis of the Strauss Divided*, 1.

10 *Crisis of the Strauss Divided*, 7.

11 Interview conducted by the Leo Strauss Center, University of Chicago, posted at https://leostrausscenter.uchicago.edu/harry-jaffa/.

12 Interview conducted by Charles R. Kesler, posted at https://www.youtube.com/watch?v=wpdM5D9C7io.

13 *Crisis of the Strauss Divided*, 8.

14 *Crisis of the Strauss Divided*, 8.

15 Similar to his own initial encounter with Strauss, some of Jaffa's students needed a second impression (or more) to appreciate him. Larry Arnn's recollection is worth recounting here:

> When I met Harry Jaffa in the summer of 1974 he was wearing a white shirt and black socks and a pair of boxer shorts. Peter Schramm, a fellow grad student who five years later would become the Claremont Institute's first president, had done me the honor of asking me to go pick up Jaffa (I was newly arrived) and take him to the first class of the semester. Jaffa didn't fully remember that he had a class…or who I was…or what the class was about. And I thought, "Goodness, what have I done?"
>
> I remember everything he said in that first class. It was on Aristotle's *Nicomachean Ethics*. We spent the whole semester, and we never got out of Book I, but read that very carefully. He began the class, "When men get to be old men like me [and I'm now older than he was then], they make a list of the hundred greatest books. But life is too short to read a hundred books. No one can know a hundred great books." He said, "I have a list of the three greatest books." The rest was a little cryptic: "Aristotle's *Politics* would require some translation to be fully relevant to modern times"; it seemed to be excluded. "The Bible is its own kind of book"; it seemed to be excluded. "Plato's *Republic* would have to be on any such list." Then he said, "Shakespeare," and something about his writing both tragedy and comedy. Then he held up the *Ethics* and said, "This is a perfect book." Right away one saw that there are some things so precious and rare that you must give your life to them to know them. And there can only be a few. And that to live a good life is to live that way. That was the first thing I learned from him.

"Remembering Harry V. Jaffa," *Claremont Review of Books*, Winter 2014–15, posted at https://claremontreviewofbooks.com/harry-v-jaffa-1918–2015/.

16 See https://leostrausscenter.uchicago.edu/audio-transcripts/.

17 Transcript of Leo Strauss course, Plato's *Republic* (Session 1, March 26, 1957), posted at http://leostrausstranscripts.uchicago.edu/navigate/2/2/.

18 Strauss course on *The Republic* (Session 1, March 26, 1957).

19 Strauss course on *The Republic* (Session 3, April 2, 1957), posted at http://leostrausstranscripts.uchicago.edu/navigate/2/4/.

20 Strauss course on *The Republic* (Session 4, April 4, 1957), posted at http://leostrausstranscripts.uchicago.edu/navigate/2/5/.

21 Strauss course on *The Republic* (Session 4, April 4, 1957).

22 For additional details on Strauss's life and work, see https://leostrausscenter. uchicago.edu/biography/.

23 *Crisis of the Strauss Divided*, 118–19.

24 Leo Strauss, *Liberalism Ancient and Modern* (Chicago: University of Chicago Press, 1968), 223.

25 *Crisis of the Strauss Divided*, 133.

26 *Crisis of the Strauss Divided*, 158.

27 *Rediscovery of America*, 11.

28 Many of these details are recounted in Jaffa's autobiographical essays "Straussian Geography" in *Crisis of the Strauss Divided* and "The Legend of Sleepy Hollow" in *The Rediscovery of America*.

29 Jaffa did not hide his identity under a bushel basket. Not long after arriving, Mansfield offered his young colleague a bit of friendly advice in response to some display of assertiveness: "Harry, if you keep this up, you'll get a reputation for being a pushy Jew." Jaffa did not hesitate in replying, "But that's what I am!" Letter to Harvey C. Mansfield, Jr., May 21, 1988, archive.

30 Letter to Leo Strauss, May 31, 1954, University of Chicago, Leo Strauss archive.

31 Brian Gaffney, "Jaffa on that Goldwater Speech," posted at https://phillysoc. org/collections/tributes/tributes-to-harry-jaffa/jaffa-on-that-goldwater-speech/.

32 Gaffney, "Jaffa on that Goldwater Speech."

33 *American Conservatism and the American Founding*, 63.

34 Lee Edwards, *Goldwater: The Man Who Made a Revolution* (Washington, DC: Regnery Publishing, 1995), 258.

35 Rick Perlstein, *Before the Storm: Barry Goldwater and the Unmaking of the American Consensus* (New York: Nation Books, 2001), 390.

36 *American Conservatism and the American Founding*, 64.

37 *Before the Storm*, 391–92.

38 Gaffney, "Jaffa on that Goldwater Speech."

39 In a 1994 letter to Jaffa, Goldwater wrote, "How well I remember that night we were putting the finishing touches on the acceptance speech, and you called your wife in Columbus, and told her precisely where a book would be, and told her what page to turn to, and what to read. That became the basis for the best speech I ever made, the one on 'extremism in defense of liberty is no vice.'" August 18, 1994, archive. Even granting Jaffa's authorship of the speech, some have questioned whether the famous lines about extremism represent sound Aristotelian thinking. But Jaffa had learned from Strauss as well as his own reading of the *Nicomachean Ethics* that the mean between the vices is a peak of excellence, not low or middling. Justice in particular only has one corresponding vice, which is injustice—a deficiency. There is technically in Aristotle no such thing as too much justice. (Jaffa compares it to health. When it is fulfilled or complete, one can go no further.) In his 1952 book, *Thomism and Aristotelianism* (p. 211), Jaffa observes that for Aristotle,

"there can be no excess of virtue because virtue *is* an extreme." (Emphasis in the original.) In a sense, Jaffa had already drafted part of those famous lines twelve years before he ever met Goldwater.

See also the transcript of Strauss's 1965 course "Introduction to Political Philosophy," (Session 12, no date):

> Aristotle also says, without contradicting himself (and this had an effect of sorts in the last election), that the mean of any virtue compared to the two opposing vices is in a sense also an extreme—especially because it stands out. Virtue is an excellence: compared with the average, it is an extreme. This landed somehow in the acceptance speech of Senator Goldwater and gave people who didn't know Aristotle an occasion to be surprised.

http://leostrausstranscripts.uchicago.edu/navigate/11/4/. It is evident in his correspondence with Jaffa that Strauss knew his student had written the speech. Perhaps he did not think it seemly to say so in class. See his letter to Jaffa, August 10, 1964, archive.

40 *American Conservatism*, xi.

41 Letter to Paul Basinski, May 5, 1996, archive.

42 Neumann, *Liberalism*, xi, xii, xix.

43 Letter to Norman Podhoretz, March 11, 2001, archive. The crime wave of the 1970s spawned the iconic Dirty Harry movies, in which Clint Eastwood plays a tough San Francisco cop whose commitment to justice exposes deficiencies in the conventional law. At a party for Jaffa's 1989 retirement from CMC, his student Ken Masugi referred to him as "the dirtiest Harry of them all." Communication with the author, December 18, 2020.

44 Letter to Richard C. Levin, March 3, 2002, archive.

45 Letter to Walter Berns, March 18, 1981, reprinted in *American Conservatism and the American Founding*, 125. Berns's comment (in a letter to Claremont professor Leonard Levy) is quoted in the engaging account of the Jaffa-Berns dispute by Steven F. Hayward: *Patriotism Is Not Enough: Harry Jaffa, Walter Berns, and the Arguments that Redefined American Conservatism* (New York: Encounter Books, 2017), x.

46 Letter to Robert Goldwin, February 6, 1983, archive.

47 Alexander Hamilton, "The Farmer Refuted," February 23, 1775, in *Selected Writings and Speeches of Alexander Hamilton*, Morton J. Frisch, ed. (Washington, DC: American Enterprise Institute, 1985), 19.

48 Letter to Henry Salvatori, May 9, 1980, archive.

49 Letter to Charles Lofgren, February 11, 1989, archive.

50 See, e.g., the 2020 essay by George Duke "Aristotle and Natural Law" in *The Review of Politics*, 82(1), 1–23. The McIntyre comment appears in *After Virtue*, third ed. (South Bend: University of Notre Dame Press, 2007), 278.

51 Richard Brookhiser, *Right Time, Right Place: Coming of Age with William F. Buckley Jr. and the Conservative Movement* (New York: Basic Books, 2011), 93–94.

CHAPTER 3

1 Letter to Walter Berns, January 14, 1981, archive.

2 Letter to Walter Berns, January 14, 1981, archive. Early on, Jaffa took to heart this lesson that intellectual errors and moral evils are not resolved simply by being ignored and that those who insist on resolving them will often be accused of unnecessary "agitations."

3 Letter to Walter Berns, January 14, 1981, archive.

4 Jaffa sometimes mentioned to friends that this was the hardest part of the book to write.

5 "Natural right" and "natural rights" are separate concepts, although they overlap in denying that all justice is conventional. The former is a classical and somewhat broader idea. (The reader may mentally substitute the phrase "what is right by nature.") Natural rights are part of modern social compact theory and refer to the inviolable claims an individual has, by virtue of being a human being, that may not justly be impinged without his consent. The closed cities of the ancient world did not recognize such rights of an individual outside or against the political community.

6 This section of *Crisis* is further examined in Chapter 6.

7 An influential mainstream historian reviewing the state of Lincoln scholarship in 2010 asserts as "unqualifiedly true" that "Jaffa's book was the first work that seriously tried to place Lincoln within the context of the Western philosophic tradition." David F. Ericson, "The Crisis in Lincoln Scholarship," *Reviews in American History*, Johns Hopkins University Press, Volume 38, Number 4 (December 2010), 664.

8 See Buckley's Foreword to *American Conservatism and the American Founding*, xi.

9 *Crisis of the House Divided*, 31.

10 *Crisis of the House Divided*, 226.

11 *Crisis of the House Divided*, 239.

12 *Crisis of the House Divided*, 225.

13 Willmoore Kendall, "Source of American Caesarism," *National Review*, November 7, 1959.

14 The intra-conservative debates from the 1960s through the 80s over the meaning of the Civil War, equality, natural rights, and the American Founding (conducted in the pages of journals such *Modern Age*, *National Review*, and *The American Spectator*) use terminology that was familiar to readers of the day but is perhaps less well understood today. Charles Kesler's 1988 introduction to *Keeping the Tablets: Modern American Conservative Thought* provides helpful definitions:

a) The *traditionalists*, or *paleoconservatives*, "saw Communism as only the latest and most radical form of the deracination of man in the modern world." Modernity had made human life "rootless, alienated, adrift; stripped of the decent trappings of custom and religion." Many traditionalists "found the roots of the problem in the Enlightenment rationalism unleashed in the French Revolution" and were opposed to "universalistic, ahistorical 'natural rights'."

b) The *libertarians* were, as today, believers in "the network of transactions and exchanges that free men make in the marketplace, whether of ideas or of economic goods and services. Any transcendent or objective ideological morality is an imposition on human freedom."

c) "The latecomers to American conservativism (they arrived on the scene toward the end of the 1960s) were the *neoconservatives* [who] tended to be academically trained social scientists.... [Their] movement toward conservatism was prompted by the New Left's open insurrection against American middle-class democracy and the American university."

Keeping the Tablets: Modern American Conservative Thought, William F. Buckley and Charles R. Kesler, eds., (New York, NY: Harper & Row, 1988), 6–8.

15 Herman Belz, "Harry V. Jaffa and American History: Philosophy Teaching by Example," *Claremont Review of Books*, Summer 1984, posted at https://claremontreviewofbooks.com/harry-v-jaffa-and-american-history-philosophy-teaching-by-example/.

16 See Chapter 6.

17 As each of these prefaces runs only a few pages, it does not seem necessary to cite a page number for each quotation. Of course, only the most recent edition of *Crisis* contains all the front matter: the 50th Anniversary Edition published by the University of Chicago Press in 2009. Through all four editions, Jaffa maintained the same pagination in the main body of the book.

18 In 2003 Jaffa wrote, "while Strauss articulated the connection between Plato, biblical religion, and medieval political philosophy, to discover the presence of classical principles in the post-classical world, he propelled my articulation of the connection between Plato, biblical religion, Shakespeare, and Lincoln." *Crisis of the Strauss Divided*, 187.

19 Jaffa, who always maintained his interest in poetry and literature, for some time nursed the ambition of producing a commentary on Sophocles's *Oedipus at Colonus* as his final work. *New Birth* apparently replaced that ambition.

20 Kesler writes: "If we were to take the comparison seriously, Jaffa would seem to be saying that, like Plato's *Republic, Crisis* showed the nature of the political or the limits of politics, whereas *A New Birth of Freedom*, like Plato's *Laws*, displays a more diluted form of natural right, a second-best regime that is more tolerable to human nature." "A New Birth of Freedom," *Claremont Review of Books*, Summer 2000, posted at https://claremontreviewofbooks.com/a-new-birth-of-freedom1/.

21 Alexander H. Stephens, Cornerstone Speech, March 21, 1861, posted at https://teachingamericanhistory.org/library/document/cornerstone-speech/.

22 *A New Birth of Freedom*, xxxv.

23 *A New Birth of Freedom*, 3.

24 *A New Birth of Freedom*, 3.

25 *A New Birth of Freedom*, 8.

26 Thomas G. West, "Jaffa's Lincolnian Defense of the Founding," *Interpretation*, 28, No. 3 (Spring 2001), 285.

27 *Crisis of the House Divided*, 239.

28 *Rediscovery of America*, 9–10. Despite a generally fair-minded treatment of Jaffa's thought by Michael and Catherine Zuckert in *The Truth About Leo Strauss*, their discussion of this particular point, which accuses Jaffa of incoherence, is itself somewhat incoherent and borders on churlishness toward the founders. The Zuckerts state that nothing in Strauss's work was more controversial than his "discovery" of esoteric writing (42–43). Yet they allege that Jaffa's explanation "derogates" the founders, who, if Jaffa is correct, were "not very astute readers" and "not intelligent enough to grasp the real Locke." The founders were "saved from falling into dark modernity only by their stupidity (to put it harshly)" (249). But why does Jaffa's explanation require the founders to be stupid? Do the Zuckerts contend that every educated person of the eighteenth century should have been familiar with esoteric writing? Was Strauss's "discovery" a great insight or not?

29 *Strauss Divided*, 21–22.

30 *Rediscovery of America*, 9.

31 *Strauss Divided*, 229.

32 *Strauss Divided*, 27–28.

33 "Jaffa's Lincolnian Defense of the Founding," 281–82.

34 "Jaffa's Lincolnian Defense of the Founding," 282.

35 *Strauss Divided*, 196–97.

36 *Strauss Divided*, 206, 214, 218, 219.

37 *Strauss Divided*, 228.

38 See especially Michael P. Zuckert and Catherine H. Zuckert, *The Truth about Leo Strauss: Political Philosophy and American Democracy* (Chicago: University of Chicago Press, 2006) and also Michael P. Zuckert and Catherine H. Zuckert, *Leo Strauss and the Problem of Political Philosophy* (Chicago: University of Chicago Press, 2014).

39 *Strauss Divided*, 242.

40 *Strauss Divided*, 242.

41 *Strauss Divided*, 244, 247.

42 *Strauss Divided*, 246.

43 Charles R. Kesler, "A New Birth of Freedom: Harry V. Jaffa and the Study of America," in *Leo Strauss, The Straussians, and the Study of the American Regime*, Kenneth L. Deutsch and John A. Murley, eds. (Lanham, MD: Rowman & Littlefield, 1999), 273.

44 Kesler may be paraphrasing Strauss's remark that Spinoza was "much more original" than Maimonides," though the latter "was nevertheless a deeper thinker than Spinoza." *What is Political Philosophy?*, 230.

45 *New Birth*, 280.

46 *Leo Strauss, The Straussians, and the Study of the American Regime* 278, 270.

47 *Leo Strauss, The Straussians, and the Study of the American Regime*, 278.

48 *Leo Strauss, The Straussians, and the Study of the American Regime*, 279.

CHAPTER 4

1 M. J. Sobran, Jr., "Governing Free Men," *National Review*, May 28, 1976.

2 Letter to Joseph Sobran, December 24, 1983, archive.

3 Harry V. Jaffa, "Aristotle and the Higher Good," *New York Times*, July 1, 2011, posted at https://www.nytimes.com/2011/07/03/books/review/book-review-aristotles-nicomachean-ethics.html.

4 Letter to Charles N. R. McCoy, April 5, 1969, archive.

5 *Strauss Divided*, 224–25.

6 *Strauss Divided*, 225–26.

7 *Strauss Divided*, 226.

8 The Platonism found throughout the works of Shakespeare, Jaffa argues, brought a form of classical thought within the reach of every literate American, even on the frontier.

9 *Conditions of Freedom*, 227.

10 *American Conservatism and the American Founding*, 57.

11 Harry V. Jaffa, *Thomism and Aristotelianism, A Study of the Commentary by Thomas Aquinas on the Nicomachean Ethics* (Chicago: University of Chicago Press, 1952), 185.

12 *Thomism and Aristotelianism*, 224.

13 *Rediscovery of America*, 252.

14 *Original Intent and the Framers of the Constitution*, 305.

15 *Statesmanship: Essays in Honor of Sir Winston Churchill*, Harry V. Jaffa, ed. (Durham: Carolina Academic Press, 1981), 8–9.

16 *Strauss Divided*, 23.

17 Communication with the author, October 31, 2019.

18 Kenneth C. Blanchard, Jr., the author of the entry on "Aristotle and Aristotelianism" in the *Encyclopedia of Science, Technology, and Ethics*, describes Jaffa's chapter as "possibly the best essay on Aristotle's politics in English." Posted at https://www.encyclopedia.com/science/encyclopedias-almanacs-transcripts-and-maps/aristotle-and-aristotelianism.

19 *History of Political Philosophy*, Leo Strauss and Joseph Cropsey, eds. (Chicago: Rand McNally College Publishing Company, 1963).

20 Letter to L. J. H. Herson, June 3, 1963, archive.

21 Jaffa withdrew his chapter in 1985 after a disagreement with Cropsey regarding the contents of the forthcoming third edition. Jaffa argued that since Edmund Burke had been previously included as a political philosopher, Lincoln merited inclusion by the same standard. Further, since chapters on Edmund Husserl and Martin Heidegger were to be added, Jaffa thought space should be found to balance them with entries on Shakespeare and Winston Churchill. After some back and forth with his old friend Cropsey (the sole editor since Strauss had passed away a decade earlier), Jaffa—to his later regret—retracted his submission. In response to Jaffa's notion that,

in the absence of his own essay, *no* chapter on Aristotle should be included, Cropsey replied, "I gave serious thought for a good eight seconds to your suggestion that I drop Aristotle from the *History of Political Philosophy* and decided against it on the ground that doing so could give the impression that I had lost my mind." Letter from Cropsey to Jaffa, November 16, 1985, archive. What Jaffa had in mind for a chapter on Shakespeare may be found in "The Unity of Tragedy, Comedy, and History: An Interpretation of the Shakespearean Universe," discussed below.

22 It is, admittedly, quite a sentence: "Every art and every inquiry, every action as well as choice, is held to aim at some good." *Nicomachean Ethics*, 1094a, Robert C. Bartlett and Susan D. Collins, trans. (Chicago: University of Chicago Press, 2011).

23 *Conditions of Freedom*, 10.

24 Harry V. Jaffa, "Natural Rights," *International Encyclopedia of Social Sciences*, posted at https://www.encyclopedia.com/social-sciences-and-law/political-science-and-government/political-science-terms-and-concepts/natural-rights.

25 *Conditions of Freedom*, 27.

26 *American Conservatism*, 264, 274. Elaborating on the first point ("the differences between men and women are the differences which instruct us in the reality of the whole of nature"), Jaffa writes, "For 'nature' refers to all those things that have their being by generation and growth. The 'natural' things are distinguished from the 'artificial' things, the things that are 'made' but do not 'grow.' We human beings are 'makers' of things, and we cause our world to be filled with artifacts, some of them wonderful indeed. But we ourselves are not artifacts. We—each of us—grow from fertilized seeds, whose life is not from any human maker. Man the maker is not the maker of man, because he is not the maker of nature. He has a nature, and he is part of nature. It is the *eros* acting in and through the generation and growth of things that are natural, by which all living things, including human things, are endowed with vitality." 264. Thomas West argues that the American founders regarded sexual practices that undermined the integrity of the family as serious criminal offenses, partly in conformity with biblical morality but primarily based "on arguments from reason, not on appeals to divine authority." Although, as West notes, "the founders judged some crimes to be minimally injurious when the conduct was not 'open and gross,' such as unobtrusive prostitution and same-sex sex. There was therefore little reason for government to focus law enforcement on these kinds of acts." *The Political Theory of the American Founding*, 228, 233–234.

27 Mary Nichols (a political philosophy professor at Baylor University) grounds Aristotle's acquisition argument in the genesis/telos distinction mentioned earlier. Aristotle sees nature as "both the origins and the ends, neither of which humanity should deny. Unlimited moneymaking is unnatural, both because it denies necessity (e.g., corporeality, death) and enslaves humanity to necessity (mere life and bodily indulgence)." *Citizens and Statesmen: A Study of Aristotle's Politics* (Lanham, MD: Rowman & Littlefield, 1992), 187. One may also note that in Aristophanes's *Clouds*, Strepsiades sends his son to

learn sophistic arguments at the "Thinkery" to help him escape his creditors. (Thanks to J. Eric Wise for pointing out this connection.)

28 *Conditions of Freedom*, 24.

29 *Conditions of Freedom*, 20.

30 Harry V. Jaffa, review of Alan Gewirth, *Marsilius of Padua, The Defender of Peace, Social Research*, Vol. 19, No. 1 (March 1952), 120.

31 See Aristotle's *Physics* II.3 and *Metaphysics* V.2.

32 In "Reflections on Lincoln and Thoreau," Jaffa writes, "Lincoln agreed with Aristotle (as did Madison) that man when separated from law is not divine, but bestial. Yet he disagreed with the opinion to which Madison gives countenance, that government is a reproach to human nature." *Conditions of Freedom*, 147.

33 *Conditions of Freedom*, 25.

34 *Conditions of Freedom*, 56.

35 *Conditions of Freedom*, 18. Jaffa is perfectly aware of the ironic character of *The Republic*. Aristotle and Plato are in agreement that the ideal city described there cannot serve as a practical model or guide. "The disagreement lies deeper," Jaffa argues,

> and concerns whether a model which transcends practice and can never be imitated in practice reveals the nature of practice more truly than a model which lies within the range of what is possible in practice. It is characteristic of the difference between Plato and Aristotle that Plato's quest for the best regime requires a construction in speech (or theory), to which nothing in practice does or can correspond, while Aristotle's quest first takes the form of an inquiry into regimes both of speech and deed, either of which might contain elements of the best regime. The first regime in *The Republic*, the so-called City of Pigs, the regime constructed out of the necessities of the bodies of men, revealed nothing of the ultimate demands of justice. For Plato, the generating of bodies by bodies does not of itself set in motion the tendencies which culminate in the truly just regime, the regime which can exist only in speech. In Book I of the *Politics* Aristotle contradicts this thesis; the families which result from the generation of the bodies of men evidently require as their complement the *polis*. The justice which makes every *polis* a *polis*, i.e. the form that justice takes in virtue of which this *polis* is a democracy and not an oligarchy, is a variety of the forms of justice. The unity underlying the plurality of the forms of the *polis* is like the unity underlying the variety of individuals of every species. It results from the nature common to all men, who are all political animals. This nature is *in* all men, not beyond them, and the truth about the *polis* like that about all nature is non-paradoxical because it is constituted, not by the duality of form and matter (to which correspond speech and deed, theory and practice) but by their unity.

Conditions of Freedom, 26.

36 *Conditions of Freedom*, 30.

37 Michael Davis, *The Politics of Philosophy: A Commentary on Aristotle's* Politics (Lanham, MD: Rowman & Littlefield, 1996), 140. Davis is a Straussian student of Seth Benardete and teaches at Sarah Lawrence College.

38 *The Politics of Philosophy*, 43.

39 *The Politics of Philosophy*, 44.

40 See *Crisis of the House Divided*, pp. 354–55, as well as the long chapter analyzing Lincoln's Temperance Address.

41 *American Conservatism and the American Founding*, 34. On the difference between Davis and Jaffa on drinking, consider Strauss's remarks in *What is Political Philosophy*, 31–32. When old, pious men engage in the act of founding and investigate the divine origins of the laws, drinking wine (even vicariously) "loosens their tongues; it makes them young; it makes them bold, daring, willing to innovate." The effect is quite different on the philosopher, for whom "wine drinking educates to moderation. For moderation is not a virtue of thought: Plato likens philosophy to madness, the very opposite of sobriety or moderation; thought must not be moderate, but fearless, not to say shameless. But moderation is a virtue controlling the philosopher's speech." In the case of political speech and the act of founding, drinking and boldness appear to be in the service of moderation and sobriety. (See also Strauss's *The Argument and the Action of Plato's* Laws, 33.)

42 *Conditions of Freedom*, 31.

43 *Conditions of Freedom*, 32.

44 *Conditions of Freedom*, 32.

45 *Conditions of Freedom*, 32–33.

46 *Conditions of Freedom*, 31–32.

47 Steve Sorensen notes Jaffa's own application of this principle in *A New Birth of Freedom*: "Jaffa argues that Aristotle, in contrast to Calhoun, 'declared politics to be an inexact science' (p. 440). Yet Lincoln's arguments are described by Jaffa as achieving 'Euclidean clarity' (p. 363) and 'mathematical certainty' (p. 364), and Jaffa says Lincoln argues in a 'quasi-mathematical' manner (p. 345). It seems it is not the mathematical character per se of political arguments which is objectionable, but the manner in which they are used." "My Country, 'Tis of Thee: Jaffa's Defense of the Noble, the Holy, and the Just," *Interpretation*, Vol. 28 No. 3 (Spring 2001), 271.

48 *Conditions of Freedom*, 38–39. Note that "legislators" in this context means those who created the original laws, i.e., the constitution—typically the founders of the regime.

49 *Conditions of Freedom*, 48, 69.

50 *Conditions of Freedom*, 33.

51 *Conditions of Freedom*, 46.

52 *Conditions of Freedom*, 69.

53 "Natural Rights," *International Encyclopedia of Social Sciences*.

54 Jaffa argues that "natural right and practical wisdom are virtually

synonymous." *Strauss Divided*, 20. See the discussion of prudence earlier in this chapter.

55 *Nicomachean Ethics*, 1134b18-30. Robert C. Bartlett and Susan D. Collins, trans. It is important to note Aristotle's clarification that some actions have no right time or place; there is never a proper way to commit adultery, for example. 1107a14-18.

56 "It may be that the given imperfect order is the best possible under the circumstances. It would then be naturally right to preserve that imperfect order, and even the man who had the naturally best for his standard would act accordingly....What is naturally best is distinct from what is naturally right. The former is the standard to which the wise legislator and statesman looks, in order to know the true *direction* of all sound policy. What is just, however, is what is fitting here and now." *Thomism and Aristotelianism*, 182–183.

57 As Richard Reeb pointed out to me, this is why Plato invokes mythology in Book X of *The Republic* to justify the city in speech.

58 Erler, now retired from teaching political philosophy at Cal State San Bernardino, lives in Claremont. In addition to getting his PhD under Jaffa, he was a friend and neighbor.

59 Edward J. Erler, "Natural Right in the American Founding: Harry Jaffa's Legacy," paper delivered at the 2015 American Political Science Association annual convention, on file with the author.

60 *Rediscovery of America*, 7.

61 Letter to Charles N. R. McCoy, April 5, 1969, archive.

62 *Conditions of Freedom*, 70–71.

63 *Conditions of Freedom*, 71. Consider Lincoln's remarks about philosophy and agriculture toward the end of his speech at the Wisconsin State Agricultural Fair, September 30, 1859, posted at http://www.abrahamlincolnonline.org/lincoln/speeches/fair.htm.

64 *Thomism and Aristotelianism*, 140–143.

65 *Conditions of Freedom*, 70.

66 *Conditions of Freedom*, 71.

67 Consider Jaffa's somewhat enigmatic preface to *A New Birth of Freedom*. The preface has three sections, separated by glyphs; the middle section has five paragraphs. The central paragraph of the central section mentions Strauss's teaching about how to read a great book and refers explicitly to "logographic necessity." In the paragraph just before, Jaffa says, "My hermeneutics are, so far as I have been able to make, those of Leo Strauss." At the beginning of the Preface, Jaffa had mentioned Plato's *Laws*, the significance of which is reinforced by the two chapters in the center of the *New Birth*, which use the words "The Argument and the Action," alluding to Strauss's *The Argument and Action of Plato's Laws*. Strauss's brief introduction to that work contains a reference to Plato's *Menexenus*, "in which," Strauss says, "Socrates rehearses a funeral speech in honor of fallen soldiers—a speech that...celebrates the

great deeds performed by Athens until about twelve years *after* Socrates' death." [Emphasis added.] The key point, Strauss adds, is that "Plato invented with ease Socratic and other stories." *A New Birth of Freedom* is described by Jaffa as a commentary on the Gettysburg Address, perhaps the most famous funeral oration in honor of fallen soldiers since Pericles. Finally, the *Menexenus* is referenced in Jaffa's response to Michael Zuckert's essay in the *Review of Politics*, discussed in the previous chapter. The *Menexenus*, in addition to revealing Socrates's interest in funeral orations, contains this remarkable line: "And while the most part of civic affairs are in the control of the populace they hand over the posts of government...to those who from time to time are deemed to be the best men...The one principle of selection is this: the man who is deemed wise and good rules and governs. And the cause of this our polity lies in our equality of birth." Jaffa uses this reference to establish the classical ground of Jefferson's remark about equality as the basis of the "natural *aristoi.*" (See Page 269, *Crisis of the Strauss Divided.*)

68   *Rediscovery of America*, 137–140.

69   *Shakespeare as Political Thinker*, John Alvis and Thomas G. West, eds. (Durham: Carolina Academic Press, 1981), 29.

70   *Shakespeare as Political Thinker*, 33.

71   Harold Bloom's 745-page *Shakespeare: The Invention of the Human* (New York: Riverhead Books, 1998) contains only one passing reference to Machiavelli, plus two instances of the word "Machiavellian"—at least as far as I am able to determine. Absurdly, the book contains no index. (Though they both wrote about Shakespeare, there is no relation between Harold and Allan Bloom.)

72   Leo Strauss, *What is Political Philosophy? And Other Studies* (Chicago: University of Chicago Press, 1988), 55.

73   *Shakespeare as a Political Thinker*, 40.

74   Letter to Angelo Codevilla, March 16, 1970, archive.

75   Letter to Harvey C. Mansfield, Jr., November 30, 1997, archive.

76   *Shakespeare as a Political Thinker*, 210.

77   *Shakespeare as a Political Thinker*, 213.

78   Regarding the sexual stigmas depicted in the play, Jaffa's concern with moral probity does not blind him to the radically different mores of contemporary America. Nevertheless, to appreciate *Measure for Measure* he insists that we must try to understand (however implausible it may seem to us) why fornication could legitimately be viewed as a capital offense. In another context, discussing *Othello*, he remarks, "One can only surmise how students for whom sex is 'no big deal' read the play. One guesses only that for them it is a black comedy about crazy people." *Rediscovery of America*, 53.

79   Consider Strauss's remarks during a seminar on Plato's *Laws*, a dialogue in which arranging marriages is held to be an essential task of the philosophic ruler. "But this question of the marriage, not so much of the rich and the poor as that of the temperate and daring, is a great theme of Plato. It goes much beyond the political discussions of Plato. According to Plato's analysis,

man on the highest level is characterized by the proper mixture of both. Both courage and restraint are integral parts of the efforts of the human mind. That is the highest problem, to which this other thing points." *Laws* (Session 9, February 12, 1959), posted at http://leostraustranscripts.uchicago.edu/navigate/3/10/.

80 *Shakespeare as a Political Thinker*, 223.

81 *Shakespeare as a Political Thinker*, 215. The desire of the "wise" to understand "true nature" through "indirect and invisible government" may unite Machiavelli and Shakespeare and perhaps even others.

82 *Shakespeare as a Political Thinker*, 220.

83 Harry V. Jaffa, Foreword to John Alvis, *Shakespeare's Understanding of Honor* (Durham: Carolina Academic Press, 1990), ix.

84 *Rediscovery of America*, 258. Just before the quoted passage, Jaffa notes, "let me hasten to add that many elements of Machiavelli are classical, and deserve to be included in an enlightened present day classicism."

85 *New Birth of Freedom*, 127.

86 *New Birth of Freedom*, 129.

87 *New Birth of Freedom*, 132.

88 *Shakespeare's Understanding of Honor*, vii.

89 *Shakespeare as a Political Thinker*, 57.

90 *Shakespeare as a Political Thinker*, 53.

91 *Shakespeare as a Political Thinker*, 52.

92 *Shakespeare as a Political Thinker*, 54.

93 *Shakespeare as a Political Thinker*, 57.

94 *Shakespeare as a Political Thinker*, 34.

95 There is, in fact, a philosopher king in Shakespeare, who is identified but not shown—or rather is not shown to reign. See the forthcoming essay by the present author.

96 *Shakespeare as a Political Thinker*, 41.

97 *Shakespeare's Understanding of Honor*, ix.

98 *Shakespeare's Understanding of Honor*, ix.

99 *Shakespeare as a Political Thinker*, 58.

100 *Shakespeare as a Political Thinker*, 58.

101 *Shakespeare as a Political Thinker*, 36.

102 Harry V. Jaffa, "Macbeth and the Moral Universe," *Claremont Review of Books*, Winter 2007–2008, posted at https://claremontreviewofbooks.com/issue/vol-viii-number-1-winter-2007–08/.

103 Leo Strauss, *Thoughts on Machiavelli* (Chicago: University of Chicago Press, 1978), 50.

104 "Macbeth and the Moral Universe." *Claremont Review of Books.*

105 *Shakespeare as a Political Thinker*, 58.

106 *Shakespeare as a Political Thinker*, 212.

CHAPTER 5

1 Though Jaffa certainly learned from Strauss the deep significance of the theological-political problem, his modified and expanded version analyzes what is almost a separate phenomenon. For Strauss, the issue centered on the alternatives of the best way of life: piety or philosophy and the irreconcilable claims of Athens or Jerusalem (reason or revelation). Christianity, as a specifically modern "problem," appears as one factor among several that led to the early-modern break with classical philosophy. It is Machiavelli, more than Christianity itself, that draws Strauss's focus because his founding of atheistic and scientific modern philosophy dispenses with concern for virtue. For Jaffa, there is a separate and in some ways larger story to be told in the way the One God of the Bible becomes, through the Roman Empire, the universal religion and thereby destroys the natural integrity of the ancient city. This creates the crisis in political obligation and the psycho-political "schizophrenia," which Machiavelli recognizes but does not solve. (Indeed, Machiavelli's solution seems to create even bigger problems, a point on which Jaffa agrees with Strauss.) The codification of religious liberty in the American founding, which solves the obligation crisis, becomes a world-historical event for Jaffa. This expanded version appears nowhere in Strauss, and—as a philosophical interpretation of America's unique role in responding to the divided loyalties and "divided mind" of Western civilization—is wholly original to Jaffa. Edward Erler expresses the point in an understated way by observing that Jaffa's 1987 essay, which first developed this thesis in detail, "was perhaps more revealing than anything Strauss wrote on the topic." See Erler's *Property and the Pursuit of Happiness: Locke, the Declaration of Independence, Madison, and the Challenge of the Administrative State* (Lanham, MD: Rowman & Littlefield, 2019), 75. This is not to suggest, of course, that no one before Jefferson (or Jaffa) appreciated the revolutionary significance of religious liberty. See the discussion of this topic in the Postscript.

2 *Rediscovery of America*, 267.

3 *New Birth of Freedom*, 257.

4 *New Birth of Freedom*, 135.

5 *New Birth of Freedom*, 141–44.

6 *New Birth of Freedom*, 152.

7 Letter to Charles Lofgren, February 11, 1989, archive.

8 *History of Political Philosophy*, Leo Strauss and Joseph Cropsey, eds. (Chicago: University of Chicago Press, 1987), 755.

9 *Rediscovery of America*, 270.

10 *Strauss Divided*, 31.

11 *Rediscovery of America*, 200–01.

12 *American Conservatism*, 253–54.

13 *Rediscovery of America*, 139.

14 *New Birth of Freedom*, xxxv–xxxvi.

15 Jaffa was introduced by George Anastaplo, the constitutional law scholar, as "the most instructive political scientist writing in this country today." *American Conservatism and the American Founding*, 48.

16 *New Birth of Freedom*, 92, 442.

17 *Original Intent and the Framers of the Constitution*, 349.

18 *Rediscovery of America*, 15.

19 One of Jaffa's strongest statements against historical determinism occurs in a discussion of whether Leo Strauss agreed with Hegel. In "Leo Strauss's Churchillian Speech and the Question of the Decline of the West" (1984), Jaffa refers to the "most eloquent rejection of historical necessity, of anything that might be called 'the wave of the future,' even if this wave was attributed to divine providence." He does not directly attribute this to Strauss, however, but says only that this sweeping and eloquent argument appears in Strauss's critique of Edmund Burke. Just before this passage, Jaffa indicates what Strauss himself "rejected, utterly and completely." That is "the doctrine that historical necessity, in any form or in any sense, *required or justified the universal homogeneous state*." [Emphasis added.] *Strauss Divided*, 112.

20 *New Birth of Freedom*, 91.

21 Letter to Norman Podhoretz, April 2, 1999, archive.

22 *Rediscovery of America*, 133.

23 Leo Strauss, "On the Interpretation of Genesis," in *Jewish Philosophy and the Crisis of Modernity: Essays and Lectures in Modern Jewish Thought*, Kenneth Hart Green, ed. (Albany, NY: State University of New York Press, 1997), 361.

24 *Strauss Divided*, 142.

25 *Rediscovery of America*, 143.

26 Letter to Rabbi Ben Beliak, October 3, 1979, archive.

27 *Rediscovery of America*, 127.

28 Samuel Cooper, "A Sermon on the Day of the Commencement of the Constitution," in *Political Sermons of the American Founding Era: 1730–1805*, Ellis Sandoz, ed. (Indianapolis: Liberty Press, 1991), posted at https://oll.libertyfund.org/titles/816#lf0018-01_head_054

29 See *Conditions of Freedom*, 172. Jaffa does not mean it would be in any way impossible to amend these provisions but rather that they are inseparable from the idea of republican government, and to remove such protections would be to destroy the basis of constitutionalism.

30 *American Conservatism and the American Founding*, 54.

31 *Natural Right and History*, 2.

32 *Rediscovery of America*, 134.

33 *Strauss Divided*, 64.

34 *Rediscovery of America*, 134.

35 *Rediscovery of America*, 106.

36 *Strauss Divided*, 115.

37 Letter to Henry Salvatori, May 9, 1980, archive.

38 *Rediscovery of America*, 135.

39 *Rediscovery of America*, 106.

40 *Strauss Divided*, 174.

41 *American Conservatism*, 70–71.

42 *American Conservatism*, 71.

43 *Strauss Divided*, 107.

44 *Strauss Divided*, 74–75.

45 *Strauss Divided*, 60.

46 *Strauss Divided*, 76.

47 *Strauss Divided*, 153.

48 *Studies in Platonic Political Philosophy*, 20.

49 *Strauss Divided*, 66–67.

50 *Strauss Divided*, 68.

51 Arthur M. Melzer, "Esotericism and the Critique of Historicism," *The American Political Science Review*, Vol. 100, No. 2 (May, 2006), 282.

52 Leo Strauss, *Persecution and the Art of Writing* (Chicago: University of Chicago Press, 1988), 16–17.

53 *Strauss Divided*, 74, 60.

54 *Strauss Divided*, 100.

55 *Equality and Liberty*, 227–228.

56 *Crisis of the House Divided*, 252, 418.

57 Leo Strauss, "Progress or Return," in *Rebirth of Classical Political Rationalism*, Thomas Pangle, ed. (Chicago: University of Chicago Press, 1989), 270.

58 *Strauss Divided*, 153.

CHAPTER 6

1 Letter to Joseph Cropsey, July 20, 1984, archive.

2 Thomas Jefferson, letter to Roger Weightman, June 24, 1826, posted at https://www.loc.gov/exhibits/declara/rcwltr.html.

3 *Strauss Divided*, 227. The allusion to W. E. B. DuBois is taken from *The Souls of Black Folk* (New York: Oxford University Press, 2007), 76: "I sit with Shakespeare and he winces not. Across the color line I move arm in arm with Balzac and Dumas, where smiling men and welcoming women glide in gilded halls. From out the caves of evening that swing between the strong-limbed earth and the tracery of the stars, I summon Aristotle and Aurelius and what soul I will, and they come all graciously with no scorn nor condescension."

4 *Strauss Divided*, 228.

5 Harry V. Jaffa, "Is Political Freedom Grounded in Natural Law?," February 1984, archive. At the end of the quotation, Jaffa is repeating an expression from Strauss's *Thoughts on Machiavelli*.

6 This topic has been a rich field of scholarly investigation for Jaffa's students.

See, e.g., Thomas G. West, *The Political Theory of the American Founding: Natural Rights, Public Policy, and the Moral Conditions of Freedom* (New York: Cambridge University Press, 2017) and Edward J. Erler, *Property and the Pursuit of Happiness: Locke, the Declaration of Independence, Madison, and the Challenge of the Administrative State* (Lanham, MD: Rowman & Littlefield, 2019).

7   *Rediscovery of America*, 134.

8   *Thoughts on Machiavelli*, 13. One should not ignore another sentence in Strauss's text: "Machiavelli would argue that America owes her greatness not only to her habitual adherence to the principles of freedom and justice, but also to her occasional deviation from them." Nor should one ignore the obvious point that what Machiavelli would argue is not necessarily what Strauss would argue.

9   *Rediscovery of America*, 134.

10 Letter to Joseph Cropsey, July 20, 1984, archive.

11 Leo Strauss, *Natural Right and History* (Chicago: University of Chicago Press, 1953), 151.

12 *Strauss Divided*, 125.

13 *Strauss Divided*, 125.

14 Letter to Joseph Cropsey, August 19, 1984, archive.

15 *Crisis of the House Divided*, x–xi.

16 *Conditions of Freedom*, 66.

17 Some commentators will deny that the issues discussed by Aristotle and Publius in this paragraph are really the same and might especially object that these are not the main focus of the Lyceum Address. Jaffa's "convergences" faced the same criticism. The solution to the problem Aristotle discusses in Book V is *education*, specifically, as Jaffa puts it, "an education that will produce a ruling class that is self-disciplined in respect to its real interests." (*Conditions of Freedom*, 67) Likewise, the famous "extended sphere" is not the final answer to the challenges mentioned in *Federalist No. 10*. (Publius still has seventy-five more essays to unwind.) As Charles Kesler observes, the more complete teaching on separation of powers in the later numbers will "encourage the people to venerate the constitution by removing it from their grasp, by elevating it above their factious passions and interests. . . . In this great achievement the extended sphere plays an indispensable but still a subordinate role: it ministers to what Abraham Lincoln would later call our political religion." (*Saving the Revolution*, p. 39) These remedies accord with Jaffa's teaching about the meaning of the Lyceum speech. In a paper for the 1977 American Political Science Association convention, Jaffa asserts explicitly, "Madison saw the political problem, as did Plato and Aristotle, as the problem of faction." See "A Phoenix from the Ashes: The Death of James Madison's Constitution (Killed by James Madison) and the Birth of Party Government." Archive.

18 *Crisis of the House Divided*, 185.

19 Abraham Lincoln, "On the Perpetuation of our Political Institutions," January 27, 1838, posted at https://quod.lib.umich.edu/j/jala/2629860.0006.103/—perpetuation-of-our-political-institutions-address?rgn=main;view=fulltext.

20 Quoted in *Crisis of the House Divided*, 214.

21 *Strauss Divided*, 18.

22 *Crisis of the House Divided*, 238.

23 *A New Birth of Freedom*, 30.

24 *Crisis of the House Divided*, 195.

25 *New Birth of Freedom*, 530.

26 *Rediscovery of America*, 152.

27 *Crisis of the House Divided*, 231.

28 Thomas Jefferson letter to John Adams, October 28, 1813, posted at https://tile.loc.gov/storage-services/service/mss/mtj//mtj1/046/046_1276_1282.pdf.

29 *Strauss Divided*, 262.

30 *Strauss Divided*, 231.

31 *Rediscovery of America*, 23.

32 Abraham Lincoln, Debate at Alton, October 15, 1858, posted at https://teachingamericanhistory.org/library/document/the-lincoln-douglas-debates-7th-debate-part-i/.

33 *Strauss Divided*, 230.

34 *Natural Right and History*, 140–141.

35 *Strauss Divided*, 122–23. Consider also the remarks of Laurence Berns:

> The most impressive attempt known to me to combine classical thought with the principles of the American polity is to be found in the work of Harry V Jaffa.... Jaffa anticipates the objection that consent is not an adequate replacement for wisdom as the ground upon which rule can be legitimated. The claims of wisdom have dubious political value because of "the fact that it is not the wise who advance under the banners of wisdom but rather pretenders to wisdom." Strauss's account of the classical position in a way admits this last point. The classics favored the rule of gentlemen, that element of society that through its wealth and leisure had the greatest opportunities to acquire a liberal education, which means an education that among other things fosters civic responsibility. This points to the ultimate justification of the rule of gentlemen: the rule of gentlemen is the political reflection of the, for almost all political purposes, impossible rule of the philosophers, the rule of "the man best by nature and best by education." Jaffa is aware of the impoverishment that would attend the removal of such political reflections.

"Aristotle and the Moderns," in *The Crisis of Liberal Democracy: a Straussian Perspective*, Kenneth L. Deutsch and Walter Soffer, eds. (Albany, NY: State University of New York Press, 1987), 156–157.

36 Consider Strauss's remarks from a course he taught on Plato's *Gorgias*:

The problem posed by Gorgias in Plato's time is fundamentally that which holds today and which is now called "the intellectual." Gorgias certainly was an intellectual. An intellectual is a man who spends most of his life reading and writing and derives his livelihood from that. That is what I think intellectual probably means. I don't know what the authorities say about it. But there is a problem in that kind of occupation. Now for Plato, the problem was simple—why he turned his mind to rhetoric. Plato was concerned with philosophy, and philosophy must be distinguished from pursuits that can easily be mistaken for philosophy. And rhetoric, as popularly understood, was such a phenomenon...What is the present day equivalent in our society to the public speaker? Well, one could perhaps say journalists and other writers, or those people who try to influence multitudes in non-specialized matters and who do not claim that their writings are scientific—people who try to put their stamp on the public mind, who aspire to become opinion leaders. [I]f you would take a supreme teacher of advertising, much beyond anything that has ever appeared up to now, then you would get something like an equivalent of Gorgias. Very good. But, if there could be a teacher of opinion leaders, in the sense in which Gorgias was one, he would be a kind of unofficial legislator for society as a whole. And an unofficial legislator may be more powerful than the official legislator for all we know. He would necessarily *appear* to be a philosopher, because the function is somehow the same. Such a man would not be a scientist in our present–day sense of the term, for science is morally neutral, or value–free. Such a man would precisely aspire to teach the opinion leaders of how to sway the multitude regarding values. Since he would have to teach both Arthur Schlesinger, Jr. and Russell Kirk, he would not be committed to either liberalism or conservatism....So he must, then, have a justice of his own. He must take a higher justice, higher than either [the] liberal or conservative interpretation of justice. The very notion of [a] teacher of opinion leaders forces us, then, to raise the question of the relation of his teaching to justice, just as Plato was compelled to raise the question of the separation of rhetoric and justice. So in other words, if we think a little bit of what is going on and what is today concealed by the term "intellectual," we arrive at the same phenomenon which Plato analyzed under the heading "rhetoric." And so it is not an old and buried story, but a very timely and topical issue [with] which we are concerned.

(Session 3, January 10, 1957), posted at http://leostrausstranscripts.uchicago. edu/navigate/1/4/.

37 *Crisis of the House Divided*, 218.

38 *Crisis of the House Divided*, 218, 221

39 *Nicomachean Ethics*, 1124b6.

40 *Rediscovery of America*, 221.

41 *Strauss Divided*, 28.

42 *Crisis of the House Divided*, 245.

43 *Crisis of the House Divided*, 247.

44 One could write a long essay simply unravelling what Jaffa says about Lincoln's references to "rational causes" and God's decrees, which "can never be reversed." Jaffa examines these in light of Aristotle's and Spinoza's metaphysical theologies. A passage on pages 251–252 of *Crisis* states:

> The quest for "rational causes" is thus a quest for causes rooted in human nature. That men should be governed in their behavior by such causes is here attributed by Lincoln to God: natural law and divine law appear to coincide. However, Lincoln's manner of reference to the divine decree is somewhat heterodox: he says that it "can" never be reversed, not that it "will" never be reversed. Traditionally the God of Israel was thought to be bound by his own promises but not by necessity. It is rather the God of Aristotle and Spinoza who is so bound.

The last sentence refers the reader to a lengthy endnote, which reads:

> The difference between a God who cannot and one who will not reverse himself has, of course, well-nigh unlimited ramifications. How far Lincoln was aware of these, we do not venture to say. However, Lincoln does say, in a later passage which must be discussed in its proper place, that the argument for Providence, like that for whisky, rests upon universal public opinion. Now it is precisely because the philosophic God is subject to ontological necessity that he cannot be conceived as changing and hence cannot be conceived as "Providence" i.e., concerned with particular beings or particular events. For this reason He could not change his "decree," while the biblical God could (and frequently did). Moreover, the argument for a God whose "decree" is subject to necessity would be an ontological argument, not an argument from universal public opinion.
>
> It may be objected that we are laying too great stress upon the distinction between "can" and "will" and that, in any case, there is no necessity for conceiving the two conceptions of deity in the form of a radical opposition. In Thomistic theology, for example, the antinomy is overcome by the proposition that all apparent "reversals" of the divine fiat are themselves predetermined by an aboriginal necessity. Without inquiring whether the Thomistic synthesis is philosophically successful, I think it clear that Lincoln's language is inconsistent with such a synthesis. For the Thomistic doctrine, while holding that the divine reversals are apparent rather than real, denies to human wisdom the possibility of penetrating to its core the necessity of the divine nature, anticipating thereby all future reversals. Revelation remains a necessity of human life precisely because central facts concerning human life, e.g., man's sinfulness and the remedy therefore, are beyond unassisted human reason. From the Thomistic view, therefore, Lincoln would have had no basis to assert as a matter of natural knowledge that the strength of the passions would always remain the same. Since Lincoln does assert this

as a matter of natural knowledge, he must have here presupposed only a natural theology. And from the point of view of a natural theology, the force of the opposition of the two conceptions of deity recurs in full. (p. 418)

John Marini argues that for the founders, "the dilemma posed by the tension between philosophy and religion, or reason and revelation, was a permanent human problem that could not be transcended or ameliorated except in a regime of civil and religious liberty." "Theology, Metaphysics, and Positivism: The Origins of the Social Science and the Transformation of the American University," in *Challenges to the American Founding: Slavery, Historicism, and Progressivism in the Nineteenth Century*, Ronald J. Pestritto and Thomas G. West, eds. (Lanham, MD: Lexington Books, 2005), 164.

45 *Crisis of the House Divided*, 252.

46 *Crisis of the House Divided*, 261.

47 *Crisis of the House Divided*, 248.

48 *Strauss Divided*, 14.

49 Harry V. Jaffa, "Political Philosophy and Political Reality," 1991, posted at https://claremontreviewofbooks.com/digital/the-long-arm-of-socialism/.

50 *Crisis of the House Divided*, 272. We see here, as elsewhere, that Jaffa forcefully condemns the dangers of egalitarianism, which he sees as a perversion of equality properly understood. One of the lessons of the Temperance Address is that all good things—not just alcohol, but also religion and philosophy—can be perverted or misused. The possibility that or degree to which the philosophic quest may be distorted to pernicious effect is another difference Jaffa had with Eastern Straussians.

51 Winston S. Churchill, speech in the House of Commons, October 5, 1938, posted at https://winstonchurchill.org/resources/speeches/1930-1938-the-wilderness/the-munich-agreement/.

52 *Strauss Divided*, 14.

53 Harry V. Jaffa, "The Peace Process is Dead. Let's Bury It," *Claremont Review of Books*, Spring 2001, posted at https://claremontreviewofbooks.com/the-peace-process-is-dead-lets-bury-it/.

54 Winston S. Churchill, *Thoughts and Adventures* (New York: W. W. Norton & Company, 1991), 177.

55 *Thoughts and Adventures*, 179.

56 *Thoughts and Adventures*, 183, 184, 191.

57 *Statesmanship*, 25, 38.

58 Leo Strauss letter to Karl Löwith, August 20, 1946, quoted in *Strauss Divided*, 75–76.

59 *Strauss Divided*, 76.

60 Leo Strauss, *On Tyranny*, Corrected and Expanded Edition, Victor Gourevitch and Michael S. Roth, eds. (Chicago: University of Chicago Press, 2013), 27.

61   *On Tyranny*, 23.

62   *Strauss Divided*, 75.

63   Letter to Warren K. Anderson, October 10, 1975, archive.

64   Strauss's remarks were delivered during his 1965 course "Introduction to Political Philosophy" at the beginning of session six on January 25. The transcripts of the first nine sessions of that course are not available online at the Leo Strauss Center but can be found in *Leo Strauss on Political Philosophy: Responding to the Challenge of Positivism and Historicism*, Catherine H. Zuckert, ed. (Chicago: University of Chicago Press, 2018). See page 123 for the eulogy.

65   This version is taken from the transcript reproduced in Catherine Zuckert's *Leo Strauss on Political Philosophy*. There are a few minor discrepancies with the version that appears in Jaffa's *Statesmanship*. Strauss's remark about the weakness of Weimar in the epigraph to this chapter is from the "autobiographical preface" to *Spinoza's Critique of Religion* (Chicago: University of Chicago Press, 1997), 1.

66   *Strauss Divided*, 77.

67   *Rediscovery of America*, 111.

68   *Rediscovery of America*, 114.

69   *Strauss Divided*, 261.

70   *Rediscovery of America*, 143.

71   Andrew Roberts, *Churchill: Walking with Destiny* (New York: Viking, 2018), 547.

72   *Statesmanship*, 3.

73   *Rediscovery of America*, 143.

74   *Statesmanship*, 9.

75   *Rediscovery of America*, 109.

CHAPTER 7

1   The wording is a paraphrase; the sentiment is Churchillian. See https://winstonchurchill.org/resources/quotes/quotes-falsely-attributed/

2   *American Conservativism*, 34–35.

3   *Strauss Divided*, 127. Jaffa once used another medical analogy in a letter to Francis Canavan: "I push arguments hard, because sometimes—at least—arguments can be conclusive, and they should sometimes both be conclusive, and be seen to be conclusive (like justice.) . . . If anyone would call our arguments 'deadly,' I don't think either of us should be offended. I would like to think that we are rather wielding the surgeon's knife, on the cancers of our time. The struggle for human decency, and the necessity to identify the claims of decency with those of reason, are desperate." Letter to Francis Canavan, December 22, 1979, archive.

4   In his Rosary College remarks, Jaffa states: "I think that we have inherited a body of—I won't say merely knowledge—but of structured behavior that is more than a mere way of knowing. We don't have to start out as

children to rediscover what Newton and Einstein discovered in order to find out what the universe is like. We may study their reasoning, and part of our education is just this. But we do not count it part of our 'Freedom' to pretend that they never lived. We inherit a great deal of information about the physical universe which enables us to become intelligent beings oriented in a universe of matter and form, of light and sound, of touch and taste, and smells and so on. Similarly, we are beings who are born into a world that has placed a great deal of reason and experience about morality at our disposal and which we would be mad to disregard merely in order to exercise some hypothetical freedom. The human mind has come to terms with the problem of moral choice in a variety of circumstances over some millennia, and that information has been reduced into various books, to a form which is accessible to us. And I think it would be insane to identify human freedom with the ability to disregard the experience—the reason and experience—of all these millennia." *American Conservatism*, 57–58.

5 Garry Wills, *Lincoln at Gettysburg: The Words that Remade America* (New York: Simon & Schuster, 1992), 38, 39.

6 Letter to Paul Basinski, May 5, 1996, archive.

7 In essay called "Willmoore Kendall: Philosopher of Consensus," Jaffa wrote: "At the end of his life Kendall became a disciple—more I think than he had ever been anyone's disciple—of Leo Strauss. In his recognition of Strauss's greatness he showed a largeness of soul that placed him head and shoulders above any American political scientist of his generation. There was about him none of the 'envy with which mediocrity views genius,' because he was no mediocrity." *American Conservatism*, 194. For an insightful and fair analysis of the disagreements between Jaffa and Kendall, see John A. Murley, "On the 'Calhounism' of Willmoore Kendall," in *Willmoore Kendall: Maverick of American Conservatives*, John A. Murley and John E. Alvis, eds. (Lanham, MD: Lexington Books, 2002).

8 Charles R. Kesler, "A Special Meaning of the Declaration of Independence," *National Review*, July 6, 1979.

9 Letter to Christopher DeMuth, November 15, 1998, archive.

10 In his foreword to Jaffa's *American Conservatism and the American Founding* (p. xi), William Buckley wrote, "It would be only a slight exaggeration to say that Harry Jaffa is uninterested in debating those who disagree with him. His most fascinating debates engage those who seem to be philosophically his next-door neighbors: Such eminent conservatives as Willmoore Kendall, Irving Kristol, Walter Berns, George Will, and Martin Diamond. These men, like himself, are patriots, lovers of freedom, principled enemies of tyranny, unmaskers of intellectual fraud."

11 Letter to Stephen Balch, March 14, 1991, archive.

12 *Rediscovery of America*, 99.

13 This is not the same Professor Steven Smith who teaches at Yale and is the author of (among other books) *Reading Leo Strauss: Philosophy, Politics, Judaism*.

14 The quotations in this section are taken from various parts of Jaffa's essay in *American Conservativism*, 111–120.

15 *American Conservatism*, 77.

16 *American Conservatism*, 76.

17 *American Conservatism*, 101.

18 *American Conservatism*, 92.

19 *Crisis of the Strauss Divided*, 13.

20 Irving Kristol's son, William, founded *The Weekly Standard* and became a vocal opponent of Donald Trump.

21 *How to Think About the American Revolution*, 6, 9.

22 In a letter a few weeks later to his old friend Frank Canavan, Jaffa wrote: "The discussion at the APSA meeting was not *too* animated. There were no 'pistols at dawn.'" Letter to Francis Canavan, October 6, 1975, archive.

23 Edward Erler, communication with the author, December 5, 2020.

24 Published in *America's Continuing Revolution: An Act of Conservation* (Washington, DC: American Enterprise Institute, 1976).

25 *How to Think About the American Revolution*, 53.

26 *Rediscovery of America*, 307.

27 *Rediscovery of America*, 305.

28 Irving Kristol, "The Character of the American Political Order" in *The Promise of American Politics: Principles and Practice after Two Hundred Years*, Robert L. Utley, Jr., ed. (Lanham, MD: University Press of America, 1989), 3–4. By a strange twist, "neoconservative" today has come to mean almost the opposite of what Kristol proposed. Whereas he argued that America, properly speaking, has no principles or theory (or that America is at its best when it ignores its own theory), the term now seems to indicate a kind of dogmatic universalism dedicated to "exporting democracy." Jaffa strongly opposed such Wilsonian adventurism, by the way, writing in a letter to *Commentary* in 2006, "the idea of bringing democracy to Iraq, or any country like Iraq, is simply utopian. [George Bush's] frequently repeated assertion that democracy is the aspiration of all peoples, and that to free any people from tyranny is to free them for democracy, has no foundation in history or political philosophy." (https://www.commentarymagazine.com/articles/reader-letters/the-bush-doctrine/)

29 *Rediscovery of America*, 323.

30 *Rediscovery of America*, 162.

31 Harry V. Jaffa, "In Re Jack Kemp v. Joe Sobran on Lincoln," *Claremont Review of Books*, July 30, 2001, digital exclusive, posted at https://claremontreviewofbooks.com/digital/in-re-jack-kemp-v-joe-sobran-on-lincoln/. All the quotations in this section are taken from this essay.

32 *The Basic Symbols of the American Political Tradition*, Willmoore Kendall and George W. Carey, eds. (Washington, DC: Catholic University of America Press, 1995) ix, xv. Originally published: Baton Rouge: Louisiana State University Press, 1970.

33 *How to Think About the American Revolution*, 32, 19, 32, 41.

34 *Basic Symbols*, 4.

35 Abraham Lincoln, speech at Chicago, Illinois, July 10, 1858, posted at https://quod.lib.umich.edu/l/lincoln/lincoln2/1:526?rgn=div1;view=fulltext .

36 *How to Think About the American Revolution*, 36–37.

37 *Conditions of Freedom*, 168.

38 Willmoore Kendall, "Source of American Caesarism," *National Review*, November 7, 1959.

39 John Murley notes that in Jaffa's "Equality as a Conservative Principle," there are "long quotations and fourteen specific citations to the 1959 Kendall review of *Crisis of the House Divided*." See *Willmoore Kendall: Maverick of American Conservatism*, 105. The Zuckerts are also correct to emphasize the importance of this review for Jaffa in *The Truth About Leo Strauss* (pp. 240–241), though I interpret Jaffa's response somewhat differently than they do.

40 These difficulties are already prefigured in *Federalist No. 43*, where the "very delicate" matter is raised regarding the status of states that do not ratify the new Constitution. Madison artfully evades the question by noting that "the flattering prospect of its being merely hypothetical forbids an overcurious discussion of it. It is one of those cases which must be left to provide for itself." See Jaffa's essay "Partly Federal, Partly National," where he notes that Madison's delicate question "ceased to be hypothetical in 1861." *Conditions of Freedom*, p. 183.

41 *Rediscovery of America*, 14, 15.

42 *Rediscovery of America*, 30, 32, 35–36.

43 *Rediscovery of America*, 44–45.

44 Letter to Charles Lofgren, February 11, 1989, archive.

45 Quoted in *The Rediscovery of America*, 196–197. Mansfield's review of *The Debate on the Constitution: Federalist and Antifederalist Speeches, Articles, and Letters During the Struggle over Ratification*, edited by Bernard Bailyn, appeared in the September 1993 issue *of The New Criterion*.

46 *The Rediscovery of America*, 197, 198.

47 *The Rediscovery of America*, 203, 204.

48 *The Rediscovery of America*, 204.

49 *The Rediscovery of America*, 212.

50 *The Rediscovery of America*, 213.

51 *The Rediscovery of America*, 216, 221.

52 *The Rediscovery of America*, 258.

53 Joseph Cropsey, *Political Philosophy and the Issue of Politics* (Chicago: University of Chicago Press, 1977), 7, 12–13.

54 Walter Berns, "Comment" on Edward R. Norman, "Christians, Politics, and the Modern State," *This World*, Fall 1983. For a recent and emphatic denial of the founders' atheism, see Robert Reilly, *America on Trial: A Defense of the Founding* (San Francisco: Ignatius Press, 2020).

55 Charles R. Kesler, "The Founders and the Classics," in *The American Founding: Essays on the Formation of the Constitution*, J. Jackson Barlow, Leonard W. Levy, and Ken Masugi, eds. (Westport, CT: Greenwood Press, 1988), 62–63, 87.

56 Letter to Eugene Miller, August 18, 1977, archive.

57 *Studies in Platonic Political Philosophy*, 21.

58 *Liberalism*, ix. Many East Coast Straussians seem to think that official orthodoxy always takes the form of traditional piety and old-fashioned morality and that therefore the philosopher (or the philosophic persona) always adopts the "heterodox" stance of aloof atheism. This is an unwarranted assumption. Jaffa insisted that Socrates always defended traditional morality against pre-Socratic conventionalism. Moreover, orthodox or elite opinion in late-twentieth-century and early-twenty-first-century America is hardly defined by old-fashioned "family-values" Christianity. Quite to the contrary, such deplorable opinions are mocked by the official piety of our secular priesthood. Many Eastern Straussians seem to miss this. Thus, some teach their students that natural right is a comforting myth, that patriotism is vulgar and embarrassing, and that philosophic liberation means transcending the ethical virtues cherished by their deluded grandparents. For Jaffa, this is neither heterodox nor Socratic. Such teachings merely reaffirm the dogmas students hear from every authoritative voice in the academy and broader culture. Who, Jaffa was wont to ask, really challenges the reigning *endoxa* of our present cave? Harry Neumann made this same point, in his usual elliptical way, by writing that "Strauss attempted to prevent the victory of liberal science over illiberal (Socratic) philosophy by justifying illiberalism in a liberal world." *Liberalism*, 87.

59 Foreword to Leo Strauss, *On Tyranny*, Revised and Enlarged (Ithaca, NY: Cornell University Press, 1963), v.

60 *The Closing of the American Mind*, 167.

61 *The Closing of the American Mind*, 309–310.

62 *Strauss Divided*, 150.

63 "Since I'm really a political scientist, as you know, I always wish you to think of the topical relevance of the conversation which is said to have taken place 2,300 years and more ago in Athens." Leo Strauss, Course on Plato's *Gorgias* (Session 3, January 10, 1957), posted at http://leostrausstranscripts.uchicago.edu/navigate/1/4/.

64 Thomas G. West, "Leo Strauss and the American Founding," in *Leo Strauss: Political Philosopher and Jewish Thinker*, Kenneth L. Deutsch and Walter Nicgorski, eds. (Lanham, MD: Rowman & Littlefield, 1994), 310–311. Strauss's essay appears in *Liberalism Ancient and Modern* (Ithaca, NY: Cornell University Press, 1968); the quotations are taken from pages 205–207.

65 See Catherine and Michael Zuckert, "Why Strauss Is Not an Aristotelian," in *Leo Strauss and the Problem of Political Philosophy*.

66 Christopher Bruell, "A Return to Classical Philosophy and the Understanding

of the American Founding," in *Leo Strauss: Political Philosopher and Jewish Thinker*, 325–327.

67 Christopher Bruell, "A Return to Classical Philosophy and the Understanding of the American Founding," in *Leo Strauss: Political Philosopher and Jewish Thinker*, 330, 328.

68 *Original Intent*, 322.

69 Jaffa's student Ken Masugi describes what he regards as the error of the Eastern Straussians this way: "For many of them 'political moderation' means purgation of political passions and political relevance. Morality (and religion) become strictly utilitarian means for carrying on the only worthy activity of life—the pleasure of philosophizing." Yet this easily becomes, as Strauss himself warned, an "unmanly contempt for politics." See, "Straussian Civil Wars," *Law & Liberty*, August 25, 2013, posted at https://lawliberty.org/straussian-civil-wars/.

70 "[I]t would be a mistake to conclude that Strauss cared about the fate of constitutional democracy only to the extent to which it was linked to the fate of philosophy. Like Socrates, he was just in more than one sense. His support of liberal democracy can be compared to his support of political Zionism. No one who knew Strauss ever doubted the depth and genuineness of his concern for Israel. Nor could anyone who knew him think that his concern was based on the belief that the fate of philosophy in some mysterious way depended on the survival of Israel. He thought no such thing." Hilail Gildin, "Leo Strauss and the Crisis of Liberal Democracy," in *The Crisis of Liberal Democracy: a Straussian Perspective*, Kenneth L Deutsch and Walter Soffer, eds. (Albany, NY: State University of New York Press, 1987), 156–157.

71 *Shakespeare as a Political Thinker*, 241. Jaffa and Allan Bloom formed an early bond through Shakespeare. The two had been friends in the 1950s, and 60s, collaborating on the 1964 *Shakespeare's Politics*. Despite their later disagreements, Jaffa persistently defended the quality and the moral outlook of Bloom's essays in that book, even many years later. In a July 15, 1998, letter to Shadia Drury, Jaffa says that Drury has "misquoted and mis-cited" Bloom regarding a subtle question of love, God, and the Bible. (Archive.) But in the 1960s, Bloom went to Paris and spent more than a year meeting and studying with various European scholars and intellectuals, including Alexandre Kojève. After this, Jaffa came to believe that Bloom gradually moved away from his early devotion to Strauss and came under the spell of Nietzsche and Heidegger. By the time Bloom published *The Closing of the American Mind* in 1987, they had already grown apart.

72 Harry Neumann, *Liberalism*, 100. He attempts to convey this distinction and its inherent, endless difficulty in a bit more detail by noting that "Socrates, like all illiberal men, herd members, never for a moment doubted the existence of an absolute good legitimating his 'truth' party [i.e. philosophers as a class]. The conflict with politics, philosophy's heart, sprang from Socratic awareness of lacking an adequate grasp of that good. This lack sparked his inability to justify either his own 'truth' party or that of the pious Athenians

who killed him. Socrates claimed only an inadequate divination (*Republic,* 505d-e, 508e-509a) insufficient to legitimize either a new 'truth' party or whole-souled rejection of the old, but sufficient to embark on his always questionable questioning." Strauss's last book, on Plato's *Laws,* centers on "the war between philosophy and politics in the philosopher's soul, a battle which must be presented exoterically to unphilosophic citizens and anti-philosophic pseudo-liberals." The latter, among whom Neumann specifically names Stanley Rosen and Allan Bloom, are those who believe philosophy means discovering the truth of atheism and nihilism. *Liberalism,* xxi, 91.

73   Leo Strauss, "Restatement on Xenophon's Hiero," in *On Tyranny,* revised and expanded edition, Victor Gourevitch and Michael S. Roth, eds. (New York: Free Press, 1991), 195.

74   *How to Think About the American Revolution,* 162–164. The Latin phrase means, "Aristotle is accustomed to seeking a fight."

75   *American Conservatism,* 141.

76   *How to Think About the American Revolution,* 166, 168.

77   In this 1965 review of Jaffa's *Equality and Liberty,* George Kateb also observed somewhat peevishly that when the respected Lincoln scholar joined the Goldwater campaign, "eyebrows were raised." *Commentary,* August 1965, posted at https://www.commentarymagazine.com/articles/george-kateb/equality-and-liberty-by-harry-v-jaffa/.

78   Walter Berns, "A Reply to Harry Jaffa," *National Review,* January 22, 1982.

79   *How to Think About the American Revolution,* 174–75.

80   *How to Think About the American Revolution,* 171.

81   John Eastman points out that the official status of the Declaration is confirmed in the congressional Enabling Acts admitting many new states to the Union:

> We have just seen how the principles of the Declaration were codified— and thus rendered enforceable—in the reconstruction-era constitutions of the old confederate states. The Declaration was made even more binding on new states admitted thereafter. As noted at the outset, Nevada and Nebraska were admitted to statehood during the war years, and in the Enabling Acts for each, Congress required that the new state's constitution, 'when formed, shall be republican, and not repugnant to the Constitution of the United States and the principles of the Declaration of Independence' (Acts of Mar. 21 and Apr. 19, 1864). The requirement was repeated in the Enabling Acts for Colorado in 1875, North Dakota, South Dakota, Montana and Washington in 1889, Utah in 1894, and Oklahoma, New Mexico, and Arizona in 1906 (Acts of Mar. 3, 1975; Feb. 22, 1889; June 16, 1906).

"The Declaration of Independence: View From The States," in Scott Gerber, ed., *The Declaration of Independence: Origins and Impact* (Washington, DC: *Congressional Quarterly Press,* 2002).

82   Vincent Phillip Muñoz. "A Learned but Dismissive Take on Conservative

Constitutionalism," *Law & Liberty*, January 22, 2020, posted at https://old. lawliberty.org/2020/01/22/a-learned-but-dismissive-take-on-conservative-constitutionalism/.

83 Quoted in *Original Intent and the Framers of the Constitution*, 85.

84 Quoted in *Storm Over the Constitution*, 115.

85 *Rediscovery of America*, 25.

86 *Dred Scott v. Sanford*, 1857, posted at https://www.law.cornell.edu/supremecourt/text/60/393

87 Abraham Lincoln, speech on the *Dred Scott* decision, June 26, 1857, posted at https://teachingamericanhistory.org/library/document/speech-on-the-dred-scott-decision/. In his essay "Partly Federal, Partly National," Jaffa notes that the Supreme Court has *legal* but not *political* supremacy, citing Madison's Report of 1800: "However true therefore it may be that the judicial department, is, in all questions submitted to it by the forms of the Constitution, to decide in the last resort, this resort must necessarily be deemed the last in relation to the authorities of the other departments of the Government; not in relation to the rights of the parties to the constitutional compact, from which the judicial as well as the other departments hold their delegated trusts. On any other hypothesis, the delegation of judicial power, would annul the authority delegating it; and the concurrence of this department with the others in usurped powers, might subvert forever, and beyond the possible reach of any rightful remedy, the very Constitution, which all were instituted to preserve." See *Conditions of Freedom*, 176.

88 Robert H. Bork, "Mr. Jaffa's Constitution," *National Review*, February 7, 1994.

89 *Original Intent and the Framers of the Constitution*, 274–275.

90 *Original Intent and the Framers of the Constitution*, 275.

91 *Original Intent and the Framers of the Constitution*, 301.

92 See Clarence Thomas, "The Virtue of Practical Wisdom," speech at Claremont Institute dinner in honor of Harry V. Jaffa, 1999, posted at https://claremontreviewofbooks.com/digital/the-virtue-of-practical-wisdom/.

93 John Eastman, "Colorblind Justice," *Claremont Review of Books*, Summer 2005, posted at https://claremontreviewofbooks.com/colorblind-justice/.

94 Myron Magnet, *Clarence Thomas and the Lost Constitution* (New York: Encounter Books, 2019), 72.

95 Ken Masugi, "Natural Justice," *Claremont Review of Books*, Winter 2020, posted at https://claremontreviewofbooks.com/natural-justice/.

96 Clarence Thomas, *My Grandfather's Son: A Memoir* (New York: Harper Perennial, 2007), 188.

97 Clarence Thomas, concurring opinion, *Adarand v. Pena*, 1995, posted at https://www.law.cornell.edu/supct/html/93-1841.ZC1.html.

98 Harry V. Jaffa, *Storm Over the Constitution* (Lanham, MD: Lexington Books, 1999), 64–65.

CHAPTER 8

1 Statement by the National Endowment for the Humanities, posted at https://www.neh.gov/award/claremont-institute.

2 Letter to Robert Horwitz, March 26, 1978, archive.

3 "Harry V. Jaffa, Conservative Scholar and Goldwater Muse, Dies at 96," *New York Times*, January 12, 2015, posted at https://www.nytimes.com/2015/01/12/us/politics/harry-v-jaffa-conservative-scholar-and-goldwater-muse-dies-at-96.html.

4 "Harry V. Jaffa dies at 96; shaped modern American conservative movement," *Los Angeles Times*, January 15, 2015, posted at https://www.latimes.com/local/obituaries/la-me-harry-jaffa-20150116-story.html.

5 Harvey C. Mansfield, "Scholars of American Politics; The contributions of Walter Berns and Harry Jaffa," *The Weekly Standard*. February 9, 2015, available through Nexis at https://o-advance-lexis-com.library.hillsdale.edu/api/document?collection=news&id=urn:contentItem:5F7D-P8N1-JBRW-201K-00000-00&context=1516831.

6 H. Lee Cheek, Jr. and Sean Busick, "How Jaffa's Critics Remember Him," *Law & Liberty*, January 26, 2105, posted at https://lawliberty.org/how-jaffas-critics-remember-him/.

7 Nathan Robinson, "Conservative hero's dark side: How an 'intellectual' icon's real legacy got sanitized," *Salon*, January 20, 2015, posted at https://www.salon.com/2015/01/20/conservative_heros_dark_side_how_an_intellectual_icons_legacy_got_sanitized/. Jeet Heer, "Homophobia and the Art of Writing," *Jacobin*, February 2, 2015, posted at https://www.jacobinmag.com/2015/02/harry-jaffa-obituary-jeet-heer/.

8 John J. Miller, "The House of Jaffa," *National Review*, January 12, 2015, posted at https://www.nationalreview.com/2015/01/house-jaffa-john-j-miller/.

9 Joseph R. Fornieri, "Harry V. Jaffa's Contribution to Lincoln Studies and American Statesmanship," *Journal of the Abraham Lincoln Association*, Vol. 37, No. 2 (2016).

10 *Claremont Review of Books*, special edition, Spring 2015, posted at https://www.claremont.org/download_pdf.php?file_name=2792Jaffa.pdf.

11 The eulogies are posted at https://claremontreviewofbooks.com/harry-v-jaffa-1918-2015/ and can be viewed on Youtube at https://www.youtube.com/watch?v=_Cn1NhIeSVM.

12 Posted on YouTube at https://www.youtube.com/watch?v=QCsIozKodJA.

13 *Nicomachean Ethics*, 1124b9-16.

14 *Wall Street Journal*, September 8, 1992.

15 "Political Philosophy and Political Reality," published by the Claremont Institute as "The Long Arm of Socialism" at https://claremontreviewofbooks.com/digital/the-long-arm-of-socialism/.

16 *The Rediscovery of America*, 95.

17 Letter to William Rusher, March 15, 1986, archive.

18 Kesler describes this Claremont center of scholarship (which broadly overlaps with Jaffa's Western Straussianism) in his Foreword to Bradley Watson's *Progressivism: The Strange History of a Radical Idea.* "Claremont" refers to "both a place and a school of thought." It is skeptical, Kesler writes,

> of all claims that historical Might or success or "owning the future" can make Right. Hence this school is well known for reopening the question of the progressive movement's justice and wisdom as a whole; and for its defense of the Declaration of Independence, the constitution, and the founder's political science against progressive attacks on them as outmoded and unjust.

Bradley C. S. Watson, *Progressivism: The Strange History of a Radical Idea* (Notre Dame, IN: University of Notre Dame Press, 2020), xvii. Watson (himself a Claremont PhD) devotes the book to critiquing the false picture of the American Progressive Era painted by many mainstream historians and limns the work of revisionist scholars correcting the record at Claremont, but also—and increasingly—at Hillsdale College in Michigan.

19 Charles R. Kesler, *I Am the Change: Barack Obama and the Crisis of Liberalism* (New York: Broadside Books, 2012), 167, 168, 187, 188, 237.

20 An essay titled "The Flight 93 Election" by Michael Anton (writing under the pseudonym Publius Decius Mus) appeared in the *CRB* on September 5, 2106, and received considerable attention for its argument that voters had to gamble everything on Trump because a Hillary Clinton presidency would mean the end of the regime: "Charge the cockpit or die." Posted at https://claremontreviewofbooks.com/digital/the-flight-93-election/. An expanded version of Anton's essay was published as a short book in 2019: *After the Flight 93 Election: The Vote that Saved America and What We Still Have to Lose* (New York: Encounter Books).

21 Communication with the author, December 20, 2020.

22 Consider Jaffa's remarks in *A New Birth of Freedom* (page 416):

> After 1776, free elections replaced the right of revolution as the ordinary means by which the rights of the people may be safeguarded. But throughout the literature of the Founding, and especially in the *Federalist*, there is a concern to prevent the tyranny of the majority as well as all other forms of tyranny. And in 1798 in the Kentucky Resolutions, Jefferson still saw the right of revolution and the threat of exercising it as necessary to the safety of the people even against the usurpations of a government they themselves had elected. One might even say that the victory of the Republicans in the election of 1800 came about because of the threats implied in the Virginia and Kentucky Resolutions. Thus the right of revolution becomes a permanent element in the electoral process, reminding both government and people that the majority loses its moral authority if it tramples upon the rights of the minority.
>
> The importance of the right of revolution is therefore missed if one thinks of it only in the negative sense. In the Declaration of Independence,

the right to alter or abolish tyrannical government is at one and the same time the right to institute new and better government.

23 For a consideration of various scenarios by which our current crisis might play out, see Michael Anton's *The Stakes: America at the Point of No Return* (Washington, DC: Regnery Gateway, 2020).

24 Abraham Lincoln, "Second Lecture on Discoveries and Inventions," February 11, 1859, posted at https://teachingamericanhistory.org/library/document/second-lecture-on-discoveries-and-inventions/.

25 As work is for the sake of leisure, so at the highest level action is for the sake of thought. Though Jaffa disparaged those who never looked beyond books about politics to actual political experience, he nevertheless agreed with Aristotle and Strauss that the life of the mind is the highest human good.

26 *Closing of the American Mind*, 332.

27 *The Rediscovery of America*, 74, 66.

28 *The Rediscovery of America*, 101–102.

29 "Political Philosophy and Political Reality: 1991," archive.

30 *Crisis of the Strauss Divided*, 116.

POSTSCRIPT

1 Leo Strauss, "Note on Maimonides' *Letter on Astrology.*" In this short commentary, Strauss observes that on the basis of astrology (a practice of idolators), the fate of men "is fully determined by the stars." By contrast, the *Torah* and "all philosophers" agree that men's actions are not "subject to compulsion." Yet "the philosophers" hold that the fate of men is a matter of chance, while the *Torah* "believes that what happens to human individuals happens to them in accordance with justice." Faith and reason both reject determinism. As between chance and justice, however, Maimonides concludes that "what happens to human beings" is not reducible to "what happens to the beasts." Unlike the beasts, human life—Maimonides seems to suggest—is governed by choice as well as chance. *Studies in Platonic Political Philosophy*, 205–207.

2 *American Conservatism*, 65.

3 Chapter 1 contrasts the unity achieved in 1800 with the disintegration that followed the 1860 election. Chapter 3 is titled "The Divided American Mind." Chapters 4 and 5 examine "The Mind of Lincoln" split into Parts I and II. Chapter 6 is on union, while 7 is on secession. The Appendix is titled "The Dividing Line between Federal and Local Authority."

4 Edward J. Erler, "The New Oligarchs Will Not Tolerate Secession," *The American Mind* (December 16, 2020), posted at https://americanmind.org/features/a-house-dividing/the-new-oligarchs-will-not-tolerate-secession/.

5 For an overview, see Michael Anton's "Are the Kids Al(t)Right?" *Claremont Review of Books* (Summer 2019), posted at https://claremontreviewofbooks.com/are-the-kids-altright/.

6 *Rediscovery of America*, 200.

7 Numa Denis Fustel de Coulanges, *The Ancient City: A Study on the Religion, Laws, and Institutions of Greece and Rome* (Garden City, NY: Doubleday, 1956).

8 From Jaffa's entry "Natural Rights" in the *International Encyclopedia of Social Sciences.*

9 "The Case for a Stronger National Government," unpublished draft, archive.

10 *The Rediscovery of America*, 147. In connection with this section, recall the discussion in Chapter 4 about "wise interventions" in Shakespeare's *Measure for Measure.*

11 *Crisis of the Strauss Divided*, 156.

12 Leo Strauss, course on Plato's *Gorgias* (Session 13, February 28, 1957), posted at http://leostrausstranscripts.uchicago.edu/navigate/1/14/.

13 *Original Intent*, 369

14 In the first chapter of *A New Birth of Freedom*, Jaffa shows that the early American debates over federalism, union, and states' rights turned on some quite recondite and theoretical distinctions. See also *American Conservatism*, page 141: "The very formulation of the problem of the One and the Many, means that the One implied in the Many, cannot be One among Many. (This is the logical defect of the Kentucky Resolutions.)."

15 *Crisis of the Strauss Divided*, 136, 156.

16 *American Conservatism and the American Founding*, 141.

17 *A New Birth of Freedom*, 71, 63.

18 *Original Intent*, 313.

19 *Crisis of the Strauss Divided*, 156.

20 *Original Intent*, 313.

21 *Original Intent*, 315.

22 *Original Intent*, 315. See also Scot Zentner, "The Philosopher and the City: Harry Jaffa and the Straussians," *Interpretation* Vol. 30, No. 3 (Summer 2003). I benefited from several email exchanges with Professor Zentner discussing this essay and Jaffa more generally.

23 *American Conservatism and the American Founding*, 35.

24 *Original Intent*, 316.

25 The following passage from Jaffa's pivotal essay "Equality, Liberty, Wisdom, Morality, and Consent" is rather long, but it is very helpful for understanding this crucial point in Jaffa's teaching. When the ancient city disappears, he observes:

> There must then be either immediate divine sanction for the laws, or a natural sanction translated from that form visible only to philosophers, to one that is intelligible to nonphilosophers. Nowhere in the *Politics* does Aristotle confront the question of how the citizens will be persuaded to obey the laws, if there are no gods to whom those laws will be ascribed. Nowhere does he confront the question of how the authority of an unmediated universal nature will replace the authority of the gods. [In the American founding the] state of nature and the social contract

supply that mediation. Aristotle recognizes that particular polities will require particular institutions—that they will be the work of legislators acting in particular circumstances. But if these legislators can no longer crown their work by appealing to the authority of particular gods as the foundation of their laws, they must appeal directly to nature. They must have some way of translating the authority of a universal nature into the ground of particular laws. . . . Moreover the idea of the state of nature, by treating civil society as a voluntary association, lays a firmer foundation for the idea of the rule of law than in Aristotle's *Politics*. It is guided, as we have shown, by Aristotle's idea of law as "reason unaffected by desire." It enshrines the doctrine of popular sovereignty—which in itself is un-Aristotelian. Contrary to what is often said, however, it enshrines not the people's will, but only their rational will. The people, in unanimously agreeing to form a civil society, may enjoin in the social contract as the ground and purpose of law only those things that are consistent with the law of nature in the state of nature. They may enjoin only as Madison said what may be willed unanimously and rightfully. Hence the rule of law, resulting from the social contract, contains guarantees against despotism, which are not guaranteed by the rule of law as described by Aristotle.

The Rediscovery of America, 44–45.

26 "The Effect of Liberty: Thoughts for Churchill's Birthday, 1993," archive. For many years, Jaffa delivered an annual lecture at a banquet to mark Sir Winston's birthday. Some were published; this one evidently was not.

27 *American Conservatism*, 136.

28 Consider, for example, the Preface to *A New Birth of Freedom*. My own speculation goes like this: The American founders' rational account of nature replaced the ancient gods as the source of political legitimacy. Yet some form of political religion remained necessary. The task of perpetuation consists in improving the *endoxa*, or bending the dominant religion toward right opinion. This challenge was especially acute in the twentieth century. The declining arc in Western man's moral consciousness, which Jaffa outlined in his Hillsdale lectures on crime and punishment, had terminated in the pit beneath the cave. Perhaps an ascending arc could be devised by transforming or shifting the false god of historicism. Historical progress or providence might be turned, through philosophic poetry, toward natural right. It is perhaps too soon to tell whether such a project could succeed. That it might not fail—or might at any rate be a worthy endeavor—can be seen in the fact that, as I would argue, without Harry Jaffa and his students, the 1619 Project would not have been necessary. (Necessary, that is, for the political agenda of the *New York Times* and its allies.) The difficulty and apparent idiosyncrasies of Jaffa's project as an exercise in philosophic prophecy or poetry may be glimpsed in this statement: "To bring reason into the marketplace is not a sufficient condition of political good. But at decisive points and moments, it is necessary. If this is to happen, right reason must not only *be* right but, so far as possible, must be *seen* to be right." Letter to Thomas Schrock, June 5, 1984, archive. Consider in this context the following excerpt from one of Jaffa's letters to Walter Berns:

Socrates' refutation of Thrasymachus was not sufficient, from Socrates' point of view, nor was it sufficient from that of Glaucon and Adeimantus, Plato's brothers (and surrogates.) But it was sufficient for Thrasymachus, who became Socrates' disciple, when he perceived that Socrates was the stronger of them. At that point Socratic natural right became political right for Thrasymachus. One might say that for Horace Greeley and the free-soil movement, natural right became the political right, when Lincoln defeated Douglas in the political dialectic of the joint debates, and their sequel, ending in the Cooper Union speech. *American Conservatism*, 138.

29 Letter to Steve Smith, December 20, 2001, archive.

30 *American Conservatism and the American Founding*, 36.

31 *A New Birth of Freedom*, 83.

32 *Crisis of the Strauss Divided*, 75.

33 John Quincy Adams, "The Jubilee of the Constitution: A Discourse," posted at https://babel.hathitrust.org/cgi/pt?id=hvd.32044044503787&view=1up&seq=11.

34 Letter to Henry Salvatori, May 9, 1980, archive.

35 *A New Birth of Freedom*, 96.

36 Because the wise do not wish to rule, anyone who asserts political authority on the claim of superior wisdom "would, *ipso facto,* be revealed as a charlatan." *Rediscovery of America*, 257.

37 *Crisis of the Strauss Divided*, 74.

38 *Original Intent*, 313.

39 An account of the history of Western philosophy is well beyond the scope of this Postscript. For an overview from the Straussian perspective, consult the Epilogue, written by Nathan Tarcov and Thomas Pangle, to the third edition of the Strauss-Cropsey *History of Political Philosophy*. Despite his disagreements with Pangle and other Eastern Straussians, Jaffa praised this essay.

40 *Liberalism*, vii.

41 *Liberalism*, 44–45.

42 A commonsense version of this insight is captured by the quotation often attributed to G. K. Chesterton: "When men stop believing in God they don't believe in nothing; they believe in anything."

43 Letter to Paul Basinski, May 5, 1996, archive.

44 Harry Neumann, *Liberalism*, 34, 134, 136, 147, 176, 178.

45 Harry Neumann, "The Man on the Moon: The question of Heidegger's 'Self-Assertion of the German University,'" *The Journal of Value Inquiry*, Vol. 13, No. 4 (December 1979).

46 Scott Atran, *Talking to the Enemy: Violent Extremism, Sacred Values, and What it Means to Be Human* (New York: Penguin, 2010), 42, 454.

47 Paul Gottfried, "Antifa: Nazis Without a Plan," *Chronicles*, August 2020, posted at https://www.chroniclesmagazine.org/antifa-nazis-without-a-plan-1/.

48 Charles R. Kesler, "Facing Mount Rushmore," *Claremont Review of Books*, Summer 2020, posted at https://claremontreviewofbooks.com/facing-mount-rushmore/.

49 *American Conservatism*, 41.

50 See, for example, "Atheistic Freedom and the International Society for the Suppression of Savage Customs: An Interpretation of Conrad's *Heart of Darkness*," *Interpretation* 4 No. 2 (Winter 1974).

51 Quite possibly, the zeal to identify enemies and impose ideological purity will end like the French Revolution: the movement will turn on itself and collapse, with much blood spilled in the process.

52 *American Conservatism*, 118.

53 *The Rediscovery of America*, 133.

INDEX

(assertion of), 149; as hero of natural right, 183; mistaken assumption regarding Aristotle and, 75; philosophy of (liberal education and), 76
"Lockistotle," 75
logomachy, 221
Los Angeles Times, 196, 197, 282
Lowenthal, David, 263
Löwith, Karl, 212

Macaulay, Thomas, 1
Macbeth, 40, 133
Machiavelli, 118–121, 134, 185
Madison, James, 277; as coauthor of *The Federalist Papers*, 255; first guide to principles of the Constitution prescribed by, 269; natural-rights theory elaborated by, 271; problem of faction described by, 192; struggles over federalism of, 246
Manifest Destiny, 55
Mansfield, Harvey, 20, 22, 34
Mansfield, Harvey, Jr., 34, 82, 250–253, 282
Manson, Charles, 40
Marcuse, Herbert, 228
Marini, John, 6, 134, 277
Marx, Karl, 152, 161
Masugi, Ken, 277
McCoy, Charles, 87, 112
Measure for Measure, 121, 136
Meese, Edwin, 270, 285
megalopsuchia, 173, 190, 212
Melzer, Arthur, 177
"metaphysics of marriage," 130
Miller, John, 283
Missouri Compromise, 55
Modern Age, 48
money, commodification of, 97
Moral Majority, 155
Morrisey, Will, 285
My Grandfather's Son, 277

Nabokov, Vladimir, 33
National Endowment for the Humanities Medal, 279
National Review, 49, 226, 237, 275, 283
natural law: Declaration of Independence and, 277; jurisprudence, promotion of, 48; jurisprudence, rejection of, 270; natural right versus, 109, 111; principles (Constitution), 269, 278; slavery and, 275
natural right: American identity and, 245; arguments for and against (seminar),

39; Aristotle and, 64–65, 101; attempt by American political scientists to escape the challenge of, 13; classical understanding of, 63, 246; debate on, 216; defense of, 67, 77, 154; definition of, 245; as "dynamite," 245; existence of (questioning of), 11; grounded (in human condition), 75; Hegel's relativism and, 148; heroes and villains of, 79; historical relativism versus, 148; incompatibility of Christian doctrine with, 254; key concept of, 109; key proposition of, 59; as living force, 14; natural law versus, 109, 111; openness to (disappearance of), 217; original discovery of, 130; permanent possibility of, 50; political right and, 63, 110, 135; proponents of, 78, 183; recovery of, 161; Socrates's first articulation of the principle of, 224; species-equality of mankind confirmed by, 293
Natural Right and History, 28, 31, 63, 67, 161, 202
Nazism, 209
neoconservatives: description of, 232; famous, 16; godfather of, 231
Neumann, Harry, 39; foreword to book (joke mentioned in), 256; moral purpose of his collaboration with Jaffa, 40; psychological tension of, 263–264
New Birth of Freedom, A, 47, 65; challenge of, 54; classical natural right explained in, 63; developments underlying America cultivated in, 139; divine right of kings discussed in, 126; human equality, world-historical meaning inherent in the proposition of, 46; Jaffa's regret regarding, 67–68; Jefferson's statement in Virginia Statute for Religious Freedom (quoted in), 310; Kesler's book as prequel to, 289; Kesler's review of 285; mob rule discussed in, 195; question of centralized government in, 246; reception of, 68; references to America's providential destiny contained in, 145
New Orleans Convention, 54
New York Times, 28, 284
Nicomachean Ethics, 23, 90; contradiction to chapter in *Politics* in; 99; famously challenging section of, 110; Jaffa's focus on, 86; Thomas Aquinas's interpretation of, 33; Washington's Farewell Address as echo of, 159

Reagan, Ronald, 17, 155; achievement of
statesmanship by, 6; Beltway blob and,
291; ideas of (loss of confidence in), 5;
kitchen cabinet of, 44; morphing of, 4–5;
party registration of, 17
Reagan Revolution, 6, 241
*Rediscovery of America: Essays by Harry V.
Jaffa on the New Birth of Politics, The*, 32,
48, 250
Rehnquist, William, 78, 270, 271
relativism: academic, 256; historical, 28, 148;
soft versus militant, 287
Repressive Tolerance, 228
Republic, The: argument about justice
presented in, 23; "climate of opinion"
(work coming from), 28; courses on,
23–24; as dialogue (versus treatise),
25; difference between *Laws* and, 72,
80; famous image from, 11; hidden
argument of, 26; inquiry encouraged by,
257; Lincoln-Douglas debate similar to
arguments presented in, 49, 65, 244; lines
copied from, 295; objections in *Politics*
laid out against, 101; pre-Roman ancient
world of, 147; use of religious poetry in,
314
republicanism: ancient (promise of),
249; Caesarism and, 45, 130; citizenry,
dependence on, 186; commercial, 120,
125; implied limitation on morality in,
186; rescue of from European feudalism,
305–306; Roman republicanism (birth
and growth of), 129
Roosevelt, Franklin Delano, 280

Salon, 283
Salvatori, Henry, 43–44, 164, 311
Saturday Night Live, 89
Scalia, Antonin, 78, 270, 272, 285
Scranton, Bill, 35
separation of church and state: definition
of, 185; founders' instituting of, 142; idea
leading to doctrine of, 165; importance of,
184; necessity of, 248
Shakespeare, William, 116–134; history
plays of, 69; landmark essay on, 34;
Machiavellian modernity, 118–121;
marriage and the mean, 121–125;
monarchy and succession, 125–133;
philosophic poet, 133–134; as political
thinker and philosophical poet, 46; sense
of justice of (self-justification), 8
Shakespeare's Politics, 46, 47

Sheehan, Colleen, 93
slavery: abolition of, 92, 241; Bork's claim
about *Dred Scott* case, 275; controversy
of, 55; defense of, 68, 196, 237; Lincoln's
presentation of problem of, 192;
misunderstood remarks by Aristotle
concerning, 97–98; obscure clauses
referring to, 52; perspective of founders
condemning, 74; protections for, 60,
273; question, focal point of, 54; study of
debates over, 12
Smith, Steven, 209, 228
Sobran, Joseph, 85, 237
social compact theory, 71, 155: legitimization
of, 60; necessity of adapting, 262
Socrates: arguments about natural right
(reenactment of), 244; arguments
between Thrasymachus and (in The
Republic), 23, 25, 49; best form of
government suggested by, 76; cataclysm
in the history of philosophy, initiation
of, 313–314; as example of "metaphysical
freedom of the human mind," 112; as first
political philosopher, 259; majority vote
to execute, 26; natural right, articulation
of principle of, 224; "opinions of the
marketplace" (questioning of), 190;
philosophic tradition originating with,
roots traced to (America), 139; political
philosophy of, 140, 230, 302, 310; political
philosophy, disagreement about meaning
of, 268; political philosophy, pre-Socratic
philosophy and, 302; principle of natural
right first articulated by, 224; prophesy
of, 118; standard of right, proposal of
nature as, 301; trial and execution of, 177;
utopia described by, 24
Southern Partisan, The, 236
Spalding, Matthew, 285
Spitz, David, 34
statesmanship (tyranny, freedom, and),
181–220; BLM protests, 196; Churchillian
magnanimity (modern ideology and
present crisis), 208–220; Declaration,
syllogism of, 183; dialectical materialism,
216; identity politics, 207; Jefferson's
aristoi letter (problem of wisdom),
198–204; Lincoln's Lyceum Address
(problem of factions), 191–198; Lincoln's
Temperance Address (problem of
fanaticism), 205–208; Machiavellian
principles, opposition to, 185;
megalopsuchia, 212; moral and intellectual